Praise for *Australia's B*

'. . . one of the most important books written about 19th-century Australia. It will doubtless achieve its stated aim of rescuing convict history from the margins.'
David Roberts, *The Australian*

'Wherever one stands, the character of convict society remains a crucially important aspect of Australian experience and this book is a vivid and scholarly reminder of the fact. It is also a brilliantly good read.'
Professor Alan Atkinson, *Sydney Morning Herald*

'Explodes many myths of the past and gives us a much better understanding of what actually happened, and the effects of this on the Australian community … should be read by everyone interested in Australian history.'
Emeritus Professor A.G.L. Shaw, author of *Convicts and the Colonies*

'*Australia's Birthstain* is the sort of history the nation needs: not a hint of ideology or left-wing resentment, but alive with the dead; characters who, each in their own unique way, shaped who we are, how we think and what we have made from our colonial experience.'
John Izzard, *Quadrant*

'. . . richly deserves to be read by those interested in Australian history.'
Paul Kraus, *Newcastle Herald*

'. . . thorough research, perceptively analysed to set the lives of the convicts and their era in perspective. By bringing their stories to life, she has made it easier to understand the society in which they lived and the way in which they were treated.'
L.A. Morling, *Western Ancestor*

Also by Babette Smith

*A Cargo of Women: Susannah Watson
and the Convicts of the Princess Royal*

Mothers and Sons

*Coming Up for Air: The History of the
New South Wales Asthma Foundation*

A Cargo of Women: The Novel

AUSTRALIA'S
BIRTHSTAIN

the startling legacy of the convict era

BABETTE SMITH

ALLEN&UNWIN

This edition first published in 2009
First published in 2008

Allen & Unwin
83 Alexander Street
Crows Nest NSW 2065
Australia
Phone: (61 2) 8425 0100
Fax: (61 2) 9906 2218
Email: info@allenandunwin.com
Web: www.allenandunwin.com

National Library of Australia
Cataloguing-in-Publication entry:

Smith, Babette
  Australia's birthstain: the startling legacy of the convict era.

  Bibliography.
  Includes index.
  ISBN 978 1 74175 675 3 (pbk.)

  Convicts—Australia—History. Convicts—Social aspects—Australia.
  Convicts—Australia—Social life and customs. Penal colonies—Australia—History.
  Australia—History—1788–1851. Australia—History—1851–1901. Australia—History—
  Colonial influence.

994.02

Index by Russell Brooks
Internal design by Kirby Stalgis
Maps by Ian Faulkner
Set in 11/14 pt Adobe Garamond by Midland Typesetters, Australia

FSC
Mixed Sources
Product group from well-managed
forests and other controlled sources
Cert no. SGS-COC-005088
www.fsc.org
© 1996 Forest Stewardship Council

The paper this book is printed on is certified by the © 1996 Forest Stewardship Council A.C. (FSC). The printer holds FSC chain of custody SGS-COC-005088. The FSC promotes environmentally responsible, socially beneficial and economically viable management of the world's forests.

Printed and bound in Australia by Griffin Press

10 9 8 7 6 5 4 3 2 1

For Penelope Nelson,
my friend since we were both fourteen

Greetings! Your Birthstain you have turned to good!

—adapted by Lord Beauchamp, 1899, from Rudyard Kipling's 'Song of the Cities'

If you cannot get rid of the family skeleton,
you may as well make it dance.

—George Bernard Shaw
(with thanks to A.G.L. Shaw, who used it first)

contents

list of maps

introduction

For many family historians in Australia, the discovery of a convict ancestor raised as many questions as it answered. At an individual level, family origins were explained and myths exploded when the 'black sheep' came to light. Family context in the wider scenario of Australian history became clear. Often, older family members or general family knowledge made it possible to deduce who hid the information, and the research process usually revealed how it was done in a particular case. But major questions remained.

The chief question was also the most obvious. Why? Dismissing the cover-up as simply due to family snobbery was too easy. Once they started investigating, family researchers realised that avoidance of convict history extended far beyond an individual story. The phenomenon was too widespread to be dismissed as a purely personal reaction. Family researchers wanted to know why Australian society came to fear its own history to this extent. How did this occur? Why was there such a fundamental national silence that the convicts as real-life characters—whose true stories abounded in success, failure, optimism and in tragedy, triumph and pathos—were forgotten? Was it the crimes they committed in Britain? Or did the source of a birthstain so terrible that it must be hidden lie in the penal colonies?

The second major puzzle for many researchers was why their ancestor's story did not fit the established view of convict experience. In so many cases, he did not go to the penal settlements of Port Arthur, or Moreton Bay, or Norfolk Island, nor was there any indication that he was ever flogged. And if the ancestor was a woman, in my case named Susannah Watson, she appeared to use the Female Factory to her advantage rather than dread being sent there, as some major scholarship claimed. Generally, published history as well as popular stories seemed melodramatic and at odds with the stories uncovered by family historians.

Family historians were right to be puzzled. For the last 150 years the idea that convict foundations were a blot on Australia's history has shaped political, social and intellectual thought to such an extent it is as though the previous 60 years never existed. The strongly developed ethos of a flourishing convict society is neither remembered nor understood. Its people have been reduced to caricature. Stripped of its 'colour', with no civil war, no War of Independence to fill the gap, it is not surprising that Australians are convinced their history is colourless and dull. Worse than that, the ramifications of the loss are widespread and damaging to analysis of contemporary Australian society as well as the past.

Australia has suffered from a major distortion of its convict history, a distortion that has been accompanied by an obvious desire to avoid the subject altogether if possible. This has been particularly evident, for instance, in the treatment of convict subjects in major national events. The Centenary of European settlement in Australia came and went in 1888. Federation of the colonies was celebrated in 1901. The Sesquicentenary of settlement was marked by further festivities in 1938. Notable by their absence from all of these was anything more than passing mention that a number of Australian states were penal colonies for up to 80 years, let alone that they were populated by a bunch of colourful, disreputable characters whose confrontations with the law, ingenious escapes and capacity for endurance were the stuff of history. When an official decision was taken in the nineteenth century to publish government records, it was accompanied by instructions to the editor to omit convicts' names unless absolutely necessary.[1] The documents chosen for publication were, of course, the despatches between dignitaries and officials who governed the penal colonies. Records concerning the prisoners were jealously guarded. Some were destroyed.

With vast areas of actual people and events corralled out of sight, the spotlight of history was forced to shine on what remained. Festive parades concentrated on merino sheep or sheaves of wheat. The gold digger with his pan became ubiquitous. In the absence of other candidates, explorers who opened pathways through the land were cast as heroes, wily opportunists were enlarged to noble gentlemen who were said to have the welfare of others rather than themselves at heart. As reality increasingly receded, lurid tales of the convict era were published which entertained while they fudged the facts even further. Increasingly, Australian history gyrated simplistically around hollow men and confected issues. The search for drama, any drama other than the real one, created villains from the very ordinary mould of squatters, pastoralists and employers (many of whom were actually convicts and descendants of convicts) and underdogs such as gold diggers, shearers and poor immigrants. A robust argument over licence fees at Eureka was inflated into the revolution Australia never had when, truth to tell, the leader of this 'revolution' ended up a conservative member of the Victorian parliament.[2] In this climate, when a British aristocrat arrived in 1899 to take up his appointment as Governor of New South Wales, he blundered from the moment he opened his mouth. On his way to his new suzerainty, Lord Beauchamp briefly disembarked at Fremantle where he responded to journalists' questions in what he felt was a complimentary fashion. Adapting the Empire's most popular poet, Rudyard Kipling, he told them, 'Greetings! Your Birthstain you have turned to good.'[3] Outrage was the local response to such unAustralian frankness on the unmentionable subject.

At the Bicentenary celebrations in 1988, it was perfectly in keeping with the Australian tradition of avoiding the convicts that the only speaker who referred to them directly was the Prince of Wales. Of course, the local discomfort by that time was shame of a different sort. For some Australians, the First Fleet was now illegitimate not because it carried a cargo of criminals but because it was the harbinger of destruction for native Australians. To avoid this unpalatable reality, the 'straighteners and naysayers' of Australian society once again came to the fore. This time, 200 years on, the First Fleet would not be allowed to disembark. Better to pretend it did not happen.

This time, silence was a mistake. Since the Sesquicentenary, something had changed. Now armed with the facts they had uncovered in the archives, the citizens wanted the convicts included. Despite the attempts of the straighteners to stop the ships sailing, the arrival of the re-enacted First Fleet, albeit forever moored in Farm Cove, produced an outpouring of emotion that was the wellspring of that anniversary. What caused the change? It could be argued that resistance to banning the First Fleet arose from cultural memory. Any close study of Australian history reveals that, throughout the transportation era and down the generations that have followed, Australians have been dogged by brigades of the righteous who feel entitled to tell them what to think and how to behave. That is itself a consequence of having been a penal colony. So is the—often mute—resistance. Australians learned long ago to take what is dished out and seethe silently, a habit which partly explains how some observers were caught by surprise at the enthusiasm for the First Fleet re-enactment. Also significant was the exponential growth of family history.

While official and academic Australia remained largely oblivious to its import, family historians had spent more than a decade before the Bicentenary deep in the archives of the convict colonies. These had become publicly accessible as far back as 1951, but for many years had been little used. Even the most comprehensive examination by a few scholars, while valuable, had only skimmed the surface of the records. Family historians changed that.

The trickle of family researchers that began in the late 1960s turned into a flood during the 1970s, and by the 1980s Australians regularly descended on the archives in droves. Initially motivated by the 1970 Bicentenary of Captain Cook's mapping of eastern Australia, they had been further intrigued about family antecedents by the popular television series created for the American Bicentenary in 1976 called *Roots*. Few had any expectations of secret wealth or the cachet of discovering their ancestor was an officer on the First Fleet. Curiosity was their predominant motive. Curiosity and an interest in relationships. In their exploration of the archives, many received a shock. Until family historians began researching in numbers in the 1970s, the extent to which convict history had been covered up at an individual level was unknown. Sometimes it originated with the convicts themselves, sometimes it was created by their descendants. Regardless of where it began, by the early decades of the twentieth century the screen erected to protect families that were founded by convicts had become genuine amnesia. Innocently tracking backwards from the birth of a parent or grandparent or great-grandparent, legions of family historians discovered something quite unexpected: the next ancestor entitled to take his or her place on the family tree had arrived as a prisoner. Most significantly, such discoveries immediately broadened the scope of family historians' research, taking them deep into the archival records.

Given the censorship about the country's origins, there is no country in the world where family historians are more important than in Australia. Unlike, say, Britain, where their significance is confined mainly to the personal, individual level, sometimes extrapolated to the scope of local studies, in this country family historians work at the cutting edge of historical research. They use primary records with confidence, blazing trails through the archives where none have trod since the colonial administrators closed the books over a century before. In fact, by tracing their family story they are uncovering the nub of the nation's history, providing information which they are uniquely placed to contribute. Where convicts are concerned, family historians know the end of the story. That knowledge in turn sheds light on convict criminality and character, on the impact of experience as a prisoner, as well as broader economic and social issues. It also re-connects convicts to the national narrative from which they were dropped for fear of the 'stain'.

Approximately 138,000 men were transported to Australia between 1788 and 1868. They disembarked in the colonies of New South Wales, Van Diemen's

Land and Western Australia, but while still under sentence or later when free, they permeated through the colonies of Victoria, Queensland and South Australia as well. Twenty-five thousand women also arrived as felons.[4] They were distributed almost equally between New South Wales and Tasmania. A number of girls or youths aged, say, fifteen, who landed in the final batch to Tasmania in 1853, let alone Western Australia in 1868, survived well into the twentieth century. Thomas Harrison, transported in 1863 on the *Lord Dalhousie*, for instance, did not die until 1931.[5] Some even lived until World War II was raging. In the early years of the 21st century, grandchildren of convicts were still alive who could remember their grandparents, their close generational link a demonstration of how the convict past penetrates modern Australia. Despite this proximity, the possibility that being founded as a penal colony had profound impact on Australian society is often met with derision. The facts suggest, however, that this topic is a real issue and should not be dismissed as someone's naive enthusiasm.

In 1999, the Australian Constitutional Referendum Study surveyed a random sample of 3431 Australians with the following question:

> To the best of your knowledge, are you descended from one
> or more of the convicts who were sent to Australia during the
> early period of British settlement in this country?

Extrapolating from this sample to the whole Australian population, Ronald Lambert concluded that approximately 2.1 million Australians would claim convict descent.[6] A similar number would agree to the possibility, slightly more of them in the former penal colonies (New South Wales, Tasmania and Western Australia) than in South Australia, Victoria, Queensland and the Northern Territory, which officially never received convicts. These assumptions revealed significant continuity between Australians in the twentieth century and arguments that raged during the anti-transportation campaign in the 1840s and '50s, when Victoria and South Australia loudly proclaimed that they were 'convict free'. At that time, according to the novelist Henry Kingsley, Victoria saw itself as 'an ocean of purity between two sinks of iniquity' (New South Wales and Van Diemen's Land). This book will show how much modern Australian assumptions still depend on historical paradigms established in the mid-nineteenth century and the extent to which they can mislead.

When the New South Wales and Tasmanian archives first became accessible in the 1950s, those academics who focused on convicts dealt in statistics and quantification rather than character and narrative. However, it is fair to say this group of scholars were pursuing a genuine issue for

Australian historians, namely the criminality of the prisoners who founded a democratic nation. In seeking to understand why fear of a birthstain impacted at a family and a public level, this book will explore the human face behind the percentages such historians established. In particular, it will examine the crimes at a personal level, taking account of individual circumstances, character and motive in an attempt to discover whether the convicts were ashamed of what they had done.

Whether the convict 'taint' lay in the crime or in the penal colonies was a key question. Seeking a source of shame so powerful that an entire society colluded in a decision not to discuss the subject meant that the experience of the prisoners after they arrived must be explored.

This book was not shaped by a predetermined hypothesis, only a general belief that fear of a convict stain had a very detrimental impact on Australia at large, and on its historiography. And an impact with cultural, social and political ramifications, whether the current residents of Australia had ancestors in the country during the transportation period or not.

Writing my earlier book, *A Cargo of Women: Susannah Watson and the Convicts of the Princess Royal*, taught me that Australian history rests on many assumptions that can mislead a researcher. Through experience I also discovered the best guide to the reality of the convict era were the prisoners. There are thousands of individual stories to know, thousands of characters in all their permutations to consider, and because the country was once a gaol records exist to help reconstruct lives that in other countries have been lost forever. Any suggestion that individual stories are too anecdotal to illustrate 'big' themes, that they are too subjective to be useful, can be soundly countered with the retort—not in Australia, they are not. Not in a country whose major themes, important stories and shared ethos arise from character and the interaction of character. In Australia, people rather than events define the nation.

In keeping with this idea, four boatloads of male convicts have been chosen virtually at random, only influenced by a decision to focus on the main transportation period and exclude the First Fleet era, which such a small percentage of prisoners experienced.[7] Added to these men are the female prisoners from *A Cargo of Women*, who arrived on the *Princess Royal*, including my ancestor Susannah Watson. Additional women are drawn from the group who arrived in Van Diemen's Land on the *Duchess of Northumberland*, the last 'ladies' transported to that colony. Also very important were women on other boats who were partners of the men.

In all, the men and women amounted to a sample of close to 1100 people.

A descendant of one of the convicts brought the ship *Sir William Bensley* to my attention, which turned out to be perfect for my purpose because its men were distributed at an early period in both New South Wales and Van Diemen's Land. The poaching story that was hidden among them was a huge bonus. The *John* was chosen because it arrived in New South Wales in 1832 at the height of the convict system and because I knew that one of the men married one of the women on the *Princess Royal*. The *St Vincent* which arrived in Hobart in 1853 was selected because it was the last boatload of male convicts to Van Diemen's Land and would also give some idea of how long convicts lived into the twentieth century. The *Lord Dalhousie* arrived ten years after the *St Vincent* and was one of the later transports to Western Australia. Collectively they were well spaced through the transportation era.

Having absorbed the widespread idea that the birthstain was a self-inflicted wound, I had my own assumptions about the outcome of this research. The prisoners disabused me, as they had done with *A Cargo of Women*. In their company, I took a voyage of discovery through convict society in search of the birthstain. No one was more surprised than I to discover that far from self-inflicted there had been an external source of the shaming. The trail the prisoners laid down took me to places I did not anticipate. It resulted in information about the creation and influence of the birthstain that was startling in its implications. At its heart was a legacy of national self-hatred among intellectual Australians, which in turn has denied the right to pride and affection for their history to the vast majority.

BABETTE SMITH

CHAPTER 1
something to hide

Shame about the convict origins of the Australian colonies and shame about convict ancestry increasingly coalesced during the nineteenth century to a point where convict topics were avoided in public discourse as well as private conversation. This reaction was well established by the 1870s when novelist Anthony Trollope, who visited all the colonies, noticed the colonists' sensitivity about the subject, their reluctance to discuss it and, in New South Wales and Tasmania, a tendency to downplay the convicts' crimes. Western Australians by comparison were convinced that their convicts were the worst kind of criminals. However, avoiding the subject was not always possible. For instance, both the Centenary of settlement in 1888 and Federation in 1901 required some public acknowledgement of history. The fact that the colonies were established by transportation was undeniable. So the colonists were forced to develop an explanation to dilute the stain that they felt it cast on their society. At the time of the Centenary, they defended themselves by emphasising the brutality of the penal system operated by Britain, the tyranny of its officials and the oppression of the suffering convict by flogging, starvation and slave labour in chains. However, as Federation included a commitment from the fledgling dominion to Britain and the British Empire, the focus had to shift from the shameful system to the individuals who had been transported. It was in this context that the nature of the convict crimes became a matter of debate.

While transportation operated, the type of crimes that the convicts committed was rarely discussed. The length of their sentences was of far greater significance to the officials and settlers in the colony, where only the crimes that were publicised by the British press assumed any prominence. Colonial crimes were a matter of frequent discussion both publicly and privately, but in most cases and to the chagrin of penal reformers in Britain, what the prisoners had done to warrant a sentence of transportation was not a matter of interest and had little or no impact on how they were treated during their sentence. In fact, before 1820 convicts were usually shipped out with their sentence carefully recorded for the benefit of the local officials but with no record at all of their crime.

Around the middle of the nineteenth century, the crimes committed by the convicts assumed significance locally in the context of a campaign to end transportation. Writing in *The History of Tasmania,* which was published in 1852, the Reverend John West justified the opposition to transportation on the grounds that 'more serious offenders' were now being transported compared with the convicts who had arrived earlier.[1] This point was reiterated more specifically at the Select Committee of the House of Commons on Transportation in 1861, at which time the only penal colony still in existence was Western Australia. Giving evidence to the Committee, Mr James Youl, who was also an anti-transportationist from Van Diemen's Land, claimed that because of changes in British law the prisoners sent to Western Australia had all committed 'some very grave offence' whereas previous convicts had been transported 'for political offences, for poaching, machine breaking, and so on'.[2] Youl's rationale for opposing transportation had obvious appeal to those who were trying to ameliorate the effects of their colonies being founded by criminals. To the extent the topic was discussed at all during the nineteenth century, this became the acceptable line.

From the early twentieth century, with transportation safely in the past, professional historians began to express opinions on the criminality of the convicts sent to Australia. Essentially, their debate, which will be canvassed in more detail later, can be summarised as a swing of the pendulum from convict as innocent victim to convict as professional criminal. There have been subsequent gyrations around notions of convicts as skilled workers forced into crime and some lateral diversions into special categories, of which social and political protesters were the most deeply explored by the early 1980s.

The first salvo by an academic historian was launched in the *Journal of the Royal Australian Historical Society* by Professor George Arnold Wood, an Englishman who had arrived in New South Wales in 1891, three years after the Centenary.[3] Wood noticed Australians' anxiety about the convict past and began to consider this professionally. In 1921, he delivered a paper to the Royal Australian Historical Society in Sydney. In his opening words, he confronted the colonists with the very issue they sought to avoid when he declared: 'The most important founders of New South Wales were the convicts.'

Wood's opinions had obviously been developed by his advisory role during the preparation of the *Historical Records of Australia*, the first volume of which was published in 1913. The project involved examining the despatches transmitted between the early governors of New South Wales and ministers in England, and Wood quoted liberally from governors Macquarie and Brisbane to demonstrate his conclusion that 'the early governors, who ruled over both emancipists and free settlers, and knew both classes well, did not think the emancipists were worse citizens than were the free settlers. They thought, in fact, that of the two classes the emancipists were the better.' Realising that misgivings about the character of the convicts were deeply entrenched in the minds of Australians, Wood enlarged his point about their worth by turning his attention to the people who ordered their transportation. 'The guilt of the condemned will be better understood if we have some knowledge of the virtue of the condemners and the reasons of the condemnation.' Among other sources, Wood cited the extensive research by sociologists J.L. and B. Hammond, which was published in 1913.[4] To support his argument that the convicts were mainly poachers or protesters driven to commit their crimes by poverty and victimisation by a wicked British aristocracy, he quoted the Hammonds' description of conditions in England: 'Men and women were living on roots and sorrel; in the summer of the year 1830 four harvest labourers were found under a hedge dead of starvation and Lord Winchelsea, who mentioned the fact in the House of Lords, said that this was not an exceptional case.'[5] Wood reinforced his point about the moral character of the convicts by telling his audience that 'men with starving wife and children at home, broke stones on the edge of immense parks in which "game" was preserved for the pleasure-shooting of the rich! Every brave fellow became a "poacher" . . . the poacher convicts were the best villagers in England.'[6]

Overriding the anxieties of the colonists, Wood had brought the subject into the light of discussion. But he faced a new impediment. The Royal Australian Historical Society was reluctant to publish his paper without change. Its members were not just doubtful about acknowledging the convicts as 'founders'; they were equally if not more dismayed by Wood's criticism of Britain. 'So no good people remained in England after the convicts left!' one of them cracked to the honorary secretary, who promptly invited Wood 'to revise his lecture to make clear that this is not what [he] meant to say'. Wood refused to compromise, insisting that his speech be published without change and adding a postscript to the published version which made it plain that he stood by it.[7]

As if to illustrate Wood's argument, the sample of convicts that underpins this book contained a group of poachers who, in 1816, became embroiled in a struggle with a member of the aristocracy in the Vale of Berkeley in Gloucestershire. Newspaper reports of the events that took place there were copious and the evidence at the poachers' trials was published in such detail that it is possible to reconstruct much of what happened, including what was said.[8]

> *Gloucester Journal, 22 January 1816:* '*"Most atrocious Murder"*—On Saturday last, an inquest was held, before William Joyner Esq. Coroner, at New Park Farm, Berkeley, on the body of William Ingram, who was killed by some poachers in a wood belonging to Colonel Berkeley . . . At a late hour last night we understood that there were three persons in custody on suspicion of being concerned . . . and from the indefatigable exertions of Col. Berkeley and his friends, we confidently hope that the whole of the murderers will meet with that punishment which they have so daringly and atrociously braved. Vickery, from Bow-street, arrived at Berkeley Castle last night to assist in discovering the villains and bringing them to justice.'

John Penny, one of the escaped poachers, was desperately afraid and running for his life. The others had been seized. He was now the main prey. Colonel Berkeley and that Bow Street cove would not rest till they had him.

Leaving behind the banks of the Severn and the parish of Thornbury, he veered across country, rushing towards Bristol and the safety of an alibi from his wife.

He found her in the kitchen, her master and mistress gone out, the baby for whom she was wet nurse asleep. They were still arguing nearly an hour later when the sound from upstairs of men arriving and talking to her master, who had since returned home, silenced their dispute. Penny heard his name and knew he was trapped.

Back to the kitchen fire, he challenged the stranger from Bow Street to take him, swore and challenged him to shoot when the man produced a pistol, struggled and swore when the constables overwhelmed him. As they forced his hands behind his back, trussing him like an animal for the kill, he yelled down at his wife, who was clinging to him, pleading that he go quietly. 'Ye betrayed me.' When she shook her head, weeping, and the Bow Street Runner denied she had helped him, he swung on her master, 'Then it was ye who did it.' Their denials fell on deaf ears.

Salopian Journal, 7 February 1816: 'John Penny, a man of most desperate character, was taken in Bristol . . . he made a desperate resistance and it required the united efforts of six men before he could be effectually secured.'

It took Colonel Berkeley a week to round up the poaching gang he suspected of committing the crime. John Penny was almost the last to be caught. In the parish of Thornbury, in a village called Moreton, another man was desperately afraid when he heard they had Penny. William Adams Brodribb, attorney at law, gentleman, was 27. He had been admitted to King's Bench and the High Court of Chancery in 1811 but before that, at the age of nineteen, he married Prudence Keen, whose family like his own were members of the Somerset gentry. They had settled in the Gloucestershire village in 1813, around the time their third child was born.[9] Now, Brodribb waited with trepidation. During the past week, his apprehension had turned to dread certainty. His friend, John Allen, had been taken last Sunday by Colonel Berkeley and his party of twenty men. Tales about the confrontation had spread swiftly round the district and every version had reached Brodribb's ears. According to most, Allen locked himself in, at which the

William Brodribb

Colonel pulled out a gun. Yelling, 'I'll have you, dead or alive', he threatened to break the door down unless the farmer surrendered. From an upstairs window, Allen called down, 'What do you want me for?' 'Murder,' was the reply. One bystander claimed the Colonel's men knocked the door down. Another, that Allen opened it. Giving evidence some months later, Thomas Clarke, one of the Colonel's pack, said Allen was standing at the head of the stairs with his hands in his pockets when they forced the door open. He agreed to come down quietly if they did not lay hands on him. All the observers agreed that this request was not honoured, some claiming that the Colonel grabbed Allen by the collar when he stepped outside before handing him over to his men. Others insisted that Allen was struck twice by the Colonel with a heavy cudgel.[10]

Flying to his master's defence came William Greenaway. Known to everyone as Shooney, he had worked for the Allen family for seven years. 'They shall not take him,' he yelled, flinging himself forward. The Colonel's fist laid him flat on the ground. 'Bring him along,' was the order. 'He may have information.' In the days that followed, Allen was imprisoned, while the Colonel, his staff and the Bow Street Runner (a member of the only police or detective force then in existence) scoured the countryside for the poaching gang. Greenaway remained at Berkeley Castle. As he put it under cross-examination, 'Sometimes I was in the servants' hall, sometimes abed, sometimes in the cook's kitchen, sometimes in the breakfast-parlour among the gentlemen.' He had been marked as a person who might confess the whole and the pressure on him was unrelenting.

Later on the day that Allen was caught, a week before John Penny's capture, William Brodribb received an invitation from Colonel Berkeley to attend the castle. His name had been mentioned, wrote the Colonel, in connection with the poaching affray.

Presenting himself at the castle as requested, Brodribb described to the magistrates what he saw on the night in question. Administering an unlawful oath was an offence established under a statute to prevent people from 'engaging in any mutinous or seditious purpose or to disturb the public peace, or to be of any association, society, or confederacy formed for any such purpose'. Brodribb later claimed that the chief magistrate, the Reverend Mr Cheston, who was taking his statement, intimated they were not inclined to prosecute him, something vigorously denied by the reverend gentleman. Nevertheless, Brodribb was franker with the inquisitors than he might have been if he had thought they were likely to charge him. Perhaps assuming that the gentlemen present, who did not include Colonel Berkeley, would accept the precautions he, a fellow gentleman, had taken against infringing the legislation, he described his careful choice of a book on which the men could swear. 'It was not the Bible. And I deliberately refrained from adding "So help you God" to the oath.' Then, Brodribb was emboldened to comment, 'Lord Ducie [another landowner] and the Colonel brought it all upon themselves by setting traps,' adding that he did not believe any of the men would ever have thought of firing upon the keepers if one of their own had not first been killed. By 'their own' he referred to the notorious death eight weeks earlier of labourer Tom Till, also from Thornbury, who was killed while poaching on Lord Ducie's preserves. Till had been killed by one of the newly invented spring guns, which could be concealed in the grass and swivelled as they spat out multiple shot. Tom Till had been found bleeding on the ground from five holes torn in his side by the leaden charge, and the villages of the Vale of Berkeley were alive with anger and resentment as much about the use of the trap as the fact of Till's death.[11]

To Mr Cheston, Brodribb's sympathy for the poachers amounted to class disloyalty which he was not prepared to let pass. 'Such observations imply you know more about the murder than you chose to disclose,' he responded. Realising his error, Brodribb attempted to recover his ground by making what was later described as 'a sort of apology'. When pressed by Mr Cheston whether he thought Till's death justified the poachers' actions, he hastened to reply, 'No. I do not think them justified.' But the damage was done. At that rash disclosure of his true feelings, the world of privilege and power to which William Brodribb had access turned against him. A week later he heard the knock he had been expecting on his door.

> *The Times, London, Friday 9 February 1816:* 'On the 28th.ult. Wm. Adams Brodribb, late of Moreton, in the parish of Thornbury, gent, was committed to Gloucester Gaol, by J.B. Cheston, clerk.'

In the Vale of Berkeley, Miss Flora Langley of Hill Court, Lord Ducie of Tortworth Court and Colonel William Berkeley of Berkeley Castle were the chief landowners, but it was the Colonel who drove the pursuit of the poachers. It is true that he was within his legal rights. The Game Laws granted landholders such as Berkeley exclusive rights and privileges to shoot game on their preserves. First instituted under Charles II in the seventeenth century, the restrictions had increased in severity throughout the eighteenth, step by step retreating from the Charter of the Forests introduced two years after Magna Carta, which generously promised that 'none shall lose life or limb' for pursuing the King's game.[12] The rapid enclosure of public land abolished the common man's opportunity to shoot a pheasant, whatever ground he stood on to do it. But it did not 'abolish' the tradition of making a living by shooting game, or the taste for eating it, let alone the idea of feeding a family by such means when no funds were available to buy food. After estates and commons were removed from public access by enclosure, the idea of 'fair game' collided with the newly instituted Game Laws. Poaching became a manifestation of the class war— a civil war in fact, which was never declared.

> *Gloucester Journal, 5 February 1816:* 'it would be difficult to bestow sufficient praise on Colonel Berkeley for his active and intrepid conduct in the discovery of the offenders of this bloody affray. He was on the alert day and night and led the party wherever there was the appearance of resistance or danger!'

In the days that followed the interviews of Allen and Brodribb, Colonel Berkeley was like a man driven. The dead keeper, William Ingram, had been in his employ five years, which was given as the reason for his master's assiduous pursuit of the poachers, but it ignored the history and the personalities of those involved, not least the good Colonel himself.

William FitzHardinge Berkeley's father, Frederick, 5th Earl of Berkeley, had been a colonel in the British Army, promoted to that rank in 1779. His son, however, was not a colonel by inheritance or by serving in the army, but because he was designated a 'colonel' of the local militia.[13] Whatever its source, it was not the title William Berkeley would have chosen. He wanted to be an earl. Born illegitimately to Frederick, William inherited his father's estates, but not the title. In 1811, he petitioned the House of Lords for a summons as the 14th Lord Berkeley but was not able to prove his legitimacy. The title went instead to his younger brother, who had been born after their parents married.[14] So the man who lived in Berkeley Castle was a disappointed man, who probably saw himself as humiliated before his tenants as well as his peers, none of which would have improved his disposition. Certainly, he was not known for a mild temperament. 'One of the most repulsive oafs and ruffians in the annals of the peerage' was the opinion of an unnamed contemporary observer. Equally scathing was the aristocratic diarist Charles Greville, who regarded Berkeley as 'an arrogant blackguard . . . notorious for general worthlessness'. Decades later one of the poachers, who was by then an old man, recalled the rivalry and ill-will that existed between Berkeley and Thornbury parishes at the time. He blamed the high-handed behaviour of the lords of Berkeley in general, but particularly regarding the preservation of game.[15] The Game Laws were enforced throughout Britain, but in the Vale of Berkeley they were implemented zealously. The constraints that arose from a long feudal relationship could still be detected a century later when local researchers politely ventured to say, 'The people of the district may have been unfortunate in having as a landlord William FitzHardinge Berkeley.'[16]

This then was the man who pursued the poachers. Someone who commanded as a consequence of birth and money, sensitive to slights, prickly about his status, famed for his combative nature and boxing skills. Someone who thrilled to the chase, ready to follow the quarry down every foxhole. The idea of calling a halt when the animal went to lair would have been dismissed out of hand.

Berkeley's determination was undoubtedly fuelled when he found himself opposed by someone whose personal qualities surmounted his lack of rank. John Allen shared some of the Colonel's characteristics, for he too was proud and feisty with a tendency to be high-handed, but he differed from the Colonel in an essential attribute: he was born with the qualities of a natural leader. The youngest son of a Thornbury farmer, Allen was 27 and married with four children and a fifth on the way at the time of the poaching affray. He combined farming with other income-producing activities—for instance, acting as the local tax collector—and he was also known 'to have a taste for game'. Whether he shot it, sold it, or ate it—or perhaps all three—is not clear, but he was known to be a good marksman with a certificate to prove his skill.[17]

It was a measure of Allen's impact on others that although not above average height, his bearing was such that people described him as tall. Widely admired for his physical strength and daring, he was acclaimed as 'the greatest leaper and wrestler' in the district, and local men regaled each other with tales of his prowess. But Allen was popular for more than his physical feats. He was also personable: 'a good-humoured man, one of the best-tempered fellows possible, and the most jovial of companions'.[18]

So when Allen took it upon himself to defy Colonel Berkeley, he had plenty of supporters. The men looked to him for leadership and they wanted to avenge the death of Tom Till not only because he had left a wife and two young children but also because, despite the use of the spring gun, the coroner had brought in a verdict of 'accidental death'. Allen's anger, however, and his determination to defy the landowners openly, clouded his judgement to such an extent that he appears to have become set on confrontation, losing all sense of self-preservation, let alone caution with other men's lives. According to evidence at the trial, it was widely known that some action was brewing against the landholders as much as a week before it occurred.

Allen always liked to taunt the estate keepers about whether the woods they guarded were full of game ripe for the plucking, but he had been doing so persistently since Tom Till's death. George Hancock, a part-time keeper for Miss Langley of Hill Court, testified that shortly after Christmas 1815 he was with farmer Daniel Long, subsequently one of Allen's group, when Allen came out of William Brodribb's house and greeted them provocatively. 'How are you, my lads? Isn't there plenty of game about Hill?' In court, Hancock continued: 'I said, "There is." He said, "I must have some of them." I said, "Why don't ye." He asked, "Where's Proudman?" That is Miss Langley's keeper. Allen said he had a knife to cut Proudman's ears. Then he asked the whereabouts of Great Long Walker: he is Miss Langley's under-gardener.' A second witness, John Jones, gave evidence of a similar conversation, but on this occasion Allen actually went to his house. 'He said he was thinking of paying Miss Langley "another visit". I told him Miss Langley had no game: he said, he knew where the game was. I told him he had better leave it off, for he would be sure to be taken. He said, he would die rather than be taken, for he could not bear the thought of prison and that he would sooner shoot a man than be taken. He said he had a list of the game he had killed that year.'

The stakes were raised even higher when Allen sent a provocative note to Miss Langley which warned her, 'I intend to visit the woods and preserve of Hill-manor on the night of the 19th. Your keepers will do well to remain in their homes.'[19] It was a declaration of war.

Looking back, William Collins, another of the poachers, wondered whether Miss Langley took any notice. 'She was a lady of spirit, not likely to be alarmed by a daring impertinent letter,' he said. 'But we saw nothing of the Hill-court keepers . . . perhaps they had joined the Berkeley men.'[20] Collins was right in noticing the Hill Court keepers were not in the woods. Miss Langley was said to have refused to let her men join Colonel Berkeley's. They may have been used as look-outs. Meanwhile, Allen's real antagonist had no doubt that battle was to be joined. Colonel Berkeley set about organising his troops so he could put a force of 30 keepers in the field.

Most of the poachers came from Allen's own village of Moreton, where his persuasive powers were strongest. In the village of Littleton, support was less widespread. For some, the dangers loomed too large and they resisted the invitation to join the group. For instance, Thomas and William Collins from Collerton Farm found Allen's request to join him irresistible, but their brother Benjamin was dissuaded by his wife and was conveniently away from home when Allen came to ask that he take part.[21] Henry Reeves also declined but his brother Jack agreed to go even though he had a wife, Hester, and three boys. On the appointed night many who had promised to come did not turn up at Allen's farmhouse.

As dusk fell, Allen went out on an unknown errand, throwing a casual invitation to William Greenaway to join the group if he wished. According to Greenaway, the men from Littleton were the first to arrive at the house around 9 p.m. Tom 'Gunner' Collins and his brother William arrived together, along with John and William Penny who lived near them. All of them were carrying guns. Daniel Long was next, carrying a stout stick as a weapon. The tallest of the group and unmarried, the 25-year-old was a farmer from Hill. He reported that two youths, 19-year-old John Burley, who was Greenaway's stepson, and another teenager, James Jenkins, were hanging about outside, hoping that Allen would change his mind and let them come. At this point, William Brodribb came in. With Brodribb was his brother-in-law, John Keen, who was a doctor in Bristol, and his friend and cousin William Pursell Hassell, a fellow lawyer with whose father Brodribb had done his articles in nearby Dursley.[22] About 10 p.m., John Allen returned, put some powder and shot and flint down on the table and invited everyone to help themselves. He was still short of men and when Greenaway reminded him of Burley and Jenkins he agreed they could join the expedition.

The rest of the gang had now arrived, including James Roach, who described himself as a farmer but, like Allen, may have dealt in game as a side-line; Robert Groves, who was also a farmer and 20-year-old blacksmith Thomas Morgan, a large, stoutly built man who had armed himself with a stick. Jack Reeves was there, carrying a gun. Also present were the two Hayward brothers, Thomas and John, who were local farmers and who both had guns, and Anthony Barton who lived at the Reeves' farm. He was a pig farmer who also acted as the local butcher and no doubt sold game too—under the counter.[23] Barton was carrying a gun. He had also blacked his face, which caused great comment among the others who thought it was an excellent idea. One by one they filed into the parlour where Allen helped them black their faces with ash from the fireplace.

At the trial Greenaway recounted, 'Somebody proposed that we should put to an oath, not to peach upon each other.' He described Brodribb leaving the parlour and returning with a book, on which he then swore two or three men at a time. Each of them kissed the book after the oath. 'After that we drank a lot of spirits and water,' remembered William Collins. The next ritual for the increasingly excited group was to chalk a white star on their hats, except for Allen's hat on which they chalked a crown. It was a distinction that was to tell against him. 'The best shot can have my double-barrelled gun,' declared Allen, who was going unarmed. There was little argument that Gunner Collins was the one entitled to it. The spare gun that John Penny had brought was passed to Greenaway. There was so strong a sense of preparing for battle it must have seemed quite natural when one of the 'gentlemen'—exactly which one Greenaway did not name—asked to see them all lined up before they left. At this sight, William Brodribb was then said to declare that 'one poacher could beat three keepers'.

The men set off into the frosty, moonlit night, along the road, cutting across fields, over gates, past Miss Langley's manor where, despite his threats, Allen did not intend to trespass. Along the way, they fired several shots at game until Allen put a stop to it, telling them they were armed because they intended to shoot game, lots of game, but on Colonel Berkeley's land. 'The spirits we had drank had made us boisterous and excited,' recalled William Collins. 'For a time we were jovial and reckless, all but Allen, who was quiet and reserved.' There was no attempt to disguise their passage. Their voices carried on the still night air. Several people, including a number of keepers, saw them pass by. Anthony Barton spotted a keeper watching them and tried to hush them, adding, 'If any of our party runs, I will blow his leg or arm off.' As they fell

quiet, William Collins began to regret that he was part of the expedition, realising how ashamed his parents would be or, worse, grief-stricken if he came to
any harm. Bereft of the poachers' voices, the profound stillness of the landscape closed in with frightening portent. 'It seemed almost like the silence of
death. It smote me with remorse,' recalled Collins. 'I wished now I could wash
my hands of the whole stupid affair, but it was too late to go back.'[24]

On the edge of Catgrove Wood on Colonel Berkeley's estate, Allen stopped
them. 'If we should meet with the keepers we are strong enough to overcome
them. And we will do so if they interfere with us. But there is to be no shooting,'
he told them. 'But what if they shoot at us?' asked someone. It was a question
to which Allen had no ready answer. According to William Collins, he paused,
shrugged his shoulders and said, 'Come on'. And they followed him into
the wood.[25]

Meanwhile the keepers had split into several groups. In the main ride,
Colonel Berkeley's keeper, Thomas Walker, showed himself just as the poachers
were forming themselves into two military-style lines. 'Huzza, boys, fight like
men,' Walker cried out to them. Allen replied swiftly, 'Never fear, we are no
cowards,'[26] and it was on. Keeping their two-line formation, the sixteen
poachers advanced on Clarke and four other keepers. Vastly outnumbered, the
keepers fell back rapidly. Somebody fired. Then a second shot hit the deputy
keeper, William Ingram, who crumpled immediately to the ground. Greenaway, positioned to the left of John Penny, insisted this shot was fired by Penny
and not by Allen, because he had no gun. Greenaway also admitted that he
fired the other shot himself. Several volleys followed. All disabled by some kind
of injury, the four remaining keepers in Clarke's group fell back in disorder. It
was a rout. With someone shouting 'Glory, glory!' the poachers rushed forward
and past them—and kept running. They were out of sight by the time rein-
forcements joined the keepers.

The poachers' forward advance turned into a rush to get away from what
they had done. Plunging headlong through the woods, across fields and over
stiles, they eventually stopped at a stream. As they washed the black off their
faces, Allen said urgently: 'We must not tell the dearest friend on earth for there
are two or three dead. We will all be hanged if we are taken.' Again, they swore
to secrecy, each kissing his own hand to confirm his oath. As they parted, Greenaway testified that he picked up a gun by the butt which John Penny claimed as
his. When he gave it to him, Penny said, 'Now Tom Till's debt is paid.'

On the Colonel's instructions, a party of his retainers including George
Hancock and Henry Hobby went out at dawn on the following morning. The
tracks of a group of men were clearly visible in the white frost and they followed
these until losing them at a major road. Undeterred, and no doubt briefed as

to his likely destination, Hobby went straight to John Allen's house and there, he said, he picked up the trail again, insisting that the snow in Allen's courtyard was trampled by many feet, leaving prints that were fresh and distinct.

Determined to catch the gang, the Colonel led a search party of game-keepers and other retainers to scour the district, searching almost every house. A number of people who had not been part of the poaching expedition were taken into custody on suspicion. One of them was Mark Biddle, who testified he was offered a reward by the Colonel even before they arrived at Berkeley Castle. 'Biddle, if you'll tell me the company of poachers, I'll give you 200 guineas and a free pardon,' said the Colonel, adding that he would give the reward to Biddle or anyone who came forward, 'except one man'. It was John Allen he was after and John Allen on whom he intended to take revenge.

Biddle was kept at the castle three days and three nights. While he was there, he overheard one of the Colonel's keepers offer the same reward to Greenaway and saw the continuous pressure that was put on him. Two days later, William Penny, a labourer at Littleton and brother of John, appeared at the castle with Thomas Collins to volunteer a statement that they had nothing to do with the events of that night. They were kept hanging around for the Colonel, who was absent with the search parties, and when Greenaway saw them there he thought they were going to confess. Fearing he would lose the chance to save his own life, Greenaway hastened to the breakfast room where various members of the local gentry were gathered either because they were magistrates or the Colonel's house-guests, or both. Their number included Berkeley resident, Dr Henry Jenner, whose late uncle was famous for his invention of the smallpox vaccine. On hearing that Greenaway wanted to confess the whole and would name the others involved, Dr Jenner took it upon himself to confirm the promise of a pardon. When pressed by Greenaway, he added a pardon for his teenage stepson, John Burley. He then proceeded to take down the statement in detail so when Colonel Berkeley returned to the castle that evening, the whole was known.

Thomas Collins and William Penny were handcuffed to one another and imprisoned within the castle while the Colonel immediately returned to the pursuit. With a party of his men, he quickly arrested Jack Reeves, James Jenkins and the blacksmith Thomas Morgan. Meanwhile, John Vickery the Bow Street Runner went on a fruitless hunt for the Hayward brothers, who had vanished. Without ceremony, the search parties entered houses and scoured outlying buildings. They found James Roach at Thornbury hidden in a cellar of his father's farmhouse. Daniel Long, who was asleep in his farmhouse at Hill, was dragged from his bed. John Penny was overlooked at first because they thought his brother William was the only family member involved, but by Sunday they were chasing him to Bristol.

> *Salopian Journal, 31 January 1816:* 'Twelve [*sic*] of the gang who committed the atrocious murder at New Park farm as stated in our last journal have been secured. One of them Colonel Berkley traced into a public house where after a desperate pugilistic encounter in which the science and bottom of the Colonel was most pre-eminent, he defeated and secured the villain.'

Robert Groves was the last to be taken. Confronting his widowed mother, whose farm he managed, the searchers managed to extract the direction he had absconded and nearly two weeks later tracked him down to Monmouthshire. The timing suggests it was Groves who had the pugilistic encounter with the Colonel. Also taken in this wild and indiscriminate round-up was Benjamin Collins. William Greenaway knew there were two Collins brothers in the party, but he had confused which ones they were. Returning home that night terrified by what they had done, William Collins had confessed everything to his parents. Recognising the grave danger, his father immediately drove him in his cart to Bristol, where he took ship for Ireland.[27] Benjamin, meanwhile, spent some days in Gloucester Gaol. When the confused identities were established he was released, but by then, William was safely away.

William Collins lived for many years in Ireland until he judged it safe to return to Thornbury. Three other poachers escaped the Colonel's clutches entirely. Anthony Barton, whose idea it was that they should black their faces, made landfall in the United States, where he founded a family whose descendants prosper today. The Hayward brothers were said to have reached the West Indies, but have vanished into history and their destination cannot be confirmed.[28]

> *The Times, London, 9 February 1816.* 'On Thursday last were committed . . . John Penny charged with the wilful murder of William Ingram . . . and John Allen, William Penny, Thomas Collins, Daniel Long, John Reeves, John Burley, James Jenkins, Thomas Morgan, James Roach and William Greenaway . . . severally charged with having been fortuitously present at the said murder, aiding, abetting, helping, comforting, assisting and maintaining the said John Penny, the felony and murder to do and commit. Greenaway and Burley were afterwards admitted King's Evidence. The whole of the prisoners are young men of decent appearance.'

The final examination of suspects took place at the county gaol in the presence of about twenty magistrates and the poachers were formally committed for trial at the next Assize.[29] By the time the Assize began on 3 April, Colonel Berkeley had succeeded in getting a second count which indicted John Allen for murder and the others for aiding and assisting him. The unexpected hero at the start of the first day was young John Burley. Picked up by Vickery, the Bow Street Runner, he had been taken to the Castle where the magistrates and Vickery advised him to confess like his stepfather and benefit from the pardon that had been arranged. Burley refused. He was then committed to Gloucester Gaol but held separately from the others in the debtors' section so Vickery could continue the pressure. During that time, he was able to talk to Brodribb through their adjacent windows and seek his advice. With what must have been a terrible urgency, the lawyer told him to say nothing, knowing that without Burley there was a chance that Greenaway's evidence would not be sufficiently supported to give it credibility. By the day of the trial, Burley was still wavering. Before proceedings got under way, he was required to swear an oath so his testimony could be admitted as King's evidence. In an act of considerable heroism, he again rejected this chance to escape the death penalty, whereupon the judge ordered that he be put in the already crowded dock with the other poachers.[30]

Gloucester Gaol where the poachers were held, newly built in 1795.

At the trial, with Colonel Berkeley sitting behind his counsel and listening closely, keeper after keeper was called to detail how they saw a group of poachers pass by, lit only by moonlight. Yes, said one of them, he was fairly sure that he recognised John Allen among them. Thomas Walker described the confrontation in the woods and in particular how the poachers surged forward after the initial shots were fired and Ingram fell. George Hancock and others described how they had tracked the poachers' footprints the next morning and what they had seen in Allen's yard. Both Hancock and John Jones testified to Allen's taunting comments about his intention to poach in the landowners' preserves. Then Greenaway was called to give evidence about who was with the poachers, how they prepared, what route they took, and what happened in the woods and afterwards. He named John Penny as firing the fatal shot, and he quoted John Penny's remark about Tom Till's debt being paid. He added detail after detail which condemned Allen as the instigator and leader of the group. He implicated not only Brodribb but Dr Keen and the attorney William Pursell Hassell as well, although the authorities were not inclined to take action against the last two.

Greenaway's testimony and a gruelling cross-examination by the defence lawyers lasted four hours. The court, which had begun at 9 a.m., sat until 11 p.m. and then adjourned until the following morning. In an attempt to shake the traitor's impact, Mark Biddle was called for the defence to claim that Greenaway's evidence had been bought with 200 guineas, but Biddle's credibility was tainted by a gaol term he had served for poaching. Greenaway vehemently denied the allegations that he had been bought. 'At first I was very unwilling,' he said. 'I confessed because my life is as sweet as another's ... a pardon was promised to me, or any man that would confess, except John Allen ... I did it on condition of pardon for myself and my stepson ... I do not do it for money but to save my life. He [the Colonel] did not promise me anything.'

The fact the poachers had charged on through the keepers even after shots were fired and a man was killed told against them in law. Better had they turned tail and run away or, given that every man in the fight knew each other so well, stopped abruptly and brought the affray to a halt. Perhaps then—if Colonel Berkeley had backed off—the coroner could have found 'accidental death' rather than 'wilful murder'.

'By law, all who went out, intending to resist every opposition, are guilty of murder,' the judge told the jury. The evidence that revealed John Allen 'as a sort of leader', as the judge put it, was remorselessly described: how the group gathered at his home, how he supplied the powder and shot, asked Greenaway to go with them, invited the rest of the group. The crown on Allen's hat told against him. So too did the fact it was he who cried 'Halt' at the stream and swore the men to secrecy again with the warning that they could all hang. 'If you believe Greenaway's testimony,' said the judge, then proceeding to enumerate all the points at which Greenaway's evidence was supported, 'the prisoners are all guilty; if you do not, there is not sufficient evidence against any one of them.'

And, having witnessed four hours of unshaken cross-examination, believe Greenaway they did. Almost as telling was the absence of a defence. Where were Dr Keen or William Hassell to deny they were there, or to testify that Brodribb had not sworn an oath, or that some at least of the men in the dock had not been present? They were a speaking silence, which the jury could not fail to heed. Indeed, their absence had been predicted by counsel for the prosecution, who made sure the jury understood its implication. After retiring for two hours, the jury returned to a hushed courtroom. Many of the jurors were so upset they wept openly as the foreman, choked with emotion, delivered their verdict: guilty against all the prisoners. John Penny was found guilty of the actual murder; the others were guilty of aiding and assisting him. Knowing death was the penalty for both counts, the jury recommended mercy for all except John Penny and John Allen. They asked that the prosecutor, Colonel Berkeley, who was present, support their recommendation which, in the words of the obsequious newspaper reporter, 'was instantly and feeling done by Mr Dauncey, in the Colonel's name'.[31] The *Gloucester Journal* echoed the feelings of the shocked community when it described the accused as 'eleven young men, nine of whom were farmers' sons and respectably connected . . . [the trial] could not but create an interest of the highest degree in the feelings of the public'.[32]

The sentence of death conferred on the poachers must have weighed heavily on Brodribb when he stood trial the next morning. Dressed in black, his face was pale and sombre. The *Bristol Gazette* described him as 'a genteel looking man'.[33] Very likely Prudence Brodribb was among those who crowded the courtroom. She had been staying with family nearby after giving birth to a son at the time of the committal hearing in early February, and later evidence suggests that it would have been in character for her to insist on attending. Two barristers, a Mr Taunton and a Mr Ludlow, appeared for Brodribb. The attorney who prepared the defence was his old master solicitor, William Hassell senior.[34] Brodribb's friend and cousin, William Hassell junior, sat with his father at the table throughout the trial in what must have been great agony of mind. The magistrates had examined him, too. His statement is noticeable for its prevarication plus a determination to avoid implicating anyone in the events of that night.[35] Perhaps at his sister Prudence's request, John Keen stayed away. Both men were vulnerable to prosecution themselves, which would have vastly increased the scale of the family tragedy that was being enacted in the courtroom. Hassell and Keen were also potentially witnesses. If they had been prepared to lie, they could have cast doubt on Greenaway's testimony. But both were professional men. It is obvious from his statement that Hassell could not bring himself to betray his personal honour or his professional oath by lying to the court.

In any event, Brodribb's defence was constrained by his earlier admission that he administered 'a form of oath' to satisfy the poachers' desire for something to bind them to secrecy. He pleaded not guilty to infringing the statute, which meant he had to prove he did not know the men gathered at Allen's house were about to do something illegal. His earlier deposition to the magistrates was tendered in court, in which he insisted he had not known the poachers would be there but had gone to see Allen on business. 'I saw a number of people there assembled which rather astonished me.' Describing some of them as 'notorious poachers', he agreed that he guessed they were going after game. Then he described how some were armed with guns and some with sticks, but he was carefully ambiguous about who carried what except in one instance. In a vain attempt to help his friend, he had stated categorically in this earlier written document, 'I am positive that Allen was unarmed.'

At the trial, Greenaway again gave detailed evidence about the oath-swearing ceremony. As someone who turned King's evidence, as informing was described, what he said required confirmation from another source. Brodribb's deposition was used for that purpose. In court, Brodribb tried desperately to counter the admissions he had made earlier. He emphasised again that he had taken care the book was not a Bible, and also that it was not he who told the poachers to say 'So help me God' as they kissed the book. However, these details were not a great help to him because the legislation simply required that those swearing the oath believed it to be binding. Fundamentally, Brodribb's statement had confirmed Greenaway's allegation that an oath was administered.

The Reverend Mr Cheston was the other major witness for the prosecution. He provided corroboration for the prosecution by tendering Brodribb's deposition and describing the circumstances in which it was made—how Brodribb had been told of Greenaway's allegations against him; how he, Cheston, had sworn Greenaway in front of Brodribb and that Greenaway had then repeated the charge. The lawyer had responded by making his statement. The clergyman was incensed at the idea that he or anyone else had suggested the magistrates were not disposed to prosecute him. 'If any such intimation had been given him anywhere, I am ignorant of it.'

Obviously feeling greatly betrayed, Brodribb persisted in the claim that he was induced to give a statement. 'Hopes of indulgence were held out to me,' he told the court. 'Mr Cheston said that if the statute could in any way be twisted to save me, it should be done.' In this, as in all aspects of the poachers' tale, one detects the fell hand of Colonel Berkeley. The law had not yet devised a system of Crown prosecutors acting for the State and by that means preventing vindictive prosecutions. In 1816, prosecution was still very much a personal affair. Even allowing for the requirements of the common law, Colonel Berkeley had the power at every turn to pursue or abandon a particular course of action. Without his thirst for revenge, John Allen would almost certainly not have been hanged, and an attempt to save Brodribb would probably have been supported.

Brodribb gave evidence in his own defence at the trial, testifying that he used his 'utmost efforts and intreaties' to dissuade the poachers from swearing an oath. In a desperate attempt to counter Greenaway, perhaps also in the hope that it could influence the judge to recommend a reprieve for Allen and John Penny, Brodribb insisted that Greenaway's evidence was doubly compromised: first by the aim to save his own life but also by the desire to prevent Brodribb from being a witness who could contradict him at the trial of the poachers. 'Greenaway has two or three times confessed to me that he was the man who murdered Ingram,' he told the court.

Probably because of the terrible outcome the day before, there was no sympathy for Brodribb and the jury took only a few minutes to find him guilty. Before passing sentence, the judge addressed him directly in words that must have haunted Brodribb for the rest of his life. 'From your education and profession,' Mr Justice Holroyd said, 'you might have been expected to know and act better. You may consider yourself as having been materially instrumental to the fatal consequences which have befallen the eleven unfortunate men who were yesterday condemned.' Then he gave Brodribb the maximum sentence for administering an unlawful oath—transportation for seven years.

John Allen and John Penny had two days to prepare themselves for death. They spent the first in a state of shocked disbelief in which anger, defiance, fear and denial intermingled. The gaol's chaplain was so concerned about their state of mind that he went back to see them a second time that day. The morning of their second day must have dawned hard and sober as reality kicked in at last to make them realise there was no escape. They were doomed to hang at lunchtime the next day. The chaplain visited again, and this time they listened to him.[36]

John Allen began to write letters.[37] To his parents: 'My Dear Father and Mother whatever Sins I have done Present to aggravate you to sin the Lord Jeasus [*sic*] Christ have Mercy on me and Pardon me for What has been done.' To his sisters begging their pardon for 'whatever Disputes have been between us' and to his wife asking hers for any 'words' that had happened between them. His grief and concern for his family poured out in another letter just for them: 'Farewell my Dear wife, and Dear four Children. I am going to leave you to God and the wide world, for you my Dear Children I do pray to the Lord to be Merciful upon you my Dear Wife and Children . . . Our Saviour was Crucified upon Good Friday and we too [sic] poor Souls is to die on Saturday.' The chaplain had done his work and, in what appears to be the last letter, religion is providing the crutch that will see Allen through the ordeal of dying. Addressing himself to everyone who was near and dear to him, he has reached an emotional stage where he has accepted his fate. Even the rage at being hanged for a murder he did not commit has been replaced by gratitude that he dies without blood on his hands.

John Allen and John Penny's final day was Easter Saturday, 17 April 1816. They attended a service in the chapel and took the sacrament, then, accompanied by the chaplain and watched by the governor of the gaol, by Mr Cooper, the visiting magistrate, the local doctor Henry Jenner and the crowd that gathered in silence around the gallows, they made their way forward without faltering. Pride came to the fore, surmounting anger and desolation in John Allen, helping him to meet this end with dignity. And his demeanour, in turn, must have steadied John Penny. From the scaffold, each told the watching crowd that he was innocent of wilful murder. They embraced each other. Then a hood and a noose were placed over their heads and they were swiftly catapulted into silence.[38]

Within the gaol, the feelings of William Brodribb and the nine other poachers when a groan from the crowd told them it was done can only be imagined. Held separately, Brodribb's anguish was private but he must have been stricken with grief made all the worse by the guilt of knowing that he might have prevented the tragedy. He was the one person to whom John Allen might have listened. When the chaplain visited the other poachers in the general felons' yard two days later, he found their indignation had drained away and many were made penitent by the horror of what had occurred. Now they were eager for the Bibles and religious tracts he distributed.[39]

The local people were not the only ones to be upset by the outcome. The accuracy of his gloomy predictions gave the Berkeley Castle chaplain no joy. He confided to his journal, 'Colonel Berkeley had run the matter of game so hard with respect to the people that I foresaw there would be a kick-up of the whole.' In his role as the village doctor, Dr Henry Jenner had been called to give evidence about the cause of Ingram's death. He had also been the recipient of William Greenaway's detailed confession at the castle. Perhaps he regretted not trying to dissuade Greenaway when he had the chance. The night before the execution, he was so distressed that he recorded in his diary:

My intention is to quit this place, rendered dreary by the tragic scene at this instant about to be acted on the horrid platform tomorrow. They certainly did not go out with the intent to commit murder. But somehow it is expected that the meanest individual in the state is to be acquainted with our penal laws and all their intricacies. In my opinion this is unreasonable.[40]

If Colonel Berkeley felt any responsibility for what occurred, it was not evident. He had been protected from public criticism throughout by a combination of fellow gentry, sycophantic employees and an obsequious press. Counsel for the prosecution took care in court to cover any questions about the Colonel's motives. In his opening address, Mr Dauncey proclaimed, 'Colonel Berkeley has felt it incumbent on him to institute the present investigation, not more for the sake of the public peace, than in justice to the faithful servant whom he has lost, and whose death has left a family fatherless and unprovided for.' Much public emphasis was given to his instruction to the Berkeley keepers that they were to go out unarmed. No one suggested that he had invited the strife by putting so many keepers into the field that night, and even more significantly, instructing them that they 'should meet the poachers like men'. They were Berkeley's proxies in his battle against the upstart Allen. His relentless personal pursuit of the poachers down every burrow and foxhole was described only in admiring terms as a 'pugilistic encounter' or likened to bravery on the hunting field or in battle. The lifelong glee he exhibited about the poachers' fate suggests his presence in the court throughout the trial was vindictive. At the very least, it would have been intimidating to his employees.

Of course this interpretation had no impact at the time. Berkeley's presence in court was mentioned only in order to praise his compassion in 'very humanely, and promptly' supporting the jury's recommendation of mercy for nine of the poachers.[41] When it was over and John Allen was dead, he remained unmoved by the tragedy to which it could be argued he was as much a party as Allen. Like a hunter who had caught his prey, he flaunted his triumph by commissioning an oil painting which depicted John Allen rallying the poachers. It hung like a trophy in the breakfast room at Berkeley Castle for many years, until moved to a less conspicuous spot after the Colonel's death.[42] But the Colonel was not satisfied with just a painting. He also arranged for the bough of a willow tree, which had been an exhibit at the trial because it was embedded with shot, to be encased in glass for display in a keeper's cottage where working men and women would see it.[43]

VAN DIEMAN'S LAND

Bebbington, Printer, 22, Goulden St. Oldham Road Manchester
and sold by H. Andrews, 27, St. Peter Street, Leeds.

Come all you gallant poachers, that ramble void of care,
That walk out on a moonlight night, with your dog, gun, and
snare;
The hare and lofty pheasant you have at your command,
Not thinking of your last career upon Van Dieman's Land.

Poor Thomas Brown, of Nottingham, Jack Williams, and Poor
Joe,
Were three determin'd poachers, as the country well doth know
At night they were trepann'd by the keepers hid in sand,
And fourteen years transported were upon Van Dieman's Land

The first day we landed upon the fatal shore,
The planters came around us—their might be 20 score,
They rank'd us up like horses and sold us out of hand,(Land.
They yok'd us in a plough, brave boys, to plough Van Dieman's

Our cottages we live in are built of clods and clay,
And rotten straw for bedding, yet we dare not say nay,
Around our cots a curling fire--we slumber when we can,
And drive the wolves and tigers oft upon Van Dieman's Land.

Oft times when I do slumber, I have a pleasant dream,
With my sweet girl sitting near me close by a purling stream
Thro' England I've been roaming, with her at my command,
And waken broken-hearted upon Van Dieman's Land.

In Britain, broadsides like this one were used to deter lawbreakers. The final verse was as follows:

> *So all you gallant poachers, give ear unto my song,*
> *It is a bit of good advice, although it is not long,*
> *Throw by your dogs and snares, for to you I speak plain*
> *For if you knew our hardships—you would never*
> *poach again.*

The Berkeley group were not the only poachers trapped by keepers and hauled before the court on charges ranging from larceny to felony to grievous bodily harm to intent to wound; nor were they the only ones sentenced to death but then transported. Indeed, on other occasions poachers were executed. However, among the many reports of poaching incidents during the eighteenth and nineteenth centuries, the Berkeley affair stood out. Harry Hopkins, who researched the subject in depth for his book, *The Long Affray: The Poaching Wars in Britain*, distinguished this particular clash from among many others as the 'long-celebrated poaching affray'. The Berkeley affair was not just famous for what occurred or the respectability of the accused. It also triggered emotional undercurrents. In the events at Berkeley, the subterranean class warfare surfaced. No one could avoid seeing the disparity of power and its potential for vengeance, which at Berkeley was fully exercised. Many would have shared Dr Jenner's sense that an injustice was being perpetrated. Some people, including his peers, were plainly troubled by the Colonel's over-zealous pursuit. Other men admired the quixotic defiance of John Allen. Deep in the country, others who identified with John Penny's flight to Bristol must have picked up their snares and nets for another night in the local woods filled with foreboding at the risk they ran. This was not a light-hearted tussle over 'fair game'. Calling it an affray could not disguise its significance. In Britain the aristocratic Colonel Berkeley and the farmer John Allen with his band of men transmogrified from individuals into figureheads, who symbolised the class battle.

> *Edinburgh Advertiser, 6 May 1816:* 'The Berkley [*sic*] poachers under sentence of death in Gloucester prison on Wednesday last received gratifying intelligence of a general reprieve.'

Along with news of the reprieve, the keeper of Gloucester Gaol was instructed to send the poachers to the hulks prior to transportation. The gaol officials immediately set about trying to delay the transfer. The visiting magistrate, Bransby Cooper, was first. In a letter which dissembled over whether the Home Secretary meant Brodribb to be included among those despatched immediately to the hulks, he proposed a plan to send off five poachers with another four to follow as soon as possible. His real aim was to spare Brodribb a sojourn on the hulks, whose fearful reputation was well known.[44] With the cooperation of the governor and the keeper, Cooper successfully delayed the movement of the poachers until 21 June, but there was no merciful delay for Brodribb. His arrival at the *Justitia* hulk at Woolwich is registered as 22 May, barely two weeks after the visiting magistrate wrote on his behalf. Before he left, he would have shared the news that the remaining poachers had been reprieved, their sentences commuted to transportation for life. A month later they followed him to the hulk. Three months later, they all sailed in the *Sir William Bensley* for Botany Bay.

Notoriety was not transported with the poachers. They sailed into oblivion when they left London. Among the earliest settlers in the country that came to be called Australia, their names and their story are unknown here.

CHAPTER 2
amnesia

Newspapers in Britain reported every detail of the events at Berkeley. Some, like the *Worcester Journal*, justified their coverage by claiming it was 'an important and most interesting trial'.[1] In truth it was for them simply a great story, and the scandal that 'eleven young men, nine of whom were farmers' sons and respectably connected' were at risk of execution kept readers transfixed for weeks.[2] From the *Times* in the south to the *Edinburgh Advertiser* in the north, every stage of the 'affray' was written about and commented upon. The names of William Adams Brodribb, gentleman, John Allen and John Penny, as well as 'the Berkeley poachers' collectively, became famous the length and breadth of Britain. On 6 October 1816, they were transferred to the barque *Sir William Bensley* for a voyage to the other side of the world, their destination a penal colony perched precariously on the edge of an ancient land, and with a tiny outpost barely a toehold in the turbulent wilds of a small island even further south. There, the poachers were among the founders of a new nation, a huge gaol which within 200 years could lay claim to be one of the oldest continuous democracies in the world.

As people of notoriety who played an early part in that amazing transformation, it is reasonable to expect the poachers' story would today be recounted by teachers in classrooms and professors in halls of learning; that they would feature in history books and learned essays and in public discourse, their character and their fate vividly illustrating the bigger issues. In their new home, unlike their old, the question of whether they were criminals or the victims of injustice could have been freely aired. In the last two centuries their characters and their fate might at least have provoked discussion. None of that occurred. For all Australians know, the Berkeley poachers might never have existed. It is as though the country is the victim of amnesia. Or of a cover-up.

A collusion of social forces at a public, institutional and at a family level created this national loss of memory. What began as an unspoken agreement to avoid an uncomfortable subject, over time turned into ignorance. The penal colony that had been the most talked about experiment in the world in its first 100 years subsequently became the object of distortion, cover-up and, finally, silence in the second.

Publicly, this occurred in various ways. Convicts, as a group, were largely omitted from major celebrations (along with the Aborigines) and from school history books. For instance, in planning the street parade in Sydney for the Sesquicentenary celebrations in 1938, much discussion ensued about whether a float featuring the convicts should be included. The debate was passionate, with people arguing fiercely for and against. Herbert Rumsey, founder of the Society of Australian Genealogists, was one who strongly believed the convicts should be represented.[3] In the end, those who were against the idea of featuring the prisoners in the parade won the argument. At the same time a decision was taken to exclude the Aborigines as well. They mounted a 'Day of Mourning' in protest, but the descendants of convicts accepted their omission silently. Their compliance was not necessarily a sign of social cowardice. In fact many would not have known they were connected to the people who arrived in chains.

Aborigines protested their exclusion from the Sesquicentenary in 1938

Convict buildings were demolished too. Having survived beside Sydney Cove since Governor Phillip's time, the sandstone Commissariat, which was not only the largest building in the first settlement but the most important because it stored the food, was reduced to rubble in 1901. Some years later, it was replaced by a building which today houses the Museum of Contemporary Art. In Western Australia, the Toodyay convict depot was demolished as late as 1934. Placenames from the convict era were also changed. In 1855 Van Diemen's Land became Tasmania. Later in the nineteenth century, not long before the first Centenary, the name of the most enduring convict encampment in the Blue Mountains—20 Mile Hollow—was changed to something that did not evoke memories of the prisoners' stockade. It became known as Bull's Camp, named after an army engineer who was not on the mountains during the peak road-building period but supervised the road's completion, on and off, and was given all the glory. Australians were apparently determined to eradicate any name that evoked the convict era, even if it was not directly connected to convicts. In this spirit, in 1879 memory of the weatherboard hut, which had become the location name Weatherboard, was wiped away, replaced by Wentworth Falls, to commemorate one of the first men to find a useable passageway over the mountains.[4] In the new colony of Queensland, they were determined to expunge reminders of the brutal penal settlement that operated there for eighteen years. Moreton Bay was renamed Brisbane, and convict infrastructure like the Female Factory building, the gaol and the commandant's house were either dismantled or allowed to crumble away.[5] In 1900, Queenslanders were blunt about their rejection of their convict past, the melodrama of their prose perfectly encapsulating the melodrama that passed for Australian history at that time.

> Shall we pass it over? We think so. Queensland's infantile days were broad arrowed with crime . . . the curse of the whippers and the prayers of the whipped was the doleful music played at its birth. Convictism hung like a pall over Moreton Bay.[6]

In fact, to the extent it has been available to them, Australians have generally shown interest in their history. In 1880, the New South Wales parliament passed an Act that made it a compulsory subject in all government primary schools. Later it was introduced into high schools. It became a field for postgraduate research at the University of Sydney from at least as early as 1915, so close in time to settlement by the Europeans that it was almost current affairs rather than history.[7]

However, in the first half of the twentieth century everyone, including academics, were constrained in their choice of topics by lack of primary sources. Until the 1960s, access to penal records was strictly limited. Colonial reminiscences abounded, but the actual records of the penal colonies were carefully guarded. Transportation ended in New South Wales in 1841, in Tasmania in 1853 and in Western Australia in 1868, but there were convicts serving sentences in all states beyond those dates and their records were operational until at least the turn of the century. Even in the early years of the new century, Tasmanian records were still being consulted by bureaucrats intent on establishing someone's entitlement to an old age pension. Angus McKay, for instance, who arrived on the *St Vincent* as a convict, applied for a pension in 1909. The application was noted on his conduct record in the penal register.[8]

There were also prohibitions on what could be revealed. In the late nineteenth century, James Bonwick was allowed to transcribe the official despatches between colonial governors and British authorities in order to compile the *Historical Records of New South Wales*, but he was under instructions to treat convict names with caution and omit them unless their historical significance required their inclusion. The sensitivities of specific descendants of convicts had to be taken into account also, since some had become prominent and influential. Relationships between soldiers and female convicts, such as Colonel George Johnson and Esther Abrahams, were potential social dynamite given the status of their descendants. Bonwick was instructed that such relationships were 'matters of a delicate nature' and must be treated 'in a careful manner'.[9] When the Commonwealth took over the project in 1912, radiologist and former physician Dr Frederick Watson became editor and, reflecting the national involvement, its name was changed to *Historical Records of Australia*. After the first volume appeared the following year, Professor G.A. Wood was appointed in a supervisory role to contribute scholarly oversight, but he too was warned to take care about confidentiality.[10] The reason given to Wood at the time was the authorities' fear that knowledge of convict ancestors would be used to blackmail descendants. Any notes taken from the records had to be vetted by the Mitchell Librarian before they left the premises.[11] The two men's privileged access to the records for this project laid the groundwork for Wood's contribution in 1921 on the character of the convicts. Given the sensitivity about the convicts as people, it was an extraordinary achievement to publish the administrative records. In effect, it was a beneficial consequence of the somewhat desperate search for 'history' that resulted from avoiding a substantial part of it. Certainly, it was a rare decision. As Brian Fletcher points out, no other British colony, except for the Cape of Good Hope, published its early records.[12] A valuable resource was now available to historians. But it was limited to the view 'from above' and at the highest level of the hierarchy. The people below, who were the subject of history, remained stored out of sight, beyond public access for decades.

When the Australian colonies federated as a Commonwealth in 1901, there was discussion about whether the convict records in New South Wales should be destroyed. Almost twenty years earlier, when the Garden Palace exhibition centre burned down in a spectacular blaze, wild rumours swept Sydney that the fire had been started deliberately to destroy the records.[13] Certainly, by the time the government wondered what to do with them, the specific records of the Superintendent of Convicts department had vanished— where and how no one knows to this day. They were numerous and their destruction would have required quite a bonfire. It is surprising no trace of what happened to them has yet come to light.

Some documents were deliberately destroyed by, or on behalf of, individuals. In Tasmania for instance, where convict records survived mass destruction, the records of some prominent citizens, such as John Davies, ex-convict editor of the *Hobart Mercury*, conveniently vanished.[14] In New South Wales some were saved—or perhaps just souvenired—by employees who kept them under their bed or in the garden shed for years. In the 1990s, for instance, the Parramatta Bench Book for May 1821–March 1822 came to light. It had been literally kept under a bed by the Brown family for as long as they could remember. 'We think our great-great-grandfather, John Brown, who was a sheriff's officer at Parramatta, obtained it somehow,' said Mrs Betty McDonell, the day she handed it over to State Records. 'He passed it on to our grandfather, barrister Alfred Brown. And it went down the line from there.'[15] Despite loss and destruction, many convict records in New South Wales did survive, including the vast correspondence of the Colonial Secretary, which remained intact at the turn of the century. On the verge of a decision to destroy these documents, the New South Wales government was struck by the thought that they were in fact Imperial records, and therefore not the local authorities' property to destroy. They wrote to the Public Record Office (PRO) in London asking what to do. The PRO took its time but eventually asked for examples of the papers in order to decide. Three sample documents were duly despatched, and there the matter rested. And rested.

Interest in Australian history gathered pace again after Federation, led in the early decades by academics such as G.A. Wood, who was the first Challis Professor of History at the University of Sydney, and later by Keith Hancock, whose book *Australia*, according to Brian Fletcher writing in the 1990s, 'set the agenda for the academic study of its subject until after World War II'.[16] Parallel with the activities of academics were those of laymen, most particularly members of the Royal Australian Historical Society, which was formed in 1901 by a group of professional and business men. Several other states also formed historical societies during the early decades of the twentieth century. They could be fierce protectors against the 'convict stain', as two young members of the Western Australian Historical Society discovered in 1931.

When a small bundle of tattered letters from a convict's wife to her husband, wrapped in an equally worn leather pouch, was handed to the society in 1931, the Research Secretary insisted that they must be destroyed, arguing that they were obviously personal letters and therefore of no historical value. The very young, recently married, Honorary Secretary, Mr Paul Hasluck, ventured to disagree. Fearing the council might decide to destroy the letters, between one meeting and the next he took them home and laboriously copied them out. At the next meeting the council decided to store them 'for the time being'. In 1934, the same Research Secretary drew council's attention to the continued storage of the letters and asked if they should be handed to the State Archives to be placed in their closed records. In her husband's absence, Mrs Hasluck took the minutes for the discussion that then raged.

The Research Secretary began by demanding, 'in a high and somewhat excited voice', that the letters be destroyed. Alexandra Hasluck recalled that she was genuinely shocked that anyone should think of destroying historical records. 'The Research Secretary, growing more agitated, retorted that they were *not* historical records: they contained no reference to historical events, places or personages; they described only the feelings of the convict's wife, and were extremely pathetic. They should not be seen by every Tom, Dick and Harry.' Some committee members agreed with the sentiment on the basis that the convict period of Western Australia's history was best forgotten. Somewhat timidly, Mrs Hasluck pointed out that the convicts were part of the state's history and could not be disregarded. This led to a discussion on what exactly the convicts had done, what buildings they made and the roads they built. 'A member of one of the Old Families of Western Australia said that the State had been founded as a free colony by gentlefolk: the convicts came later and unwanted and should not be associated with it.' 'But no one would associate them with the founding, only with the making,' said someone else, to which the 'Old Family' replied firmly, 'That was immaterial: they were not there at the beginning, they did not take any of the risks.' At this point, Alexandra Hasluck says she 'quelled her diffidence' to insist in her turn that the council had no right to destroy the letters. '[T]hey were letters that [the convict] had apparently valued and had kept carefully in a pouch made specially to preserve them. Such a thing was a trust to the people who found it . . . It was the Council's duty to take them into safe-keeping.' In the face of that, there was nothing more that could be said. Mrs Hasluck herself composed the minute that disguises the controversy that had engulfed them all. 'After some discussion, it was decided that only official papers should be handed over [to the Archives], the letters being retained by the Society.'[17]

In 1932, six years before the Sesquicentenary of Australia, the Society of Australian Genealogists added to the venues where Australians could pursue their interest in history. It was from this platform that president Herbert Rumsey fought his battle to get the convicts included in the festive parade. Having been outvoted on that issue, Rumsey was determined that the convicts should be commemorated somehow. In a limited edition, he printed a list of convicts on the First Fleet. It was the first time their names had been published.[18]

NO INVITATION.
"Buzz off or I'll book you!"

Convicts were 'not invited' to participate in the 1938 celebrations. The caption to this Bulletin *cartoon read: 'No Invitation. "Buzz off or I'll book you!"'*

At the same time, interested individuals were writing history. Among them was the High Court Judge H.V. Evatt, who in 1938 published *Rum Rebellion*. In 1941, inspired by fury at the treatment of the Aborigines and the convicts during the Sesquicentenary, novelist Eleanor Dark began her trilogy of novels with sound historical underpinnings which depicted both groups. The first volume was called *The Timeless Land*.[19]

In the decade after World War II academics like A.G.L. Shaw and Manning Clark and Lloyd Robson began major professional research into Australian topics. Not surprisingly, they quickly confronted the paucity of original material available to them. Clark's reaction was to publish in 1950 *Select Documents in Australian History, 1788–1850*, which pulled together a range of primary material of use to historians and teachers. Once again, the activities of interested laymen ran parallel to the academics. Journalist Malcolm Ellis published substantial biographies of Governor Lachlan Macquarie and the early pastoralist John Macarthur. Significantly, Ellis also wrote a biography of Francis Greenway, who was transported for forgery but was also the architect of the few remaining buildings from the convict period in Sydney. Relatives of the Henty family who settled in Victoria and of James Milson, an early settler in New South Wales, published family letters and other documents. The Australian public bought these books with enthusiasm. From 1956 their interest in historical topics was further met by productions from the new medium of television: ABC Television's drama series about Governor Macquarie, for example, was particularly popular. Meanwhile, in Western Australia they were still throwing out convict records. In the 1950s a workman at Fremantle Gaol who was helping to clean up after it ceased operation as a prison was confronted by hundreds of photographs of convicts. He asked someone in authority what he should do with them. 'Destroy them. Throw them in the ocean if you want,' was the instruction.[20]

Tasmania established a State Archives Authority in 1951 and New South Wales in 1961, each initially within the relevant State Library. In Tasmania, the records of the Convict Department, which had been stored 'in no particular order with many volumes, including a volume of the convict indents, on the floor, and the whole vault needing cleaning', were the second group of documents transferred to this new home.[21] For some years, the release of the information they contained was left to the discretion of the Archives Authority. Restrictions in both states were loosened for bona fide scholars.[22] An examination of his bibliography for *Convicts and the Colonies* reveals that A.G.L. Shaw had unlimited access to convict material held in Australia during this decade. So did Manning Clark for his *History of Australia*, which was researched during the same period. New Zealander and former war correspondent Charles Bateson was also allowed access for his 1959 book, *The Convict Ships*, which is an example of a layman's scholarship that became a standard text. But whoever the applicant, a letter had to be written, credentials explained, testimonials produced. A family historian who approached the Mitchell Library or the State Archives had no direct access to convict information and probably received little encouragement from archivists because the topic was cumbersome to manage, given the policy restrictions, and sometimes controversial if a First Fleeter turned out to have arrived in irons.

Then in 1961 a visiting American scholar precipitated a crisis of policy-making in Tasmania by telling the media that he was there to study records relating to convicts and their families. Uproar ensued. Questions were asked in the Tasmanian parliament. Letters were written to the editor of the *Hobart Mercury*. In self-defence, the Library Board decided they should formulate 'a directive' for the Archives Officer. After considerable discussion about how to do it, they finally decided that 'access to convict lists will only be granted to those who have made prior application in writing to the Board indicating the nature of the records required and generally the purpose for which such records are required'.[23] The catch for applicants was that the board would judge the worth of their project. Not only would it decide whether they were bona fide scholars, it would also form a view about whether their research had sufficient historical value to warrant permission to wander among the records. The first application considered under these new rules was from Dr George Rudé, then based at the University of Adelaide, who went on to write a seminal text on the convicts called *Protest and Punishment*.[24] Rudé was easy for the board to approve because he was only interested in the 'respectable' convicts—those who were transported for political protest of some kind and who had been put forward with the poachers by G.A. Wood in 1921 as more victims of circumstance than criminals.[25]

Dr Lloyd Robson's request shortly after was much more sensitive because his project was about the origins and crimes of all the convicts. Having drafted his book based on research in the archives, Robson applied to publish the prisoners' names. The board refused, but Robson's request did precipitate a change in policy. Foreseeing that Robson would not be the last applicant, the Library Board added a new condition for scholars who wished to use archival material. Henceforth, they must agree 'to abide by the Board's decision in relation to the publication of names and other particulars going to identity'.[26] It took nine years before this provision was abolished. Robyn Eastley, now a Senior Archivist at the Tasmanian office, recalled that it was a book by Dr Peter Bolger called *Hobart Town* which, as the local newspaper put it, 'set the academic cat among the Tasmanian family pigeons with a vengeance'.[27] Like Robson, Bolger had been granted permission to use the records and then asked permission to publish the names. According to Eastley, the Library Board panicked when they received the application. After much anxious scrutiny of the text, careful notes of the names mentioned, legal opinions obtained and staff interviewed, they declined Bolger's request. At the same meeting, however, probably warned by lawyers that their position was untenable in the long term, they cancelled the requirement to seek their approval for publication of names. Bolger's book was, in fact, published with names, but it contained a disclaimer protecting the local authority. According to Bolger, information about convicts was obtained from records in Britain and not from the Archives Office in Tasmania.[28]

In the 1960s, as academic requests for information gathered apace, so did those from members of the public. In New South Wales the Mitchell Library, recently separated officially from the State Archives, asked the Society of

Genealogists to help out by handling the family historians. The library was then able to introduce a policy that access to its documents would require a reader's ticket, which would only be granted for purposes of valid historical research and not for family history.[29] The society immediately found itself with the same problem as the library and the Archives: 'We were inundated,' recalled former president Keith Johnson. 'At that time, the Society had similar restrictions to the library on access to records. If someone wanted information about ancestors who were likely to be among the more than 30,000 names in the 1828 Census, they had to wait patiently while the Honorary Research Secretary produced the copy of the census from its locked cabinet, scrutinised the list and then handed them a note of the relevant information.'[30] Another decade passed before Johnson and his colleague Malcolm Sainty decided the time was right to publish the 1828 Census in its unexpurgated glory. Then—and this was 1980—they were taken aback when Dr Frank Crowley greeted their scholarly work with barely concealed anger. 'I protest on behalf of my ancestors,' he wrote. Fortunately, more enlightened academics in the form of Ken Cable and Brian Fletcher hastened to assure the editors that they 'should take no notice'.[31]

Meanwhile, the Tasmanian Archives had become embroiled in a battle with the owners of a kiosk at Port Arthur who, it turned out, had been in possession for many years of the documentary archives of that dreaded penal institution. How they got them was never discovered. Fortunately they deposited the documents with the Archives before demanding payment. The battle that ensued when the Archives refused to pay on the grounds they were government property anyway kept both sides occupied for years.[32]

In New South Wales, the Mitchell Library was part of an initiative to increase the convict records available to Australian researchers. First proposed by Sir Keith Hancock and the National Librarian Sir Harold White, the Australian Joint Copying Project (known as the AJCP) aimed to microfilm documents of significance to Australian history which were held in Britain. Former Mitchell Librarian, Phyllis Mander-Jones, was appointed research officer for the project on her retirement from the library. Her job was to identify what should be filmed in the Public Record Offices (PROs) in London and Edinburgh and the various county repositories throughout Britain.[33] Filming commenced in the mid-1960s and the scheme continued over the next fifteen to twenty years. As a result, microfilm of hulks and prison registers, shipping indents, surgeons' journals, war office musters, private correspondence and diaries became available in Australian locations.[34] As a precaution, the opening frame of each film contains a condition for eager researchers: 'By order of the Council of the Library of New South Wales, the information contained in these records must not be used in any manner likely to cause pain or embarrassment to any living person.'[35]

A side benefit of the AJCP filming was the return of the sample documents sent to the PRO at the turn of the century. New South Wales archivists knew there were gaps in their records, but knowledge of the correspondence with the PRO had been lost in the intervening years. Scanning an AJCP film one day, senior archivist Dawn Troy spotted three documents that she was sure rightly belonged in Australia. The earlier correspondence was unearthed and a carefully pitched reproachful letter was sent to the PRO. The local archivists waited in suspense. To their relief, no argument was raised about ownership and the two printed convict indents as well as records of convict bank accounts were returned.[36] During this period also, Dawn Troy prepared what became the definitive *Guide to the Convict Records in the Archives Office of New South Wales*, a publication of such high calibre that it was fundamental in making those records readily accessible to legions of family researchers over the next 25 years.

By the mid-1970s a younger generation had assumed positions of influence within the records repositories. The same occurred among historians, politicians and community leaders. Attitudes were changing rapidly in the community and the restrictions on access to convict information seemed increasingly outdated. With the rising requests for information, management of the records became increasingly difficult when access could not be facilitated to meet demand. In 1976, Tasmanian archivists successfully petitioned the Library Board asking for this 'needless censorship' to be removed.[37]

In fact, officials and institutions could not have taken their stance on keeping convicts' details secret without tacit community agreement. From the mid-nineteenth century, and in some cases earlier, information about convict ancestors was being erased at a personal and family level. The widespread cover-up involving ordinary families (as opposed to the middle class) began in the 1850s and gathered pace during the following decades. As we shall see, there was external impetus for this expansion of shame. Until that time, the idea of an indelible birthstain was more often in the eye of the beholder than the bearer of it. Attempts to hide the convict taint during the transportation era were confined to a few families who had acquired wealth and status and whose antecedents were a handicap. In the 1820s in New South Wales, for instance, a sequence of official musters culminating in the 1828 Census, all of which have survived, make it possible to detect a far-sighted ex-convict such as Mary Reiby recording a different ship of arrival to help her descendants keep their disreputable forebears secret. Mary Reiby was among the earliest convicts transported. After she had acquired respectability and riches, she paid a visit 'home' to Britain. When she returned to the colony she used the name of the ship on which she returned to her advantage. Transported as a young horse thief, Reiby had arrived in New South Wales in 1792 on the *Royal Admiral*, but she appears in the 1828 Census as a settler who 'came free' on the *Mariner* in 1821. If she had been less well known, this stratagem would have created a major puzzle later for family researchers.

The erasure of convict links is a phenomenon that professional historians have not taken seriously. In fact have often denigrated. One academic historian, Dr Alison Alexander, asked her class of 127 students at the University of Tasmania whether they were descended from convicts. Of the nearly 20 per cent who knew they were, 60 per cent had only discovered the information through research done by a family member since 1970.[38] The knowledge had not been passed down through the family. Ronald D. Lambert, a sociologist, conducted a survey of genealogists in 2002 that was somewhat marred by the disparagement contained in his premise that they 'have developed an array of generic arguments for neutralising their ancestors' stigmatised status—for themselves, for their families and for their communities'. His sample of 46 people included 38 who were direct descendants of convicts. The overwhelming majority of them told Lambert that they were unaware of their convict ancestry before they started genealogical research.[39] Vast anecdotal evidence exists about the topic among family historians but apart from Dr Alexander, the only other survey is one by this author who found in a sample of 100 convict descendants collected during 2004–05 that 80 per cent had no idea they were connected to convicts before they began their own research.

Generally speaking, Australians who were most publicly proud of their ancestors were people who thought they had come as free settlers or among the military on the First Fleet. Their knowledge was usually based on oral tradition. Initially accepted without scepticism, oral history is something every family historian has since learned to distrust. The family of James Wilde provides a typical example of what can occur, in this case when someone has leapt at the idea they were descended from Sir John Wylde, the convict colony's Deputy Judge Advocate. This was the family story until it was discovered recently that their ancestor, James Wilde, was a prisoner on the *John* in 1832. At some stage the Wildes had created a link to someone prominent that subsequent descendants believed. Getting past these well-established stories is frequently the first challenge of family historians. Some give up when they cannot prove the legend, but many more have found their way past the myth to the reality behind it. Nevertheless, a few have had great difficulty accepting that their family story is false.

Forty years ago, desperate denial described the reaction of some of the First Fleet descendants who would do anything to preserve the idea of a freely arrived pioneer settler. Some families who discovered their ancestor was a convict on the First Fleet became notorious for attempting to substitute a soldier's musket for a prisoner's manacles. In the 1960s and '70s, stories of their reaction were circulated widely and with mirth, unfortunately stereotyping all family historians as pretentious sentimentalists incapable of rigorous research and loose with the truth. After John Cobley published *Crimes of the First Fleet* in 1970, including the first substantiated list of names, the dismayed protestations by some descendants gradually gave way to acceptance. It took ten years for the furore to subside, but by the 1980s a convict ancestor had become as much a cause for pride as a soldier. Despite some controversy, interest in First Fleet ancestors was a significant factor in the growth of family history in Australia. The Fellowship of First Fleeters, which was founded in 1968, derived extra impetus from the impending bicentenary of Captain Cook's visit to eastern Australia. The 1788–1820 Pioneer Association was also established in the late 1960s and members of both groups, as well as those who wanted to be members, for the first time created public pressure for information from the convict archives.[40]

The Captain Cook Bicentenary in 1970 raised the profile of Australian history, but it only laid the groundwork. Bearing down six years later came the bicentenary of the American Revolution. Australians had no particular attachment to American history, but the American celebrations added to the general consciousness of national history. Specifically, the television series *Roots*, which told the generational story of a family of slaves from their beginnings in Africa, had enormous impact. Australians read the book, then watched the television show in their thousands and began to wonder when their own family first arrived. Simultaneously, in the press and on radio, Philip Geeves was popularising Australian history, answering readers' questions and doing surveys about convict connections. In 1979, when the New South Wales Registry of Births, Deaths and Marriages decided to release the historic indexes for general research, many people had reached a stage where they thought, 'I can do that'.

The trickle of interest swelled to a flood and Australians in their hordes descended on the archives and the libraries. Membership of the Society of Australian Genealogists in Sydney climbed steeply from 629 members in 1972, through 7500 in 1982 and to nearly 10,000 five years later.[41] The momentum peaked in 1988 with the Bicentenary—a celebration which, despite its subject, refused to allow a re-enactment of the first white settlers going ashore. With the innocence of ignorance, thousands of Australians accessed the newly released births, deaths and marriages indexes, obediently working backwards from their parents and grandparents in the best genealogical tradition, until they were pulled up short by the revelation that they had discovered a convict ancestor, sometimes more than one. In some cases, a whole new generation of Australian ancestors came to light. As the research widened, tenth cousins once removed were reunited, each a descendant from convict great-great-great-grandparents whose large family had been unsuspected, and they usually brought some item or information which helped to piece together the puzzling whole.

Family amnesia about the convicts was explained in a variety of ways. As well as the respectable or prominent ancestor who happened to have a similar name, there was minimisation, or even complete fudging, of facts which had probably long ago been lost anyway except for the basic issue that an ancestor had come to Australia for a somewhat disreputable reason:

> Later generations were told that Thomas was a 'remittance man' sent out and supported by his family to avoid disgrace for some misdemeanour, variously described as fixing a boxing match, stealing money collected for a good cause or rick burning. My cousin and others believed such stories and passed them on until we discovered in 1981 that Thomas was a convict. However some members of the family in the male line had apparently been told the truth.[42]

If the information about a convict ancestor was passed down, it was often to the eldest son. Sometimes only the boys were told, on the assumption that girls needed to be protected from hard reality. How many knew and kept the information quiet in some pact with their parent or grandparent is impossible to establish.

William Brodribb's eldest son, also William Brodribb, is a case in point. Around 1834 he left Tasmania, where his parents lived, with the intention of taking up pastoral land on the mainland. In the classic style of the Australian squatter who was establishing himself, Brodribb drove stock up and down the backblocks of Victoria, New South Wales and Queensland, squatting on land, buying land, selling land, leasing land, buying livestock and selling it. Sometimes he worked as a manager. Sometimes the run was his own. By the 1860s he was a wealthy pastoralist, a prominent citizen and a member of the Victorian parliament. In these roles, he was conscious of the need to attract immigrants to Australia, which was not the destination of first choice for many. Paying his first visit to England in 1863, he gave speeches and wrote pamphlets about life in Australia with the aim of convincing prospective immigrants to settle here. In 1883 he published his autobiography, *Recollections of an Australian Squatter*. Its opening line is an example of both the dilemma and the cover-up of convict ancestry in action. Brodribb wrote: 'In the year 1818, I arrived from England with my parents, who settled in Tasmania …' Did he know? Young Brodribb was ten when he sailed with his mother Prudence, sister Lavinia and other siblings on the *Friendship*. In Gloucestershire, he may not have known of his father's trial and conviction, but he grew up in Van Diemen's Land where he would have been too old not to have discovered that his father was transported.

William was probably an example of an older son who was entrusted with the truth and in the climate of the late nineteenth century was not going to advertise it.[43] In later generations, some branches of the large Brodribb family knew they were descended from a convict, but others did not. In 2004 David Scott, a descendant of young William Brodribb, recalled, 'My mother and uncle knew of the convict origin of the Brodribbs but liked to keep it quiet. I only found out when I discovered the reference in documents I was reading for political science at the university in the late fifties. Then they said they had always known . . . but did not tell me!'[44] By comparison, the information was not passed down at all through descendants of the Brodribbs' daughter, Lavinia. According to one of them, Jo Watson, 'My own grandmother certainly did not realise William Brodribb was a convict. As a teenager, I can still remember her musing, "what an intelligent man Grandfather William must have been . . . being chosen to come here and help set up the new colony". My father was the descendant but it was actually my mother who found reference to Brodribb's transportation in a history book.'[45]

Descendants of the Berkeley poachers typify the descendants of many convicts. Like many other family researchers, by the late twentieth century most of them were unaware that the ancestors they were looking for had arrived in Australia as convicts.

Descendants of Daniel Long had no idea that he had come to Australia as a prisoner, let alone any knowledge of the poaching events in Berkeley. They did not ask questions. Why would they when the tale they were told was perfectly satisfying and there was no reason to suspect its accuracy? Daniel Long as a convict received a grant of land and later owned a pub in the Tasmanian hamlet of Sorell. His descendant Linda Forbes described how these facts were the basis of their family story. 'My father was told that Daniel had "come out with Governor Sorell and was given a grant of land at Sorell—we should own the town by rights". The convict bit had been erased from the family stories but I've been unable to find out at what point this happened. I suspect one of my grandfather's brothers knew the truth, but he never admitted it to anyone and expounded the same family story.'[46]

The Long family typified the range of responses that can occur when a convict was discovered. Linda Forbes, who uncovered the information, reported how her relatives reacted to the news. 'My father and grandfather (direct descendants of Daniel) were a bit uncomfortable about it, but relieved that at least he hadn't been an axe murderer or a rapist! Their wives, who both came from lower middle-class shopkeeper/bookkeeper type stock, were not at all sympathetic. My grandmother always pursed her mouth tight when it was mentioned and started muttering "no one's ever interested in my family" which would mean I had to down tools researching the Longs and dig up something on her side to keep her happy. My mother whooped at the news and declared to my father, "I might have known you came from a family of illiterate criminals."[47]

By comparison, descendants of Jack Reeves were one of the few families who knew about their convict ancestry, although it was somewhat whitewashed. They were told that 'Jack Reeves was a poacher. And that he farmed after getting his ticket-of-leave and then became licensee of a pub. There was no mention of the murder of a game-keeper . . . he was made out to be a simple poacher.' His descendant, Lauris Crampton, explained that her family were apparently more concerned that Jack Reeves failed to marry his partner (ex-convict Elizabeth Burrell) than by his criminal conviction. Family history had always described the couple as married and someone had altered their son's birthday by twelve months so he was born after Reeves had obtained his ticket-of-leave when the couple were living together. In fact the boy was born in the Female Factory and baptised under his mother's name. According to Lauris Crampton, 'There was definitely no mention of Jack's wife and three sons back in England.'[48]

In a publication designed to mark the bicentenary of white settlement in Tasmania, Alison Alexander described her ancestor Jane Baird, who was charged with assault and theft in 1840:

> She told the court that one Thomas Lamond had come to the alehouse one night a little intoxicated and became more so as the night wore on. The next day he was led away by his daughter. Jane denied stealing any money from him, but said he gave her some money to keep for him, which her husband later gave back to Thomas's son and daughter when they came for it. [While there] the daughter Janet became intoxicated and broke some dishes. Jane denied throwing a bottle at Janet and cutting her head but said that the two Lamonds were so noisy and riotous that she went out to the road and enlisted the help of three men to keep the Lamonds in order. The Lamonds offered to fight the men, and Jane got rid of them and secured her door. The men returned and threatened to break down the door, but as there were plenty of passers-by, they did not do it.

The court listened to this story but was not persuaded. Jane was found guilty and sentenced to seven years transportation. Her career in Tasmania was as disreputable and feisty as the scenario that resulted in her exile but, as Alison Alexander recalled, after family research had uncovered her story, a large crowd met to celebrate. 'Jane . . . had many descendants, who kept extremely quiet about their ancestor's criminal career, which was unknown to later family members. Research brought it to light in the 1970s, and a gathering of all Jane's descendants was held. My parents returned highly entertained: to commemorate the life of this turbulent woman was collected a group of the most respectable and well-behaved late twentieth century Australians that could be imagined.'[49]

William Honeyman was convicted in Edinburgh in 1815 and travelled to Australia as a prisoner on the *Sir William Bensley*. His descendants began researching his daughter Anne when one of them discovered her grave in Tasmania and wondered how a Honeyman came to be buried there, remote from any family connection. A book about Honeyman families generally, which was published in 1909, speculated about Anne's father, stating that 'he was probably Alexander but may have been William, and that he was an architect in Scotland'.[50] The author had also accumulated some details about Anne's brothers, Alexander and William. These had been supplied by a daughter of the younger boy, William, who was herself therefore the grand-daughter of the William Honeyman transported to Australia.

According to this daughter, who was obviously reliant only on what her father chose to mention, 'My father, William, was reserved and did not say much about his parents. He and his eldest brother Alexander spent much of their early lives at sea. Father told me he was born in Falkirk and that his mother's name was Ogilvie, her parents being shipbuilders of Glasgow. He spoke of his father as being an architect and a very clever man, but did not state his name. His mother married again.'

There were grains of truth in some of this, as there were in another story handed down through the family, which suggested that Anne and Alexander and young William's father, the senior William Honeyman, had died at sea 'on the voyage to Australia'. But as contemporary Australian researcher Jill Roy explained, 'Much dedicated searching finally proved that their father's name was William, not Alexander, and it was then that an amazing story unfolded. The truth has all the elements of a soap opera—grand theft, arrest and trial, death on the high seas, orphanages, mystery and tragedy.'[51] It is a story that will be explored fully in later chapters.

The origins of family amnesia were many and varied. Sometimes they arose from tactics initiated by the convicts themselves to disguise their background, the truth of which was never revealed to descendants. A favourite ploy was also the simplest. Often the convict just changed his name. An alias could begin in England with a series of convictions under two or sometimes three different names. Such a collection of identities usually caused the desired confusion at the time but it did not necessarily defeat later family research. If the men stuck to just one of their aliases in Australia, uncovering their tracks was easier. The greatest problem for family researchers was when the prisoners varied their names after they arrived in the colony, particularly if they arrived with one name but married and were buried under another. And the disguise adopted in Britain was not always a working alias. Sometimes it was just an impudent gesture. At face value, for instance, a legendary highwayman appeared to have cloned himself. The ship *Layton* transported both a 'Dick Turpin' and on the same voyage a rascal from County Galway who dignified himself as 'Richard Turpin'. The *John* also brought a 'Richard Turpin' to New South Wales. An alias like this was usually discarded after a convict served his sentence and was free of the penal record-keeping. John Smith or White or Brown were also popular pseudonyms adopted by prisoners who wanted to disguise their origins but they were more likely to be retained for longer, which made the task of uncovering the truth harder for assiduous descendants.

One 'John Smith' was brought undone decades later by his family. Originally known as George Evans, he was transported by the *Tortoise* to Van Diemen's Land in 1842, leaving behind in Sussex a wife and four children to whom he never returned. Instead, George married another convict in 1850, while his first wife was still alive. Together they raised five children. After their marriage, when the family moved to Rushworth, Victoria, George took the opportunity to change his name. Presumably to disguise his convict past, but perhaps to disguise his bigamy too, he became John Smith. Several generations later, his descendants were stumped. They traced him back to Rushworth, but every attempt to get further than that drew a complete blank. Only when a more experienced researcher, Robert Saunders in Tasmania, gave them some help was a breakthrough achieved. With Saunders' assistance they managed to link John Smith to a convict named George Evans via marriage details and the birth records for the first two children born in Van Diemen's Land.[52]

Working backwards from an assumed name and linking to a convict who arrived with another name is one of the significant contributions that family historians make to Australian historiography. An unrelated researcher who begins at the ships' indents is far less likely to arrive at the truth, having no reason to suspect trickery when they lose the trail. They just accept the research avenues are exhausted. Descendants, on the other hand, know full well that a particular person existed up to a certain date because they usually have his or her death certificate. When their ancestor simply vanishes, they are more likely to become suspicious. They also have the advantage of family knowledge about siblings and children and locations of importance to the family.

The convict James Freeman set his descendants a challenge that would have defeated anyone less committed than those for whom he was an ancestor. Transported for stealing a horse, he arrived in Hobart in 1828 on board the *Bengal Merchant*. When his sentence was over he did not move to New Zealand or Victoria as many others did. Instead, he stayed put in Van Diemen's Land, married and had children but then changed his surname to Prince. To complicate matters his children, except for one son, changed their names too and in the case of the daughters they married, thus doubly obliterating their tracks. Trying to find the death of James Freeman and his wife Mary, or even the outcome of their lives, took many years for their descendant Leonie Mickleborough, for whom the documentary traces simply evaporated at every turn. In the course of her research, she spread notices of her problems throughout the global network of family historians. Finally, a descendant of the son who had not changed his name made contact to say she had a family Bible, which supplied the missing link between James and Mary Freeman and the name 'Prince'. Inscribed in the Bible was the following: 'To Mr James W. Freeman [and] Mrs James W. Freeman, A present from his mother Mrs James Prince on his wedding day June 3rd 1865 . . . Grandmother Mary Prince died 9 April 1871 aged 57 years.'[53]

Occasionally, echoes of the penal system lingered in a family even when specific knowledge was lost. After Trevor Carey uncovered two convict ancestors in the 1980s his uncle, who was born in the early years of the twentieth century, remembered family talk about 'a one-armed overseer of convicts in Tasmania called Gunn and that he was very cruel'. The memory was accurate. William Gunn, who was the Superintendent of Convicts in Tasmania for many years, was believed by the prisoners to have a superhuman memory of them and of their misdeeds. He lost his arm in a fight with bushrangers. Trevor Carey himself recalled that during his childhood his many uncles all frequently used the phrase 'he deserves a good flogging'.[54]

The women prisoners are no easier to track than the men, although their name changes tend to have more legitimate purposes. Some female convicts were convicted under their maiden name but transported by the married one, often declaring themselves 'the wife of Joe Blow' in the hope they would be reunited with their husband. Women who simply lived with a man, or two or three men consecutively, took his name for the duration of the liaison and registered his children by that name. Susannah Watson, who arrived as a prisoner in 1829 on the *Princess Royal*, was one of these. Transported as (Mrs)

Watson, she lived as Clarke for the bulk of her fourteen-year sentence in order to trick the authorities into thinking she was married to fellow convict John Clarke, who had only a seven-year sentence. When he gained a ticket-of-leave, Susannah was assigned to live with him and could serve out the rest of her sentence to all intents free, as a wife and mother. Like many women prisoners, she took care to record the fathers of her Australian children within their baptismal name. Charles Isaac Moss Watson was the son of Isaac Moss, and John Henry Clarke Watson the son of John Clarke. It was her descendants' good fortune that she registered Charles, at least, as Watson, probably because she did not have a continuous relationship with his father. John's birth was harder to trace because he was listed as Clarke. Once free, Susannah reverted to her legal name, Watson.[55]

The tricks the convicts used to try to blur their tracks through the system were continuously inventive—wrong surname, wrong spelling, different first name with one surname, different surname with first name, several first names with the original surname. Few realised at the time, however, that the great identifier for the authorities—and over a century later for their descendants— was the name of the ship that brought them to Australia. Occasionally a prisoner decided that muddling the ship would be a useful way of hiding their identity. John Clegg, for instance, declared in the 1828 Census that he was transported on the *Sir William Bensley*, yet is nowhere to be found on that ship's indent. In fact he arrived the year earlier on the *Ocean*. There were others like him, but most prisoners did not detect the trap set by their ship's name.

Another stratagem employed by convicts or their descendants was similar to that of John Smith (aka George Evans): move away, move interstate or move to another country altogether. It was in this way that the 'ocean of purity between two sinks of iniquity', as Victoria liked to describe itself, shared the convict stain almost as much as the rest of Australia. It was not only gold or the prospect of employment that prompted Vandemonians to move in great numbers across Bass Strait to Victoria in the latter part of the nineteenth century. It was also the opportunity to put their convict past well behind them. For the same reason, Western Australian convicts moved east in significant numbers. South Australia was often their destination of choice, but some kept going to Victoria. Convicts also took their families to New Zealand, where although they broke the link to their past misdeeds their demeanour was not always convincing. As a New Zealand descendant explained, her family just knew their ancestors were hiding something, but it seldom occurred to anyone it was a criminal past. 'My great-great grandmother, Emma Tyror, was the daughter of two convicts but she never talked about her origins in Australia. It was assumed this was because she had Aboriginal blood.'[56]

James Jaye was an example of a convict who simply omitted uncomfortable facts. Convicted at the Old Bailey of stealing lead, the 22-year-old pastrycook was transported for seven years. He landed in Sydney in 1832 on

the *John* and was assigned to work with the surveyor J.B. Richards, who laid out the town plan for Bathurst. Granted a ticket-of-leave four years later, Jaye then married Ann Storrett, who was also a convict. At fifteen, she had been the youngest girl transported on the *Princess Royal*.[57] The gold rush in 1851 transformed Bathurst from a small settlement serving the surrounding pastoral stations into a rapidly growing town. Jaye was well positioned to take advantage of the changes. When Bernard Holterman visited the district in the late 1850s and photographed the business of tinsmiths J. Jaye & Co., he captured on film the stake that Jaye had established in the community. Approximately twenty

James Jaye disguised his convict past

years later, by which time he was approaching 60, Jaye wrote a letter to his eldest son in which he carefully established a respectable family history:

> In a young country like ours, a man who bears a family ought,
> I think, to let them know something of their origin . . . Your
> mother was the daughter of Sergeant Storrett of the Scotch
> Grays . . . My grandfather was Robert Jaye of the County
> of Suffolk, by trade a thatcher . . . My father was also
> Robert . . . [58]

There was no mention that 'your mother' arrived as a convict on the *Princess Royal* in 1829, and not even a hint that Jaye had also arrived as a felon. The reason he wrote the letter is unknown, but slurs about ancestry were commonplace from the mid-nineteenth century. Perhaps some insult was flung at Jaye, or his son, by another Bathurst worthy who knew Jaye's history. In the country town of Braidwood around the same time, parish clerk and former convict John Yeates thought it worth taking his neighbour before the Bench of Magistrates for describing Mrs Yeates as 'a damned convicted bitch'. Actually his wife, Mary O'Driscoll, was a free Irish immigrant. But the incident

J. Jaye & Co. tinsmiths. Jaye's wife, ex-convict Ann Storrett, stands in the doorway. Note the slogan above the window on the left: 'Live and Let Live'

demonstrates how the convict taint was used by ordinary working people against each other after transportation ended.[59]

A common tactic by descendants was to skip a generation when talking about family history. The descendants of Gloucestershire highway robber Joseph Barrett did that. Everything focused on Joseph's son, Abraham, who was a prominent citizen in Launceston during the last half of the nineteenth century. As descendant Pauline Connell put it, 'the family story "started" with Abraham and it was believed the family "came from New Zealand"'.[60] Brian Barrett, another descendant of Joseph, had a vague memory of being told that the family originally came from Scotland. As we shall see, there was a small seed of truth in some of this. But the existence of Joseph Barrett, the convict, had been completely lost.[61]

By the late twentieth century, the extraordinary life and character of Susannah Watson was unknown to her family because it too had skipped a generation, erasing Susannah from the collective memory. We knew nothing of her arrival on the *Princess Royal* in 1829, of the husband and children she left behind, of her two Australian sons fathered by two different men, of her ruse that fooled the authorities into thinking she was married to one of them, or of two further marriages followed by a long, legal widowhood until her death at 83 years singing 'Rock of Ages'. My family, Susannah's descendants, believed that branch of the family began when Charles Watson (subsequently discovered to be Susannah's bastard son) migrated to Australia, bringing with him a printing press which he used to establish a string of country newspapers. The initial duplicity appears on his death certificate in 1886, which recorded his birth in the Hawkesbury region of New South Wales, where many free settlers established farms. His mother's name was only recorded as Susannah, without a surname. In fact, Charles was born at the notorious Female Factory in Parramatta at the height of the convict system. The dissembler was probably Susannah's daughter-in-law, Eliza née Yeates, who was herself the daughter of a London pickpocket. At the time of Charles' death, she would have been the only person in a position to know where the truth needed blurring and what details should only be partially recorded.[62]

Where once families dreaded exposure of their convict connection, today the discovery that a convict belongs in the family tree is a matter for celebration. For one thing, it places an individual family in a very specific historical context. For another, there is also the bonus of bountiful records. Prisoners far outstrip free immigrants in terms of the traces they left behind. The convict records tell family researchers the colour of their ancestor's eyes, whether his hair was dark or fair, whether he had whiskers, if her skin was pale and smooth or marked by smallpox. How tall they were. How fat or thin. Some records in Tasmania reveal what they said about their crime. Archives in both Sydney and Hobart contain petitions from convicts applying for their families to be brought out by the government, seeking a ticket-of-leave or attempting to manipulate the system in some way to their benefit. Despite the formal language, in these documents the family researcher is privileged to catch a glimpse of a real person. However disconcerting the information—and sometimes it is—researchers have learnt to value it, warts and all.

Contrary to their popular reputation, family historians do not fear unpalatable truths. With the exception of a few high-profile descendants in the past, they in fact have a tradition of pursuing the truth regardless of consequences. However, the well-publicised early reaction of First Fleet descendants may have been a factor in shaping the attitude of some professional historians, which too often can only be described as contemptuous. Attending a meeting in connection with the 1988 Bicentennial, John Spurway experienced academic disdain for family history first hand. He recorded hearing a senior historian declare about family history 'that the practice belongs, with its adherents, in the realms of the "great unwashed" and has no significance for real history'.[63] In 2004, the Tasmanian-based academic, Professor Emeritus Michael Roe, was far more positive about the contribution of family historians. In his opinion, 'The "burden of history" indeed has weighed heavy upon this [Tasmanian] society . . . The burden has taken long to lift, awaiting the past thirty years or so. Crucial in the process have been people prepared and even happy to acknowledge convicts in their own genealogy.'[64] The negative opinions expressed in Spurway's hearing fifteen years earlier confirmed that Alan Atkinson had the right of it when he wrote about family history in 1989, 'This willingness to embrace the convict past does not yet prevail everywhere. It is a popular rather than an official attitude.' Atkinson was one academic who, with his colleague Norma Townsend, thought family history had something to offer the profession.[65] Along with Ken Cable and Brian Fletcher, they did much to forge early links between the two.

When Atkinson expressed this opinion he was reviewing Mollie Gillen's vast undertaking published in 1988 as *The Founders of Australia: A Biographical Dictionary of the First Fleet*, a publication whose examination of the primary sources was so rigorous that it is now the definitive reference on the 1500 people who made that significant voyage.[66] At a time when the Bicentennial Authority was disavowing all things convict, Gillen had been nurtured in her immense task by family historians, without whom it would not have seen the light of day. Supported by individual subscribers, two former presidents of the Society of Australian Genealogists, Malcolm Sainty and Keith Johnson, ensured Gillen's work became available through their publishing house, the Library of Australian History. The intense anger of many Australians about official treatment of the Bicentennial was reflected in their foreword. Here, Sainty and Johnson were explicit about what they described as the 'vigorous and at times malicious' opposition to the First Fleet re-enactment by the Australian Bicentennial Authority, even to the extent that 'the Authority asked the City of Portsmouth to have nothing to do with it'. Fortunately, it was a request that the Portsmouth authorities chose to ignore. Herself the descendant of a convict, Gillen had written previously about her ancestor, John Small, a work described by Brian Fletcher as 'justly received as an outstanding contribution to family history'. In *The Founders of Australia*, Gillen transcended her personal interest and produced something of national value.

By publicising the details of the First Fleeters, Gillen was continuing a worthy tradition among family historians that began in 1937, when Herbert Rumsey privately published the first list of names of convicts on the First Fleet.[67] Family historians' desire to reveal the truth deserves respect. As we have seen, Sainty and Johnson were responsible for the publication of the 1828 Census. It was also a twenty-year campaign by genealogical societies around Australia, spearheaded by the late Nick Vine Hall, which succeeded in preserving the 2001 Census. Unlike, say, Britain, which has a treasure trove of nineteenth-century censuses, from 1841 Australia's were always destroyed to placate convict descendants. In the late twentieth century, privacy issues were put forward by advocates supporting their continued destruction. But today, millions of Australians are given the option at each census to choose whether their information is preserved for researchers in the future. Having used the 1828 Census in their own work, family historians know how important a complete national snapshot can be and how greatly its value is enhanced if every Australian participates.

We should not be surprised that it was family historians who made most use of the archives of the penal colony once they became available. Convicts and their families began the cover-up. It is only fitting that convict descendants should dismantle it. However, there are broader issues than the reaction of individual families to their criminal ancestor. Having examined the multifaceted ways that convict topics were hidden at a public and private level, it is time to return to the question of why.

G.A. Wood's paper delivered in 1921 to the Royal Australian Historical Society is very revealing about Australians' attitude to their history. Much of what he said was an obvious attempt to allay some deep anxiety which he detected about the morality of the convicts. His tone is reassuring. More than once, he emphasised that 'it would be wrong to believe that the morality of New South Wales was of a lower standard than the morality of England'.[68] Equally apparent in his paper, however, is his assumption that it was the prisoners' crimes in Britain that were the source of this concern. Plainly, any search for a reason why Australian society saw its history as a birthstain must include an examination of the convict crimes.

CHAPTER 3
an amazing cast of characters

G.A. Wood's reassurance in 1921 that the convicts were of good moral character lasted 40 or 50 years at a popular level until family researchers could examine the archives for themselves. But at an academic level Sir Keith Hancock was expressing doubts within ten years about Wood's elevation of the convicts to (almost) innocent victims. In his book *Australia*, Hancock wrote in 1930, 'The tendency of a folk to idealise its origins is universal among mankind and may be observed even in Australia where the popular imagination has created the legend of a typical convict "sent out for snaring a rabbit" . . . and in Australia it is considered not only legitimate but virtuous to snare rabbits.'[1]

It was not until after World War II that a number of academics comprehensively followed up Hancock's doubts. From the 1950s, with the archives now accessible to academics, these historians examined the convict indents (lists of those transported, grouped by ship) to analyse the crimes that were recorded there, usually in one or two words such as 'highway robbery', 'larceny' or 'stealing money'. From this they made deductions about convict character and sought to establish whether the convicts were as innocent as Wood claimed or were the products of a criminal class. While A.G.L. Shaw was still researching his major work on the subject, Manning Clark examined the indents. Based predominantly on these plus some secondary sources such as the Catholic Vicar-General Father Ullathorne and Henry Mayhew, a nineteenth-century social researcher, Clark asserted in 1951 that 'the convicts who came to Australia were, in the main, not men and women pushed into crime by some temporary economic or social crisis, but men and women who were permanent outcasts of society, who had run the risk of avoiding the deterrents society used for such types and who scorned all attempts at their regeneration'. Most of the convicts, he argued, were professional criminals.[2] In due course, Shaw agreed with this general conclusion, but his extended scrutiny had made him conscious that the subject was complex and there were more layers of information that needed to be probed. In his book *Convicts and the Colonies* (and subsequently), he urged that detailed follow-up studies be undertaken. In 1965, Lloyd Robson published *The Convict Settlers of Australia*. Robson agreed with Clark and Shaw and his research, which was based on a statistical sample of the indents, gave their conclusions about the crimes of the convicts a useful quantitative base. Being an academic of his time, that was as far as Robson could go. As noted earlier, he was refused permission to publish the names of convicts. At the close of the 1960s, therefore, a more penetrating assessment of convict crimes and character remained a subject for others to take up.[3]

In the following decade, feminist historians were more intent on making a broad case about women's position in Australian society than considering women as individuals or challenging the issue of whether they were criminals. Then, in 1978, George Rudé published *Protest and Punishment*, in which he tested Wood's general premise that social and political protesters made up the bulk of the convicts. On a definition of protesters as people 'who acted together with others, or appeared to do so, in pursuit of common political or social goals', Rudé concluded that out of the approximate total of 162,000 convicts only 3600 would fit that category.[4] This number included 120 women, most of whom were arsonists, and people Rudé described as 'marginal' protesters, who included poachers, cattle maimers and arsonists generally. As the names of many protesters were already known, there was no objection to their personal stories being told publicly. Consequently, Rudé's work produced a more three-dimensional portrait of his sample of convicts than any previous study.[5]

As a result of the academic focus on proving or disproving whether the convicts were criminals, there was not much progress on anything else. In 1988 the publication of *Convict Workers*, edited by Stephen Nicholas, introduced a new angle on the issue of criminality. Again based on a statistical sample, Nicholas' contributors argued that the convicts were really ordinary working men and women who should be assessed within a global context of forced migration. Nicholas strongly challenged the earlier conclusion that they belonged to a criminal class. 'Such an interpretation does much violence to the understanding of Australia's white past. It has bequeathed to a generation of Australians a popular image of convict society as brutal, unproductive and sterile; and of convicts as unskilled professional criminals . . . The convicts transported to New South Wales were representative of the British and Irish working classes. This meant that they brought a cross-section of useful skills, many immediately suited to the needs of a growing colony.'[6]

The profession appeared satisfied to leave the matter there. Indeed, in the 1990s, one senior historian claimed, 'Everything that can be said about the convicts has been said' (recounted to the author by the recipient of this observation). But there was another level to which the debate could be taken, one that was particularly important in a nation that had no large-scale historical events in the sense of a civil war, or a battle for independence. The Australian story was always one of character and interpersonal relations rather than sweeping themes. Historians' various contentions needed to be tested, and this could only really be done by looking beyond the ships' indents and conducting an extensive appraisal of individuals. Only at that level could a judgement really be made on the issue of criminality. Only there would be found the drama, tragedy, comedy and pathos—the 'colour'—that so many Australians thought their history lacked.

On stage at the Old Bailey, 1809

The debate between the historians from G.A. Wood in the 1920s to Stephen Nicholas in the 1980s did achieve a useful consensus on the categories of crimes committed by the convicts. Generally, historians over seven decades agreed the categories covered thieves, burglars, highwaymen, receivers, protesters (including arsonists and poachers), as well as violent criminals, some of whom committed murder. Based on the indents, it was agreed by all that the great majority were thieves. Percentages were assigned to these categories.

As previously mentioned, the sample that underpins this book comprises approximately 1100 convicts. Of these, 870 male prisoners who arrived on four boats are its core group. Two hundred of them arrived on the *Sir William Bensley* in 1817. Two hundred came on the *John* to New South Wales in 1832. Two hundred and seven men arrived in Van Diemen's Land on the *St Vincent* in 1853, and 270 arrived in Western Australia on the *Lord Dalhousie* in 1863. Although the focus here is on men, female prisoners also feature in this book. Some of the women, such as those who arrived on the *Lord Melville* and the *Maria* in 1817 and 1818, were the wives and girlfriends of the men, in this case on the *Bensley*, most of whom came as prisoners themselves. Other women were part of my previous study of 100 convict women on the *Princess Royal*, which landed in New South Wales in 1829, or are drawn from those on the *Duchess of Northumberland*, who were the last female prisoners to arrive in Van Diemen's Land.[7] These men and women will be the guide to an examination of the convict crimes in an attempt to establish whether this was the source of Australia's birthstain.

The much-discussed poachers were a consistent flow of convicts for Australia, although a small proportion of the total. They did not come in large waves like the agricultural (Swing) rioters of the 1830s. Or spasmodic, spectacular groups like the rebels from Upper and Lower Canada between 1838 and 1840 and the Fenians in the 1850s. Sometimes there was a batch from a particular incident, like the Berkeley poaching clash. In the main, however, they came in dribs and drabs, one here, a couple there, reflecting the fact that most poaching was an individual, solitary act. Rudé calculated that 226 poachers were transported, but they are hard to detect. Indents for the early ships did not record transportees' crimes, but even in the criminal registers created in Britain, the crime of 'poaching' rarely appears. For example, 'murder' was the crime listed against the names of the Berkeley poachers. Of the other five poachers or would-be poachers in this sample, the crime of only one was described as 'poaching' to the muster clerk who compiled the *John*'s indent. And that in itself was a touch of defiance on the part of the poacher, **Isaac Fisher**.* A woollen weaver by trade, Fisher was affected by the decline of cottage industries and small manufactories. Aged 29, he was also a widower with a son. Tried at the Gloucestershire Assizes, the charge against Fisher did not mention 'poaching' once. Instead, he was charged with 'feloniously, unlawfully and maliciously assaulting, cutting and wounding John Gay'. It took the *Gloucester Journal* to reveal that Gay was a gamekeeper. By 1831, it was possible for the

---

*   Names printed in **bold** in this chapter are of convicts whose stories are elaborated upon later.

judge to deliver a sentence of 'Death Recorded', which meant an automatic commutation into transportation for life and this was Fisher's fate.[8]

Another poacher sailed on the *Lord Dalhousie* in 1863 but his crime was listed as 'shooting and wounding', with no mention of poaching. Thirty-year-old **Caleb Stapley** was one of a family of agricultural labourers in Sussex. Dusk was falling on a wet, misty winter's day in 1861 when he was confronted in the wood on the Adamson estate near the village of Seddlescomb. According to the keeper, Samuel Burdett, a gunshot attracted his attention, and when he found Caleb he was leaning against a tree with a gun in his hand. Burdett made 'a dash' at the poacher but the ground was slippery and he fell. Caleb ran. Struggling to his feet, Burdett yelled, 'Staples, I know you!' and gave chase again. At those words, Caleb swung round and fired at him. Limping along, Burdett yelled again, 'I'll have you', but he was wounded and could not keep up. Cross-examined in court, Burdett was unshaken. It is impossible to know to what extent need or greed motivated Caleb. It could have been both, but he was employed at the time and not completely poverty-stricken. When asked by Constable Bexhill whether he had been at work that day he replied, 'No, I left off about half past three. Then I went to the pub and had a pint of beer.' Several witnesses appeared in the court to give him a good character but the jury found him guilty. The law had changed by 1861 and a death sentence was no longer applicable. Instead, Caleb Stapley received a sentence of six years penal servitude.[9]

Thirty-two male arsonists were included in this sample and they were less prominent on the earlier boats. The *William Bensley* carried one in 1816, a farmer called John Andrew Lovell from Northampton, who served his sentence in Van Diemen's Land and returned to England once he had a free pardon. In 1832, there were none on the *John.*[10] By comparison, there were five arsonists on the *St Vincent* in 1853 and 26 on the *Lord Dalhousie* in 1863. Protest, resentment, malice, fraud and sheer bravado are revealed by a detailed look at their crimes. Poverty lurked behind many a blaze, but not all.

Throughout the transportation period, there are examples of men and women using arson as a means to an end. In 1847 **John Hobbs**, for instance, set fire to a haystack to change his life. In a statement to the police, Hobbs said that he and his mates, Tom Webster and Robert Lewer, had to beg the money for the toll to cross Kew Bridge on London's outskirts that morning. They spent the day wandering around the farmland on the other side. Hobbs did not say whether they were looking for work. Nor did he mention whether they had spent the balance of their begging on a pint at the pub, although he was to claim later that he was drunk that evening. Whatever their real purpose, as dusk fell they converged on a farm they had passed earlier in the afternoon.

There, to the puzzlement of the farmer, Frederick Piggot, and others who testified to what happened, they laid some faggots under a large haystack, then used Hobbs' pipe to light three lucifers so each could participate in setting it ablaze. There was no personal grudge involved. They were unknown to Farmer Piggot and neither he nor any of the witnesses had ever seen them in the parish of Richmond before.

The local police sergeant who had been called to the fire found the trio waiting at the police station for his return. 'We've come to give ourselves up for setting fire to the hayrick,' they told him. 'I'm willing to hear anything you might have to say,' he replied, but cautioned that it could be used in evidence. Nevertheless, they insisted. So, as the sergeant put it, 'They were all three together—as one made a statement, I asked the others if they agreed with it and they said "Yes".'

'We were the whole day in Richmond without anything to eat,' said the three young men, after first describing how they had begged for the bridge toll to cross the river. 'Our lives for some time past have been spent in such misery and poverty we were determined, when we left London this morning, to do something to alter it. We looked out for a stack to set fire to.' Then, they gave details of how they set the fire. Declaring, at the policeman's insistence, that they made the statement voluntarily, they signed it. Just to be sure he wasn't being taken for a ride, the sergeant took away the men's shoes and matched them to the footmarks in Farmer Piggot's field. At the trial in London's Central Criminal Court on 10 May 1847, Webster, who had a previous conviction, lost his nerve and claimed he was innocent but Hobbs, aged 23, and Robert Lewer, who was only sixteen, stood firm. The judge gave them hefty sentences: twenty years for Webster, fifteen for Hobbs and ten for Lewer.[11]

Two years later, while John Hobbs laboured in Gibraltar with other men who would sail in the *St Vincent* to Van Diemen's Land, **Eliza Morrison**, a freckle-faced Irish girl with red hair and blue eyes, cast her fate to the wind by setting fire with her friend Mary Nowlan to the house of Margaret Cavanagh in Ballymore Eustace. 'I was in bed,' the Widow Cavanagh testified indignantly. 'My child and I were inside. We might have been burned to death.' She swore that she did not know the prisoners. Constable Cox, who attended the fire, also said he had never seen the girls before; they were strangers, arrested on suspicion. However, Cox told the court that one said when he took them, 'There's no use denying it. It was we that did it. With matches.'

When the constable said that, one of the jurors quizzed the girls directly. 'Did you set the house on fire?'

'Yes' was the reply, presumably from Eliza who had pleaded guilty even though her friend was trying to claim innocence.

Then it was the judge's turn to check the extent of their culpability. 'Were there persons living in the house?'

'Yes, my Lord.'

At that, the judge lectured them at length 'on the heinousness of the crime, and the fatal consequences that might have resulted, if an alarm had not been given'. Then, he sentenced them to transportation for life. But they were not downcast. 'A long life to Your Honour,' they chorused.[12]

In Van Diemen's Land, the red-haired Eliza met the dark-haired John Hobbs, who was by then also sporting an equally dark beard. It is not hard to imagine the conversation that triggered their special relationship.

Irish women arsonists like Eliza Morrison are a distinctive group of convicts, distinctive because there are so many of them but also because so many claimed to do it deliberately. George Rudé noted this phenomenon in 1978, but no historian followed up until Diane Snowden's doctoral research in 2005. Covering the period 1841–53 in Van Diemen's Land, Snowden examined the 248 Irish women who arrived with convictions for arson. She concluded that at least 79 of them were actively using arson as a way of emigrating. 'By the early 1850s, it was entrenched as a means of engineering transportation among women, a fact recognised by the Irish courts and frequently commented upon in Irish newspapers.'[13]

Arson was rarely committed by English women. One exception was a young servant girl, Mary Ann Marjoram, who was sentenced to death at the Suffolk Assizes in 1812 for setting fire to a house. Because she was only sixteen and it was her first offence, the sentence was commuted to transportation for life. In 1819 she married Will Coates, who arrived on the *Sir William Bensley*.[14] The *Princess Royal* carried 100 women in 1829, but there were no arsonists among them. In 1853, the *Duchess of Northumberland* carried two arsonists among a total of 216. Mary Ann Hurren was an 18-year-old dairymaid who committed her first offence when she set fire to a stable in Ipswich. By contrast, Ann Jones or Johnson, who was also a dairymaid, had a previous conviction for arson when she set fire to a bed in the Frome Workhouse. Both women were sentenced to ten years.[15]

Historians from Wood to Shaw, to Robson, Rudé and more recently Diane Snowden agree that whether transported arsonists were criminals or protesters can only be decided case by case. No blanket guilt or innocence can be declared. Some did it as a protest or from malice against a master or landlord, some in order to get a free passage 'beyond the seas', some for the insurance or just to cause a sensation. This sample included examples of all these motivations.

Henry Sherry, who sailed on the *Dalhousie,* set fire to his father's house while his father, John Sherry, and his sister Eliza were inside.

Eliza Sherry was a reluctant witness at his trial. She wept as she told the court how she and Henry lived with their father at Stourmouth near Sandwich in Kent. The two men had quarrelled while all three were sitting round the table having their midday dinner. John Sherry was complaining about the time Henry spent at the pub. Possibly, Henry was already drunk. 'Cross and excited', as Eliza put it, he stormed out declaring, 'I'll burn the house down'. They did not see him again that afternoon and, not believing for a moment that he meant it, they went to bed as usual that night. But Henry had gone back to the pub. His friend, Harry Andrews, described how he was already drunk when he stopped by his shop. 'He asked me to go and have some beer with him. He told me he'd had a few words with his father and that he would burn the place down that night.' Later that night when Andrews heard the cry of 'Fire', he rushed out and discovered a barn blazing fiercely near the Sherry family's house, which was also alight. Meanwhile, Eliza Sherry was rushing round inside their house. She, too, had heard the cry of 'Fire'. 'I looked out the window and saw the barn in flames. Downstairs, I found the thatch on our roof at the back of the house was on fire.' She threw some water on it and thought it was out. Shortly after, she discovered that the fire had broken out somewhere else. It was under the thatch. 'I could not reach the thatch this time,' she said. She heard her brother's voice in the crowd outside, but did not see him. Harry Andrews, who had been helping to put out the fire in the barn, saw Henry watching from the road. According to Andrews, Henry was disappointed to learn that the fire in the barn was out. 'I was going to give it another touch,' he told Andrews, who was shocked. 'You don't mean to say you set your father's house on fire?' he exclaimed, to which Henry Sherry replied that he did, adding: 'And the barn and stable also.'

Henry's counsel tried to argue that Henry was insane. Eliza gave evidence of how Henry had been in the army, fighting in the Crimea. She told the court, 'He came home with a fever and has been ill from time to time ever since. He was ill [shortly] before the fire. At one time, when he had rheumatic fever, it was necessary to have two men to look after him.' But the judge said setting fire to a house while people were inside was one of the few crimes, short of murder, for which capital punishment still applied. 'Death will be merely recorded against you. It will not be carried into execution,' he told Henry, adding, 'But you can be sure that you will not have your liberty until many years have expired.'[16]

By far the greatest number of arsonists in this sample were on board the *Dalhousie*, which supports Rudé's conclusion that the number transported to Western Australia was particularly high. He calculated a total of 361 arsonists, all but one English, among the nearly 10,000 men transported to that state. They were all men, since no women were transported to the western colony, and they arrived at a steady but increasing rate on the 37 ships that took convicts there. The number peaked during the years 1863–66, when more arsonists arrived than in all the other years combined. In total, Rudé calculated that 1000 arsonists were transported to Australia.[17]

Despite the huge variety among the prisoners and their crimes, predominantly they were thieves—thieves of anything that moved, anything left unattended, thieves from inattentive people oblivious to their property or their person, thieves of money, livestock, watches and jewellery, of building materials and cloth, of dresses, shoes, hats, ribbons, handkerchiefs and livestock including rabbits, ducks and fowls, alive and dead. Robson's study found that 80 per cent of the prisoners were thieves and the sample scrutinised here supports his figures. To some extent individual research can flesh out the human being beneath the statistic, but the records available for the hundreds and thousands of mundane cases of theft vary enormously. In many instances, it is only possible to find information about the type of goods stolen, their value and perhaps the location and name of the prosecutor. Motives or circumstances were rarely described. For many, the only record that remains are the bare facts. For instance, 20-year-old **Valentine Wood** was a labourer who originally came from Dublin. In March 1816 he was sentenced to seven years transportation at Shrewsbury in England for stealing 'one velveret coat value 5 shillings, one striped waistcoat value 2 shillings and one pair breeches value 1 shilling' from William Evans of the parish of St Chad. No other information survives. It is a sparse record for the pivotal moment in the life of a young man whose turbulent career in the penal colonies ended in his execution in Sydney for highway robbery in 1822.[18]

In 1850, the information about **William Whittaker (alias Baker)** was little better. Aged 28, Whittaker was a farm labourer from Stafford who pleaded guilty to larceny, in his case stealing a topcoat, a jacket and other (unspecified) articles. His previous conviction for a felony, for which he had served twelve months, ensured that this time he would receive a sentence of transportation. He showed no dismay at the news. According to the *Staffordshire Advertiser*, he 'impudently thanked the Chairman' of the Quarter Sessions.[19]

More detail survives for **Thomas Plows**, who was tried at the Old Bailey in 1816 on a charge of stealing clothes. The circumstances of the offence and the decision of the prosecutor to charge Plows are more typical of the earlier transportation period than later, when the development of a police force was accompanied by a greater requirement for witnesses and other evidence such as footprints and the like. The story behind Plows' conviction could probably stand for many others in the early years.

John Evans, servant to Benjamin Hall, Esq., told the court how he found 16-year-old Plows hiding behind Evans' bedroom door in the Mayfair house where he worked. Plows was dressed like a London confectioner. 'I asked him what business he had there? And he said he had come from Mr Gunter's, the confectioner in Berkeley Square, for orders.' Plows claimed he had been looking for the kitchen and had gone into the wrong room by mistake. 'I was just coming out when the gentleman stopped me.' But he was no slick thief. Caught on the spot in what may have been a fateful impulse, he was too frightened to dissemble successfully. Evans said he was 'very much confused and made a great many stammers when discovered'. It was enough to make Evans suspicious, and after sending Plows on his way to the kitchen he did a quick check of his possessions. 'I just put my head into my own room to see if all was right. I saw that my coat which had been hanging on the other side of the room, and my hat, which had been in a box had been moved from the far side of the room . . . to the chest near where the prisoner was standing when I first pushed the door open.' The clothes never left the premises, and there was some discussion in court whether moving them across the room met the definition of 'larceny', which in legal terms involves taking *and* carrying away. But the jury found Plows guilty of stealing a coat, value £2, and a hat, value ten shillings. He was sentenced to seven years transportation.[20]

Fifteen years later, 14-year-old **Samuel Rowney (sometimes Rooney)** also received a sentence of seven years transportation when he was convicted of stealing a coat in October 1831. In this case the victim was his father, for whom he had been working as a sweep. We can only guess what possessed the man to prosecute his own son. An elder boy, George, was already in New South Wales as a convict and perhaps Samuel's father thought it was for the best. But as will become apparent in later chapters, it seems likely there was ill-will between them.[21]

James Jaye (sometimes Jay), the 22-year-old son of a Suffolk thatcher, sailed with Rowney in 1832. He had no previous convictions when he was charged with stealing lead (affixed to a building) in London in April 1831. His reason for being in London is unknown. His skills and work experience were described as 'pastrycook and indoor servant' but he had either come to the metropolis because he could not get work in Suffolk or he had lost his job in London. When he turned to crime in December 1830, he was living in the Asylum for the Houseless Poor in London where he earned his keep by acting as a helper and stoker. He had been there ten weeks when Constable William Attfield spotted Jaye and another man, Reeves, in the street not far from the Asylum. 'They were carrying a heavy load which was wrapped in a jacket and a pair of trousers,' he told the court. Attfield summoned help to take them before they could sell the lead. His colleague, Constable Scotchmer, tied their hands together. Protesting loudly, one of the prisoners revealed he understood the law. 'What are you going to do with us?' he demanded. 'You can do

James Jaye stole lead from the roof of the Houseless Poor Asylum

nothing. Where is the prosecutor? Where is the man that owns it?' But Attfield had guessed where they came from. In court, he produced the overseer of the Asylum as a witness who confirmed both men had been staying there and described how he had gone to the roof and found all the lead stripped from the trapdoor. The assiduous Attfield then testified how the stolen lead fitted the vacant space perfectly. James Jaye tried to insist that he had run into Reeves in the street, who asked for help carrying the heavy load. Reeves dovetailed his story to Jaye's, claiming that he had been asked to take the lead out. The jury did not believe them. Found guilty, both were sentenced to seven years transportation.[22]

Examples of the proverbial stolen handkerchief could be found from the beginning of transportation right up to the system's closing years in Van Diemen's Land and Western Australia. By the later dates a record of prior offences were taken into account when deciding sentence. All three culprits below pleaded guilty, which reduced the details available to a bare outline of the crime.

> **Richard Welsh**, age 21, tried Central Criminal Court, London, for stealing 1 handkerchief value 3 shillings, from the person of Samuel Highley. Two prior offences. Ten years penal servitude. (Transported 1853 to Van Diemen's Land.)

Patrick Brian, age 24 from St Giles, London, occupation stonemason (imperfect). Convicted at Clerkenwell Sessions, London, 25 September 1849 for stealing a handkerchief from the person. Two prior offences. Ten years penal servitude. (Transported 1853 to Van Diemen's Land.)

Thomas Tomlinson, age 20, pleaded guilty to stealing a handkerchief from the person of an unknown man, having been before convicted. 'It was stated that the prisoner had been seven times previously convicted.' Sentence six years penal servitude. (Transported 1863 to Western Australia.)[23]

Picking pockets was another crime gratefully seized upon by Australians who were trying to explain away the convict stain; the very name made the crime sound innocuous and trivial. In fact, the records reveal that 'picking pockets' encompassed a variety of methods, not all of them involving a thief's hand in a victim's pocket. In the early transportation era, there were many pickpockets transported to Australia, and most at that time were from London. At the Old Bailey between 1800 and 1834, for instance, 3656 people were found guilty of being pickpockets, of whom 2607 were transported.[24] The *Sir William Bensley* had eleven on board, all Londoners, all one way or the other just like the stereotypical pickpocket, jostling people in public places, swift, casual, snatching and running away. **Joseph Williams** was a good example. At the Old Bailey, Hannah Wallis, married woman, told the court she was walking down Tower Street about seven o'clock in the evening. 'My shawl was suddenly snatched off my neck from behind. I cried "Stop Thief" . . . I turned quickly around and saw the shawl in the prisoner's possession.' Hearing her cries, two men rushed to help. One of them stuck out his foot and tripped Joseph up. Constable Pope, who rushed to join the melee, said Joseph swore badly then, even though he had the shawl in his hand, tried to claim he did not take it. A tall, fair young man, 21-year-old Joseph was a printer—an occupation that was to stand him in good stead in the years ahead. Apparently an orphan, he told the court he had been brought up for eleven years by the Philanthropic Society. 'I was on my way there to get work,' he said. 'A person threw the shawl into my arms.' But Old Bailey juries were not gullible. They had heard that kind of story many times. They found Joseph guilty and he was sentenced to transportation for life.[25]

In 1832, the *John* carried only four pickpockets to New South Wales. In the main they continued the pattern of those on the *Bensley* except for 22-year-old **James Wilde (sometimes Wild)**, who was convicted as a pickpocket but in strange circumstances. A turner and machine-maker originally from Manchester, Wilde seems to have been convicted as a pickpocket by association. At the trial, the real culprit was identified as Thomas Haw who, it was alleged, took the pocketbook from a farmer who had hired him to act as his substitute in the North Lincoln militia. Haw must have blamed Wilde, who was then tracked to Lincolnshire where he was caught with the pocketbook in his possession. Both men were convicted and sent to the *Cumberland* hulk at Chatham to await transportation. From there, Wilde petitioned the King claiming that he alone committed the offence after overhearing Haw and the farmer arguing about whether Haw deserved more money for doing the militia service. According to Haw's own petition, Wilde had wanted to address the jury when he heard the verdict but was not permitted to do so at the time. Subsequently he was so compelling in writing that both the chairman of Quarter Sessions and the committing magistrate wrote to support the plea that Haw be discharged.[26]

'A gang of pickpockets' screamed the *Preston Chronicle* when **John and Ellen O'Neil** were arrested in January 1850. In reality, they were family rather than a gang. Ellen and her brother, Richard Clark, worked the scam; John and his mate, Tom O'Gar, stood by to carry away the loot. But Inspector Rigby had noticed the group staring in a shop window. Suspecting they were up to something, he kept an eye on them. 'The female prisoner went into the shop, and the other two followed,' he testified. Richard Clark was already inside. The inspector must have crossed the road to peer through the window. 'They crowded round Miss Ann Boys as she chose her purchases,' he continued. 'Then the two men came out.' Inside the shop, Ellen continued the deception, buying some white stockings before she left. Separately, Richard bought some black silk. How could anyone guess they were thieves?

Inspector Rigby, meanwhile, had detained the two men. Searching them at the police station, he found a purse, a watch key, one sovereign and other money in O'Gar's hat. John O'Neil was carrying £2 3s. in silver and various copper coins. Suspicions confirmed, Rigby immediately went in search of Ellen. He caught her in Fishergate, just as she must have thought she was safely away. Amounts of money that she could not account for were found on her, too, along with the white stockings that linked her back to the shop. Her brother, Richard, was picked up shortly after. At first Ellen tried to protect him by denying they were in any way connected, but eventually had to confess the relationship. Once Miss Boys described how she had missed her purse and listed its contents, they were well and truly caught.

Ellen was sixteen and John twenty when they were tried. Despite their youth, both had police records for petty pilfering—sentences of three months and six months 'for stealing tills' as John put it, and of one and four months for picking pockets. Ellen told the authorities in Van Diemen's Land she had served six months for stealing money, but this was not listed on her record in Lancashire. Whatever the real history, their experience showed in the careful planning for this crime. Their motive is unclear. The involvement of Ellen's brother and later information about her father, John Clark, suggests that Ellen had a stable family background. Nothing is known of John O'Neil's family, nor his circumstances, but in the prison register his occupation is given as 'steam loom operator' so he had apparently worked in one of the Lancashire cotton factories.

Though worldly and cunning in their street activities, there was also a strange naivety about the O'Neils. They pleaded guilty, each of them emphasising at every turn that they were married. Perhaps they were expecting six months or a year in the local gaol. If so, the judge's sentence of transportation must have come as a shock, particularly if it initially applied only to John. Ellen was the only woman on a long list of men, and the only one listed without a previous conviction, yet a sentence of transportation by 1850 required evidence of an earlier offence. In the criminal register, someone has underlined her name as though pausing for thought. Did she beg to go too? Or was seven years transportation for both of them the reward for saving the court time with a guilty plea? The O'Neils' crime does not fit the stereotype of pickpockets. It is closer in style to the common pattern of 'stealing from a shop'. In fact, on their ships' indents, the O'Neils were not listed as 'pickpockets', an anachronistic term by 1850. Instead, they were each simply described as thieves who stole money. However, when John O'Neil described his crime to the muster clerk in Van Diemen's Land he stuck to the colloquial term as 'picking pockets'.[27]

Young **Thomas Fleming** who sailed on the *St Vincent* was described in some records as convicted of 'stealing money' but his crime had the more traditional elements of a pickpocket. His victim Mary Fisher told the court she was looking in the draper's window on High Ousegate in York when she felt someone pulling at her gown. Turning round she saw Fleming withdrawing his hand from her pocket. He was clutching her purse. She chased him down the street, yelling, 'Stop, stop, my pocket has been picked.' A shoemaker named George Thompson joined in the chase and, together, they caught Fleming. The police proved that he had been convicted before in 1846 and he was transported for felony for seven years.[28]

Some thieves stole large amounts of money. At the Lent Assizes at Newcastle-on-Tyne in 1828, **Ann Storrett**, a 15-year-old kitchen girl, pleaded guilty to stealing a receipt in the sum of £500 which had been deposited with her employer Jonathan Bachhouse & Co., who were bankers. She was sentenced to seven years transportation and sailed to New South Wales on the *Princess Royal*.[29] Over twenty years later, **Henry Taperell**, aged eighteen, sailed on the *St Vincent* after he was convicted at Exeter City Sessions in Devon in July 1850 for stealing five promissory notes valued at £5 each and other monies amounting to £30 from the office of his employer Mr Drake. Poverty was not his motive. Not only was he employed, he also came from a middle-class family.[30]

Edward Hillier and **William Simpson** were transported to Western Australia after their trial at the Liverpool Borough Sessions on 11 April 1862. According to the *Liverpool Journal*, they were caught 'swindling an Irish emigrant'. Both in their forties, the pair of rogues had worked out that people coming to buy a passage on the emigrant ships that left from Queen's Dock in Liverpool would be carrying large sums of cash. On 18 March 1862 they spotted young Bryan Patterson, who had just arrived from Ireland, and dubbed him 'the Galway Grecian'. As they watched, Patterson boarded the *Queen of the Seas* in order to book a berth. There, as if by chance, he met Hillier who asked him if he was going to Australia. 'That I am,' replied Patterson. 'I am glad to hear it. So am I,' said Hillier. 'We'll be company for one another.' He suggested they go ashore and have an ale together. As they were nursing their drinks, Simpson appeared. Introducing himself as though he had never seen Hillier in his life before, he claimed to have just come into £7000 which he wanted to lend out at 5 per cent interest.

In the conversation that followed, the two tricksters got the Galway Grecian to the stage where he was asking to take a loan from Simpson. At that point, Simpson left to get a stamped bill, leaving behind a bag supposedly containing money as security. He soon returned saying that he could not obtain a bill. Hillier then escorted Patterson in search of one, the young Irishman leaving £18 10s. in cash behind as a demonstration of good faith. Of course when Patterson returned Simpson had vanished with the cash. Hillier, who had made an excuse to fall behind, never reappeared. Despite the seriousness of the case for everyone involved, the description of how the swindle worked and the defendants' nickname for Patterson made the court rock with laughter. The judge was not at all amused. 'You have been guilty of one of the most wicked and heartless robberies that I have heard of,' he told Simpson and Hillier before sentencing them to ten years penal servitude each.[31]

Generally, the women's crimes were not as varied as the men's, although the statistics were similar. One per cent committed a violent crime such as murder or manslaughter, but otherwise they were overwhelmingly thieves. Unlike the men, they did not commit highway robbery, nor did they 'break and enter' unless they were part of a gang of burglars. Their crime was usually straightforward stealing from a shop or a market, from a client when the woman was working as a prostitute, or from an employer. For some crimes such as coining, they worked in conjunction with their man. There was little change in the women's crimes whether they occurred in 1818, 1828 or 1853.

Susannah Watson was 34 years old and the mother of six children when she was convicted at the Nottingham Assizes in April 1828 of stealing from a shop. It was not her first offence. She had been convicted of theft twice in the previous decade, but a close examination of her circumstances revealed the extent to which poverty had driven her to crime. She was married to a frame-

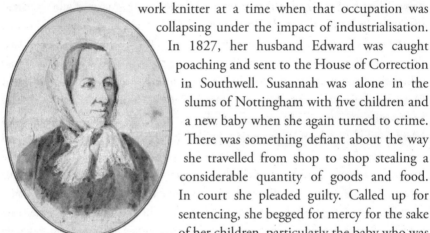

work knitter at a time when that occupation was collapsing under the impact of industrialisation. In 1827, her husband Edward was caught poaching and sent to the House of Correction in Southwell. Susannah was alone in the slums of Nottingham with five children and a new baby when she again turned to crime. There was something defiant about the way she travelled from shop to shop stealing a considerable quantity of goods and food. In court she pleaded guilty. Called up for sentencing, she begged for mercy for the sake of her children, particularly the baby who was only fifteen weeks old. She said she had been 'driven by necessity' but admitted it was no excuse, adding 'I could not bear to see my children starving'. The judge was unsympathetic. 'It would be beneficial for your children to have you removed from the country,' he told her before sentencing her to transportation for fourteen years.[32]

Drawing of a woman convict, c. 1800

Many thieves were transported for stealing small livestock such as fowls, geese and rabbits, snatching them from markets or farms in an almost impulsive fashion. Contrary to popular legend, this kind of crime was not confined to the early days of transportation. Nineteen-year-old James Barnes was convicted in November 1850 for stealing one tame rabbit, valued at two shillings. A prior offence was taken into account and he was sentenced to seven years penal servitude, which later became transportation to Van Diemen's Land.[33] Stealing larger animals required more premeditation and men who stole horses or sheep were often members of gangs that earned a living by this means.[34] None of the cases studied here provided evidence of gangs, but many of the men appeared to take a professional approach to the theft. They were not rank amateurs, grabbing a sheep or a horse on impulse. In 1816, the *Bensley* carried nine men who had been convicted of stealing sheep or horses on a small scale. In each case, their butcher was convicted with them. The *John* carried nine men convicted of stealing animals and whose behaviour revealed at least some premeditation. Prominent among them were brothers **Abraham West (alias Stapleton)**, age 31, and **Francis Stapleton (alias West)**, aged 21, who were convicted together at the Derby Assizes in 1831. Sometime during the night of 2 May they stole a three-year-old chestnut colt and a six-year-old brown mare from a stable near Pontefract in Yorkshire. Intent on putting as much distance as possible between themselves and the scene of the crime, they then set out on an arduous trek. By dawn, they had reached Alfreton where a butcher, Benjamin Taylor, spotted them resting beside the road. 'Both men and horses seemed jaded and knocked up,' he told the court. 'The horses were covered with lather and dirt.' Later that day he saw them again. This time they had stopped to feed the horses at a pub called the Harrow near Ilkeston in Derbyshire. They had travelled 62 miles. Noticing their state, the landlord was suspicious. 'You must have rode these horses a good way, this morning,' he remarked. 'We only brought them from Chesterfield,' Abraham West replied quickly, but he sensed the landlord would not be satisfied and got ready to leave. It was too late. The landlord had summoned some neighbours. Together they took the brothers and the horses into custody on suspicion, until the original owner, hastening over from Ponte-fract, identified the horses the following morning. In court, the Stapletons were sentenced to death for their crime, although the judge indicated immediately that he would recommend a reprieve.[35]

In 2004 the grand-daughter of **Angus McKay** remembered he 'had a springy gait and would make a clicking sound with his tongue as he went along'. An old man's habits, perhaps, or shades of the 16-year-old shepherd who could bound from boulder to boulder of the windswept hills of the Isle of Lewis in northern Scotland, clicking his tongue to match his strides. Born on the island in 1833, the young McKay had begun shepherding not long after his sixteenth birthday. Barely six months after McKay began working for a tenant farmer named George Mitchell, a warrant was issued for his arrest on suspicion of being part of a 'system of sheepstealing' in the parish of Uig. Claiming to speak only Gaelic, the youth had to rely on an interpreter. The local clergyman Reverend David Watson translated during his examination by the magistrates. How wide the sheepstealing net extended is not clear from his interrogation, except that it was well organised, with more than one safe house to hold the stolen sheep between theft and sale, with facilities for re-branding, and with ready buyers available for the stolen animals. George Mitchell lurks suspiciously passive in the background, but according to McKay a Malcolm McLean, who was Reverend Watson's former servant, was the instigator of the plan. McLean also coordinated the processing of the four-legged stolen property. McKay told them, 'The bargain for the sheep was done at the house of my master, Mr Mitchell. McLean came one night after I was in bed. He'd often urged me to get him some sheep. He paid me seven shillings on condition that I would not mention it to anyone.' McKay admitted that both he and McLean took part in the essential re-branding that would disguise who owned the sheep. 'McLean held them to me and I burned them with a marking iron on the right side of the nose, like he told me.'

McKay twisted every which way under the cross-examination of the magistrates, at first claiming there were three sheep, later admitting to earlier thefts. Desperately trying to reduce the charges, he even claimed that one sheep belonged to his father. His parents, John and Margaret, and his brothers Hugh and Donald all lived in the parish. Suddenly, they too were at risk. The following week, John McKay confirmed that he did have some sheep of his own, but denied that the one sold by Angus was his. 'I did not give my son a lamb or hog to sell this season.'

Committed for trial before the Aberdeen Circuit Court of Justiciary in 1850, McKay pleaded guilty and received a sentence of seven years transportation. After nineteen months in Scottish gaols he was sent south, initially to the *Stirling Castle* hulk, then to the newly completed prison at Portsmouth. There he laboured for twelve months and fifteen days at unspecified 'public works'. With a little under three years of his term completed and conduct that was uniformly described as 'good', the authorities decided he was ready for transportation. He was issued with a ticket-of-leave and put on board the *St Vincent*, which sailed for Van Diemen's Land on 21 December 1852.[36]

After stealing, burglary or housebreaking was the most common crime committed by the men. All four boats carried large numbers of burglars— around 19 per cent, with little variation from the *Sir William Bensley* in 1816 to the *Dalhousie* in 1863.

In 1815, 24-year-old **William Honeyman** kept a public house in Falkirk, Scotland, not far from the flourishing Carron ironworks where Honeyman had worked as a youth. He was well known in the district, had a reputation as 'a sober and industrious young man',[37] was running his pub, and had a wife named Jean Ogilvie and three children. He supplemented his income by working as a bricklayer for the ironworks, repairing furnaces at all hours of the day and night. But the idea of stealing the company's payroll was on his mind. On 8 September 1815, Honeyman waited in the street outside the ironworks while his friend, a seaman named **John Smith** who was described as 'a small, thin lad', slid through a tiny window and passed out the money from the payroll office. Their spoils amounted to nearly £1500.

The robbery occurred on a Friday. The following Monday, Honeyman turned up bold as brass to install bars on the window of the pay office, loudly declaring to all and sundry, 'I'd hang the robbers if I caught them. And burn them at the gates of Carron.'

Only ten days later he was singing to a different tune. The ironworks' cashier had meticulously kept a record of the serial numbers of bank notes and the investigators followed the money trail to William Honeyman and then to John Smith. Both men confessed to the crime, they claimed, on the promise that their lives would be spared. Certainly their confessions enabled the authorities to recover the money, which Honeyman had buried in the ash pit of his cellar and Smith in the pigsty of his mother's home, but despite their earlier admissions both men pleaded not guilty at the trial. After various legal complications caused by these conflicting positions, they were sentenced to death, later commuted to transportation for life.[38]

Charles Clephane was another Scottish burglar. A tall young man with a swarthy complexion, he was twenty when the Glasgow Court of Justiciary sentenced him to death on 3 May 1816.[39] Although he may have acted on the spur of the moment, his actions indicated experience. While Charles had no previous conviction, two of his cohort, **John Grindley** and Alex Napier, had several. They were known, as the Scottish law puts it, for being 'habit and repute thieves'. Nevertheless, the night of the robbery began innocently enough. It was Christmas Day 1815. Having gathered at Clephane's mother's place, they decided to go to a dance. Six of them, all very young men, set out together. Walking down Clyde Street, Glasgow, either Napier or Grindley spotted an opportunity. While Clephane watched, Napier gave Grindley a leg up and through the window of a house. William Campbell, one of two boys who had been lagging behind the other four, saved himself by describing what happened. Grindley was inside. 'He handed out cloth and a red box to Napier who passed it to Clephane . . . We took the box to Mrs Clephane's. It was forced open by a piece of iron.' Grindley was still in the house when they left and must have been passing out more loot to Napier on the street because the following day they needed a trunk to carry it all. Having stowed the goods temporarily at Mrs Clephane's in the Gorbals, the group went to the dance as planned. There they picked up several girls whom they took back to the Gorbals for the night. Lizzie Robertson, who had spent the night with Charles Clephane, described how Grindley and Napier went out early to move the trunk. Clephane remained in bed but Lizzie added, 'He said Napier and Grindley were stupid. They ought to have taken the stuff away the night before.' Enraged when he heard this in court, Charles Clephane yelled at her, 'You are a liar, you whore!' The evidence of one witness at the trial who saved herself by cooperating with the authorities revealed that Clephane's father had been convicted at the Glasgow Circuit Court six months earlier. The witness claimed Charles Clephane played on her sympathy by telling her they expected his father's house to be sequestrated by the Crown. 'He said the trunk contained his mother's best clothes,' she testified.[40]

When Clephane and Grindley were sentenced to hang, neither showed a flicker of emotion. A reporter from the *Glasgow Herald* who was watching closely recorded, 'They did not seem to be in the least affected by their awful situation.' After some weeks, their sentence was commuted to transportation for life and they sailed on the *Sir William Bensley* three months later.

Charles' father, **Andrew Clephane**, had been tried in Glasgow on 29 September 1815. Variously described as a hawker, a silversmith, a jeweller and a former publican, he kept premises at the Saltmarket, which was notorious for the 'ladies of the night who lived there, but also for number of young thieves who frequented it'. The Glasgow city officers had Andrew Clephane marked as a receiver of stolen goods, for which he had been convicted once previously. But in September he was charged with Robert White and James Edgar, who were just boys, of breaking into a haberdashery on 1 July and stealing a vast quantity of silk shawls, handkerchiefs, lace squares and other goods a travelling hawker could readily sell. The pattern of persuading someone else to store the stolen goods was the same as that followed by his son six months later. Andrew Clephane was convicted of receiving and sentenced to fourteen years transportation. He was still in the gaol when his son was caught at Christmas.[41]

Fifteen years later, in 1831, the contents of 19-year-old **Tom Stacey**'s pockets revealed him as a professional burglar. Five skeleton keys were found on him, together with a bag of tools containing a chisel, a centre-bit, a gimlet, a knife, and a phosphorus-box or lantern with matches and wax candles. In the cellar of the house at 63 St Paul's Churchyard in London he had left behind another phosphorus-box or dark lantern with a candle burning in it, a crowbar, a chisel and a centre-bit with its brace but no stock. He had chosen his target carefully, for Jabez Woodhill operated a well-established jeweller's shop on the ground floor of the house, which offered rich pickings. Woodhill also rented two floors above the shop and usually slept there, but he was away from home when Stacey broke in. In Cannon Alley, the chain that held the grating fast presented no problem to a man who had come prepared with appropriate tools. Stacey swiftly let himself down into the cellar, but inside things began to go awry. Woodhill knew the value of his goods and the door at the head of the cellar stairs was locked. As Stacey tugged and shook it, he woke John Smith, assistant to the jeweller, who was asleep barely three feet from the door. Smith set off the alarm and woke a house full of sleeping servants. The most damning testimony came from a shop assistant named Guy Clarke. Woken by the alarm, he looked down from his window and saw Tom Stacey heave himself out of the cellar and turn to run. Clarke shouted 'Watch! Watch!' Hearing the cry from nearby Paternoster Row, the watchman George Nichols moved so fast that Stacey got no more than a yard from the cellar before he was caught. Clarke was there to swear that the man Nichols caught was the same man he had seen fleeing from the cellar. The verdict was guilty, and the sentence was death. But Stacey sailed on the *John* a few months later.[42]

Two other men who would travel on the *John* were tried at the Gloucestershire Assizes on the same day, 10 August 1831. Twenty-five-year-old **Richard Nicols** was a stonemason by trade and literate. In April he had been committed in the parish of Stroud on the charge of burglariously breaking and entering the store of Edward Sharp at Stonehouse, from where he was alleged to have stolen two sacks containing three bushels of flour and a cheese. At twenty, **George Wheeler** was considerably younger, but he had already served four years in the Royal Marines and the scars on his back revealed that he had been flogged. Since military service at that time was for life, it is not clear how he came to be at large in Gloucestershire. He described his occupation as labourer and told the gaoler that he could neither read nor write. Wheeler was charged on two counts of burglary, once for breaking and entering the house of Elizabeth Nash to steal clothes, and secondly for breaking into the house of John Slade and stealing a silver watch as well as clothes and other items. Both young men had 'Death Recorded' against them, and in both cases this sentence was commuted to transportation for life.[43]

Contemporary drawing of a convict in the dock

George Rawlinson, a 23-year-old shoemaker, was one of many burglars on the *Lord Dalhousie*. He was caught in Hertfordshire, having crossed the county border to steal away from his home near Aylesbury, Buckinghamshire. Although up for two counts at the Lent Assizes in Hertford in March 1862, it appears he was in effect a first offender. No prior convictions were produced by the police. But when they first charged him with stealing five watches from George Clark of Tring, he confessed of his own accord that he had also stolen a pair of boot trees belonging to Francis Kingdrell. His sentence was six years penal servitude. Having been held at Hertford Gaol for six weeks, Rawlinson then passed through Millbank prison and on to Pentonville, where he spent nearly six months in separate confinement designed as a rehabilitation measure. In October 1862 Rawlinson was moved to Portland, from where he was selected for transportation to Western Australia. Evidence to the 1863 Select Committee on Transportation revealed that 'selection' was often a case of gaolers calling for volunteers. Young and single, Rawlinson may well have been one of those who was keen to go.[44]

Highway robbery was another type of theft committed by many convicts transported to Australia. Highwaymen have a long and romantic tradition in British culture: the very term conjures images of a dashing caped figure in an intriguing black mask, mounted on a charger and demanding his prey 'Stand and deliver'. These assumptions, along with the idea that highwaymen robbed only the rich, often to help the poor, have been deeply embedded in most people of British descent since the time of Robin Hood. Rogues they might be, but never violent or ugly. Rather, gentlemanly and honourable and kind. Almost noble. If anyone was killed or injured it must have been an accident or rough justice. For Australians, it is tempting to assume that convicts whose crime is described in the records as 'highway robbery' fitted this mould—indeed, sometimes the convicts themselves made the link, as the occasional use of 'Dick Turpin' as an alias indicates. The reality, however, is a long way from the romantic image. Highway robbery was usually a fast, violent assault, on foot, carried out by desperate men with no time to waste on courtesies. The victim was often injured, sometimes quite badly. The description 'highway' meant the robbery occurred on a public road. In later decades, this terminology vanished and crimes with exactly the same elements were simply described as robbery with assault or robbery with violence.

In 1816, the *Sir William Bensley* carried sixteen men convicted of highway robbery.[45] **Joseph Barrett**, age twenty, was convicted at the same Assizes as the Berkeley poachers. His reprieve from death arrived with theirs, and he shared the emotion of their final departure. In the parish of St George near Bristol, he left behind two brothers, Daniel and Stephen, and two sisters, Sarah and Eliza. Whether their parents were still alive is unknown. Close to the River Avon, the parish was an area of extensive market gardens and since Joseph gave his occupation as 'gardener' it is likely that he worked in one of these.[46] Little detail survives about Barrett's crime. There was no suggestion that he had an accomplice but the money was not recovered, which indicates someone else was involved. Joseph was a slight man of middling height and it is hard to imagine that he accomplished the hold-up without help, even though the indictment mentioned assault 'with force and arms', which means he had some kind of weapon. The victim was Henry Hobbs who was (whether walking or riding is unknown) on the King's Highway at the time of the offence. Given the size of Joseph's booty, the target was obviously specially chosen. The takings included one silver watch valued at £7, another watch valued at £7, a gold seal plus a second seal, together worth 18 shillings, two watch chains valued at 2 shillings each, a leather pocketbook worth 5 shillings, a hat valued at 10 shillings, three 3 shilling bank tokens to the total value of 9 shillings, three 'silver coin called shillings' valued at 3 shillings total, two promissory notes on the Worcester Old Bank worth £5 each, a note commonly called a Wantage Bank Note in the value of £1, a promissory note for the value of £17, and ten bank notes for the payment of £1 each. In 1816 the value of goods stolen as well as the circumstances of the crime affected the sentence, so it is not surprising that once the jury found him guilty the judge sentenced him to be hanged.[47]

Nearly 40 years later, the *St Vincent* carried only two men identified on landing by the crime of 'highway robbery', but there were many others on board whose crimes contained the elements described that way in earlier days. Twenty-four were convicted under the description 'assault and robbery' or 'robbery with violence', although these include four Irishmen whose crime had political overtones. By 1863, the term 'highway robbery' had vanished entirely. Instead, the *Lord Dalhousie* carried 23 men convicted of assault and robbery or robbery with violence, most of them indistinguishable from the crime earlier described as 'highway robbery'.

The men in this category on the *Dalhousie* tended to be the older ones, seven being aged over 35 years, the youngest 21. **Joseph Sowden (aka Joseph Sowden Ledger)** was 37 when he committed his crime in Scarborough in Yorkshire, and it was far from his first offence. He had seven prior convictions. The case papers have not survived, but from the sketchy information available it appears the police were determined to get him conclusively this time. On 16 July 1862, Sowden was convicted at the York Assizes of 'robbery with violence in company with others upon a man called Charles Smith'. This offence had occurred in April but Sowden had not been arrested for it until four days before the Assizes began. Just to be sure of a conviction, the police charged him with receiving the property as well. Found guilty on the charge of robbery with violence, he was sentenced under the name of Thompson Sowden to four years penal servitude. Two days later, but within the same Gaol Delivery for the York Assizes, Joseph Sowden was found guilty of robbery with violence upon a man named Christopher Warwick. Someone, possibly one of his cohort from the first robbery, turned King's evidence in time to ensure the police could get a second conviction. On the strength of a second conviction for felony, the sentence to penal servitude was increased to ten years.[48]

The trials of the later transports reveal how much the legal system had changed since the *Bensley* men were given fifteen minutes, if they were lucky, before being sentenced to death or transportation. In 1816, the person wronged was the prosecutor in the court. Legal counsel on either side was the exception rather than the rule. By the early 1860s, the Crown was always represented by a lawyer and defendants frequently were. Through the changing decades, the enduring safeguard for all the prisoners was the jury: a hard-headed, practical, sympathetic bunch of citizens ameliorating through their group ethos any vindictiveness from an individual. They were no soft touch, however. Scrutinising details of the men and women they convicted, it is apparent that the jury rarely got it wrong in deciding guilt or innocence of a particular crime. Any injustice lay in the definition of an appropriate penalty, or the context in which many of the crimes were committed.

Another change was the development of a police force. By the time the *St Vincent* sailed in 1852, the days of a prosecutor/victim calling in a Bow Street Runner were long gone. Now police walked the beat in every town. They were on every street. To someone committing a crime it must have felt as if they were around every corner. Worse still, in a relatively small population, even in London, the police had a remorseless memory for an old offender. Many a convict returning illegally from transportation was spotted by the eagle eye of a bobby who had dealt with him before.

Last in the chain of theft were the receivers of stolen goods. Receiving was what might be called a steady job in a life of crime, considered rather than impulsive, passive rather than active. Receivers tended to be older criminals and relatively stable because success required they stay in one place so their clients knew where to find them. Not surprisingly, so did the police. Among my sample of 877 men, sixteen were convicted as receivers, a figure which almost matches Robson's findings. Two travelled on the *Bensley*, three on the *John*, five on the *St Vincent* and six on the *Lord Dalhousie*.

Peter (sometimes Patrick) Quigley and his wife **Mary O'Hara** were convicted of receiving in Glasgow in 1816. Irish born, they told the magistrates they had been together as man and wife for two years. Peter claimed to have been in business in Ireland but had met with some 'setbacks' that caused him to move to Scotland. He was operating an unlicensed pub at the time they were arrested. Mary initially swore she had been married to Peter for thirteen years, then changed her statement to match his, explaining that those thirteen years were spent with her first husband. The pair were brought down by three young boys who were caught after dismantling a shop window and stealing pieces of tartan and gingham cloth valued at the large sum of £20. The boys and their older accomplice, who called himself John Smith, split on the

Quigleys in an attempt to save themselves. In fact, the boys were so effective at incriminating the Quigleys that the judge concluded they deserved only one year's imprisonment in the Glasgow Bridewell. 'You were tools in the hands of Quigley and his wife and seduced by them to the commission of the offence,' he pronounced. Keen to ensure the Quigleys were convicted, the city officers paraded several other witnesses with allegations they had sold stolen goods to them, but none was as conclusive as the three young boys. One witness testified that Peter Quigley had told him he would act insane in an attempt to avoid conviction. Whatever the motive, Quigley misbehaved on a grand scale. The *Glasgow Herald* described him as speaking 'very violently and disrespectfully to the judges'. The *Glasgow Chronicle* reported that when called on to plead, he behaved in a 'a very indecorous and disgusting manner and reflected on the administration of justice in Scotland'. During the whole trial he behaved with the utmost levity and 'appeared to entertain much enmity to the city officers'. The Quigleys were transported for fourteen years.[49]

In the hierarchy of counterfeit money, coining was the lowest of the low. An attempt to earn a living by the desperately poor. One police detective, named Wensley, said of coiners, 'They are the most wretched of criminals. I have known scarcely a coiner who was not almost penniless and living under the most squalid conditions.'[50] Two people were usually involved in coining operations: one to make, then hold the mould; the second to pour the hot metal. They were frequently husband and wife. The makers of the counterfeit coins would sell a quantity at say five pence for a shilling's worth. Sometimes they would protect their identify by selling initially to an agent who would then sell the coins again, reducing the ultimate return even further. Finally, people whom the law called 'utterers' but their peers referred to as 'smashers' would pass the money in the community. Having bought the coins they would use them to pay for goods and make change in markets, shops or public houses. At all levels, it was usually subsistence living.[51]

Forgery of bank notes was no more profitable for most participants. As with coining, those who ran the risk of uttering the notes were the most exposed for the least profit. In the early years of the nineteenth century, forging bank notes was relatively simple for a skilled artist or calligrapher, but as the century progressed the police became more professional in their approach and methods of detection improved. Bankers and shopkeepers grew more suspicious. Expert eyes now scrutinised the weight and colour of the paper, its watermark and the style of engraving. In response, forgers upgraded their tactics. Notes were deliberately dirtied to make them look used. However, it was common for a shopkeeper to say on being offered a note, 'Just wait while I ask the bank to check it.' To avoid this trap, utterers would pose as travellers and buy goods with forged notes over the weekend, leaving town before the bank opened on Monday. Sometimes women would dress as servants and pay a tradesman or purchase goods, ostensibly on behalf of their master and sometimes even giving a false address. Successfully gulled, the tradesman would often not discover the notes to be false until several days later.[52]

Bank notes were not the only written instruments that could be forged. Cheques, promissory notes, bills of exchange, bills of lading, wills and conveyances were also vulnerable to the counterfeiters' ingenuity.[53] Financial crime also included embezzlement. Defined as 'the crime of a servant appropriating to his own use the money or goods received by him on account of his master', embezzlement in nineteenth-century Britain was not constrained by class or gender. Underworld investigator Henry Mayhew concluded that it was 'perpetrated in the metropolis by persons both in inferior and superior positions'. Nor was it limited to men. Mayhew found examples of female embezzlers before the courts.[54]

In post-Napoleonic-war England, the *Bensley* carried thirteen men convicted of coining, uttering, forgery and embezzlement. In many cases, their wives or partners were convicted with them. For example, **Peter Barnes**, aged 33, had moved to England from Longford in Ireland. At the Lancaster Assizes in March 1816, he and his wife Jane, aged 30, were charged with coining and putting off counterfeit sixpences at Liverpool. The actual indictment gave some more detail of their operation, claiming that they had been 'feloniously and traitorously colouring with materials producing the colour of silver, two round blanks of base metal, each of them being suitable to be coined into counterfeit milled money resembling the silver coin of this Kingdom called 6d'. They both received a death sentence, which was subsequently commuted to transportation for life. They sailed for Botany Bay around the same time, Peter on the *Sir William Bensley* and Jane on the *Lord Melville*.[55]

Many who sailed with Peter Barnes were trying to supplement their earnings by financial crime. Among them were the brothers **Henry and Robert Dye**, aged 22 and 33, who were tried together at the Old Bailey on 29 May 1816. Originally from Norfolk, both were tall men, at 5 feet 8 inches and 5 feet 10 inches. Henry was a 'ship's caulker' and Robert a baker. Originally indicted for forgery, they both pleaded guilty to the lesser charge of possessing forged notes, for which they were each transported for fourteen years.[56]

Thomas Wells was one of two embezzlers on the *Bensley*. Employed as a clerk and servant by a firm of land surveyors called Messrs Driver & Co., he was 'entrusted by them to receive monies and valuable securities on their account'. An underwriter at Lloyd's Bank named John Rasch told the court that he was in debt to Messrs Driver for what he described as 'a little balance' when Thomas

Wells called to collect the money. 'The sum due was £23 19 s., but I told him that a deduction ought to have been made,' Rasch recounted. He asked Wells to put his case to the Drivers, telling the court, 'I had no doubt that they would take something off.' The following day Wells returned. 'It's not customary, but the gentlemen will take off five guineas,' he told Rasch, altering the account accordingly. Rasch then paid by cheque for which Wells wrote a receipt. Of course his employers knew nothing about this transaction. Edward Driver gave damning testimony. 'We never authorised him to make any deduction in the account of Mr Rasch, or even knew that he applied to him for payment. He never rendered any account whatever of this money to us. I have examined the book in which such money ought to have been entered and no entry is made of it whatever.' Thomas Wells was married with children, but whether greed or necessity motivated him is not revealed by the court records.[57]

There were financial criminals on every boat in the sample, although their numbers were smaller in the middle years when the *John* (1832) and the *St Vincent* (1852) sailed. There were nineteen on the *Lord Dalhousie* in 1863. Coining was flourishing again and men who would sail to Western Australia were doing much the same as many of their predecessors had done since Peter and Jane Barnes' operation in Lancaster in 1816. Although the death penalty no longer applied, sentences remained harsh and the police had become extremely vigilant. In London, the terror of every coiner was the Brannan family, father and son. The London Mint had poached the elder James Brannan from the police force where he was formerly an inspector, but his authority to pursue counterfeiters was not diminished. His son, also James, was still in the police force with the rank of sergeant. Together they constituted a formidable foe, as one of the *Dalhousie* coiners discovered.

Henry Milford, aged 22, was making coins in a tiny room in Spitalfields when the door, which he had carefully locked, burst open under the blows of a sledgehammer. Taking in every detail at a glance, ex-Inspector Brannan later described the scene vividly to the court. 'I saw Milford sitting by a clear, bright fire, in his shirt sleeves, with a plaster of Paris mould in one hand, wrapped in a pad, and a pipkin containing molten metal in the other.' At the sight of them, Milford set down the pipkin on the stove, flung the mould to the floor and stamped on it. Determined to preserve vital evidence, the older Brannan pushed him into the waiting grip of young Sergeant Brannan and the two men struggled violently. Meanwhile, two girls who had been working at the table with Milford sprang to their feet. Emma Theobald aged 22 and Jane Dyer, eighteen, had been scouring metal coins with sand to prepare them for silvering. Emma flung a cup full of sand and water in the inspector's face. A shower of sixpences and fourpenny pieces rained down from it but Brannan's reflexes

An Old Bailey trial in the 1840s

were good. 'I caught the cup between my arm and body and did not let it fall to the ground,' he recounted, producing the coins for inspection by the jury. 'Here are twenty-four dated 1856. And sixteen of 1823.' As Emma flung the cup, Jane Dyer launched herself towards the inspector's back, hands outstretched as if to strangle him. Inspector William Broad was one of the five officers who then rushed the room. 'I caught Dyer by her hands, then let go one and held her by the other while I picked up from the floor eight sixpences and four groats.' Emma Theobald accepted defeat when Bryant took five counterfeit sixpences wet with sand from her hands. 'You have been scouring these,' he accused her. 'Yes,' she replied, 'I suppose I have.'

As Milford was hauled off, the former inspector remarked triumphantly, 'I was told to look out for you. I was to try and put a stop to your dealing.' Milford tried a disingenuous response. 'I have not been long at it Mr Brannan. Not more than three or four months. Indeed, I might say this is my first time.' But Brannan knew differently. After the three prisoners had been found guilty by the jury, and the two girls received sentences of eighteen months in prison, he stepped up to tell the judge, 'Milford lives by coining. He employs women and children to pass it, in shops where there are old persons or children serving.' He did not mention any previous conviction but the judge apparently took into account the evidence of a large-scale racket and handed down a sentence of six years penal servitude.[58]

Three of the forgers on the *Dalhousie* were passing notes on a small scale, but some were part of counterfeit operations to a grand design. In April 1862 Cholm Reichberg, aged 45, a jeweller, Abraham Josephson, 32, a travelling jeweller, and Woolfe Harwitz, 22, a commission agent, were charged with forging and possessing plates for the manufacture of five-rouble and ten-rouble notes of the Russian Empire. This was the final stage in a sensational fraud case. Described by the *Times* as 'foreigners', the three men were Polish Jews from Odessa. Together with **Abraham Rosenberg**, 55, a frame-maker, and Kaufman Weber, 35, a tailor, who were tried with Reichberg two months later, they had systematically planned to circulate forged Russian notes. After two extensive trials, they were all sentenced to penal servitude—Reichberg and Rosenberg to eight years; Josephson, Harwitz and Weber to six years each. All but Harwitz would sail on the *Lord Dalhousie*. Among the witnesses at the trial was one who had asked Josephson why they were carrying out their scheme in Britain rather than Russia. He testified that Josephson replied, 'In England they are not so severe. In Russia they would send our wives and families to Siberia.' How he felt when he discovered his destination was Western Australia is not on record but he and the others settled successfully there, travelling backwards and forwards to Europe as they needed.[59]

The *Dalhousie* carried two lawyers convicted for forgery. One of them, **Joseph Shaw**, was tried at the Derby Assizes in March 1862. Shame for his crime was evident during the trial as he rested his elbows on the dock rail, a hand shading his face from onlookers. The court was packed with people he knew, some of them sympathetic, many of them aggrieved clients, all of them curious to gauge his every reaction in this last stage of a Derbyshire scandal.

Joseph Shaw, known as Josh, was a 29 year-old solicitor. He was also High Bailey of the District Court of Derbyshire, an appointment secured for him the previous year by his influential mother-in-law, a member of the wealthy Cantrell family. On 5 August 1859 Shaw had married 19-year-old Maria Cantrell and they settled in Tideswell near Derby, where Joseph continued to practise law. Over the next five years they had three children—Thomas, John Francis and Alice. Unknown to Maria, however, within two years of their marriage her husband was weaving a false and increasingly complex web of mortgages, conveyances, money advanced, money delayed, promissory notes and correspondence promising, explaining, delaying . . . Deeds of all kinds were exchanged. Some were genuine. Some were not. Many of these documents were attested to or bore the signature of Joseph Shaw. Some carried the signature of his clerk or agent in Ilkeston. As the interlocking network unravelled, it was the clerk who first came under suspicion. By the committal hearing he was desperately reiterating his innocence. Another solicitor's clerk 'showed me some deeds with my name upon them, but I denied they bore my signature. Upon my oath I did not tell him they were my signatures. I did not tell him that I had signed many deeds and papers for Mr Shaw. I said I had signed papers, but they were all writs . . . [T]he signatures upon the deeds shown to me were not mine, nor did I acknowledge they were mine [previously] at Ilkeston.'

At the Assizes, Shaw was arraigned on eleven counts of forging and uttering. In the hushed court, the clerk read them over in an interminable roll-call: forging and uttering a deed purporting to convey certain land, forging and uttering a promissory note for £52, forging a deed of conveyance . . . His voice low but steady, Shaw answered each one in turn, guilty, guilty, guilty. He was sombre but calm. Next morning, however, when his counsel, Mr O'Brien, addressed the court regarding his sentence, Shaw's composure finally cracked. O'Brien began by telling the judge that Shaw had instructed him to emphasise 'the great shame and sorrow' he felt. There was reference to some 'imprudence of which he had at an early period of life been guilty' and which, it was inferred, led him into every-increasing debt. Was it gambling? Or drink? No details were given. Nor was any attempt made to excuse what Shaw had done. When O'Brien touched on the life he might have led and the prospects now before him, Shaw sobbed aloud as he buried his face in a handkerchief.

After a brief expression of sympathy, the judge moved swiftly to his broader duty. 'You, from your high character and apparent respectability, solicited and enjoyed the confidence of the public and of your clients,' he told Shaw, 'but desperate to maintain your position, you plunged into a career of fraud and perjury which has few parallels in the history of crime, a career, which as you well know a very few years ago must have been closed by the forfeit of your life upon a public scaffold.' He sentenced Joseph Shaw to fifteen years penal servitude.[60]

From his examination of the convict records, Robson found ten bigamists among his sample of 6131 men. At the Old Bailey between 1800 and 1834, 177 people, mainly men, were found guilty of bigamy. Sixty-seven of these were transported.[61] Bigamists were transported through the duration of the penal colonies but they fell off in numbers in the later period.[62] There were two in this sample, Henry Bayley Holland who was transported on the *St Vincent* in 1853, and Francis Bodenham who sailed on the *Bensley* in 1816. Although transported 37 years apart, each man received a sentence of seven years. Bayley Holland was unlucky. Prosecution of bigamy continued unabated in Britain during the nineteenth century but, generally, the penalties became more lenient. By 1847 a bigamist at the Old Bailey who used the same defence as Francis Bodenham 30 years earlier—'She knew I was a married man at the time I married her. It is her fault not mine'—received only a six-month sentence.[63]

Francis Bodenham was above average height for his time, with pale skin that refused to tan, fair hair and grey eyes. This appearance, along with his education and the lack of tattoos, scars or marks of any kind, distinguished him from many of his shipmates on the *Sir William Bensley*. The details are hard to disentangle from the record but Bodenham was 22 when he married Amy Petty in February 1812 in the then rural village of Mortlake in the parish of Kingston-on-Thames outside London. After their marriage, the couple lived with Amy's mother and, according to his mother-in-law, conceived two children before he left Amy. His trial for bigamy took place almost three years later, in January 1815. There, it was revealed that he went to live in Heston, in Middlesex, where barely eighteen months after his wedding to Amy, he married Eliza Keattch. Miss Keattch testified that she and Francis were fellow servants for a Mr Lewis and during that time the prisoner 'came courting to me'. She swore Francis told her that his wife died in childbirth. She also testified that she had been married to Francis on 4 June 1813. The marriage was confirmed by the parish clerk of Heston, who gave the date as one year later. Francis defended himself by claiming that Eliza Keattch 'fully understood I was a married man, but she threatened to destroy herself if I did not marry her'.[64] Cross-examined about this point, Eliza 'positively denied' it and the parish register of St Leonard's, Heston, supports her. There, for all to see including descendants of Francis, he is described as 'widower of this parish'. The fact that his wife Amy gave birth to a daughter in November 1814 and the persistence of his mother-in-law were no doubt factors in bringing Francis to trial, but Eliza also had an urgent agenda. In 1815, she gave birth to a son, Harry, who had been fathered by Francis.[65] Found guilty by the jury, Francis was sentenced to transportation for seven years.[66]

As Francis sailed away to Van Diemen's Land, **Sarah Franks**, who was to become so important to him, was convicted of theft at the Old Bailey. One of her co-accused, Sarah Pinnion, had been tried before with another member of the Franks family, a boy named Samuel, which suggests that stealing and receiving may have been the family business. The professional nature of Sarah Franks' crime is obvious. She appears to have been one of a group who were criminally active in the East End and she disposed of the property in a very business-like manner to four different pawnbrokers under at least two different names. This was a young woman who knew what she was doing.[67]

Some crimes in this sample involved violence and bloodshed. Men were convicted for murder, manslaughter, cutting and wounding and doing grievous bodily harm. In addition to the nine poachers on the *Bensley* who were convicted of murder, there was a stonemason named **John Belcher** whose crime was cutting and maiming. Two men on the *John* in 1832 were convicted of manslaughter and one of murder. Twenty-year-old Francis Wilson was also on the *John*. As a stonemason he had a weapon readily to hand when a fight broke out at the pub where he had been drinking heavily. He confronted his antagonist, William Liddale, holding his mason's knife in both hands. On 13 April 1831 at Knaresboro in Yorkshire, Wilson was charged with assaulting and stabbing Liddale in the right thigh with intent to murder, plus four other counts—intent to maim, intent to disfigure, intent to disable and intent to do grievous bodily harm. Wilson pleaded not guilty to all but the jury found him guilty on the last count.[68] The *St Vincent* carried eight men who had been convicted of crimes that ranged from manslaughter to maliciously wounding, including Robert Ward who was convicted of the manslaughter of his wife during a quarrel. On the *Dalhousie*, the convictions of twenty men were described as manslaughter or wounding with intent or murder and two as wilful murder. They amounted to 10 per cent of the total. One in this group was the poacher, Caleb Stapley. The most sensational in terms of publicity in Britain was Richard Reeves, the perpetrator of what was known to the British press as 'The Strand Murder'.

Teenager **Richard (Dick) Reeves** lived in Drury Court, London, with his father Thomas, who was a basket-maker, his stepmother Mary and his ten-year-old step-sister Mary Ann, known as Polly. His stepmother had cared for Richard since he was seven years old. The case excited enormous sympathy for the 'mild and inoffensive-looking youth', so much so that some unnamed people arranged free legal defence for him.[69] Crowds gathered outside the Bow Street Police Court to catch a glimpse of Dick as he was led from the police station. Aware of the interest, the *Times* reported every detail, including the opinion that he looked much younger than his age. 'He is of very boyish aspect . . . His countenance is intelligent, open, and rather handsome than otherwise, though slightly pitted by smallpox. His dress though of common texture was particularly clean and tidy.'

Dick's stepmother was among the witnesses. About 45 years old, she appeared with a large patch of sticking plaster immediately above her eye. According to the *Times*, she was very agitated and had difficulty answering questions. The report also observed that the family was 'dissipated and ill-tempered'. Certainly, Mrs Reeves' evidence gave some indication of the pressure Dick Reeves must have experienced daily working as a basket-maker with his father in the business that was run from a back room on the ground floor of their house. Dick had developed a habit of leaving home to get away from his violent father, supporting himself by pawning his clothes. Mrs Reeves described her husband's severe drinking problem, reporting that since their marriage in 1852 he had been in St Bartholomew's hospital twice suffering from delirium tremens. 'Unfortunately he has been in the habit of drinking a good deal,' she told the court. 'The previous time when he was under restraint was twelve months ago when he had the same thing the matter with him.' Mrs Reeves also gave details of a family history of what might have been epilepsy. 'There was an uncle that died at Hanwell who was subject to fits,' she said. 'I believe he died quite out of his mind.'

But Dick's problems were not confined to his father. His half-sister liked to play power games with him, and the two were constantly quarrelling. When Mrs Reeves went out, she entrusted her keys to her daughter Mary Ann, but the girl used them to lock the cupboard containing bread and other food, which meant Dick could not get anything to eat. Neighbour Ellen James had overheard a typical tussle between them on the morning of the murder. Through tears, she told the court that she heard Dick calling to Mary Ann; who was upstairs. 'Polly, Polly,' he called. He wanted to start work in the back room but Mary Ann brushed him off, saying impatiently, 'What do you want, Dick?' Mrs James heard him ask, 'Polly, I want the key for the back place [the workshop]. Bring me the key of the back place.' When she replied, 'I don't know where it is Dick,' he told her, 'It's on the table against the window.' There was a pause. Finally Mary Ann said, 'All right Dick, I've got them.' Shortly after, Mrs James heard her go downstairs. At this point Mrs James broke down, sobbing violently, exclaiming, 'Oh your worship, he was always a good boy.' Pressed about the relationship between the two children, she said that she had heard Dick Reeves threaten the girl many times. Asked to give a specific example, she said, 'When the step-mother has locked the cupboard and she [Mary Ann] has taken away the key so he could not get any bread, I heard him say, "You little bitch".'

On 15 November 1861, when Mrs James overheard this latest exchange between brother and sister, Mr and Mrs Reeves went out together. When Mrs Reeves returned, she could not find her daughter. She asked Dick if he knew where Mary Ann was, but he answered 'no' and ran off.

Dick Reeves had many friends in the neighbourhood, including John Lynes, the porter at the Exeter Hall Hotel. Dick told him that his little sister was lost. He asked Lynes and another friend, William Carney, if they would walk along The Strand with him to look for her. The trio went as far as St Clement's Church when Dick announced, 'It's no use looking for my sister in the streets. Go home and tell my father if he wants Mary Ann, I have strangled her. She is in the coal cellar.' As the two men ran back to the house, Dick continued on his way down The Strand. Lynes and Carney found Dick's father, very drunk but eventually agreeable to looking in the coal cellar. The neighbours, Ellen James and a second woman named Mrs Griffiths, joined them, Griffiths carrying a candle which she held high as John Lynes pulled open the trapdoor to the cellar. At the sight of Mary Ann lifeless on a heap of coals, Mrs Griffiths screamed 'Oh, my God. It's

Polly.' Lynes jumped into the cellar and lifted up the little body. 'It was all in a heap, on its side with some coals lying on her cheek . . . I noticed a rope or clothesline tied round her neck,' he recalled.

Meanwhile Dick was halfway down The Strand where he met another friend, 18-year-old Jemina Kadge. 'I have strangled my sister,' he told her. When she did not believe him, he insisted 'I have done it.' Questioned by the lawyer about Dick's demeanour, Jemina Kadge replied, 'He was in a very good temper when he spoke to me about it. He had a smile on his face.' Police Constable Charles Venus said much the same thing. He knew Dick by sight and went looking for him, eventually finding him leaning against a lamp post on the corner in Carey Street. When Venus said, 'I want you,' Dick straightened up saying, 'I know what for. I did it.' Although cautioned, he repeated, 'I did it. She aggravated me to it.' In court, Constable Venus described Dick as 'Perfectly calm. He had the same indifferent look that he has now. Quite cool and collected.'

At his trial in the Central Criminal Court the jury found Dick guilty, but they too strongly recommended him to mercy 'because of the bad example set to him at home'. The judge sentenced him to death as required by law, but said that he would recommend that it be commuted.[70]

Killing someone was not only a male crime. Women convicted of murder or manslaughter were also transported to Australia. Their numbers were not large—about 1 per cent of the total number of female convicts. Fitting this pattern, there was one, Margaret Hartigan, among the 100 women transported on the *Princess Royal* in 1829. The number of female convicts transported for murder increased later in the transportation era. There were five on the *Duchess of Northumberland* which docked at Hobart in 1853, all of whom had killed their children.

Eliza Dore was 22 when she was indicted for the murder of her six-week-old daughter at Newport in Wales. Her lover, Abel Ovans, who was also 22, was charged with her. The arrival of a baby threatened to end their relationship. As the weeks passed, Abel would not touch his daughter and showed no love for her, telling a neighbour he did not like children when they were cross and that he wished the child dead. The tension between the couple worsened when they could not pay their rent and were turned out of their lodgings on a wintry Sunday. They stayed at a nearby pub, but by Wednesday evening they were homeless again. Abel was growing angrier and he was taking it out on Eliza. As they walked to yet another lodging house, carrying their belongings in a large bundle, accompanied by wails from the baby, he made up his mind. On the Mill Street bridge he stopped dead, swearing at Eliza, 'If you don't give me that child, you won't live with me because I won't keep it.' Grabbing the child, he left Eliza weeping on the bridge while he walked off down the side of the canal. When he came back he was carrying the shawl and clothes, but the baby had gone. Between tears, Eliza kept asking him what he had done with the child. 'I've done away with it,' he snapped, 'for I'll not keep it.' Eliza wept even harder at this, but Abel had no sympathy. 'Don't make that noise here. Come to the lodgings.' The more she cried, the angrier he became, finally threatening to beat her unless she stopped.

The next morning the naked body of a baby was found floating on the edge of a large pool called the Mill Pond, not far from the Mill Street bridge. With no identification on the child, the inquest simply recorded 'Found dead' and the tiny body was buried in the churchyard at Stow. A reward was offered for anyone who could identify her.

A woman convict in the mid-nineteenth century

Two weeks passed, during which Eliza kept up the pretence that all was well with her baby. But when people asked Eliza how the baby was she told different stories to different people. To one she said, 'She's famous'. To another, 'She's a little cross. I can't run out when she's asleep.' A third person was told, 'She's at my mother's at Boxhill.' But of the baby herself, there was no sign. In the end, someone suspected foul play and told the police.

Abel was arrested first but denied all knowledge of a child, while the stories Eliza told the police were hopelessly contradictory. Then, as they took her to the station, she said suddenly, 'If I did not do it myself, they cannot punish me', and she asked where the baby was buried. When she was told, something changed and she began to confess, although pleading anxiously with the police, 'Don't tell Abel that I said he treated me ill.' It was not until her mother arrived that Eliza described exactly what happened.

Abel kept denying the child was his, but when they had heard all the evidence the jury did not believe him. Both were found guilty, although the jury recommended mercy for Eliza, who was transported for life. Abel was hanged.[71]

There were no rapists on the *Sir William Bensley* or the *John*, probably because men who committed rape were usually hanged. By 1853, however, and when the *Dalhousie* sailed in 1863, a reprieve was more likely than it had been in the past. Few details of the crimes survive because the case papers were not kept and the newspapers did not report anything more than a brief outline. There had originally been two rapists on the *St Vincent*, but one jumped overboard. Fifteen men out of 277 on board the *Dalhousie* had been convicted of rape, two of whom raped children. Neither of the latter were young men. Johan Herrold was 42 years old and Thomas Barclay, a London glass-blower, 32. Both men received sentences of life.[72] Two others for whom some details were available were accused of raping young women. George Dean, for instance, was an 18-year-old potter who was convicted on his own confession of assaulting and robbing Mary Ann Hancock in Staffordshire and also of raping her. His confession may be the reason his sentence was six years penal servitude.[73] Peter Swayne was a labourer, aged 28, who assaulted a young woman named Martha Petty in Wiltshire. Swayne also pleaded guilty, which so concerned the judge that he asked counsel to ensure that the prisoner understood the implications of what he was saying. But Swayne insisted and was sentenced to eight years penal servitude.[74]

Soldier convicts formed significant numbers among the convicts sent to Australia. The war with France had ended when the *Sir William Bensley* sailed in 1816, but the ship carried a 45-year-old 'Band man', Nicholas Barris, who had been court-martialled in Abbeville, France. Most ships that sailed from England during this early period, as distinct from Ireland, carried court-martialled soldiers as prisoners—usually four to eight at a time, but sometimes many more. In 1812, convicts on the *Guildford* included nineteen soldiers. In 1811, the *Admiral Gambier* carried eleven.[75] Soldier convicts are one of the interesting aspects of the penal colonies that have been hidden by lack of discussion of Australia's convict origins. After more investigation, they may prove to have been more influential than the much-discussed social and political protesters.

The *John* carried fourteen soldiers among the total 198 prisoners who landed in New South Wales in 1832. They had mainly been convicted in places around Britain where troops were used to keep order during those domestically turbulent times. The soldiers on the *John* had been court-martialled at Chatham, at Aberdeen in northern Scotland and the fast-growing midlands town of Manchester, plus the metropolitan locations of King's Mews in Whitehall and the Tower of London. On this ship, only two reflected the increasing spread of the British Empire: **William Crooks** and **William McGhie** were court-martialled on the same day in Bombay and shipped back together to London. Later in the transportation era, soldiers sentenced to transportation in India and other colonies were sometimes sent directly to 'the Empire's gaol', as Governor Arthur described Van Diemen's Land. In earlier times, and again during the Western Australian convict era, they usually went back to England first.

A chequered career as a convict reveals **Patrick Quigley** as the quintessential Irishman: irrepressible in adversity, self-reliant, accountable to no one, opportunistic, all accompanied by a touch of the blarney which helped him ease even the most dreadful situations in which he found himself. When he was sentenced to transportation in 1831, Quigley was a 26-year-old private in the 17th Regiment of Foot, known as the Leicestershires. He had 'taken the King's shilling', as enlistment was termed, at Cork, not far from his birthplace in the parish of St Mary, Limerick. At the time he was about seventeen. Unlike others in need of money, Quigley did not then desert only to enlist again with another regiment. He stayed with the army for nine years, but he developed a habit of wandering off. Each time the army brought him back, whereupon he did it again, and they rounded him up again, court-martialling him each time with a sentence of corporal punishment. Each time, the War Office publicised his details alongside absconding convicts and tales of robbery and murder in the *Police Gazette; or, Hue and Cry*. Of middling height at 5 feet 5 inches, Quigley was described then and consistently in the future as 'stout-made', with a distinctive round face and small mouth in a large chin, dark hair and eyebrows and, at the time of his desertion at Chatham, clean-shaven. He walked off wearing his regimental trousers and his red fatigue coat. And in this first of many similar descriptions, his occupation is described as 'tinman'.[76]

The court-martial ordered that Quigley receive 300 lashes in addition to his sentence of transportation, in which case the following description might just as well have fitted him, occurring, as it did almost simultaneously with his own punishment:

> Another unfortunate miserable wretch has been flogged until human nature could no longer bear the torture. On Saturday morning last, the 1st Battalion of the 1st Regiment of Grenadier Guards mustered at the usual place in Knightsbridge barracks, when a private soldier named Griffiths, belonging to the battalion… was brought out from his place of confinement to hear the minutes of a court-martial read over by the adjutant of the regiment . . . It appeared that his crime was desertion, and the court found him guilty, and sentenced him to receive 500 lashes. The unfortunate man was instantly tied up and the drummers went to work with their cats. Griffiths is a very fleshy man, and his cries were dreadful. After receiving

260 lashes his back was in a dreadful state and it was quite evident that he had received as much flogging as he could bear . . . he was released from the torture and conveyed to the military hospital, to be cured of the laceration which he had received.[77]

The records of the *John* reveal that three of Quigley's shipmates had been sentenced to 500 lashes at some time in the past and one, James Lynn, had received 600. The full sentence was not always completed, if for no other reason than the purely practical one that the army would frequently have flogged its miscreants to death, and later records reveal that Patrick Quigley received 'only' 150 of the 300 lashes awarded against him.[78] Floggings received by convicts in Australia pale by comparison with soldiers in the British Army, where the men continued to be flogged for many years after transportation ceased. The number of lashes permitted in the army was reduced to 50 in 1846, in theory at least if not in practice, but the last stripes were not inflicted on a soldier's back until 1881.[79]

Quigley's fourth desertion convinced the army that, despite any number of lashes, he was irredeemable. The court-martial sentenced him to fourteen years transportation and, after a brief spell on the hulks at Chatham, he found himself on the *John* bound for Botany Bay. Once on board, he quickly adopted the 'old soldier' persona to negotiate a deal with the detachment of troops from the 31st Regiment who were sailing with the ship to guard the prisoners. Quigley would grease and clean their weapons, a chore he knew from experience they would be happy to avoid, in return for the right to walk about the decks. It is unknown how many side deals he did with individual soldiers to obtain the occasional plug of tobacco or a pot of grog. His negotiations would have been even easier when ten members of his old regiment joined the guard as part of an arrangement where the 17th Foot was being transferred in batches for service to New South Wales.[80] But Quigley's efforts to ensure himself a comfortable sea voyage did not end with the soldiers. Before long he had so successfully ingratiated himself with the surgeon James Lawrence that the medical gentleman came to rely on Quigley and his crony William Crooks, also a soldier, to assist with the management of other prisoners.[81]

All the soldiers on the *John* were transported for desertion, which was the main crime committed by military convicts, although Philip Hilton, who has done the most research on the subject, notes, 'there is a foggy lack of clarity about what defined desertion and what distinguished absence from desertion'.[82] For many years, it was the army's practice to brand deserters with the letter 'D'.[83] Only two of the fourteen soldiers on the *John* bore the imprint (former Guardsman William Dunn from Donegal and the Scot, William Muire Eagle) but nine men on the *Dalhousie* carried this mark. One of the Western Australian group, John Kenny, had taken 'desertion' a step further than simply leaving himself. While stationed at Halifax, Nova Scotia, as a private in the 63rd Regiment, he was found guilty of urging other soldiers to desert and of holding meetings to plan their desertion. The British Army had long been nervous about desertion and mutiny among forces stationed in North America. The anxiety was a legacy of the rebellions in Upper and Lower Canada 30 years earlier, but also because the United States was temptingly close. British newspapers reported examples of Americans 'enticing' British troops across the border and then angrily describing a British military raiding party which crossed into the United States to recover the deserters as 'this act of invasion of our soil and insult to our national authority'.[84]

In 1853, the *St Vincent* carried nine soldier prisoners to Van Diemen's Land. They included a hard core of experienced older men. Isaac Povey, 36, had served eleven years in the Grenadier Guards, James Ross, age 33, nine years in the 7th Fusiliers, and William Scheal, 29, nine years in the 88th Regiment. Most were convicted of desertion. In Van Diemen's Land also, convict soldiers tended to be older than the thousands of young criminals who sailed with them, a pattern that changed in Western Australia if the *Lord Dalhousie* is indicative. Among the 43 soldiers transported by that ship in 1863, the ages of the soldier convicts ranged from 22 to 41, but nearly two-thirds of them were in their twenties.

Along with differences in age were changes in the type of offence committed. In the Western Australian group only four soldiers were convicted of desertion. The great majority were transported for striking their superior officer, or threatening him, and in one case of killing his sergeant. Of all prisoners on the *Dalhousie* who were transported for life, ten, or almost half the total, were soldiers. Since the greater violence and resistance to authority was among the younger soldiers, it may indicate a generation less prepared to tolerate the British Army's disciplinary practices. But there is another possible explanation for their attitude. A majority of the soldiers were Irish by birth. Despite having taken the King's shilling, men like John Farrell, at 41 the oldest among the *Dalhousie* soldiers, knew where their loyalty ultimately lay. The harp of Erin was tattooed on his right arm and above it the words 'Ireland Forever'.[85]

'Insubordination' was another military crime that was open to interpretation. In his book, *Adventures of a Guardsman*, transported officer Charles Cozens described how a tussle of wills with his corporal-major escalated into threats to put him on a charge, which was followed by a rash response from Cozens: 'If you do that, it will be the last time because I'll *do* for you.' The outcome for Cozens was transportation to New South Wales for ten years.[86] 'Insubordination' featured often in the crimes of the soldiers transported on the *St Vincent* and the *Lord Dalhousie*, but it was frequently accompanied by actual assault.

While a prisoner in Bermuda, the Irish exile John Mitchel discovered that some soldiers deliberately sought transportation to escape the army.[87] **John Conway** may have been one of those. The 23-year-old had a continuous history of courts-martial at all levels—general, garrison and regimental. Convicted in Malta in August 1857 of using threatening language to his commanding officer, he set about making the authorities pay for incarcerating him. Originally sent to Dartmoor, presumably because he convinced someone he was only fit for light duties, he was hastily removed for using threatening language towards the assistant surgeon and Police Warder Shepherd and for 'General Bad Conduct'. An investigation into this incident concluded that 'this man is utterly unfit for association on the public works', a decision that was very likely exactly what Conway wanted to achieve. They sent him to Millbank where he was lashed with twelve stripes for 'filthy and insubordinate conduct', to Portsmouth prison where he was lashed for 'mutinous conduct in striking his officer' (in this case a prison warder), as he was later still at Millbank for 'shouting, singing, swearing, cursing and using filthy, disgusting language'.[88]

Few soldiers recorded any information about 'kin' in the prison registers. Most of them were single. Soldiers were not allowed to marry without the permission of their regiment, and even if this was given there was still the difficulty of maintaining a wife and family unless they were able to live 'on strength', which few were allowed to do. Hilton calculates that only 20 per cent of the convict soldiers were married, which is much lower than the figure for convicts generally.[89] Among the married men on the *Dalhousie* was 22-year-old **Richard Farrell**. Born in Ireland, he had been serving in St Helena when he was convicted by general court-martial of 'shooting with intent' at his superior officer. Even though he had no previous transgressions, Farrell was sentenced to life. When he sailed for Western Australia he left his wife Mary behind in England with their young son, Robert.[90]

Life as a common seaman was no easier than for a soldier. Naval courts-martial were just as unrelenting and harsh. There were numerous sailors and merchant seamen among the prisoners sampled here. The *Bensley* had eight on board—a couple of midshipmen, a sailmaker, and in **Robert or Henry Dye** a ship's caulker. Three were Scots including young burglar Charles Clephane who was, as he put it, 'bred to the sea'. In 1853 the *St Vincent* carried fewer sailors but it did include a captain among its numbers.

William Kidd was 38 years old when he landed in Hobart in May 1853, but his grey hair and greying whiskers must have made him look much older—

a real Old Salt. And in reality, that is what he was: many years a master mariner, four years captain of the ship *Jane and Isabella*. Until he sank her.

In May 1848, the *Jane and Isabella* lay in Liverpool taking on 95 tons of salt for passage to Bulmer, Northumberlandshire. Cargo loaded, Kidd sailed her north, circling the tip of Scotland to come down the east coast. But he never reached Bulmer. Instead, he called at Scranish on the island of Tyree. The herring season was at its peak, salt was in great demand, and Kidd's cargo mysteriously vanished. In Scranish also, an 80-fathom hawser, a chain cable and other articles belonging to the *Jane and Isabella* were sold to local fishermen.

Having replaced the salt ballast with sand, Kidd sailed south. Off the island of South Uist, at the entrance to Lock Skebort or Skipport, calamity supposedly struck the *Jane and Isabella*. Overriding the pilot in the wheelhouse, Kidd took the helm himself and drove her bow forward wildly on the surge— straight into the rocks. The jib boom, the bowsprit and the figurehead broke into pieces and were carried away by the swell. But still she floated. Undeterred, Kidd swung the wheel over so she surged hard against the rock. This time her side was stove-in and she sank in deep water, taking the ballast of sand to the bottom with her.

It is not known how long the purchasers of the salt, the ship's owners and the insurers of the *Jane and Isabella* pondered their loss. Or when they began to think that the captain had done something dastardly. Presumably insurance investigators tracked the items sold in Scranish. Maybe they talked to the ship's crew or discovered a disgruntled pilot. Even when they decided that Kidd was to blame, they were unsure in what way. The lawyers argued about the appropriate charge. Was it destroying the ship, the theft of its cargo, intent to defraud the insurance company or a breach of trust? They turned to a barrister who dropped the breach of trust, retained the attempt to defraud and advised that the grounds for the charge of theft should be clarified.

Meanwhile William Kidd spent time with his wife and children in Aberdeen. He even took another voyage, this time to South Australia, perhaps anticipating that he might soon be down that way in very different circumstances. Finally, in October 1849 he was arrested and confined in Tolbermory Prison. His trial was held in the following February. After he pleaded guilty Mr Logan, Kidd's lawyer, negotiated a plea bargain that involved conviction for theft of the salt but escape from the death sentence required for the wilful destruction of ships. Logan then attempted to mitigate the length of sentence. 'The prisoner has always borne a most excellent character with those he has served previous to the *Jane and Isabella*,' he told the court. He described Kidd's voyage to South Australia in the *Warrior*, pointing out that the prisoner had conducted himself in a proper manner throughout. Then he came to the nub of Captain Kidd's wild action.

'The owner of the ship my lord was indebted to the prisoner for a considerable sum of money. He had allowed the vessel to sail from Liverpool without being properly "found". Had the prisoner in his capacity as master merely sold a portion of the cargo to defray expenses, so far all would have been right. But having once broken bulk in the Western Highlands, my lord—and it being the heat of the herring fishing—he confesses my lord that he sold the lot.' On the prisoner's behalf, Logan admitted that the ship had been destroyed to screen the robbery of its cargo. He told the judge that Kidd had sent the owners £40 already towards compensating them. In accordance with his confession, the jury found William Kidd guilty and the judge sentenced him to seven years transportation.[91]

All four boats surveyed here included social and political protesters who fitted Rudé's definition, that is, 'people who acted together with others, or appeared to do so, in pursuit of common political or social goals'. During 1830 and early 1831, for instance, England was wracked by rural protests across many counties, particularly in the agricultural areas of the south-east where there had been a rise in rural poverty and unemployment and a decline in cottage industry that had not been offset by other growth.[92] Agricultural labourers were the main protagonists in a defined and collective movement against the conditions of their lives. Machine breaking, arson, threatening letters and angry meetings about wages and living conditions were a feature of the period, as were riots and, sometimes, robbery. Known colloquially as the Swing Riots, the protests of this period resulted in boatloads of transportees to Australia early in 1831. Ships such as the *Eliza*, the *Eleanor* and the *Proteus* carried nothing but protesters of this type, amounting to some 500 men.[93] By contrast, the men on the *John* were mainly thieves. The only 'protesters' on board were the Merthyr Tydfil rioters, who will be described below. The *Lord Dalhousie* carried no distinctive group, but Western Australia did not escape the dissident element because there were 26 British arsonists on board, some of whom were protesting in their individual way. Other boats to Western Australia carried groups of the Irish political activists known as Fenians.

The first of the protesters who acted collectively in this sample were on board the *Sir William Bensley* in 1816. They came from the village of Littleport, near Ely.

Richard Rutter was no hot-headed lad at the time of the 'disturbances' at Littleport. Already 41 years of age, he was married with one child. He even owned two cows, which was no small thing for an agricultural labourer in England in the summer of 1816. Life could have been good if work was regular and sufficiently paid. Among Rutter's friends in the village was **Joseph Easey**. At 35, Joseph was close to Rutter in age and he was also married, with a two-year-old son called Joseph. The two men would have worked together often, harvesting and ploughing and sowing fields for local farmers. Joseph, who stood barely five feet, was known to all and sundry as 'Little Easey' to distinguish him from another villager named John Easey, who was a tall 5 feet 9 inches.[94]

On the evening of Wednesday 22 May 1816, Rutter and the two Easeys gathered with 50 or so agricultural labourers at the Globe public house in Littleport. It was an annual event, for everyone present belonged to a precursor of what were later called friendly societies, in which the members pooled funds to help those in need. That night, they were shocked to discover that everyone was in such a dire position that none could help any other. They were all vulnerable to the steep rise in the price of wheat, work was uncertain because the harvest was poor, and in any event, those who were employed were paid wages so low they could barely survive. On average, their weekly wages were nine shillings when the price of a loaf of bread was nearly a shilling (eleven and a half pence in fact).[95] Furthermore, those who owned property could not access help under the Poor Laws: Rutter would have had to sell his two cows to become eligible. Over a beer, the men became angrier and angrier, inflamed by the news that one of the local farmers, who was also a magistrate, had sacked three of his labourers. Eventually, Joseph Easey rushed round the village sounding a horn to call others to join them in seeking money from the better-off villagers, such as farmers and shopkeepers and local clergyman the Reverend Vachell, who was also the local magistrate.

They rampaged through the village armed with bludgeons and pitchforks and a few guns. They broke shop windows. They forced their way into homes demanding money and destroying property if it was refused. Carried away with their success, the group set off for Ely, some of them riding on a horse and cart, on which they had mounted two fowling guns. Meanwhile, the Ely magistrates had been warned of what was happening. One of them, Reverend Sir Henry Bate Dudley, known as the 'Fighting Parson', sent a messenger to the First Royal Dragoon Guards who were stationed in Bury St Edmunds, then swore in the tradesmen of Ely as special constables and prepared to face the rioters.[96]

At dawn the two groups confronted each other. For the rioters, the key was the power exercised by the magistrates, sitting in civil quarter sessions, over the Poor Law regulations. 'Our children are starving, give us a living wage,' they demanded. Another request was that the poor rate be the equivalent of the 'price of a stone of flour per day'. Even when the three clerical magistrates agreed that these demands would be met, the protesters would not go home but spread through the city. After some delay, the magistrates issued a statement to the crowd in the marketplace:

> The magistrates agree, and do order, that the over-seers shall pay to each family two shillings per head per week, when flour is half-a-crown a stone; such allowance to be raised in proportion when the price of flour is higher, and that the price of labour shall be two shilling a day, whether married or single and that the labourer shall be paid his full wages by the farmer who hires him.[97]

The rioters had won everything they sought and most of them went home well satisfied. But Richard Rutter did not. The agreement made no difference to him unless he sold his cows. When urged to leave, he refused. 'I might as well be hanged as starve,' he said. 'I'll be damned if I'll not be fed in Ely. They can hang me from the nearest thorn-bush if they please.'[98]

When Rutter finally returned to Littleport, he joined the other rioters who, expecting retaliation from the authorities, had barricaded themselves inside the George Inn. The First Royal Dragoon Guards came the following day under the command of the Fighting Parson, who demanded their surrender. Shots were exchanged and one man was killed before the Littleport men were defeated. Three weeks later, they were tried at a Special Assize. Little Easey, marked for blowing the horn that summoned the mob and for threatening a landholder named Henry Martin, was convicted of stealing and sentenced to death, later commuted to life. Richard Rutter was found guilty of robbery and sentenced to fourteen years transportation, John Easey to seven years for stealing from various shopkeepers. Together with Aaron Chevell, a local tailor, John Jefferson and Richard Jessop, who were all convicted for stealing, they were shipped to Botany Bay on the *Sir William Bensley*.

The sentencing judge pronounced that 'The conduct of the rioters cannot be attributed to want or poverty, the prisoners were all robust men, in full health, strength, and vigour, who were receiving great wages; and any change in the price of provisions could only lessen that superfluity, which, I fear, they too frequently wasted in drunkenness.' However, A.J. Peacock points out that pay for agricultural labourers, the price of bread and the regulations of the Poor Laws were creating turbulence across England that summer. The authorities cast these as matters of law and order but, according to Peacock, it was 'a revolt of desperate men; the criticisms were those of a class which had divested itself of the responsibilities it once had to the poor and oppressed'. The background of the riots in Littleport was that of a society in transition, from what E.P. Thompson termed 'the old moral economy' to the economy of the free market when, according to Peacock, community leaders shed the last of their obligations towards the poorer sections of society. The once 'deserving' became the 'designing' poor.[99]

The protesters on the *John* were four men convicted for the Merthyr Tydfil riots in Wales in June 1831. The issues there were complex but included parochial concern with the activities of the Court of Requests and its bailiffs, the level of wages at the ironworks and the practice of 'truck', whereby the ironmasters paid their workers in tokens which could be used for purchases from the company's store. (The Truck Act, which forbade this practice, passed through parliament just before the riot.[100]) More broadly, and like their compatriots elsewhere in Britain, the workingmen of Merthyr had their hopes pinned on parliamentary reform. The rejection of the first Reform Bill in spring 1831, the forthcoming elections for a new parliament that would consider a second version, created a volatile social and political climate across the country. Organisations of 'radicals' in favour of reform and of others devoted primarily to the interests of workingmen were coming into existence. Only days before the riots, a mass meeting of thousands of workers not far from Merthyr had been addressed not only by advocates of reform and speakers on local issues, but by men known as proponents of unions. William Twiss, organiser of the new colliers' union for the National Association for the Protection of Labour, is said to have visited Merthyr *before* the riots.[101] Subsequent research has uncovered other men who were later distinguished as leaders of the Chartist movement.[102] In the months following the Merthyr riots, union lodges mushroomed across the valleys as Wales became—and remained—the heartbeat of the working-class quest for equality.

The trouble began on Wednesday 1 June 1831, when thousands of workingmen rioted through the streets of the mining village of Merthyr Tydfil. Their target was the Court of Requests, which lent workers money to ease the periodic slumps in the mining industry but confiscated their property when they could not repay the debt. The court's actions were compounded by its ruthless bailiffs and by some shopkeepers, particularly Thomas Lewis, 'a notorious and hated huckster' who gave some small credit and then took advantage of the court's debt recovery process and forced sales.[103] The bailiffs had repossessed a trunk owned by **Lewsyn yr Heliwr (in English, Lewis Lewis)**, and forcibly recovering it from the shopkeeper who had it for sale was a trigger, perhaps a premeditated one, to the subsequent action. In the days that followed, this trunk became a kind of trophy. It was carried at the head of processions. Lewsyn himself was also treated like a trophy, carried on high with his trunk and set up on top of it, like a commander at the centre of the action. From that perch he made a speech in Welsh outside the home of the President of the Court of Requests. Shortly after, fireballs were hurled through the windows.[104]

The next morning, the crowd marched on the village, striding out behind a Red Flag with a loaf of bread impaled on its staff and blowing a horn all the while—a call to arms to others who joined them, or perhaps to mark the presence of the Huntsman, Lewsyn, at their head. By his side were a group of older men, including David Hughes, 40 years of age and a miner who was described as 'much respected' and, as events would prove, capable of 'arguing down magistrates when angry'.[105] Once in the village, the marchers moved systematically among the houses, identifying confiscated goods and encouraging their original owners to repossess them. The house of the much-hated Thomas Lewis was invaded. During this encounter, a young miner named **Tom Vaughan** burst through the door, hit Thomas Lewis so hard he sent him sprawling, then hit his wife Elizabeth so she fell on top of him.[106] Meanwhile, 24-year-old **David Thomas**, nicknamed Dai Llaw Haearn or Iron-Hand because he was a skilled 'puddler' (iron-worker), was particularly active outside the houses of the bailiff Thomas Williams. Mrs Williams later testified, 'He said he'd be damned if he wouldn't get everything back.' Flourishing a pick-handle, Thomas shouted to the crowd, 'Now is your time. If they have anything belonging to you, take it!' And they did. As each item was carried out, they cheered.[107] Over 100 houses and shops were visited in this way.[108]

It was outside Thomas Lewis' house, standing on his chairs in the doorway, that the magistrates J.B. Bruce and Anthony Hill tried to read the Riot Act. The crowd, by now two thousand strong, was pushing and heaving and yelling 'Reform!' When Bruce appealed to David Hughes, he got short shrift. Hughes replied, 'It's no use to speak to us. We're having the goods out and the Court of Requests down.' At this point Lewsyn yr Heliwr intervened physically to push the crowd back and allow the magistrates to read the Act, first in English and then in Welsh. When they had finished, the crowd drove them off their chairs and down the street before returning to the recovery of confiscated goods.[109]

The next day, surging in their thousands outside the Castle Inn where the magistrates had taken refuge, the rioters found themselves in direct confrontation with 70 soldiers of the 93rd Regiment who had been summoned from Brecon. A deputation of workers including Lewsyn yr Heliwr, David Thomas, David Hughes and a young man named Dic Penderyn met with the magistrates, but when they returned to the crowd outside with nothing to report, a wholesale battle broke out. Staves, sticks and fists met bayonets and rifles. Lewsyn was in the thick of it, encouraging the men to disarm the soldiers, urging them not to let the military get their backs against the Inn wall. Dic Penderyn was glimpsed waving his hat in the air and cheering, but witness after witness revealed that people were watching Lewsyn yr Heliwr not Dic Penderyn. In the melee, Private Donald Black was stabbed through the thigh with a bayonet. Asked in court if Dic Penderyn did it, he replied that although Dic was nearby, he could not say because he was watching Lewsyn, who was working his way behind him. Black testified that he did not see Dic Penderyn or Lewsyn yr Heliwr lay hands on anyone, but he described how he saw Lewsyn confront Captain Sparks when the captain pushed a man back into the crowd. 'You would not do so to me,' Lewsyn challenged the captain, to which the captain shook his head and gave a 'sort of laugh' which, Black implied, angered Lewsyn further.[110] It was a bloody and hard-fought battle in which rioters were transformed into rebels. The soldiers were vastly outnumbered and the workers were having the best of it until someone inside the inn gave the order to fire. Sixteen men, women and children fell dead. An unknown number of wounded dragged themselves away. An unknown number died and, for fear of reprisals, were secretly buried.[111]

The seething crowd in the front of the inn broke up but the battle continued. Lewsyn was seen 'running with a musket in his hand. "Stand your ground! Stand your ground!" he was shouting as men with captured guns went racing round the rear of the Inn.'[112] The rebels took up position on a slope behind the inn and exchanged shots with the troops until the soldiers ceased firing.[113] That night, the rebels withdrew, but only to regroup, and thousands of men flocked to join them. Displaying the skills and tactics of military campaigners, they blockaded the town. The Swansea Yeomanry hastening to support the 93rd were ambushed and relieved of their weapons. The rebels had taken the town and they held it for nearly four days. The local authorities wrote to the Lord-Lieutenant for Wales, Lord Bute, 'We need every soldier we can get hold of.'[114]

The workingman's victory could not last. On Monday 6 June, extra troops arrived in numbers. By nightfall, most of the rebel leaders were captured. On Tuesday, Lewsyn yr Heliwr was caught in the woods near his home. Three weeks later, the trials began. Lewsyn yr Heliwr and Richard Lewis (no relation to Lewis Lewis) known as Dic Penderyn were charged with stabbing Donald Black, but only Dic was found guilty of this offence. Lewsyn was found guilty of robbing Thomas Lewis during the attack on his house, although according to Gwyn Williams, evidence at his trial ranged far more widely over his activities and leadership of the rising. Both men were sentenced to death. Dic Penderyn was hanged but the sentence of Lewsyn yr Heliwr was commuted to transportation for life.

Williams had no doubt that the Merthyr Rising, as he called it, was a planned insurrection. It appears that the government was concerned to play it down.[115] Taking depositions at the committal stage, magistrates were so alarmed at what they were hearing that Evan Thomas, chairman of the Glamorgan Quarter Sessions, wrote to Lord Bute for advice about how to frame the charges. 'The depositions already made in Lewis Lewis's case have disclosed facts of so serious a nature that I think it would be very desirable to have the advice of some Legal Man on behalf of Government as to the Commitments.'[116] The *Cambrian* reported that a charge of high treason was likely.[117] But Lord Melbourne's government did not want the nature and scope of the Merthyr

Rising to be publicised and Melbourne rejected a charge of high treason, commenting, 'There seems to me no ground for this. The men may be committed for rioting (the simplest of all cases). If afterwards the charge is of a higher nature, they may be prosecuted accordingly.'[118]

Behind this display of calm, however, the government was frightened by what had occurred. Just how much was revealed eight years later at the time of the Chartist march on Newport, when Melbourne declared 'It is the worst and most formidable district in the kingdom. The affair we had there in 1831 was the most like a fight of anything that took place.'[119] As Williams points out, the Rising in Merthyr was different from bread riots or 'affrays' of the kind the British government was used to managing. It was different also from election demonstrations that surrounded the Reform Bill. In terms of people killed by the troops, it far outnumbered the infamous Peterloo Massacre near Manchester. In the determination and skill with which the workingmen, led by Lewsyn yr Heliwr, fought back, it was unique.[120]

Historians disagree about the character of Lewsyn yr Heliwr. David Jones described him as a 'ringleader' who may have escaped the gallows because of his influential friends or because he betrayed Dic Penderyn to save his own life. Jones suggested that the closure of the court for part of Lewsyn's evidence was when he betrayed his comrade. Jones also quoted a newspaper report of four Wesleyan chaplains saying that they heard Lewsyn weeping in his cell after Dic Penderyn was hanged. They claimed he cried aloud, 'Richard is innocent! For I know him not to have been there. I was by the soldier. If I had been sharing the same fate, I would have disclosed it on the scaffold.'[121]

More recently, Gwyn Williams described Lewsyn as a 'charismatic figure', a man to whom other men listened, someone 'they would follow against muskets and bayonets'.[122] With the benefit of more recently discovered documents, he found no evidence that Lewsyn was an informer or that there was a conspiracy to spare him. In fact, he concluded that Lewsyn yr Heliwr was even more than that:

> he was also, clearly, a man of *chware teg*, fair play, with a painful sense of honour. When he took a chest of drawers from a poor woman who had bought it from the debtors' court and restored it to its 'lawful' owner, he made sure the woman got her money back, even if he had to commit a capital offence to do so. He protected magistrates and a hated constable from his own men . . . 'Honour! Honour! He's had enough!'... He was one of those men which communities like his produce the world over, 'the man who makes himself

respected'. In the June of 1831, it was his neighbours who made him the man who would 'make the working people of Merthyr respected'.[123]

On 13 August 1831, Lewsyn yr Heliwr joined David Thomas, David Hughes and Tom Vaughan on a hulk, all of them sentenced to transportation for life. With the exception of Tom Vaughan, all left behind wives and children. In January 1832, they sailed together for New South Wales on the ship *John*. During the long voyage Lewsyn occupied himself teaching his fellow prisoners to read and write. It is unlikely that he confined himself to teaching them their letters. No one so committed to the workingman's cause would have passed up the opportunity to influence a captive audience of 200 men.[124] Had he stayed in Wales, Lewsyn yr Heliwr might have become an active Chartist. In New South Wales, there was nothing to distinguish him from the other felons, and with the help of Australian historical amnesia this man, who some call a hero, vanished from history.

The *St Vincent* carried four Irish protesters in 1853, although their convictions were for 'assault and robbery'. The facts of the case and the violence against the victim do not contradict the convictions under common law, but the context of their actions entitle them to be described as protesters.

Michael Nash, aged 48, was their leader. A big man, more than 6 feet tall, he would have loomed over his compatriots at a time when most were between 5 feet 5 inches and 5 feet 9 inches and many were shorter. Clean-shaven but with bushy black eyebrows, a prominent nose and strong jaw, he must have been seen as a man who should not be trifled with. With these qualifications, it is not surprising to find him in charge of what was plainly a cell of Ribbon men.[125]

The Ribbon sect was one of the longer lasting and more widespread of many secret societies that operated across Ireland from the eighteenth century, beginning with the Whiteboys in Tipperary in 1761. Another society, the Defenders of Ireland, whose activities culminated in the 1798 Rebellion, delivered some of Australia's most prominent convicts. Individual acts of arson, assault, cattle-maiming and threatening letters were part of the protest mix, but the underground societies were the most organised means by which the Irish fought back against their conditions.[126] In *Convict Settlers of Australia*, Lloyd Robson quotes an insider's description of Ribbonism from a newly arrived prisoner:

> Ribbon sects are illegal combinations sworn to obey their
> chief, to take the arms of the Protestants and turn them out

of the country. County delegates travel over Ireland giving the Ribbon men new signs and making appointments to meet at certain times. They also travel through England and Scotland. The members of the Society choose their delegates by a polling. They assemble every quarter. The oldest delegate is appointed chairman and has the general superintendence of the delegates. Parish masters are under the delegates and under the parish masters are Guardians who have the power to dismiss delegates. Each guardian is over twelve men. One parish master is over them and one delegate over all the parishes in the country.[127]

Michael Nash was waiting in Nolan's public house in Shannagolden when one of his henchmen brought a new recruit to meet him. Terence Feehan, who turned King's evidence, told the court that Nash bought him a drink and, pressing half a crown into his hand, asked him to join them in attacking Lord Monteagle's steward, Loughlin Sharpe. When Feehan asked what he had against Sharpe, Nash replied, 'He's starving the poor. He's only giving them a shilling a week for draining. And he will give a shilling to any man that would kill a poor man's horse that would go [stray] into Lord Monteagle's demesne.'[128]

Lord Monteagle's defenders argue that his public duties as a member of parliament kept him in London and that he and Lady Monteagle 'exercised close and continual influence and authority at home'. Unlike his fellow Irish landlords, he did not employ rapacious agents to manage his estate, but instead relied on his son and an able and loyal staff 'to look after day-to-day business . . . staff and household were in capable hands'. His only agent was confined to handling the accounts.[129] However, Michael Nash was in a position to know what he was talking about. He was employed as a wood-ranger at Mount Trenchard, the home property of Monteagle's estate, and was also involved in herding some of the cows.[130]

The gang, which included **Patrick Dempsey**, Feehan, **Michael Culhane** and **John Hennessy**, gathered at Michael Nash's house to blacken their faces before setting out. Nash sent them on their way with the instruction, 'Break Sharpe's feet and hands and drive him out of the country.' From her garden, Mrs Sharpe saw them approaching the house. Desperately, she tried to slam the door in their faces but they forced her backwards. 'I'll knock your brains out with this,' threatened Patrick Dempsey, waving the stone he carried. Once inside, they fanned out through to the kitchen where they found her husband. Feehan placed himself in the parlour with Culhane while the rest of the gang confronted the steward.

'When we came out, Culhane struck Mr Sharpe with a hedge-hook in the ear,' he said. Then Sharpe was knocked to the floor. 'Hennessy had a leg on his throat. He asked for a bayonet to pick out his eyes,' continued Feehan. Before they left, someone either beat up or shot the steward's legs. Feehan described how Culhane and Walsh were near his prone figure, Walsh with a gun in his hand. 'I saw Mr Sharpe's legs bloody before we left,' he said. 'I asked who did it and Culhane said that Walsh did it.' On that they parted, hitting Mrs Sharpe on the way out.[131] The damage they did to the steward was terrible, as the *Limerick Chronicle* described in heart-rending detail:

> Mr Loughlin Sharpe . . . is an elderly grey headed man, respectable and intelligent. He was helped up the steps [of the witness box], with a crutch, and wore slippers; his voice was very weak—his left ear was cut off by the ruffians who had assaulted him; one of the fingers of his left hand, and the bones of his nose were broken. His back was also hurt and he appeared to have endured much bodily suffering, from the barbarous punishment inflicted on him, by those whose instruction it was to mutilate him for life or to murder 'a faithful steward'.[132]

The steward's evidence put a different complexion on what happened. He suggested there were malicious reasons behind the attack, telling the court how Michael Nash had given orders to feed the cows on hay twice rather than once a day, which he had countermanded 'because there was a great waste of hay'.[133] It appears to be a question of when good stewardship becomes penny-pinching and, if Michael Nash was right, whether that occurred at the expense of the poor. But who knows what pressure the financial agent in Tralee was putting on Laughlin Sharpe?[134]

The jury found Michael Nash, Patrick Dempsey, Michael Culhane and John Hennessy guilty and they were sentenced to transportation for seven years.

In 1855 the British parliament passed the *Penal Servitude Act*, which effectively ended transportation as a punishment. Some convicts would still be sent to Western Australia, which needed their labour, but in the previous decade the system proposed by penal reformers for over 50 years had taken hold. The hulks were only slowly phased out and were still in existence in 1857, but new prisons had multiplied across Britain and the concept of solitary incarceration plus periods of public labour as the way to rehabilitate prisoners was being implemented. As the system changed, the prisoners on the hulks became increasingly mutinous about their conditions, their anger aggravated by constant changes in policy concerning who would be selected for transportation. Sometimes the 'most hardened' (for which read 'most troublesome') offenders were sent. At others, it was those the authorities regarded as best behaved. Of course the policy was always being subverted. Ex-guardsman Charles Cozens, who was on board the *Justitia* hulk at Woolwich in 1840, reported intense competition to get on the list for 'the Bay ship'.[135] One evangelical surgeon-superintendent was shocked to his moralising core to learn that money often changed hands to ensure a passage.[136] Whatever the policy currently operating, an expectation had developed that a man could do a portion of his time in Britain, which would conclude with a conditional pardon or a ticket-of-leave and a voyage to the, by then, symbolic Botany Bay. By 1851 a gold rush in the colonies made the prospect even more enticing and prisoners were outraged by the passage of the *Penal Servitude Act*. What? No transportation? The men who sailed on the *St Vincent* and the *Dalhousie* were caught by these changes. Once convicted, there was no certainty they would be sent to a penal colony.

On a close look, the convicts defy categorisation by character as much as the crimes defy categorisation by motive. The men and women who were transported stand revealed as an amazing cast of characters exhibiting the full spectrum of humanity with all its frailties and strengths. Individual studies call into question the reliability of any data recorded in the indents. As people living on the edge of necessity, most convicts learnt criminal tricks such as constant name changes, varying descriptions of their skills or trade, and the usefulness of raising or lowering their age. Highway robber Tom Smitherman's age went from fourteen to nineteen in the space of eighteen months. John Hobbs' occupation changed from labourer at his trial in England to french polisher on arrival in Van Diemen's Land. George Wheeler claimed illiteracy but later despatched eloquent petitions to the governor. Arguing about whether they were idle layabouts or ordinary workers is shown to be irrelevant because neither trade nor employment is a valid yardstick. Many committed their crimes while employed, some because they could not earn enough to live but some for no obvious reason. For others, lack of income meant crime was the only way to survive. It could also be an expression of anger or revenge. At best, the indents can provide only a superficially accurate sketch. But when detailed individual research is combined with the extended genealogical information of family historians, an amazingly full picture can be created of people who have been known to Australians only as percentages in categories. Case-by-case examination of the convicts makes it plain that there can be no black-and-white conclusion about whether they were members of a criminal class or 'just' poverty-stricken working-class people who turned to crime. They were all of those things.

Evidence from a range of sources indicates that most convicts were not ashamed of their crimes. Their behaviour in court, for instance, is an important indicator. Many examples exist of prisoners thanking the judge or the jury for the outcome, sometimes with heart-felt gratitude but more often with cheek or bravado. William Gray, who was transported on the *Dalhousie* for arson, swept the judge a mock bow as he said, 'Thank you my lord'. Eliza Morrison's cheerful response—'A long life to Your Honour'—was typical of many. Others like Charles Clephane heard the most terrible sentences without a flicker of emotion. Susannah Watson begged to be spared transportation for the sake of her children but she was unashamed, explaining what she did in terms she hoped the judge might understand, that 'I could not bear to see my children starving'. There were exceptions, of course. The demeanour of solicitor Joseph Shaw revealed his shame. The Richard Turpin who sailed on the *John* told the constable who arrested him for the death of his baby that he was drunk, adding, 'I didn't mean to do it.' But if there had been wholesale weeping and promises by the prisoners to mend their ways, we can be sure the newspapers would have reported every detail. Such reports are few and far between, in fact virtually non-existent. Most prisoners were pragmatic, understood the risk they ran and accepted the consequences. According to Surgeon Peter Cunningham, the more professional thieves assessed their career according to how long they lasted without getting caught. He described overheard conversations when a new batch of prisoners disembarking at Botany Bay met old acquaintances from England. 'On inquiring how Bill or Tom or such-a-one fares, and hearing he is still "a-going at it", [the old acquaintances] exclaim in surprise, "What a lucky dog! What a *good run* he has had."'[137]

Male prisoners enjoyed telling stories about their exploits, competing with each other about who had done the most skilful, amazing, daring, extraordinary deeds or who had most cleverly outwitted their pursuers, prosecutors, judge or jury. They entertained themselves on the long voyage to Botany Bay by conducting mock trials, regular Old Bailey Sessions with 'the chief justice of England, perched upon a three-legged stool with a bed [mattress] under him for a cushion, a patchwork-quilt round him for a robe of office, and a huge swab [mop] combed over his dignified head and shoulders in lieu of a wig. Barristers with blankets round them for gowns, pleaded eloquently the causes they were engaged in, brow-beating and cross-questioning the witnesses according to the best-laid-down rules and chicanery of law; while the culprit stood quaking in the dock, surrounded by the traps of office, awed by the terrific frowns which the indignant judge every now and then cast upon him.'[138] This was not the behaviour of people who were ashamed and nor was it a solitary example. A decade later, an exasperated employer described a youth who boasted of his skills as a thief and who excelled at imitations of the leading barristers and judges in London.[139] These men's lack of shame or repentance was described by clergymen such as Father William Ullathorne, who told the Molesworth Committee in 1838 that 'there is a sort of spirit of bravado, a spirit of pride, and an *esprit de corps,* which leads them to converse much on their crimes, and to mix their conversation with a good deal of obscenity'.[140]

Transportation was certainly not regarded as shameful. According to the Commissioner of the Poor Law in 1837, Reverend Henry Bishop, 'the punishment of transportation was no punishment at all; the terror was nothing; that in fact they looked to it as a reward'. And he added, 'the transport would consider he was going out to emigrate, in fact, there would be very little difference between those who went out as emigrants and those who went under sentence of transportation'.[141] The only check to what he termed 'anticipation' was if they were married. Single men were not the slightest bit worried about going. Dr Morgan Price, a surgeon who made seven voyages on transports, reported the same thing. 'Convicts do not express much feeling of regret, except in the first instance in parting with their friends.'[142] At a personal level, colonial official Alexander Maconochie, Private Secretary to the Lieutenant Governor of Van Diemen's Land and later Commandant of Norfolk Island, claimed that the convicts 'neither regretted their crimes, nor offered atonement'.[143]

One area in which shame is occasionally recorded is the effect of transportation on the prisoners' relatives in Britain. Protecting family was sometimes the reason the convicts used an alias. In addition, a few examples exist of sorrowful letters apologising to a parent or wife for the shame that has been caused them by the penitent's crime. Offsetting this, however, are many examples of young men, notably older sons or brothers, who risked transportation to help relatives survive. As later evidence demonstrates, men like George Rawlinson, Joseph Sowden Ledger or Joseph Barrett would not have felt the need to apologise, nor would apology have been expected.[144] Ultimately, whether the convicts were shameless because they were deplorable characters who were professional criminals or because they believed their circumstances justified their crime can best be judged by examining how they behaved in the penal colonies.

CHAPTER 4
a convict community

When the *Sir William Bensley* dropped anchor in New South Wales in 1817, the total population of the colony was approximately 16,000, of whom 5795 were serving convicts. With the military, government officials and a handful of settlers accounting for fewer than 2000 of the free residents, emancipists dominated the community. The free population also included around 3500 children, most of whom had convict parents.[1] Had it come to a struggle for power, the prisoners had the numbers to overthrow the authorities. Failing any such attempt since an abortive rebellion in 1804, the settlement was in effect a convict colony 'by consent'. Any analysis of Botany Bay has to take account of these proportions and their impact on the attitudes and culture that were established during those years. Their effect was far more profound than the (tiny) upper-class disdain for the convict taint on which so much emphasis has been placed.

Two issues had been significant in establishing the tone of the settlement. The first, which occurred soon after the Europeans' arrival when they were facing starvation, was Governor Arthur Phillip's decision that all people regardless of rank should share equally in the remaining supplies.[2] In issuing that order, Phillip overturned every expectation of the class-ridden society from which the colonists had come, making it clear that the humanity of the most lowly convict was as important as his own. From that moment, sharing on an egalitarian basis became entrenched in the ethos of the convict community and, as we shall see in Chapter 5, was common practice among its residents by the 1830s.

No less significant to the tenor of society were the early theatrical enter-
tainments. Held in a makeshift theatre, the first occurred in June 1789 and the
second on 16 January 1796.[3] Written, staged and acted by convicts, the performances were attended by everyone from the Governor down. Captain Watkin
Tench was present in 1789 and recorded in his journal:

> Some of the actors acquitted themselves with great spirit and
> received the praises of the audience: a prologue and epilogue
> written by one of the performers, were also spoken on the
> occasion; which, although not worth inserting here, contained
> some tolerable allusions to the situation of the parties, and
> the novelty of a stage-representation.

In other words, the actors sent themselves up as well as mocking the oddity
of a stage show in a penal colony. In 1802, a prologue said to be this one was
published in London. It was allegedly written by George Barrington, who was
notorious on both sides of the globe as a pickpocket, but by 1796 Chief
Constable at Parramatta and soon to be promoted to Superintendent of
Convicts.[4] Although twentieth-century research has cast some doubt on
whether this prologue was the one actually spoken in the colony, let alone by
Barrington, throughout the nineteenth century the colonists believed it was
Barrington's and made it their own. Its famous opening lines embodied the
self-deprecating, some would say shameless, humour of the interaction between
the governed and the governing in this upside-down world. No doubt to gales
of laughter, the convict actor proclaimed what would become the lasting terms
of (social) engagement in the colony (whether these words are an accurate
rendition or not):

> From distant climes, o'er wide-spread seas we come,
> Though not with much eclat or beat of drum
> True patriots all, for be it understood,
> We left our country for our country's good.[5]

In common with most convict voyages, the *Bensley*'s, which lasted 186
days, was uneventful. William Brodribb and the Berkeley poachers had been
joined on board by Richard Rutter, 'Little Easey' and the Littleport bread
rioters. With them were 185 thieves of one kind or another from all over
Britain, including the Scots Charles Clephane, William Honeyman and Peter
Quigley, the Lancashire coiner Peter Barnes whose wife arrived on the *Lord
Melville* two weeks before him, highway robber Joseph Barrett, bigamist Francis

Bodenham and the London embezzler Thomas Wells. They had lost one of their number at sea when William Young from Surrey jumped overboard, but were otherwise healthy and without any significant illness or accident.[6]

Since 1815, a retired naval surgeon had been allocated to every convict ship. Armed with complete authority over the welfare and discipline of the prisoners, the surgeon's presence was designed to counter any abuse of power by captains such as Donald Trail of the *Neptune* and to handle other threats such as the outbreak in 1814 of typhus on the *Surrey* and of dysentery on the *General Hewitt*, which made their voyages the proverbial hell-on-earth for the convicts.[7] It became the usual practice for the surgeon to keep a journal about the health and conduct of the prisoners in his charge but on the *Bensley*, for some unexplained reason, this task was allocated to the Chief Officer. Lieutenant Richard Bastard kept a detailed log of his management of the prisoners while the surgeon, William Evans, apparently confined himself to their health care with help from Berkeley farmer Daniel Long.

From Bastard's log we learn by the designation *Mr* Brodribb and *Mr* Wells that their status as gentlemen took precedence over that of convict. In fact, both probably shared the cost of a cabin that allowed them to avoid the prison deck below. Very likely they also ate in the captain's mess with the passengers rather than eating with their fellow prisoners. Both made themselves useful during the voyage, Brodribb by supervising the distribution of rations after the steward fell ill and Wells by offering to read Divine Service each Sunday. A scene erupted at each service when 60-year-old Edward Davis loudly abused everything to do with religion and refused to take part. When Bastard resorted to ordering him flogged, Davis responded, 'I'm being transported through spite. Now I'm to be punished for the same reason.' Some research into Davis' background reveals that his bitter resentment was very likely generated by the clergyman in Staffordshire who committed him to trial for stealing a horse collar and harness.[8] Throughout the voyage, Lieutenant Bastard and his fellow officers, along with the detachment from the 46th Regiment who were acting as guards, were kept alert by a mutinous, unruly crew, an accidental fire caused by the explosion of casks of rum and the unrelenting industry of the prisoners in preparing to escape. The Scots were particularly disruptive, William Honeyman, John Grindley and Charles Clephane all being handcuffed for stretches of 48 hours for possessing knives or razors, or making threats of violence to the sentry. Clephane also spent time in the cuffs for refusing to eat his bread ration and trying to incite others in his mess to do the same. But they were in the minority. Most of the men, including Joseph Barrett, Francis Bodenham and the boy Tom Smitherman, avoided drawing attention to themselves.

The *Bensley* made only one voyage as a transport and may have been specially chartered for this trip because she contained the space necessary to transport the next Lieutenant Governor of Van Diemen's Land, Colonel William Sorell, his wife Louisa, their four children and three servants. A good-looking man with a strong-boned face and high forehead, Sorell was in his early forties and had recently resigned from a long and successful career in the army. Serious and somewhat reserved by nature, his unpretentious, pleasant manner made him well liked and readily accessible to people regardless of class or background. Louisa was fifteen years his junior and described by those who knew her as 'very pretty and interesting'.

Unknown to those on board the *Bensley*, Sorell and Louisa's love affair was a scandal of immense proportions. Despite Sorell's reputation as 'a steady, reserved and highly respectable' man, he had cast it all away for Louisa, describing their feelings for one another as 'an attachment . . . not to be effaced'. Their departure for the other side of the world strategically removed them from the public exhibition of this passionate relationship in the law courts, where Louisa's husband was suing Sorell for criminal conversation with his wife.[9] It also left behind the complications of a wife, Harriet, who was telling all and sundry that her husband had left her penniless and abandoned their children. He had certainly kept her short of money but this appears to have been a clumsy, harsh attempt by Sorell to get her to let him bring up the children. When they sailed for Van Diemen's Land, Sorell and Louisa were not in fact man and wife. Legally, Louisa was still Mrs Kent, the wife of Lieutenant Kent of the 21st Light Dragoons, but in the colonies she was known as Mrs Sorell. She and William Sorell had fallen in love when both men (Sorell without his wife) were stationed at the Cape of Good Hope between 1807 and 1811.[10] The *Bensley* spent Christmas and New Year, nineteen days altogether, at the Cape during the voyage to Botany Bay. Even though Lieutenant Kent had returned to London, the time there must have contained some moments of exquisite difficulty for the Lieutenant Governor and his lady.[11]

Lieutenant Governor
William Sorell

Calling at the Cape gave William Brodribb a chance to write to Prudence, and what he told her—probably reflecting long conversations with Sorell—was sufficiently optimistic to settle any doubts she may have had about following him. Female courage was not confined to convict women. Reared in the narrow world that Regency polite society thought suitable for the daughter of a provincial gentleman, Prudence rose to meet a very big challenge for a young woman of her background. She could not have received word from William much earlier than February 1817, but she must have been waiting and planning for it. Little more than four months later, on 3 July, she and their four children were ready to sail on the ship *Friendship* for New South Wales. She liaised with Thomas Wells' wife, Charlotte, who also sailed on the *Friendship*. They were accompanied by wives of other convicts as well as 101 convict women.

The surgeon was held responsible for the behaviour of the prisoners and the *Friendship*'s surgeon, Peter Cosgreave, was anxious from the beginning that he would be accused of endorsing prostitution. When the ship called at St Helena he went so far as to apply to the admiral in command there for help to stop the women and the crew cohabiting. Two post captains held an enquiry on the spot and reported back to their admiral, but neither the *Friendship*'s surgeon nor her master was informed of the outcome. Nothing changed. On arrival in Sydney, Cosgreave reported that prostitution had begun before the ship left England. Three local magistrates found the charges 'most fully proved' but exonerated the surgeon and the master from any blame. In these proceedings, Charlotte Wells supplied a supporting statement for the surgeon, but Prudence Brodribb did not.[12] Her refusal suggests that she did not agree with the surgeon's opinion of the women's behaviour. Perhaps her relationship with them was different.

One of the prisoners on that voyage, 35-year-old Elizabeth Burrell, alias Leveston, became the long-term partner of farmer Jack Reeves from Berkeley. Convicted with another woman of stealing a large quantity of muslin from a draper's shop in Newcastle-on-Tyne, Elizabeth described herself as 'a country servant'. She was the perfect choice to help Prudence with the children and, after landing in Hobart, she may have continued to work for the Brodribb family. In April 1819 her first child by Jack Reeves was born and by 1820 she was living with him.[13] Both the lady passengers on the *Friendship* would have been dismayed had they known that the surgeon was compiling a report on their character together with comments about the other women, free and bond, on the ship. Charlotte, who was helpful to the surgeon, was described as 'inoffensive' and given the ultimate accolade of being 'a good mother'. Prudence was simply described as 'well behaved and inoffensive'. The surgeon's verdict on Elizabeth Burrell was 'inoffensive and industrious'.[14]

Lachlan Macquarie had been Governor of New South Wales since 1810 and throughout those seven years Van Diemen's Land had been an intractable, if distant, problem. The sudden death of Lieutenant Governor David Collins at Hobart in 1810 had virtually coincided with Macquarie's arrival in the senior colony. A succession of military officers acted as commandant in his place, but all proved unsatisfactory to Macquarie. So also, when he was finally appointed by London in 1813, did Lieutenant Governor Thomas Davey. Macquarie described him as displaying 'an extraordinary degree of frivolity and low buffoonery in his Manners'. There were mixed views about Davey, but the undeniable truth was that he liked a drink and was as happy carousing in a pub as he was at a family dinner in Government House. By the end of four years under Davey, and given the seeds of problems sown by his predecessors, Van Diemen's Land was a lawless place, its settlement on the verge of collapse.[15]

Governor Lachlan Macquarie

On meeting Sorell, Macquarie formed the opinion, which was supported by others who met the Lieutenant Governor, that he would deploy the kind of firm, decisive management that would bring order to Van Diemen's Land.[16] Furthermore, Macquarie immediately liked Sorell. The two men saw their role as building for the future in a social as well as a physical sense. They were of the same mind about how to approach colonial society with its strange mix of prisoners, ex-prisoners or emancipists as they were called, and the small group who for a variety of reasons had come free and therefore felt themselves exclusively entitled to be regarded as polite society. 'Polite society' in the colonies consisted mainly of people who would not have qualified for that status at home, which made them all the more determined to establish boundaries that defined and enhanced their position in the colony. The idea of a convict stain that would forever mark the bearer already existed, but at this point it was mainly in the minds of the small group who arrived free. And because they were few in number, try as they might it did not dominate the tone of the wider community. The crimes of the prisoners and any prospect they would feel ashamed of being a convict evaporated for most when they landed. Most who had become free led their lives with blithe disregard for their former condition as prisoners because almost everyone they mixed with had a similar past. Their most noticeable response to the attitude of the 'exclusives' was to be fiercely possessive of the land that offered them a future despite their background. Botany Bay was regarded as *their* colony, and immigrants were resented because the former prisoners feared they would create a society that was a replica of Britain. Only the few emancipists who had achieved wealth and wished for recognition were stung by the discrimination displayed towards them. It was this group in particular that Macquarie through his patronage sought to integrate fully into colonial society.

During the nearly three weeks that Sorell was in Sydney, the Berkeley poachers were among the many topics of conversation between the two administrators. Macquarie would have read about the trial in the English newspapers and Sorell could pass on London gossip about the behaviour of Colonel Berkeley as well as his own opinion of the poachers. Through Sorell, Brodribb and Thomas Wells had an interview with Macquarie that was a prerequisite to his agreeing that Sorell could take them to Hobart as part of his own 'suite' on board the colonial barque *Cochin*.[17] Wells served the Lieutenant Governor as his private secretary throughout his time in the colony. In the first instance, Brodribb became clerk to the Bench of Magistrates. Later he would be appointed Deputy Provost Marshall. Sorell had spent much of the voyage scrutinising the convicts on the *Bensley*. When the muster was completed in Sydney he marked with a small cross those he particularly wanted with him in Van Diemen's Land. Among them was Richard Rutter and all the poachers, including James Roach, who Sorell would later describe to Governor Arthur as 'one of my best men'.[18]

While Brodribb and Wells proceeded to Van Diemen's Land with Sorell, the rest of the *Bensley* men disembarked in Sydney. Eighty-four were immediately distributed to the major areas of settlement around the Cumberland Plain west of Sydney. In four approximately equal groups they went to

Windsor, Bringelly, Liverpool and Parramatta. At these centres, a handful were assigned to specific settlers such as William Cox, William Howe, James Meehan, Captain Banks and William Lawson. The rest were retained for general distribution to local settlers or kept in clearing parties or road parties to be utilised collectively. The group for general distribution at Windsor included the burglar William Thomas. Nineteen when he arrived, Thomas stayed in the area for a decade or more, working mainly for Stephen Tuckerman on his farm at Wilberforce. Twenty years later, he became part of Surveyor General Major Thomas Mitchell's exploration team and accompanied him on two major overland expeditions, including the one designated 'Australia Felix' because of the vast expanse of land it opened up. A bullock driver on the first trip in 1835, Thomas added the job of butcher on the second in 1836. He was rewarded for his efforts in 1835 with his ticket-of-leave, which was due anyway, and £5 was also lodged to his bank account. In 1836 he received a conditional pardon for the life sentence awarded him at the Old Bailey so many years before.[19]

Two of the men Sorell had hoped would follow him to the Derwent, excise officer Will Coates and Yorkshire militia officer William Fisher, were instead sent to Bringelly, where Fisher held the post of Overseer of Government Stock for three years. Seeking emancipation in 1821, he reminded the Governor that he had been actively involved from the beginning in the project of 'reclaiming the wild cattle in the cowpastures'. (They ran away in the early days of settlement over 30 years earlier and multiplied while left to themselves.) Fisher's wife, Frances, and his daughter Maria joined him in 1822 and the family made a new life on their own land grant at Cobbity, near where Fisher was first assigned.[20]

Thomas Plows, the young thief who moved the coat and hat across the room, was sent to the Liverpool area. He was free by 1824 and worked for a while as a baker in York Street, Sydney. By 1828 he had become very respectable. Now aged 27, Plows was listed in the census that year without the usual identification of the ship of arrival. Although his convict origins were revealed by the designation 'free by servitude', his entry went on to describe him as 'settler' at Appin. He had been married the year before at Campbelltown to Jane Stanton and in the following fifteen years they produced ten children. After Jane died in 1847, Thomas married again to Bridget Connor. He died ten years later at nearby Camden aged 62, his occupation described as 'farmer'.[21]

Three men from the *Bensley*, William Macphilamy, coiner Peter Barnes and Thomas Ashby, a shoemaker from Warwickshire, were recorded on the list as 'distributed' to their wives even though both parties were convicts. Of course the women had brought several children with them who would need support, and it was not unusual for a male or a female prisoner to be assigned to their spouse who came free to the colony. But assigning one convict to another was definitely prohibited. For some reason it appears the officials thought these men's wives were free. The women had arrived first on the *Lord Melville*. Perhaps they got word to the men, which enabled them to deceive the authorities.[22] In 1822, Ashby's request for an assigned servant brought the error to light. His wife, Esther, who had always acted as his shoebinder, had died in childbirth the previous year and he was in need of a new assistant for his business as shoemaker and farrier in Parramatta. Replying to the Colonial Secretary's request for information, the Superintendent of Convicts' office revealed their books showed him 'assigned in 1817 to Joseph Bradley and never returned to the Superintendent's charge'.[23] Somewhat acerbically, the Colonial Secretary then asked for details of 'the general pass under which Ashby has been on his own hands for the last five years'.[24] None was forthcoming. In any event, they decided it was not worth pursuing the matter. Ashby had caused no trouble. They assigned him a convict from the latest batch, thus continuing the egalitarian, socially mobile environment that enculturated so many newly arrived prisoners. Totally unconcerned by the idea of a convict stain, emancipists of Ashby's standing usually shared their living arrangements with their convict servants and maintained 'little if any Distinction' between them.[25] Rather than being locked away behind brick walls, or chained together on the roads, the recent arrivals lived and worked with one of their own who had achieved socioeconomic stability beyond his—or their—reach at home.

Forty-five men were not on the list for general distribution in New South Wales, nor among those who were sent to Van Diemen's Land. Some were assigned to individual settlers in Sydney. Most were allocated direct to government projects because of the trade skills they possessed. Stonemason John Belcher was one of these. William Honeyman was another. Using the bricklayer's skills that had always kept him in jobs around the Carron ironworks, Honeyman spent at least part of his initial period in New South Wales helping to build St Matthew's Church, Windsor. Then, some time in 1822, he spotted a chance to escape.[26]

Meanwhile around 84 men sailed south on the colonial brig *Elizabeth Henrietta* in September 1817, following Sorell to Van Diemen's Land. Half disembarked at Port Dalrymple in the north and the balance continued to Hobart. The local settlers had wanted any northern town to be on the site later known as Launceston, but Macquarie had decreed that the northernmost town should be called George Town and was to be sited at the mouth of the Tamar River. At the time the north was known generally as Port Dalrymple. The

Hyde Park Barracks, completed 1819. Bensley *men, such as stonemason
John Belcher and bricklayer William Honeyman, probably helped to build it*

Bensley men who disembarked there included Joseph Barrett, Charles Clephane, who was calling himself James at the time, Valentine Wood, the young thief from Shrewsbury, one or perhaps two of the Dye brothers—it is hard to be sure because although both were on the list drawn up in Sydney, one of them vanishes around this point. With them was Richard Rutter. The other Little-port men and all the poachers went on to Hobart.

Some men who landed in the north, such as Rutter and Joseph Barrett, were assigned immediately as agricultural labourers to settlers in the Launces-ton area, but most of them were there to build George Town. They joined a community of approximately 100 prisoners who were guarded by five privates in the town, plus two more at the Low Head look-out. Additional control was in theory provided by the prisoners and ex-prisoners who acted as super-intendents and overseers under the direction of Principal Superintendent of Building and of Convicts, William Leith. Management of the prisoners as well as the progress of building work was impeded by the constant state of warfare between Leith and the Commandant, Major James Stewart, who was based at Launceston, and to whom Leith reported.[27] These circumstances created opportunities for the prisoners that they were not slow to take up.

Acrimony and outbreaks of lawlessness in the north was just one of the problems facing the newly arrived Lieutenant Governor. Hobart was little more than a straggle of houses, and these were more than usually crowded with settlers who had left their rural properties for fear of the prisoners who had become bushrangers and were roaming the island at will. Tackling law and order was an obvious priority, but only one of many. Everything was in short supply: no spare weapons, insufficient tools, food production that could not feed the settlement. Land communication with the north was unreliable and dangerous because of the bushrangers, slow and difficult because the road was little more than a track. Administrative arrangements were makeshift and inadequate. The *Bensley* men were one of the resources immediately available to Sorell and he deployed them in key areas. Thomas Wells was given the task of bringing method to the paperwork. Brodribb's job was to improve the administration of the law and he was appointed Registrar of the Lieutenant Governor's court. Within two months Sorell also made room for him as clerk to the Bench of Magistrates, a position formerly held by Thomas Fitzgerald, who combined the role with being the colony's only schoolmaster.[28] There were precedents for their appointment to such pivotal roles in the administration of the colony. An emancipist, Thomas Crowder, had held the position of Superintendent of Convicts for many years.[29]

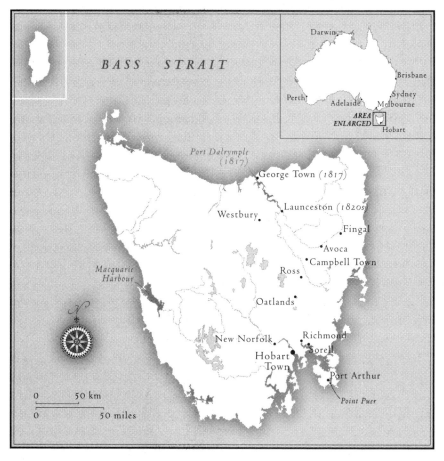

Van Diemen's Land, with locations mentioned in this book

Brodribb found himself accommodation somewhere in town, possibly with a gentleman emancipist introduced to him by Sorell. There was nothing privileged in this arrangement. In Sydney, Macquarie had nearly finished building a splendid barracks to house the government prisoners when they were not working, but in Hobart the arrangement that had existed since first settlement in Sydney still operated. The prisoners were required to find their own lodgings in the town, for which they paid a set amount of five shillings from wages earned while working for government. If there was no spare accommodation they would live in a makeshift skillion attached to a house for which they paid by doing chores such as cutting wood. Working hours usually ended at 3 p.m. From then on the day was the prisoner's 'own time' during which he could lie about and drink or work to earn extra money as he chose.[30] Three weeks after he arrived, Brodribb was sufficiently well introduced to be included in a gathering at fashionable New Town a few miles out of town. Dining at the home of Mr and Mrs Whitehead and their guests, he met Reverend Robert Knopwood for the first time. Thomas Wells, who must have been very busy with Sorell, came in towards the end of the meal.[31]

Knowing that Prudence would come swiftly, Brodribb set about acquiring land, sometimes in his own right and sometimes in partnership with Thomas Wells. Once they held a ticket-of-leave, convicts were entitled to a grant of land but there was nothing to stop them buying property from others if they had the funds. In what may have been their first purchase, Brodribb and Wells jointly bought 75 acres from William Paterson.[32] Free settlers were entitled to grants of land proportionate to the funds they brought with them, and although initially Brodribb was barred from access to this benefit he did receive a grant from Sorell of 300 acres after he had received a conditional pardon in 1818. Meanwhile, he bought land and proceeded to erect a house to accommodate the family when they arrived. The Land and Stock Muster in October 1819 recorded that he held 400 acres of land, some under cultivation, plus 30 cattle and 560 sheep. At that stage he had seven assigned servants, at least one of whom would have been helping Prudence with the children, including their latest son who was born in 1819.[33] Thomas Wells had also acquired 100 acres, all under pasture on which grazed sixteen cattle and 720 sheep.[34]

Writing to Governor Arthur approximately five years later in an attempt to persuade him to grant extra land, Brodribb set out his estate and its improvements in detail. On property of 380 acres he had built what he described as 'a neat residence with suitable out buildings', improvements which cost £500 over and above the purchase of the land itself. It is likely this was the Brodribb family's first home. In the intervening years he had also erected 'a spacious house on the New Town Road by the bridge costing £1,200' and had 'further invested nearly £700' which he had received from England, possibly by way of a legacy from his father-in-law. He had a small herd of 56 cattle, which he said were mainly females. Unfortunately, Brodribb was in the middle of a battle with the authorities over a plan to drive the main north road through part of his property at New Town. In these circumstances, Governor Arthur was not at all disposed to cooperate, noting on the memorial that, 'Until the business of the road through Brodribb's garden is settled this application for a grant of land cannot be attended to.'

In other ways Brodribb tried to cooperate with the Governor. He gave evidence to the Committee for Affairs of the Aborigines that Arthur established early in 1830 to find ways to counter the increasing attacks. Brodribb's eldest son, William junior, had been speared. Three years earlier, in December 1827, Richard Rutter, farming his own land near Launceston, had been attacked and killed. The coroner's jury could not pinpoint the date or clarify the circumstances. They simply concluded that his death was 'wilful murder . . . by one or more of the black native people'. Rutter's family had not joined him in the colony and he died alone aged 51.[35] Rutter's death, as well as the spearing of his own son, would have been in Brodribb's mind when he suggested that winter offered the best opportunity to 'harry' the Aborigines. A watch could be kept on places they were known to frequent, such as one near Campbelltown where they collected flint for their spears. Later that year, William junior took part in the military-style operation to round up the Aborigines that came to be known as the Black Line.[36]

Land records provide an early example of Brodribb's tactic for disguising his convict antecedents. In the Land Commissioner's Report for Van Diemen's Land compiled over 1826–28, Brodribb is recorded as holding land at South Esk River. Listed as Deputy Provost Marshall and Solicitor, he is accurately described as arriving in the colony on 8 April, but the year is given as 1818, a small but significant error of twelve months and one that his eldest son repeated many years later. At the social level occupied by the Brodribbs, the convict stain was felt far more acutely than among the lower ranks, to most of whom it meant nothing. Even Sorell's patronage could not protect Brodribb from daily slights, frequently delivered by people who would have been lucky to cross his doorstep at home. There is no evidence that he reacted angrily or even discourteously, but he must have writhed inside when people drew a line he was not to cross.

In evidence to Commissioner Bigge, who was sent in 1819 by the British government to investigate the state of the colony under Governor Macquarie, Lieutenant Archibald Bell clearly described the attitude that Brodribb encountered and which has always been regarded as the reason that descendants hid their convict ancestry. Asked his thoughts about admitting ex-convicts to Society and how he would behave in these circumstances, Bell replied, 'I have considered them as having been once tainted, unfit for associating with afterwards; and though I have no objection to meet them on public occasions, I certainly would not wish and never intend, to make them the companions at my table or of my society.'

But discrimination could also apply to 'public occasions'. In Van Diemen's Land, emancipist George Gatehouse, who was well regarded for his discreet manner and well-conducted business as a brewer and orchardist, did not receive an invitation to the festivities that marked Sorell's arrival. Presumably, Brodribb too sat on the sidelines, the camaraderie of the voyage broken now they had made final landfall. In those times, the allocation of pews in church was an important indication of social status. Fortunately, since it was a matter of interest to Commissioner Bigge, Sorell had taken the precaution of consulting with the Deputy Judge Advocate and Reverend Knopwood about the seating arrangement for the newly built St David's Church. He was able to explain to the Commissioner that their decisions were guided (in the usual way) by the principle 'of relative Rank and property' of the congregation. In this arena too, Hobart society liked to distinguish clearly between the emancipated and the free settlers. Brodribb, Wells and another prominent ex-prisoner William Jemott were publicly grouped together in the first rank of emancipists, in front of the other ranks from the army and the servants who sat right at the back, but behind the two rows kept vacant for visiting 'strangers'.[37]

Commissioner Bigge examined Edward Abbott, Judge Advocate of Van Diemen's Land, about the character, role and status of local emancipists. Asked if he knew of any who were now settled upon estates and living with respectability, he named William Jemott, George Gatehouse and Brodribb. When the Commissioner wanted to know about their crimes, Abbott could answer with a fair degree of accuracy about two of them. William Jemott, he understood, as supercargo of a vessel, ran away with it and sold the proceeds in America, for which he was sentenced to death. Mr Brodribb, he told the Commissioner, had been convicted of administering unlawful oaths. He had no information about the crime of George Gatehouse. (In fact Gatehouse arrived on the *Coromandel* in 1804 under the alias John Simpson, crime unspecified on the indent, served his time and went back to England when he became free, only to return in 1816 as a settler with a large amount of capital.)[38] 'Do you know that any of these Persons have been admitted into Society or are received at Government House?' asked the Commissioner. Abbott's answer revealed that George Gatehouse had some grounds for being offended that he was excluded from the welcome dinner for Sorell. 'I have never seen them in Society myself,' the Judge Advocate replied. 'Nor would I willingly meet them anywhere as members of Society. And I have only once seen Mr Gatehouse on a Public occasion at Government House. It was a Dinner either on the King's or the Queen's Birthday.'[39]

Before talking to Brodribb, the Commissioner questioned his boss, the Acting Provost Marshall, John Beamont. Once again, he probed for details of Brodribb's conviction. Beamont was vague. 'He came out as a convict, but I am not certain whether he is emancipated.' (In fact Brodribb had received a conditional pardon in December 1818.) 'Was he transported for life or for a shorter term?' asked Bigge. 'I am not certain,' said Beamont. 'He entirely executes the duties of your office?' asked Bigge, the bland text of the interview disguising any incredulity. 'Yes he does,' answered Beamont. The Commissioner then wanted to know if Brodribb was taking something off the top of the fees set in the schedule and was told, 'None that I am aware of.' Beamont then explained that the Deputy Judge Advocate drew up the Schedule of Fees and he thought, but was not sure, that it was then approved by the Lieutenant Governor. The Provost Marshall was entitled to the fees the office collected, presumably after deduction of expenses incurred. He told Bigge that he allowed Brodribb half the fees by way of remuneration. They then discussed the bailiffs employed by Brodribb, who turned out to be a ticket-of-leave man named White and 'two or three others' whose names Beamont could not remember but he did know they were convicts.

Armed with information from Beamont and from Edward Abbott, the Commissioner was ready to interview Brodribb, although it was two months before they met on 25 May 1820. The interview was relatively brief. Bigge checked who appointed Brodribb (Mr Beamont was the reply, which countered any allegations of undue patronage from Sorell), and how long he had filled the office of Deputy Provost Marshall (about twelve months). Someone had plainly suggested to Bigge that Brodribb's appointment was nothing but a sinecure that rewarded him for no effort. Bigge then asked Brodribb directly whether he did the work himself or simply delegated it to someone else. 'I have assistants,' Brodribb replied. 'I could not possibly do it all myself. We have had 149 causes and from 100 to that number in most Terms of the year, except the last, which is immediately before the Harvest.' Quizzed about the fact the assistants were convicts, Brodribb explained the history of their employment, how he had begun by hiring a free man at a cost of £50 per annum but now employed a man named Heywood who held a ticket-of-leave, plus a convict who had been assigned to Mr Beamont but now also held a ticket-of-leave. He was then asked if he went in person to Port Dalrymple when writs were to be executed there, or whether he sent someone else. 'I have gone on two occasions myself,' said Brodribb. 'And I have sent someone three or four times there. A person has been appointed at Launceston for some time for this purpose. His name is John Dell.'

Before he closed the interview Bigge returned to the subject Brodribb feared. The Commissioner had been in the colonies since early 1819. Colonists like Brodribb knew that his investigation threatened Macquarie, who had been criticised for his treatment of emancipists and the generosity with which he handed out tickets-of-leave and pardons. Seven years had not elapsed since Brodribb was sentenced in Gloucestershire. Macquarie's actions might be reversed by Commissioner Bigge. Brodribb must have broken into a cold sweat as Bigge asked, 'When did you receive your emancipation?' He replied, 'About fourteen months ago. His Excellency Governor Macquarie promised it to me in two years when I came into the Colony.' Smooth as silk came the follow-up: 'And when did you arrive?' Brodribb knew it could be checked. 'In April 1817,' he replied.[40]

An area in which Brodribb experienced both frustration and humiliation was his profession. Admitted to the Court of King's Bench in Westminster, member of the Inner Temple, he was no longer adorned with the lustre of these qualifications. An experienced practitioner, he could no longer exercise his professional skills. He was a lawyer but no longer a member of the legal profession. In 1817, there was no court based in Hobart, only a full bench of magistrates and the Judge Advocate. A Supreme Court judge resident in New South Wales occasionally sat in Hobart, but most cases, and all major criminal matters, went to Sydney. By default, Brodribb was able to appear locally for clients in a capacity described as 'agent'. He also handled chamber work, drawing up wills and conveyances and other documents. In January 1819 he formalised this role by placing an advertisement in the *Hobart Gazette*:

> Mr W. A. Brodribb (late regularly admitted Solicitor of the Court of King's Bench Westminster) begs to acquaint the public that he has opened an office at the Veranda House, Elizabeth Street for the practice of Conveyancing, Assignments, Leases, Wills etc. [which] will be prepared with accuracy and dispatch.[41]

Brodribb's decision to advertise his practice in this way was almost certainly prompted by a sitting of the Supreme Court that was scheduled later that month. In effect, his advertisement was a challenge to the judge to forbid his appearance. In Sydney, emancipist attorneys were a controversial issue and Mr Justice Barron Field held strong views that were well known in both colonies. Initially, luck was on Brodribb's side. The two solicitors whom the judge had almost certainly insisted should appear for their clients in Van Diemen's Land were delayed. It was a question of accepting Brodribb or postponing the sittings. Reluctantly, the judge gave in, but not without a fight. In a public address to the court, he expressed his regret about the absence of the solicitors. 'Their arrival is hourly expected from Sydney,' he told the assembled company. As Brodribb stood waiting in the courtroom, he continued, 'As a necessary expedient for the accommodation of suitors in this island, and for the more effective administration of justice, the court is pleased to accede to the application of Mr William Adams Brodribb . . . to act as an Attorney in the court *pro tempore*.'[42]

It was a victory of sorts, but only a temporary one. The following year an English attorney, George Cartwright, set up practice in Hobart.[43] In the months that followed, Hobart was flooded with attorneys. By 1823, only a year before Van Diemen's Land acquired a Supreme Court of its own with a resident judge, three more solicitors were admitted to the court, and in February that year all four newcomers advertised that they intended to appear at the sittings of the Lieutenant Governor's court. Not long afterwards, the procedure in the Lieutenant Governor's court officially changed. Agents like Brodribb were no longer acceptable.[44]

Since August 1821 Brodribb had held an absolute pardon, but he was tainted in the eyes of those who came free. Because of his conviction, he was barred forever from practice as a lawyer. In an interview with Commissioner Bigge, the Judge Advocate Edward Abbott described the situation which would have confronted Brodribb at home every bit as much as it did in Hobart. First telling Bigge that if Brodribb applied to appear in his court, he would refuse him permission, he then explained his general attitude to emancipist attorneys. 'In the first place I consider them positively disqualified by Law; and in the next Place, when they appear as attorneys in Court, by reason of their former condition they are unfit persons to conduct legal Business.' His rider was a concern specific to the colonies: 'And I likewise think that, if admitted as attorneys, their pretensions to higher offices would immediately follow.'[45]

In fact Brodribb could have returned to England since his pardon was not conditional. The longing to see family and old friends would have been very strong and he and Prudence must have discussed whether they should go. But despite the slights, something held them in Van Diemen's Land. Very likely, they concluded that Brodribb would suffer the same snubs, probably worse, in England. In any event, after five or more years they were settled and very comfortable. It was still a pioneer society, but far more soundly established as a result of the reforms Sorell had implemented, as well as the ever-increasing flow of free settlers in addition to convicts who were now disembarking at Hobart rather than going to Sydney first. Furthermore, and of great importance to them both, the colonies offered unlimited prospects for their family, which would soon total eight children.[46]

William Brodribb was not the only *Bensley* voyager deployed by Sorell as he set about bringing the colony to better order. Some were used for his personal comfort. Others because of what they could contribute to the colonial workforce. Richard Armstrong, who had been a groom in England, was appointed groom to Government House. In 1823 he married Sarah Randell who had been convicted like Richard of possessing forged bank notes. Sarah had sailed on the *Friendship* with Prudence Brodribb. She was one of those who incurred the ire of the ship's surgeon, who described her as 'Prostitute. Regardless of remonstrance.' Only eighteen months after their marriage, Sarah died, probably in childbirth. There is no record that Armstrong married again. He left Government House when he received his ticket-of-leave but his skill with horses was always in demand. When he died in 1834, 'near upon 50 years' old, he was working as a horsebreaker for a settler, Mr Kade.[47]

Under the supervision of the Acting Engineer and Inspector of Public Works, two men convicted for passing forged notes—Edward Yates who had been a blacksmith in Shropshire and William Lindsay, a 'waterman' from Lincolnshire—were assigned to build the government corn mill and associated watercourse. Despite a blasting accident that cost Edward the sight of one eye, they worked with such dedication that the mill began grinding barely a year later. In December 1818 Edward Yates was appointed superintendent of the Government Mill at a salary of £50 per annum. The same month both he and Lindsay received conditional pardons for their 'intelligence and industry'. With Sorell's backing, Yates was among those who petitioned for assistance to bring his family to Hobart. In September 1820 his wife Jane and their four children arrived on the convict ship *Morley*. Yates continued at the Government Mill for nearly three years before branching out on his own by opening a new, water-driven flour mill in Liverpool Street in partnership with James Tedder. In anticipation of the family's arrival he also built a two-storey house in Elizabeth Street. Apart from a fine for working during Divine Service in 1819, his only brush with the law after his arrival was an altercation with two constables when he was bound over to keep the peace for 'removing his son James Yates from their custody'.[48]

Robert Groves had been given the job of the Lieutenant Governor's 'bird-stuffer',[49] but the other Berkeley poachers were encouraged to return to what they knew best—farming. After landing, Daniel Long was appointed overseer of the Government Farm and a constable at New Town. He received a conditional pardon at the end of 1818 and was farming his own land by 1823, having received a grant of 50 acres at Ormaig (near Colebrook). In February 1824 he married Mary Ann Fetters, who decades later was said by her descendants to have been 'late of India'—a suspiciously vague description that sometimes covered very disreputable ancestry. Nothing has come to light, however, that suggests Mary Ann had come to the colonies in any manner except free. She may have been the daughter of a soldier. A few months after their marriage, Daniel also became the licensee of the Plough and Harrow in the main street of the hamlet called Sorell.[50]

Jack Reeves worked for the government in some unnamed capacity that, like Long's, probably took advantage of his agricultural knowledge. After receiving his ticket-of-leave in mid-1819, he rented a farm at Browns River.[51] James Roach, Will Penny and Tom Collins were assigned as agricultural labourers to settlers, but Roach amassed sufficient funds to purchase 30 acres, and as early as 1819 was living on a well-established farm with crops of wheat, beans and potatoes and 50 sheep grazing on 21 acres of pasture. Roach was caught up as a witness in a case of cattle-stealing which Sorell used as an example to reduce, if not entirely stamp out, the widespread practice of taking other people's livestock. Otherwise, the only encounter Roach had with the law was in 1830 when he was prosecuted 'for keeping one dog liable to duty without a licence', but for which he was acquitted on the grounds that there was 'no proof that the dog is liable to duty'.[52] William Penny worked for Mr Henry Thrupp, in whose employ he remained for some years. When he received his ticket-of-leave in 1818 Tom Collins took a job with Richard Naylor of Norfolk Plains, where he was quickly appointed overseer of the farm, that being, as he put it, 'a line of Life I was brought up too [sic]'. They were all granted tickets-of-leave quickly by Sorell. He also supported anyone who wanted to bring out their wife and children, although not all families were willing to make the voyage. Sorell was equally swift with his support when the Berkeley poachers applied for emancipation. It was necessary to send the applications to the Governor in Sydney and, on Tom Collins, in 1820 Sorell wrote for Macquarie's benefit, 'This man, one of those convicted in the case of poaching in Gloucestershire, is entitled to my strong recommendation to His Excellency for a conditional pardon.'[53]

One of the Berkeley poachers did not seek Sorell's help. In November 1818, barely eighteen months after they arrived, young John Burley died. Whether it was an accident or illness that killed him was not recorded. Either way, the unlikely hero of the poachers' trial was given no time to discover whether life in Van Diemen's Land offered him a better future.[54]

The Littleport rioters were another group who attracted Sorell's support. Despite the distance, Sorell did not forget Richard Rutter, sending him a note on his memorial for a ticket-of-leave and asking the Commandant at Launceston to have it delivered to him.[55] Several of the Littleport group, including Joseph Easey, wanted their families to come to Van Diemen's Land. The first application was submitted in 1817 but nothing eventuated. A second, with

Sorell's specific support, was forwarded in 1819 and met with mixed results. Edward Yates' family, who were on this same application, arrived the following year but there was no similar happy outcome for any of the Littleport men.[56] The families may have been deterred, as many were, by horror stories about the voyage and melodramatic descriptions of depravity at Botany Bay. Sometimes the men heard nothing and were left to worry and wonder until, in most cases, they finally gave up. But Little Easey never resigned himself to the loss of his wife and children. After obtaining a free (absolute) pardon in 1824, he returned to Littleport. There he found that Elizabeth had formed a new relationship in his absence of nearly a decade. Accepting this reality, Joseph remained at Little-port anyway. After a while he started a new relationship himself with a local woman named Sarah Freeman who bore him a son, John. After Elizabeth died in 1843, they were married.[57]

The *Bensley* men were significant in the early development of Hobart. By 1820, Samuel Nash was the Water Bailiff, and stonemason James Aikman acted as the Overseer of Stone Cutters. The young printer, Joseph Williams, found his skills were in short supply. By 1820 he held the position of Assistant Government Printer in Hobart, in which capacity he would have worked frequently with Thomas Wells producing Sorell's official notices and regula-tions. When Joseph was re-transported to Newcastle, someone—Thomas Wells perhaps—thought that labouring in irons was a waste of his ability. Word reached Sydney that there was a trained printer on the loose and this attracted the attention of Robert Howe, editor of the *Sydney Gazette*.

Francis Bodenham disembarked in Hobart with the first group of *Bensley* men in September 1817. Despite his status as a prisoner, there was every reason why he should have found success in the colony. Educated and personable, although not actually a gentleman, he must have had a certain air of quality about him. With his London experience as a servant—and a crime that did not involve theft—he would have been snapped up very quickly by one of the settlers, who were always looking for good servants. But Francis also had the technical skills of an engraver and silversmith. That, combined with the fact that at 27 he was no callow youth like most of the others, meant that the authorities marked him out for something more useful. By late January 1818 he had been appointed an overseer of the working gangs. By July he was a constable in Hobart Town. But his skills offered the opportunity to earn good money in his own time and he intended to make the most of them. Optimistic about his future, he placed an advertisement in the local paper two months after gaining the appointment as constable. In it, Francis Bodenham offered his services in watch-mending and engraving from premises next door to The Bricklayers Arms in Elizabeth Street. But then, almost simultaneously with the establishment of this enterprise, his nemesis arrived in the form of Sarah Franks.

Soon after her trial at the Old Bailey, Sarah sailed for New South Wales on the *Maria*. From there she was trans-shipped to Hobart by the *Elizabeth Henrietta*, arriving on 14 November 1818. She brought with her all the streetwise experience of stealing and, more to the point, receiving and disposing of stolen goods, that had been her way of life in London. Like everyone else, Sarah Franks and Francis Bodenham were looking for a partner and their eyes alighted on one another. Twelve weeks after she landed, they were married. Nine months later, Francis' trouble-free run in the colony came to a crashing end. In September 1819 he was convicted by a Bench of five magistrates of receiving watches stolen from a Mr Thomas Devine. He lost his job as a constable. He was sentenced to two years labour in the gaol gang. Most devastating of all, he was sentenced to be flogged. Until that moment, Francis Bodenham's skin was unmarked. His body did not display even one of the fancy tattoos so beloved of his fellow prisoners. Now he had to bear the degradation and shock of 50 lashes. To a man not hardened by army service, nor by the toughness developed from life on the streets or in the crowded slums—to someone with no record even of fisticuffs—it must have felt like a gross violation. That year, 1819, was a turning point for Francis Bodenham, although his full tragedy took decades to play out.

Meanwhile, as Francis laboured in the gaol gang, Sarah was active in some way that resulted in her confinement, in February 1820, 'to the Gaol during the Lieutenant Governor's pleasure'. Of course, this may have been deliberate on her part because it put her in the vicinity of Francis, who returned with the gang to the gaol each night. Nevertheless, she must have been assigned some time in the following months and it is possible that Francis gained some remission of his sentence to the gang. Wherever they were, eighteen months later in July 1821, they were caught together 'out after hours'. Francis was ordered 'to labour the same hours as the Gaol Gang for a week'. Sarah was punished by three hours in the stocks. Whatever the exact details of the stolen watches in 1819, she had acquired a reputation in the town as someone who would dispose of stolen property. In February 1822 she was accused but acquitted of receiving a shroud knowing it to have been stolen. Then on 1 June she and Francis were both committed for trial for receiving four baskets of tobacco and sundry articles which had been stolen by George Harrison from the stores of his employers, Messrs Kemp & Co. Van Diemen's Land still had no superior court. Serious crimes such as this one were usually tried before the Court of Criminal Jurisdiction in Sydney. On 22 June, Sarah and Francis left Hobart and the prospects it might have offered them, sailing on the *Jupiter* for New South Wales.[58]

In January 1822, only a few months before the Bodenhams left Hobart, the ship *Amboyna* arrived in Sydney. When the anchor dropped, her master wrote immediately to tell the Colonial Secretary that he had embarked four convicts in Calcutta. One of those he listed was the irrepressible, determined William Honeyman. When last sighted, Honeyman was using his bricklayer's skills to build the new church at Windsor in New South Wales. Originally let to a private contractor who had failed, the expertise of the government trade gangs had been brought in to finish it.[59] Then, in November 1820, the Principal Superintendent of Convicts posted a notice in the *Sydney Gazette* to inform all and sundry that Honeyman had absconded 'from the Bricklayers Gang'. Whether he was still working on the church when he vanished or had been brought back to Sydney for another of Macquarie's many building projects is not clear, but very likely he was close to the harbour and mixing with the many sailors who took leave in the port between voyages.

Sydney could be a lucrative port for a sailor. From the seamen, the prisoners learned where the ships in harbour were heading, who was travelling, when they were departing. Many were prepared to pay every penny they possessed for help in escaping. Many did escape with the connivance of ships' crew. The Colonial Engineer, Major Druitt, confirmed this to Commissioner Bigge when he testified, 'They have tried to escape in numbers. And many have effected it.'[60] The government talked of fining ships' masters in an attempt to stop their complicity but, payment aside, a captain would risk a fine if he needed another pair of hands to make up his crew. In 1819, Macquarie appointed a couple of coxswains in two guard boats that would row between the ships at anchor during the night. In Van Diemen's Land, Sorell was doing the same. Meanwhile men swam through the dark waters, hauled themselves up the side, slipped through hatchways. After a ship cleared the port, but before it left the harbour, it was smoked. Constables were stationed on each vessel to catch the absconders as they came coughing and spluttering from every nook and cranny. Despite this precaution, many got away. Honeyman was one of those who defeated all the traps the government set, wriggling his way on board the *Agamemnon*, which was transporting troops to Madras.[61]

Far from being the mythical place 'beyond the seas' from which there was no return, Botany Bay leaked like a sieve throughout the transportation era. Escape was a constant preoccupation. The long voyage provided the prisoners with a comprehensive lesson in global geography and there were enough sailors and soldiers among their number to fill in the details of the places they did not see and the routes their transport did not follow. In the very early years, some men took the mickey out of their mates by convincing them that China lay beyond the mountains west of Sydney. The fact that some believed this and went looking for China became the authorities' standard joke to demonstrate the stupidity of the prisoners. In England, they spread the story widely by broadsheet as a warning that escape was hopeless. But the convicts had arrived by sea and most turned to the sea for a way out.

The *Bensley* men were indefatigable escapers. Some of them vanish so completely after arrival in Sydney that it has to be assumed they got away. For example, Christian Brabazon, who was tried at the Old Bailey, although a native of Ghent, is never heard of again after landing in 1817. Described as 'a linguist' on the *Bensley*'s indent, he probably escaped as ship's crew under cover of being a foreigner. James Burns stowed away on the *Frederick* in Sydney harbour but was discovered in Hobart. In January 1818, Richard Baker, convicted with his brother William of burglary in the cottage of a retired naval officer, was charged with 'concealing himself on board the ship *Pilot* with intent to escape from the colony'. He was sentenced to work six months in the Hobart gaol gang. With him on the *Pilot* was John Burley's friend among the Berkeley poachers, James Jenkins. According to the *Hobart Gazette*, they were ordered to work in irons in the gaol gang. They did not stay there long.[62]

Contemporary drawing of a convict

Up north the situation was even worse—from Sorell's perspective, that is. From the prisoners' point of view George Town and its surrounds were an absconder's paradise. Near the mouth of the Tamar, it was well positioned for access to Bass Strait. There were few guards. In fact, the prisoners outnumbered their guards and overseers, many of whom were ticket-of-leave men anyway. Only months after they arrived, Valentine Wood and shipmate Thomas Harlow were among those who overwhelmed the small troop of soldiers, torched the town and then fled into the bush. Harlow lived in the bush for nearly two years, but Wood did not cope in the wild and was soon recaptured. Described by Sorell, who knew him from the voyage, as 'an incorrigible vagrant who will someday be the means of forming a Band of Plunderers', Wood was sent to Sydney for trial, where he was sentenced to two years at Newcastle. In 1822, he was executed for highway robbery near Sydney.[63]

John Smith, who was William Honeyman's accomplice in the Carron ironworks robbery, was an active absconder. Disembarking at Port Dalrymple in September 1817, he too was soon in the bush, where he linked up with notorious bushranger named Peter Geary, an associate of the even more notorious Michael Howe. Wounded at Black Brush, where Geary was killed by soldiers, Smith was sent to the gaol gang in Hobart. There he was soon devising a new escape plan with shipmates James Jenkins and Richard Baker. By April, all three had absconded into the bush. After a year in the colony, the men were beginning to get the measure of the place. Baker and Jenkins had only seen Hobart, but Smith knew the lay of the land generally, as well as the layout and personnel at Port Dalrymple. He hatched a plan based on that local knowledge. Robert Henry Dye was also in the gaol gang, consigned there for stealing four pieces of iron off the wheels of a cart. While his shipmates took to the bush, perhaps in a diversion, Dye with five others got clean away. Under cover of darkness, they slipped two government boats from their moorings in Sullivan's Cove and collected Smith and Jenkins from some prearranged spot. Richard Baker, who missed the rendezvous, was back in the gaol gang two months later. As they made their way down river, they managed to steal an anchor and a water cask from one of the settlers.

Like weapons, boats were in short supply in Hobart. Smith's pursuers wanted the boats back almost more than the men. The tone of the government notice was urgent. 'All Constables and others are hereby commanded to use every Exertion in their power to apprehend the said Felons, and lodge them in His Majesty's Gaol at Hobart Town,' it thundered. Knowing how many would sympathise with the prey rather than the hunter, the notice tried to intimidate

James McCabe, Matthew Brady and Patrick Bryant: three of
Van Diemen's Land's many bushrangers

the sympathisers by warning, 'all Persons are cautioned not to harbour, maintain, conceal or in any way aid or comfort the said Felons, on pain of Penalties that will thereon ensue'. Two boats gave chase, one in charge of the Acting Naval Officer, Lieutenant Robinson, the other under the command of Superintendent of Convicts Walter Peerhouse, who knew the absconders by sight because he shared their voyage on the *Bensley*, but as a passenger. James Kelly, commander of the local brig *Sophia*, set sail too, intent on following the gang into open sea if necessary. All day the wind blew hard from the south. When the pursuers concluded finally that escape into the ocean was impossible, they narrowed their search to the coves and inlets of the river.[64]

In fact the party had passed beyond the mouth of the Derwent. From there they sailed up the east coast to Port Dalrymple. No doubt they intended to find some supplies near George Town. Perhaps also, they planned to collect Robert Dye's brother Henry, who had disembarked there. In Bass Strait a few miles from the mouth of the Tamar, they were spotted. Some hours passed before a search party could be mustered and the 'pirates', as they were called, once again escaped. But they were starving, so hungry that John Smith and another man went ashore and gave themselves up. Meanwhile, a whaleboat from the *Rosetta*, which was at Port Dalrymple, went in pursuit. On board was Lieutenant Cuthbertson and men from the 48th Regiment who knew the neighbourhood well. Northerly gales gusted in from the Strait. Once again, it seemed impossible that the pirates could have made the open sea. And indeed they had taken shelter. The lieutenant caught them by surprise 'in the first Western river', capturing most of the men, the launch and some tools. Dye and Jenkins and their remaining companions joined Smith on a long overland march under guard to Hobart. Valentine Wood, who had been brought in from the bush, was sent with them. One of the Dye brothers never reappeared. A week later they were all before the Bench of Magistrates. Robert Dye, John Smith and James Jenkins were sentenced to 100 lashes each and transportation for three years to Newcastle.[65] Orders to the Commandant there described them as 'pirates from Van Diemen's Land to be kept in double irons and closely watched being dangerous and desperate characters'.[66] Jenkins would never see the other Berkeley poachers again.

Escapes like this are typical of many attempted by the convicts, yet they are not part of the folklore about the penal colony. Until recently, convict escapes were only ever mentioned in passing, and then always from the perspective of the authorities. Did such events cause trouble for Governor Davey? Was Sorell successful in stopping them? The daring and enterprise of the prisoners in attempting escape were ignored. Their interconnected relationships remained unnoticed. Like William Honeyman, they were lost in the silence about the convict colony.[67]

It took Honeyman's descendants to uncover his story, prompted by the chance discovery of the solitary grave of his daughter, Anne, in Van Diemen's Land. How did she get there, they asked themselves. Why was a 17-year-old girl called Honeyman buried in a family plot belonging to a totally unconnected family? And why Van Diemen's Land? As canvassed in Chapter 2, the family history was a mixture of fact and fiction, real names and false. Years passed as Honeyman descendants pieced together the real story. Honeyman's hair-raising expedition to India becomes even more tragic with the knowledge that his family had meanwhile set out to join him. In 1822, wife Jean, with Anne, her sister Margaret and her two boys William and Alexander, who were six and three, sailed on the *Castle Forbes*, probably in the entourage of a free settler named Alexander Reid and his family. They landed in Hobart, only to find that Honeyman was supposedly in New South Wales. Family research has concluded that Jean left the two girls behind in service to the Reids while she and the boys sailed north. Subsequently, Anne married but died in childbirth only seven months after the wedding. Strangely, given the devotion that had brought Jean across the world to find her husband, she became involved with one of the crew on the voyage to Sydney. She was already pregnant by him when she attended the Superintendents of Convicts' office to make enquiries about William Honeyman. There they would have produced for her the letter written by the commander of the *Amboyna*, who had sent an extract of the ship's log to explain what happened on the voyage from Calcutta to Sydney.[68] Dated 16 August 1821, it read:

> Midnight departed this life, William Honeyman, one of the convicts sent on board at Calcutta for NSW, having hurt himself by a fall from his hammock in the Gale of 7th July last in the Bay of Bengal by which he unfortunately burst some blood vessel and has lingered ever since.

William Honeyman had died only a few months, weeks even, before Jean left Scotland. Honeyman was literate and there had been time to write home since the *Bensley* arrived. Had he heard nothing in reply? Is that why he gave up waiting and set about making his own way home? India must have been a shock beyond anything he had imagined, not least in the way poor white men stood out in a crowd. He must have realised that making a living in India, let alone the chances of catching a ship to Scotland unnoticed, were almost impossible. By comparison, New South Wales seemed an attractive destination. When they picked him up, he asked to be returned to the convict colony. If he had made it back, he would have discovered that many of his shipmates had reached a similar conclusion.[69] In Honeyman's absence, many of them had received a ticket-of-leave or a pardon. Many were taking the first steps to establishing a stake for themselves in a society where there were no replicas of Colonel Berkeley and his ilk, no social structure that kept his power intact while consigning them permanently to the 'lower orders'. And no shame at having been one of the chosen people, selected for transportation by the best judges in England. That was an experience most inhabitants of Botany Bay had shared.

CHAPTER 5
outward bound

The authorities came closer to matching reality to their rhetoric about the impossibility of escape when the system tightened from the mid-1820s. The two penal colonies were run by Governor Ralph Darling, who arrived in New South Wales in 1826, and Governor George Arthur who was in charge in Van Diemen's Land after replacing Sorell in 1824. Like Macquarie and Sorell, these representatives of His Britannic Majesty were in perfect accord about how to approach the management of their domain. But their attitudes were the complete opposite of their predecessors'. To Darling and Arthur, New South Wales and Van Diemen's Land were gaols first and last. Indeed Arthur had a grand vision of Van Diemen's Land as the gaol for the entire British Empire.

The population had grown since the *Sir William Bensley* arrived, but despite some free immigration during the 1820s, it was still a convict society. The census in 1833 revealed approximately 60,000 people now lived in New South Wales, of whom 24,543 were serving convicts and 26,064 free adults. Forty-five years after settlement at Sydney Cove, the balance between free and bond had tilted towards the free, but most who were free were still emancipists.[1] The number of children now totalled 10,187 of whom, applying John Molony's calculations in his book *The Native Born*, 90 per cent had convict and ex-convict parents.[2]

It was a *laissez-faire* society. Tattooed on more than one convict arm, 'Let all the world say what it will, Speak of me as you find', proclaimed the dominant community ethos of judging a person on their character rather than by the usual markers of class, wealth, education and propriety.[3] And what of the taint of crime? Since all but a minority shared a criminal conviction, there was rarely reason to remember it. In fact the former prisoners were notorious for their lack of shame, as the following poem published by the Presbyterian clergyman Reverend Dr J.D. Lang in the 1830s demonstrates:

> Who would not live a year or two in Sydney
> To get acquaint with all its nonpareils;
> To dine with people of a certain kidney
> And bask all in the sunshine of their smiles?
> They don't live quiet, as they ought, and hid. Nay,
> Proud of their expulsion from the British Isles,
> Some glory in their shame! Very strange tales
> Are told of gentlemen of New South Wales.[4]

In their optimism about this new society, described by one fascinated visitor as the 'land of contrarieties',[5] the former prisoners frequently overcompensated by being distinctly possessive. As James Macarthur told the 1837 Select Committee on Transportation, 'They believed the colony was theirs by right.'[6] Particularly noticeable was their attitude to 'new chums' who arrived free. Pride in the community and affection for the land that offered them a chance had been obvious since at least the early 1800s,[7] and the locals hoped desperately to keep things that way. In his reminiscences, Lang reported Governor Macquarie saying in a burst of exasperation after a confrontation with one of the free settlers, 'This country was established for the reformation of convicts; free people had no right to come to it.' To which Lang, who had lived among them for 50 years, added: 'This feeling was very common among the emancipists of all classes.'[8] Nothing changed with the passage of time. In the 1840s, one visitor fumed helplessly, 'The fact of being a drunkard, or a convict, is not looked upon in this country, among the *class*, as any disgrace; on the contrary . . . no shame whatever is evinced by the very best amongst them; and they look upon all "self-imported devils" as beneath them, and not worth consideration.'[9]

When the *John* arrived in Sydney, polite society was still no more than a pimple on the social surface. The mores in the streets, the pubs, the shops, among the locally born professional and business men, among the tradesmen, the seamen, labourers and servants were those of the prisoners—a confident, hard-drinking, blasphemous, humorous society, but energetic and optimistic, confident that they had found a place which they could make their own. Pride in their homeland was particularly visible on 26 January in the regattas held to celebrate the arrival of the First Fleet. At the dinner on what was then called

Anniversary Day the most popular toast was, 'The land, boys, we live in'. As noticeable as affection for the land was the insistence that newcomers adapt to local ways. As Russel Ward put it, 'Before 1851, the colonial contempt for new chums had sprung mainly from a feeling of nationalism, which in turn closely associated with a lower-class *esprit de corps*. Even an Englishman might be rapidly forgiven his unfortunate heritage provided he did not give himself the airs of a "swell".'[10] More than anything else, the ex-prisoners dreaded an influx of immigrants who would overwhelm them with the class and moral strictures of British society, relegating them once more to being outcasts.

The *John* disembarked its prisoners into this society on 10 June 1832, a few months after Governor Darling's departure. His replacement was Richard Bourke, a Protestant Irish liberal whose views were shaped by the early influence of his kinsman and lifelong mentor, Edmund Burke. Governor Bourke's advocacy of issues such as trial by jury, freedom of the press and emancipists' rights, as well as free immigration and public education, was more reminiscent of governors Macquarie and Sorell than his immediate predecessors. This would be crucial to advancing the transition of the penal colony of New South Wales to a representative democracy. When Bourke arrived, there were approximately 21,800 convicts serving sentences, with an average of 1700 arriving annually over the six years of his appointment. All of them, including the men from the *John*, benefited directly from Bourke's reforms to the magistracy and particularly from the limits on flogging and the circumstances in which it could be carried out.[11]

Except for one tragic event, the *John* had an uneventful voyage, sailing direct between London and Sydney in 120 days, which was much shorter than the 186 days it took the *Bensley*, even allowing for the *Bensley*'s stop at the Cape. The *John*'s surgeon, James Lawrence, treated patients in his hospital, assisted in the usual way by one of the prisoners, in this case John Keating. Also as usual, Lawrence kept a detailed journal of the ailments he treated. In fact the prisoners on this and most other voyages received a standard of health care they had never previously experienced. Some sought out the surgeon at the first sign of a sniffle, and liking what he did for them they came back several times. Others took the opportunity to get treatment for long-standing problems like haemorrhoids or rheumatism.[12] Generally speaking, the death rate of prisoners was very low.[13]

Nevertheless, deaths did occur on the voyage and the *John* was no exception. But in this instance, the death of one of the prisoners, John Clifton, was really triggered by the ever-present fear on transports carrying male convicts that they would in some way hijack the ship. Threats to take transports were frequently made. Tools prepared. And verbal confrontations between prisoners and their regimental guards were commonplace. Nevertheless, there were few actual mutinies and most so-called attempts were in the minds of jittery sentries. The tragedy on the *John* almost certainly occurred this way, despite the chief mate's claim to the police magistrate that 'The conduct of the prisoners has been very refractory.' There was just one thing wrong with the tactic of blaming the prisoners. The men appointed by the surgeon to oversee Clifton's punishment were in a pivotal position to support the surgeon's claim to have acted properly or to undermine him. Not surprisingly, they turned out to be the two ex-soldiers, William Crooks and Patrick Quigley.

Appointed a prison guard by Surgeon Lawrence, Quigley was on duty as the men settled for the night. The regimental guard paced the deck above. All was peaceful until a sentry spotted smoke rising through the forward hatch. He yelled down to Quigley to find out what was happening. As Quigley went to look, the sentry heard someone say, 'Damn and bugger the ship, I wish she was the one on fire now.' Below deck, Quigley found a small pile of oakum and shavings on fire by the foremast. The surgeon told the magistrate it was near No. 5 mess. Quigley was more ambiguous. 'I didn't see any prisoner near the foremast when I discovered the fire, but afterward they all flocked round. Any of the men might have discovered the fire where I found it.' According to the surgeon, the captain of No. 5 mess, Robert Morgan, pointed out John Clifton. According to Quigley, 'Clifton said subsequently that he wished the ship was on fire.' Tom Vaughan, who belonged to the same mess as Clifton, defended him. 'I did not hear him say he would like the ship to burn. A man named Morgan accused him of saying it.' But Robert Morgan stuck to his story. 'Clifton slept in the same berth with me, next but one. I told the truth about what he said.'

In any event, the surgeon decided that Clifton must be punished. The next day he ordered him to walk the deck for two hours and appointed Crooks and Quigley to supervise. Clifton was to carry a bed on his back while he walked. Presumably, it was some kind of mattress although it was just described as 'a bed'. It was a very hot day, 80°F in the shade when Clifton began his walk, ironed on one leg but not carrying his bed. He was angry and lurching about violently. Since he had brought no bed on deck, Crooks made him run. In fact the surgeon, who came on deck about three-quarters of an hour after the punishment started, said 'Crooks applied a rope end to his breech and forced him to run.' The surgeon claimed he put a stop to this, told Clifton to walk and had a bed brought up so the punishment could be carried out as ordered. Then he went below.

When Clifton collapsed and died, everyone ran for cover. Conscious that he was vulnerable, Surgeon Lawrence asked Governor Bourke in Sydney to appoint someone to investigate 'while everyone is still on board who witnessed my treatment of the convicts'. He testified that when he examined the body it gushed water. That raised the question of whether Clifton died from consuming too much liquid while overheated. If so, who gave it to him? It turned out several people did. When Clifton first called for water, his messmate Tom Vaughan gave it to him. Quigley said Clifton had received his standard issue of lime juice and water and he also insisted that both he and Crooks gave Clifton water. Of course, Crooks confirmed their humane gesture. 'He had two pots of water from Quigley and myself,' he told the magistrate.

Any reading of the evidence suggests that Crooks was enjoying his power over the unfortunate Clifton, but both convict soldiers were exonerated by the word of a serving soldier. Private William Foreman testified that he 'saw no cruelty by the persons placed to keep the prisoner walked'. Was the punishment too severe? A unanimous chorus claimed it was not. In what sounds a suspiciously boastful and certainly self-serving tone, Quigley declared, 'I should not have thought anything of the punishment if it had been inflicted on me.' But even Tom Vaughan said it was not unreasonable, claiming that he had been punished the same way but he had to walk the deck for twelve hours. Harsh or not, Vaughan probably provided the clue to Clifton's collapse. The doctor had described Clifton as about 22 years of age, apparently in good health and was 'not particularly stout'. However, Vaughan revealed, 'He had something the matter with his breast. He wouldn't go to the doctor.'

With the investigation complete, the prisoners were allowed to disembark. In the fifteen years since the *Bensley* dropped anchor, the arc of settlement around Sydney had widened enormously. The colonists spent 25 years after they first landed gazing at the mountain range that blocked the way west and wondering and wondering what lay beyond. Since Blaxland, Lawson and Wentworth finally crossed it in 1813, explorers, pastoralists, governors, travellers and prisoners had gone across and back, across and back in a never-ending, ever-increasing procession. Governor Macquarie was one of the first across the mountains, journeying as far as the plains beyond, where he chose a site near the river to be the place for a town that would be called after Lord Bathurst. In 1822, he gave a hand-picked group of settlers, including at least one ex-convict, grants of land to settle there. By the early 1830s, a steady flow of new settlers had increased the traffic even more. All these travellers demanded improved infrastructure. In the Vale of Clwydd, ex-convict Pierce Collits built an inn for travellers to rest before or after making the torturous journey to or from Mount Victoria. At the windswept plateau named by Macquarie as Black Heath another ex-convict, Andrew Gardiner, established an inn. Further down the mountain, the Weatherboard Hut was regarded as offering acceptable accommodation. The track marked by Blaxland, Lawson and Wentworth had been developed by surveyors and engineers and convicts into something resembling a road. The first of what would be several versions of a hazardous descent from the western escarpment to the gentler foothills below had been cut. A series of stockades was being developed to house the road gangs.

New South Wales, with locations mentioned in this book

The colony had opened out south-west and north-west as well. In the north, settlers had pushed inland up the valley of the Hunter River from Newcastle as well as cross-country from the Hawkesbury and Castle Hill. A northern road had been completed in 1831 but it was still easier and quicker to sail up the coast, particularly if you were transporting prisoners.[14] By 1824 Newcastle had been superseded as a place of secondary punishment by Port Macquarie, which by 1832 had itself been opened up for free settlers. It was also used as a place to send infirm or disabled prisoners or those designated 'special' in some way because of education or reputation in England. In 1832, the secondary punishment settlements were further north at Moreton Bay and on Norfolk Island. The south-west had changed least in fifteen years. Although villages such as Liverpool and Campbelltown (known as Airds) were more densely settled, there were only a few pastoral stations beyond Goulburn. Hume and Hovell had trekked down to Port Phillip, but Surveyor General Mitchell had not yet opened up the overland route to Port Phillip and the mouth of the Murray. William Thomas from the *Bensley*, who would act as his bullocky and butcher on two of those expeditions, was still an assigned servant in Windsor.

Sydney was a bustling seaport. Transports and naval vessels, whalers from the United States, merchant ships from India and Batavia and China crowded the harbour. Sailors still crowded the port. Prisoners were still determined to escape. Money still no doubt changed hands in return for information and for help. The 1830s were the height of the convict system in New South Wales, with 31,200 prisoners arriving in the decade, compared with 15,030 who arrived in the 1820s.[15] Among the citizens going about their business in Sydney in 1832 were *Bensley* men such as Peter Quigley, who was a shopkeeper in Market Street. John Jacobs was a watchmaker, also in Market Street. Daniel McMahon was a shoemaker around the corner in York Street. William Cuthbert was a coach proprietor nearby. Thomas Ford was a constable based in Liverpool Street. Most who had servants employed ex-convicts, but some of them had applied for and been assigned men and women who were still prisoners. Sentenced to two years at Newcastle for stealing a box of tobacco from Edward Lord in Hobart, the compositor Joseph Williams had been made a constable at Patrick's Plains before Robert Howe of the *Sydney Gazette* managed to track him down. Persistent applications by Howe finally succeeded in getting Joseph assigned to him in 1825. By the time the *John* arrived in 1832, he was working in Sydney for printer George Williams at the *Australian*, which was owned by W.C. Wentworth and Dr Robert Wardell. In 1837 Joseph married Sarah Jones and three years later was the father of two daughters, Elizabeth and Emma.[16]

The 'pirates' of Van Diemen's Land had settled down in the ten years since their transportation to Newcastle. Robert Dye married and returned to settle in Van Diemen's Land. Poacher James Jenkins settled near Bathurst, where he began farming. He was still a bachelor in 1832 but much later, at the age of 66, he married a widow named Rebecca Batreep. They continued to live in Bathurst until Jenkins was killed in 1867 when the wheel of a dray ran over his chest.[17] Francis Bodenham and Sarah were living in Sydney. Having been sentenced to seven years at Port Macquarie in 1822, Francis once again impressed someone in authority and was appointed to the position of gaoler.[18] Both Francis and Sarah were required to give evidence in Sydney in the case of *R. v. Bradney*, but during their time in the town they were confined in the Sydney gaol despite an attempt by Francis to get permission to live in lodgings while they waited for the criminal sessions to start.[19] In 1829, Francis finally obtained his certificate of freedom which covered both his original seven years for bigamy in 1815 and the extra seven for receiving stolen goods in Hobart. But Sarah had been given a life sentence for receiving stolen goods in London, which meant she was still a convict when the seven years at Port Macquarie ended. Well acquainted with the colonial regulations, Francis applied to the Colonial Secretary for Sarah to be assigned to him. Much paperwork ensued at the Secretary's office. Francis had to swear an affidavit proving their marriage by Reverend Knopwood in Hobart before the authorities were prepared to agree to the request. The couple returned to Sydney the following year, where Francis successfully applied for the appointment of 'turnkey' at the Penrith lock-up. He lasted in the job only two months before being dismissed for drunkenness.[20] He had now held a succession of low-level government appointments ranging from overseer of the working gangs in Hobart to this latest position, but with the exception of the position as gaoler at Port Macquarie he had lost every one of them. Thrown on his own resources, Francis fell back on his technical skills to earn a living as a watch repairer or engraver.[21]

Susannah Watson and the women of the *Princess Royal* were also in New South Wales. A minority had been in continuous trouble over the three years since they landed, either through drunkenness or by absconding from their employer. Some, including young Ann Storrett, had fallen foul of the disciplinary rules. Within six weeks of their arrival in 1829, Ann was taken into custody by a constable late one evening for being found with another prisoner, Eliza Green, in a disorderly house. In evidence to the magistrate, the constable said, 'The house is a disorderly one and a number of people were therein at the time dancing, there was a fiddle playing and the prisoner Stort [*sic*] had a pint of porter before her.' Although the picture is one of people harmlessly enjoying themselves, the magistrate agreed with the constable. Blaming the masters rather than the women, he sent Ann and Eliza to the first class (non-penitentiary) of the Female Factory at Parramatta. Ann was eventually sent over the mountains to work in the Bathurst district, where a few years later she would marry James Jaye from the *John*.[22]

By the end of 1832, 40 per cent of the *Princess Royal* women had already escaped their sentence by the best option open to female prisoners: that of marriage. Susannah Watson had denied herself this option, perhaps because she was expecting her husband Edward would follow her with their four children, perhaps because she did not realise how detrimental it would be to reveal she was already married. Edward never came but when Susannah did meet a single, free settler named Isaac Moss, there was no possibility they could marry. In fact, the relationship only complicated her life further. Already caring for the infant she brought with her, Susannah was returned to the Factory when it was apparent she was pregnant. However, and like many of the prisoners, Susannah came to understand the system and found a way to subvert it to her advantage. Some time in 1833–34, she met up again with John Clarke, whom she had known as a fellow prisoner in Nottingham. Together they deceived the authorities into thinking they were married to one another. When John, whose sentence was only seven years, received his certificate of freedom in 1834, Susannah was assigned to him and was able to spend a large part of her fourteen-year sentence as a wife and mother.[23]

In the early 1830s, many of the pastoralists who held grants on the Cumberland Plain around Sydney were taking up additional land in the new areas. While retaining their original properties, families with well-known names like Macarthur, Lawson, Ogilvie, Dumaresq, Badgery and Cox were in the process of obtaining large grants in the far reaches of the Nineteen Counties that Governor Darling had declared to be the limit of settlement. Some had been in the colony for many years. Some of the younger generation had been born there. They were experienced in managing a convict workforce, and after years of practice they had an eye for a good man even when he appeared before them as magistrates for some transgression. These established families had been joined since the 1820s by new arrivals. Many were Scottish, encouraged by Reverend John Dunmore Lang, who returned to Scotland several times to bring back boatloads of emigrants. They included crofters displaced by the highland clearances, for whom emigration meant a chance to achieve something more in life than bare subsistence, but some were middle-class merchants or professional men. The latter group were looking for status and fortune on the land in New South Wales, but were ambivalent about local society. Scottish newspapers, and the *Edinburgh Review* magazine in particular, had been running highly coloured commentary about the penal colony for years. It affected attitudes to migrating there, and in the climate created by a hyperbolic press, the intending emigrant could be greeted with a chorus of derision when he announced his decision to go. Once resident in New South Wales it was difficult to admit you liked the place in case that stained your own reputation by association. Writing home after some years in the colony, Glasgow merchant William Panton still felt obliged to make a deprecating reference to 'this land of kangaroos and convicts'—a quote from one of Sydney Smith's explosive critiques in the *Edinburgh Review*.[24]

A number of wealthy ex-convicts were included among the employers of men from the *John*. Samuel Terry was the subject of such fascination to the British that when he died in 1838 the *Times* ran a large obituary of 'The Botany Bay Rothschild' accompanied by an illustration of the emancipist on his horse. Terry was allocated 23-year-old Thomas Bottoms, alias Swain, from the *John*. A boilermaker from Manchester, Swain was still with the Terry family nine years later.[25] Ex-convict merchant and brewer Robert Cooper was allocated the Gloucestershire poacher Isaac Fisher as well as 18-year-old William Taylor from Yorkshire. Both men had life sentences, which from an employer's point of view made them prize labourers who would potentially be in their work-force for many years. Cooper had sons on the land near Goulburn and it is likely that Fisher, at least, was sent there because when he finally obtained his ticket-of-leave it was for the Goulburn area.[26] The assignment of the two men to Cooper totally disproves the assertion of a historian as recently as 2000. Making a case for discrimination against the native-born because they were the children of convicts, John Molony claimed, 'The magistrates repeatedly refused to sign the applications made by the Coopers for assigned servants which, at the time, effectively deprived them of a labour force.'[27] The archives tell a different story from the gossip of the day, and the discrepancy confirms how the long years when the archives were not accessible created undue reliance on newspapers or published reminiscences for Australian historians.

The assignment of the men from the *John* reflected the contemporary spread of settlement. On the initial list, 35 were assigned to the Hunter area, including Maitland, and 67 were assigned in Sydney. But comparing this initial list with where the men were eventually located changes the totals to at least 46 to the Hunter, and 54 assigned in Sydney. The other major assignment area was the newly developing south-west through Narellan, Campbelltown, Sutton Forest and Berrima. A couple of men went further to St Vincent and Gundaroo. Sixteen went no further west than Parramatta, but at least five continued over the mountains to Bathurst. The Cumberland Plain, which had been the boundary of distribution for the *Bensley* men, was very much a secondary area for those assigned from the *John*.

Some employers liked to assess their new servants before deciding what to do with them. In 1828, for instance, George Bowman put the teenage Martin Cash through some stern tests of both labour and discipline before sending him to the Bowman station in the far Hunter Valley. Cash survived the testing time because he had been forewarned to keep his mouth shut regardless. Straight off the ship, walking through Windsor under the escort of a constable, he met some Irish friends and seized the opportunity to ask them about Bowman. 'I learned from my friends that he was a bit of a martinet. Also that

I must observe the utmost caution or I might make matters much worse than they were at present.' Intent on making him understand the importance of deferring to his master's demands, Cash's friends gave him vivid examples of ways 'circumstances could become much worse' for him. Cash took these warnings to heart in New South Wales. He would regret later that he forgot them in Van Diemen's Land.[28]

The young Martin Cash, with bandaged head

Like Cash, a significant number of the prisoners assigned in Sydney were in fact destined for their masters' holdings up country. In many cases the destination shown on the assignment list reflects the collection point or a temporary location. By 1832, according to a rule introduced earlier by Governor Darling, employers were supposed to collect their assigned servants from Sydney. But many still assumed—or hoped—the men would be delivered somewhere near their rural destination. The Superintendent of Convicts, Frederick Hely, tried hard to enforce the rule by reassigning prisoners to another employer if they were not collected promptly. Failure to collect their assigned men was the reason Hely gave in the *Government Gazette* for changing the allocation of several convicts from the *John*.

Four men were sent to the Australian Agricultural Company (AAC) at Port Stephens north of Newcastle. The AAC was a pastoral company established by some of the oldest landholders in the colony with investors in Britain. In return for the capital backing of the company, the Crown granted very large tracts of land at Port Stephens and, later, around the Peel River near present-day Tamworth. The company had brought out a number of working families as free settlers but it also utilised assigned labour. The records suggest that men could work with some contentment for the AAC if they were so inclined. None of the four men from the *John* can be found absconding or disorderly. Two of them were still with the AAC nine years later and the remaining two may have been also, but by then they had obtained their certificates of freedom and it is harder to be certain. Joseph Laycock from Yorkshire, a stuff weaver by trade, a highway robber by crime, stayed with the AAC for a very long time, becoming sufficiently trusted to be granted a passport in 1842 which allowed him to travel alone between the company's land at Port Stephens and their holding on the Peel River. In 1845 his ticket-of-leave was extended for Port Stephens. In Britain, Laycock was married with a son and it is possible that, with the company's help, he brought his family to the colony. Unfortunately, he died young at 39 years in 1848.[29]

On the evidence of the *John's* men, the Assignment Board, which included the Superintendent of Convicts, tried to match the prisoners' skills to their future employers. But the results were mixed. The two pastry-cooks, James Jaye and James Woods, were assigned to gentlemen who could make use of their talents, in Wood's case to Campbell Drummond Riddell, the Colonial Treasurer. Former soldiers Edward Gill, who described himself as 'officer's servant', and William McGhie, who said he was a 'groom', were allocated to Mr Donald McIntyre and to Supreme Court judge Alfred Stephens. All but one of the seven men who declared themselves 'colliers' or 'miners' were assigned to the Mineral Survey Department only a month before Mineral Surveyor and engineer John Busby started building a bore to carry water from ponds at the present-day Centennial Park to Sydney Town.[30] This group included all but one of the Merthyr Tydfil rioters, two soldiers, George Thompson and Joseph Mellons, who were miners and colliers before they enlisted, and a Derbyshire miner named William Weightman.[31]

In accordance with legend, there was some gross mismatching between skills and assignment, but there was also evidence that the Assignment Board knew what it was inflicting on the employer and tried to balance some of the stranger assignees with someone of more obvious value. For instance, Henry Bayley, a pastoralist at Mudgee, was allocated William Anderson, a working jeweller and goldsmith from Oxford, but he was also given William or Charles Bussey, who was an experienced farm labourer. Samuel Welsby, who could plough, milk, reap and sow, was assigned to John Webber, whose pastoral station Penshurst was in the Hunter Valley. Francis Robertson or Robinson, a 16-year-old lacemaker from Middlesex, was also assigned to Webber. It seems that John Webber called personally to collect the two men and may have rejected Robertson as unsuitable because within the month the boy was instead allocated to Charles Sims at Penrith.[32]

Sixteen-year-old Edward (more commonly called Henry) Johnston was a farmer's boy convicted in Glasgow of robbing a shop. Despite his claim to know something about farms, he was a mixed blessing to his employer when it came to managing sheep. Assigned to Archibald Bell in the Upper Hunter, he was supposed to carry out the duties of a shepherd, but in April 1833 Bell's overseer Samuel Owens reached the end of his tether. He took Henry before the Bench on not one but two complaints, explaining that he would have brought him earlier for the first problem except for the 'considerable inconvenience' in attending the court. Owens told the Bench that Henry was under standing instructions to bring back the carcass of any sheep he found dead. Instead, he returned one night bearing the ear of a sheep in his pocket. Asked to explain, Henry told the magistrates that he was in charge of a young flock of sheep. 'I couldn't drive the flock and carry the sheep. Last time I carried a sheep and the flock got away from me.' They punished him by adding an extra six months before he could get a ticket-of-leave. Moving on to the second complaint, the overseer explained that a few days earlier Henry had returned home with only half his flock. 'He told me that a native boy had rushed his flock—that part of them got away from him and he could not bring them home.' Owens had then gone out himself and had found the flock, except for three sheep. Of course Henry could have made up the story of the 'native boy', but if not it suggests the local tribe had perfected an easy trick to hive off some meat from inexperienced young shepherds. The Bench must have believed Henry because they let him off without penalty.[33]

Contemporary drawing of a convict

James Atkins was not so lucky. An 'indoor servant' from London, James had been assigned off the ship to James Glennie's family property in the Hunter Valley. His was not a case of mismatched skills because he was employed around the house. Dr Glennie had taken up more land over the range on the Liverpool Plains, leaving a younger generation of Glennies in charge of the household in the Hunter. This might explain why after three years with the family, during which he did not appear before the Bench, James was taken before the local magistrate in 1835. Mr Alfred Glennie testified that Mrs Henry Glennie had found a blanket on the prisoner's bed in the kitchen and when she asked him about it he tried to claim it was one she had given him. When she searched the bed and found the original blanket he was accused of lying. James testified in his own defence that, 'The nursery maid brought the blanket into the kitchen on Monday last. She wanted to iron some clothes on it. She left it there and I thought there was no harm putting it on my bed.' He called the nursery maid, Ann Linder, to give evidence for him but his case was not helped when Ann, who was Jewish, refused to take the oath as a matter of principle. Cross-examined by the magistrate, Charles Forbes, Esq., Ann told him that her father on his deathbed made her promise never to swear an oath. Nevertheless, she supported what James had told them, saying she often took blankets into the kitchen and might have left this one behind. Forbes gave James no latitude. In what appears an extremely harsh decision for a young man who had been with the family so long, he was found guilty of telling a falsehood to Mrs Glennie and sentenced to 25 lashes. Despite this incident, James served the whole of his seven-year sentence in the Glennies' employ. It will take a descendant to reveal what became of him after that.[34]

Richard Nichols from Gloucestershire was more prepared for country life than most, but it was his stonemason's skills rather than his rural background that determined where he was sent. On arrival, he was assigned in Sydney to Benjamin Lloyd, who had himself arrived as a convict on the *Asia* in 1820 and was now established in business as a quarryman.[35] At some point Richard changed employers. By 1837 he was working for Mr Thomas Burdekin, also in Sydney, but this relationship failed in April 1840 when his master charged him with 'disorderly conduct, drunkenness etc.', the kind of misdemeanours that in Britain might get a servant dismissed but in the penal colonies had more serious consequences. Tried before the Sydney Quarter Sessions, Nichols was sentenced to twelve calendar months in irons, which he served in the New-castle area.[36] Given Nichols' track record as a prisoner before and after this event, it was a surprising lapse of caution. It may have been caused by the behaviour of his master but he had been with Burdekin at least three years with no other problem surfacing in the records. News from home may have been the real cause of his 'disorderly' behaviour. Nichols had left a wife and two sons behind and as he was literate he could correspond with them. It is possible that he got drunk on learning that his wife would not follow him, or even perhaps that she had died or taken up with someone else.

After his year in the gang, Nichols was assigned in the Hunter Valley. When he obtained a ticket-of-leave in 1843 he was working at Patrick's Plains, later called Singleton. The following year he married Jane Munro, whose father Alexander had brought his family to New South Wales as free settlers in 1839. The couple settled in Singleton, where Nichols prospered buying land and building houses. They had six children and Nichols passed on his knowledge of the stonemason's trade to his eldest boy, James, who became a leading citizen of the town, served as an alderman on the local council and for some years held the licence of The Tradesman's Arms. Richard Nichols lived long enough to see the opening in 1881 of the fine two-storey Commercial Family Hotel in John Street that James had built and which proudly advertised '12 bedrooms,

2 dining rooms, 6 or 7 parlours, a billiard room and a bathroom, the latter supplied by a force feed pump from a large underground tank'.[37]

Despite telling the muster clerk that he was a hatter, Henry Alphan was also assigned to the Hunter district. Born and bred a Londoner, he was convicted at the Old Bailey of stealing jewellery and, although a first offender, sentenced to death. On the face of it, there could have been few men on the *John* less suited to life in the New South Wales bush. Perhaps Henry thought so too at first. Perhaps his employer, Alex Flood, decided he was a useless station hand and returned him to government. Either way, by 1836 Henry was working in Sydney. Then in 1840 he obtained his first ticket-of-leave and a strange thing happened: the Londoner chose the bush after all. Returning to the Hunter Valley, he took a job with the settler Patrick Leslie at Scone. The area was no longer at the edge of settlement and in 1842 Mr Leslie obtained a passport for Henry (and Henry's recently acquired wife Ellen O'Donnald) to accompany him to the new frontier of the Darling Downs.[38] Recalling those times, Leslie could not praise the men who worked for him too highly. 'We had twenty-two men, all ticket-of-leave, or convicts, as good and game a lot of men as ever existed, and who never occasioned us a moment's trouble: worth any forty men I have ever seen since.'[39] A competent stockman and now very familiar with the bush, Henry made his mark by discovering a new stock route (Spicer's Gap) from the Downs to the coastal plains. And his personal story was part of a larger pattern. Unknowingly, his choice of a life in the bush confirmed the evidence given to Commissioner Bigge a decade earlier by the then Superintendent of Convicts, William Hutchinson. Asked by Bigge, 'How long does it take to make a London thief a good farming man?' Hutchinson replied, 'Two or three years', adding in answer to a further probe about how often such transformations occurred, 'Very frequent'.[40]

The men from the *John* who were sent to stations around the Hunter Valley found themselves in circumstances unlike any gaol they had ever experienced. With settlement pushing steadily northwards, the home station was often far to the south—nearer the developing village of Maitland, for instance—and the prisoners were sent by their masters to newly acquired land further out. They were frequently unsupervised, sometimes with just one other man for company, or maybe a small group of three or five, visited at irregular intervals by an overseer. In 1832, the upper reaches of the Hunter were the edge of settlement, very remote and strange to a Briton far from home. A man was thrown on his own resources. To survive, he must adjust to the weird trees and strange rock formations, turn the daring and nerve deployed as a criminal in Britain into steadfastness against new or imagined terrors. Summon his courage against fear of a native spear and his wits in the hunt for lost livestock in unknown territory. Turn the skills previously used in a crowded, damp, unforgiving city into resourcefulness that could fashion his situation to his needs—make a table from a piece of wood, build a shelter from bark and branches, husband a fire when the leaves were damp.

Harassed unmercifully both before and after they became prisoners, such men could recognise that the peaceful life had advantages. Martin Cash served his seven years in the Upper Hunter in the 1830s and summed up the relief provided by the space and the solitude: 'though a measure cut off from society at the time (more "like a great spot in the desert"), our calm and undisturbed mode of life [was] free from the daily annoyances and petty tyranny which at that time men of my class were generally subjected to and which has ever been the bane of my existence'.[41]

Contemporary drawings of convicts

Forced to travel vast distances alone, the men became adept at living in the bush. Some became friendly with the natives, describing them as 'always friendly and obliging'. But they learned new skills from them too. 'In the enjoyment of comparative liberty, I fraternised with the natives, and in a little time became thoroughly acquainted with their manners and customs.'[42] Fishing, for example, was a favourite occupation, fine perch being in abundant supply. But the prize was the local mullet, which was so popular with the Aborigines they refused to barter it with the convicts. Finding their own methods of catching the mullet far less successful, the men watched and learned how the indigenous people did it.[43] But not all encounters between the two races were so benign. Only a few years later, convicts and emancipists slaugh-tered a large number of natives at Waterloo Creek and Myall Creek, murder for which some of them were hanged. At least two of those men were in the upper Hunter with men from the *John*.[44] Nevertheless, as the mullet-catching episode shows, there was also friendly interaction between the two races.

Later generations would depict these convicts as aliens at odds with a foreign world, but that judgement underestimated the men. Contemporary evidence suggests that many, although not all, adjusted to and even admired their new abode. It is not far-fetched to suggest that many shared the feelings of Martin Cash when, after clambering up a steep slope in search of lost sheep, he gazed with something like affinity at the view spread out before him. 'I soon made the top of the range which is the highest land in that part of the Colony, and the fertility of which I believe is not to be surpassed in any quarter of the globe, the grass as far as the eye could reach having all the appearance of young barley when about eight inches high and fully as thick. The land on the opposite side of this range forms a succession of undulating hills intersected by deep ravines and gullies.'[45]

Any close and wide-ranging study of the sources soon reveals that Australian egalitarianism was not forged on the goldfields, as tradition would have it. Equality began in the penal colony, one significant factor being the employment of newly arrived convicts by ex-convicts, another occurring in the far reaches of the bush on outstations like those to which the men from the *John* were sent. Boiling the billy for callers was the normal practice, regardless of class differences. '[A]t this time Captain Bingley, his superintendent and any other gentleman travelling through the bush was not above sharing our hospitality, it being a general understanding throughout the colony.'[46] Life in the bush offset the lack of ethics developed by a life of crime, where lies and dobbing in someone else to improve your own situation were a way of life. Some continued these practices—informers never vanished entirely—but shared hardship resulted in shared resources. Over time that translated into loyalty and a willingness to be dependent on another man or a group of men. Rations were often short-changed, whether the prisoners were working freely in the bush or chained to one another on the roads, and there were incidents when dog ate dog in a vicious, corrupt hierarchy. But shortage of food was also the moment when they learned to share.

> At Captain Pike's farm I have seen the rations of meat for forty men weighed off in the lump, which had afterwards to be divided into individual shares by the men themselves . . . Some of them by this process could not possibly receive the authorised complement of 7 lbs for their week's allowance . . . amongst Captain Pike's servants were to be

found men of all trades: blacksmiths, shipwrights, carpenters, wheelwrights, all of whom shared alike . . . I believe it to be a fair representation of nearly all others throughout the colony.'[47]

This defining experience of life in the bush was not confined to the Hunter. Men assigned to other parts of the colony shared it too, including the miners from Merthyr Tydfil. Someone must have written to Governor Bourke or to the Superintendent of Convicts, Frederick Hely, about Lewsyn yr Heliwr, perhaps warning that he was a dangerous agitator and should be watched. He was allocated on the first assignment list to a settler in Bathurst, very likely because he described himself at the shipboard muster as a farmer as well as a collier. On the supplementary list that re-allocated those whose employers did not collect them, the superintendent's own name was down as Lewsyn's employer. What this meant in practice is hard to determine. Lewsyn may have worked in the superintendent's office for a few months while Hely formed an opinion about him. Or he may have been assigned to help John Busby with the bore. When Lewsyn's employment record was canvassed a decade later, it began in 1835 with his assignment to John Sullivan, a Commissioner of Crown Lands.

Like so many of the prisoners, Lewsyn brought the burden of tragedy and loss, guilt and remorse with him to the colony. Travelling with Sullivan on long forays through the bush, under high blue skies with a sense of limitless space and possibility, the emerald valleys of Wales with their smoky skies and gritty air would have fallen away to a dream that in itself healed the scars of what had occurred there. Many times he must have wanted to share this new world with his family. Within months of receiving his ticket-of-leave in 1840, Lewsyn petitioned for assistance to bring them out. His wife could be found through the Rumney Iron Works, he told the authorities, and he had three children— Margaret aged sixteen, Jenkin aged fourteen and Lewis who was eleven. When making these applications, prisoners were also required to supply references of people in Britain. In light of the politics surrounding the riots in Merthyr Tydfil it is significant that Lewsyn gave the name of the iron master, Josiah Guest, Esq.

In September 1841, Lewsyn was advised that his application had been approved and forwarded to London. And then he waited, working as a carrier around the Port Macquarie district as his ticket-of-leave required. In June 1846 he was granted a passport to work for Mr Charles Steele at the Macleay River for twelve months. Before moving north he applied for a conditional pardon, the only way a lifer could end his sentence. Since transportation to New South Wales ended in 1841, he would have known his chances of success were high.

Sadly, he never knew that a pardon had been granted, or whether his family had decided to travel to the colony. On 6 September 1847 the Superintendent of Convicts received a letter from the Macleay River advising him that Lewis Lewis Prisoner No. 32/1169 had died suddenly. No cause was given. No accident described. His sudden death in his early fifties was apparently from natural causes, perhaps a heart attack.[48]

The other Welsh rioters had mixed fortunes in the colony. Young miner Tom Vaughan had the good fortune to be assigned to James Macarthur, whose family knew a thing or two about the balance between encouragement and control. The Macarthurs, for instance, were one of the few employers who included grog as part of their men's rations, carefully measured of course, and classed as a reward rather than a right, but a heart-warmer nevertheless to a man who had been labouring for them.[49] David Hughes was officially assigned to the Mineral Survey Department based in the south-west at Airds. From there it is possible he was 'lent' to the Macarthurs and sent with Tom Vaughan to their land in the Burra Lake district 100 miles to the south-west. Called Richlands, the Macarthur property was a full day's ride into the bush beyond Goulburn. Barely established in 1832, by 1839 it was a thriving enterprise with around 40 workers employed there. As it was so remote it was vital it had enough supplies and was self-sufficient. Storage in particular was essential. Traces of the miners' work for the Macarthurs remain today in the form of 'bottle bins' at both properties. Deep bottle-shaped holes, some of them over 20 feet deep and perfectly round, the pits were cut down into solid rock. Built by men who knew what they were doing, properly waterproofed with plugs in the top to make them vermin proof, they were excellent for storing wheat. Similar 'bottle pits' are to be found in the coal-mines of Wales, but they are very rare in New South Wales and the ones at Burra have been classified as national heritage.[50]

David Hughes was still in the Airds district, now called Campbelltown, and still working for the Mineral Survey Department in 1839 when he applied to bring his family to New South Wales. He listed them as wife Margaret, living in Merthyr Tydfil, and four children—Mary aged twenty, Betsy fifteen years, Margaret fourteen years and Evan aged eight. Before approving his application, the Convict Department checked their records of Hughes' time in the colony and reported to the Colonial Secretary that he had not transgressed at all. Then, like Lewis Lewis, Hughes waited for news. It was a small community and he had revealed more of his personal circumstances than was wise for a prisoner. Sure enough, when he began living with a local woman, someone remembered his application for a wife in England. The ticket-of-leave he had received in 1842 was cancelled for 'immoral conduct'. Two months later, however, at the behest of someone more worldly and kind, it was restored.

Hughes received his first ticket-of-leave for the Campbelltown district in 1840, by which time he was working as a sawyer, and a ticket-of-leave passport in 1841 allowed him to cart timber to the markets in Sydney. His family never came to the colony. In 1846, when his life sentence ended with a conditional pardon, he married Harriet Craig. Their first child, Charlotte, was born shortly after, with two more children in 1849 and 1856.[51]

Tom Vaughan meanwhile had settled down too. He obtained his ticket-of-leave in 1840 for the Goulburn district, followed by a conditional pardon in 1849. In between, he married Mary Ann Croker, the daughter of an immigrant family who had arrived in 1839 on the *Kinnear*, sponsored by the Macarthurs. While not rich, the Vaughans were well established and well known in the area. Tom acquired land in the parish of Bolong near Laggan, on which he built a stone house named Springwood where the family lived and farmed. When gold was found at nearby Tuena in 1851, it must have stirred an old miner's heart. Very soon after, he purchased his first property at Mianna Creek, but it did not turn out to be a goldmine. Tuena was a lively area, made particularly notorious by several visits from the bushranger Ben Hall who was after the gold, but according to legend danced with the local girls before he left town. The son of convicts himself, Hall had much in common with the smaller settlers.

Tom and Mary Ann had three children. Only young Tom survived to adulthood, but he multiplied the Vaughan clan by producing twelve grandchildren. A 'rioter' in Lord Melbourne's eyes, old Tom became a respected local citizen on the other side of the world. Just a glimpse of his youthful defiance remained detectable in his reputation for being 'the only citizen to arrive at church riding in a sulky, but without a coat and tie'. He is buried at Bolong cemetery and shares his grave with a favourite seven-year-old grandson who died before him. Their burial place is described by a descendant as 'one of the most peaceful cemeteries in Australia, looking out over a huge valley from high on a hill . . . over his beloved Bolong River and the rainbow trout he had chased all his life'.[52]

David Thomas from Merthyr Tydfil spent much of his time as a government man, like David Hughes, working for the Mineral Survey Department. In 1842 he received a ticket-of-leave for the Newcastle district, followed twelve months later by a passport allowing him to proceed to New England in the service of the Land Commissioner, William Denne. No word of him surfaced for five years until he turned up in Newcastle in April 1848. There his good record turned upside down when he was charged with indecent assault on a girl 'less than ten years of age'. According to the evidence the girl had been playing with her ten-year-old brother when Thomas approached and asked if she would shake his hand and give him a kiss. According to her brother she refused at first, but then did kiss him when he gave her a penny. He then persuaded the girl, whose name was Ann Birrell, to walk with him in the bush, telling her brother to go away. The boy ran home to tell his father. Inexplicably, Mr Birrell stayed at home but told his son to run back to his sister immediately. Consequently, the evidence that Ann was screaming in the bush when he arrived, and crying as they made their way home, depended on the testimony of a boy. Only then did the father and a friend go in search of Thomas. It must have been a passionate confrontation, with the father telling Thomas he would 'pull him', meaning before the Bench, and Thomas trying to dissuade him. Denying that he assaulted the girl, he told Birrell that if he was pulled, he would 'get another lagging'. He then left Newcastle, Birrell reported him and Thomas was picked up ten days later in Muswellbrook. He was not charged with rape and the judge took some care to distinguish for the jury the need to decide on whether he actually committed an indecent assault with intent to rape. David Thomas appears to have accepted fatalistically that he was lagged. According to the *Maitland Mercury* he 'did not make much of a defence', but he did call several character referees. Sentenced to seven years hard labour on the roads or public works of some kind, he was granted a ticket-of-leave for the district of Broulee in 1852 but disappears from the record after that.[53]

Isaac Fisher, the poacher who cut and wounded a gamekeeper in Gloucestershire, spent only a short time in the service of Robert Cooper. Convicted of a colonial crime in 1835, he was sentenced to Norfolk Island. Arriving back in Sydney on 30 November 1839, he was forwarded to Cockatoo Island for the balance of his sentence.[54] When finally released, he returned to the Goulburn district where he had been first assigned, obtaining a ticket-of-leave there in 1841. At the time of his conviction in England, Isaac was a widower with one son. In Goulburn, he married Sarah Blakeley in 1852, but she died twelve months later, aged 48. The following year, Isaac developed a relationship with Elizabeth (surname unknown) and the pair subsequently had five children. He was 85 years old and the events in Gloucestershire and, for that matter, in Norfolk Island, were far behind when he died in 1887.[55]

Also in Goulburn were the brothers who walked two stolen horses through the night in Yorkshire and whose names eventually proved to be Stapleton, not West. The older brother, Abraham, managed to switch his original assignment from the ship to Sir John Wylde so he could join Francis, who had been sent to John Richardson at Six Mile Creek. The brothers stuck together for some years. By the 1837 Muster, for instance, they were both working for John Skinner at Raymond Terrace near Newcastle. Francis received a ticket-of-leave for that district in 1840, and the following year the ticket became a passport that allowed him to accompany his employer, John Kelso, up the Hunter and over the range to New England.[56] By that time, Abraham had moved away. He may have been working for someone else, or he may have received a colonial sentence. When he obtained a ticket-of-leave in 1843 he was in Goulburn, where he settled and married Mary Ellingham in 1853. Some time in the next six years, Francis fell ill. He was with his brother in Goulburn when he died aged 46 in 1859. Abraham lived in the Wollondilly area near Goulburn until he too died in 1871.[57]

James Wilde, who had insisted on taking the blame for pickpocketing so his co-accused Thomas Haw could return to his family, was sent further afield than most, to the far south-west at Yass Plains. His employer, Henry O'Brien, was the major settler in the area and also acted as the local magistrate. The two men got off to a difficult start. O'Brien had asked for a carpenter, so he was disappointed when Wilde turned up. On the other hand, although convicted in Nottinghamshire, his newly assigned servant was born in Manchester, where he acquired skills as a turner and machine-maker. Only 22 he was also, as the confession in England demonstrated, a man of some character. He would not have taken kindly to having his ability derided by O'Brien, who complained bitterly to the Colonial Secretary that Wilde was 'assigned as a carpenter of which profession he was quite ignorant'. O'Brien was told in effect to take him or leave him and he managed to make do for over two years, but from Wilde's point of view they must have been unpleasant. In late 1834 matters came to a head, at which point

Contemporary drawing of a convict

Wilde either absconded or, as O'Brien later claimed, was returned to government. In any event, he had to walk the several hundred miles to Sydney. Distance may have confused the issue because Wilde's arrest was announced in January 1835. As punishment for being at large, he was sent to iron gang No. 8, based west of Sydney. From there, only two months later, an unnamed labourer was assigned to Henry Cox at Penrith. Very likely this was James Wilde, who appears in the muster eighteen months later as working for Cox.

Wilde must have been happy as a gardener at the Cox property, Glenmore Park, because he stayed with the family for a long time. While there, he met Edward Cox's 16-year-old servant girl, Elizabeth Laurence, and when James received his certificate of freedom in 1839 they married at St Thomas' Church in nearby Mulgoa. The first four of their twelve children were born at Glenmore before they left the Cox family in 1850 and moved into the growing town of

Penrith, where James worked in the construction industry as a water carrier. Like many ex-convicts, he remained vulnerable to charges of theft or other criminal offences. If something was missing, fingers quickly pointed at the person who was known to have been a government man. And James liked a drop to drink, which increased his risk. In 1849, one of his drinking mates charged him with theft of three £1 notes and James was searched. The money was found at his feet but he denied it came from him. In court, the evidence that both parties were very drunk at the time, plus the refusal of the prosecutor to identify the money, resulted in the jury delivering a verdict of not guilty. Despite this close shave, James continued to enjoy a drop, and very likely 'one too many' was the reason he died after falling from a bridge on New Year's Eve, 1864. He was 54 years old.[58]

James Jaye had trained as a pastrycook, although he was unemployed in London when caught stealing lead from the roof of the Asylum for the House-less Poor. His name appears on the first assignment list for the *John* as allocated to D.G. Howard, but he was in fact assigned to J.B. Richards, a surveyor, who had been mapping the country west of the mountains since the previous year. In Richard's employ, Jaye travelled in a wide circle around and beyond Bathurst, out to Wellington and Orange, to Cowra and down the Lachlan River. Along the way they surveyed farms and designated roads, laid out the town plan for Carcoar and completed the task of laying out the streets of Bathurst to a plan approved by Governor Darling. Richards settled in the town and later owned the property Carwyman at nearby Kelso, where he grew grapes and made wine in the 1870s. James Jaye obtained his ticket-of-leave in 1836 and he too settled in Bathurst. Since Richards continued his survey work until at least 1843, it is likely that Jaye continued working with him. Meanwhile he married Ann Storrett, the youngest girl on the *Princess Royal*, who may have been working as a servant for Mr Richards. By the time James received his certificate of freedom in 1840, they were the parents of Rachael, the first of their seven children. The Jayes raised their family in and around the Bathurst and Orange area, and when the gold rush began near Ophir in 1851 they were in the thick of it. In another example of an enterprising ex-convict spotting an opening, James began to advertise his services as a tinsmith—selling tin trays and dishes to the thousands of miners arriving daily in the area. In time, he went into partnership with William Freeman, who later married the Jayes' daughter, Rachael.[59]

Most of the convicts were young men in their early to mid twenties, and the men of the *John* were very youthful indeed. In fact, the ship might well have been termed a 'boatload of boys'. Of the 200 prisoners on board, 40 per cent were aged twenty or less, ten being under sixteen, including a twelve-year-old named Daniel Croker. He was a tailor's boy convicted of stealing spoons. With a little freckled face, fair skin turned ruddy from the sunshine of months at sea, he stood 4 feet 1 inch tall when he landed at Sydney. His companions included the fourteen-year-olds Edward Hulbert, who was a stable boy convicted of stealing linen, Daniel Hammond, an errand boy who stole money, and John Stanford, a brickmaker's boy who stole a cap. Dublin-born John Deal had worked in a cotton factory in Lancashire. Samuel Rowney or Rooney was a chimneysweep convicted of stealing a coat from his father. It would be nice to think that his father had prosecuted his son in order to send him to a new life with his brother George in New South Wales, but it is unlikely. The boy bore a grudge against older men who ticked him off like his father.[60]

In earlier days, child convicts were left to fend for themselves, but by 1830 the colonial authorities were desperate to find a solution to the problem of an increasing number of them arriving as prisoners.[61] In Van Diemen's Land when the *John* arrived, Governor Arthur was about to establish a settlement especially for boys called Point Puer, on the long finger of land across the bay from the penal settlement of Port Arthur. In New South Wales it had become the practice to send youths to Carters' Barracks in Sydney to learn a trade. There were also two orphan schools, which had been relocated away from the town environment by Governor and Mrs Macquarie. The male school was a farm near Liverpool. The Female Orphan School, designed by Mrs Macquarie in 1813, was on the banks of the Parramatta River at Rydalmere.[62] Other options for placing youthful convicts were the government-run Grose Farm in Sydney and an establishment at Emu Plains. Since 1825, the Church and School Corporation, which administered the orphan schools, had also operated a farm-cum-school at Bathurst. It closed in 1832, but when the *John* arrived a school was being built to replace it at the soldier settlement reserve at nearby White Rock.[63] Several of the boys were sent there.[64]

In the first instance, however, the ten youngest of the *John*'s convicts were sent to Carters' Barracks, where some of them immediately played merry hell with the authorities. John Stanford and Samuel Rowney were the ringleaders. Much of an age, they were both constantly in trouble, but as rivals rather than friends. In November 1832 Samuel received 'six stripes on the back' for allowing a window blind to be 'injured' while he was in charge of the ward. The week after, John Stanford absconded and spent six days in the cells when he was returned. The week after that, Samuel absconded, for which he spent three days in the cells. In December, they both spent time in the cells again for absconding, but separately. Samuel had taken another boy, Daniel Hammond, with him this time. Soon after, Daniel was sent off to Bathurst, no doubt to get him away from 'bad company'. Also in December, John Stanford was sent to the cells for two days for beating Samuel. Next, Samuel received another six stripes and a day in the cells for having 'dirty slops on Sunday morning'.

Every time either boy absconded, he was picked up around Sydney and returned by an exasperated police magistrate at Hyde Park Barracks. In May 1833, less than a year after their arrival, he finally sentenced both John Stanford and Samuel Rowney separately to an iron gang. It was an extraordinarily harsh decision and the Superintendent of Carters' Barracks intervened to suggest they be diverted to work on Goat Island instead.[65] Whether Samuel and John benefited from this suggestion is not clear. They may have been sent to Bathurst instead because each can subsequently be found in the area assigned to private employers, but John Richie, a boy from another ship who was with them at Carters' Barracks, ended up in an iron gang at Cox's River.[66]

To varying degrees, all the boys received some instruction in a trade while they were at Carters' Barracks. Daniel Croker and Joseph Collier learnt the skills of a harnessmaker. Edward Hulbert and John

Stanford were in the wheelwrights' class. Joseph White and James Brewer learnt to be coopers, Daniel Hammond to garden. Samuel Rowney's chosen trade was ropemaker.[67] Their fortunes in the colony were mixed. Samuel's career will be traced in the next chapter. Little Daniel Croker proved hard to track. He appears to have been sent to Bathurst from Carters' Barracks. After receiving his certificate of freedom in 1839 he can be traced to the Bathurst–Wellington district by letters sent to him at the post office in 1844, 1845, 1846 and 1848. After that, he vanishes.[68]

Contemporary drawing of a convict

Some of the children can be traced in assignment. By mid-1835, and probably earlier, Joseph White was working for the pastoralist James Mudie in the Hunter Valley. Mudie was notorious for the harsh regime at his station implemented by his superintendent John Lanark. Twice in quick succession, Joseph was in trouble for losing sheep. In July he was sentenced to 25 lashes for losing one. In September he was charged with failing to deliver the full complement of 39 lambs and 41 ewes from his flock into another man's flock. Questioned by Thomas James, the sheep overseer, about what he had done with the missing six, Joseph replied, 'Bugger it, I never had them.' Taken aback at this insolence, James threatened to stop his tea and sugar rations, at which point Joseph compounded his sins by laughing as he replied, 'What the hell if you do.

I'll have someone else's.' Far from being intimidated before the magistrates, Joseph insisted the overseer had not counted the lambs as he claimed and called two other shepherds as witnesses. They proved unhelpful, however. Richard Perry testified that the overseer did count the lambs before sending Joseph off with them, although his testimony also revealed that Joseph was simultaneously responsible for 350 older sheep. At this point Charles Forbes, who was sitting as magistrate, made up his mind and sentenced Joseph to 50 lashes. When the convict muster was taken about a year later, Joseph had managed to change employers. He was listed as working for the partnership of Uhr & Jones further up the Hunter at Cassilis, where he stayed until 1841, when he was given a passport by the Scone Bench to travel with pastoralist Richard Cobcroft to the Liverpool Plains. The following year he received a ticket-of-leave for the district of Maitland. Five years later, he finally received a certificate of freedom.[69]

The convicts were objects of curiosity, speculation, denigration and amazement from polite society. Their character was debated constantly, and never more so than their performance as servants. Whether or not the convict maid had stolen the grog, or the gardener had forgotten to dig over the vegetable patch or worse still had been too drunk to do it, was the subject of endless, enjoyable conversation in the colony. In Britain, it was more their 'depravity' of language, behaviour and attitudes that occupied the dinner tables and the parliament. Everyone who visited the colony had an opinion. George Bennett, who was there in 1834, described an assigned convict as: 'An individual who is well fed and clothed—insolent and indolent and takes care that the little work he has to do is badly done.' Frequently, such condemnation was triggered by some personal experience that was not acknowledged. Easier to appear as a considered voice of wisdom than reveal that some cocky, good-for-nothing Shropshire thief had given you cheek. Other contemporary visitors agreed with Bennett, describing the convicts as 'men of the most dissolute character' whose 'vicious depravity' immediately reappeared when they were free as 'idleness, drunkenness'. There was never a consensus, however. Many landholders who knew the prisoners first-hand claimed they were 'trustworthy, hard working, civil and obedient'. Some commentators were 'struck with the ruddy, healthy and athletic looks of the young convicts'. And why not? They were not brutalised old men. Most of them were little more than teenagers. Their 'good behaviour' was also remarked upon, but social class shaped opinion about this. Alexander Harris, who mixed with the lower orders, described them as people of 'manly independence of disposition', while to Commissioner Bigge whose sources were 'the best informed inhabitants', they displayed 'vanity and ostentatious appearance'. Same convicts. Different point of view.

The prisoners, of course, had their own opinions. Since expressing some of them would lead to a flogging, they found other ways. Robert Howcroft, a Yorkshire errand boy who had been convicted of stealing books at the age of thirteen, worked for the solicitor George Wigram Allen, who was a devout Methodist. The battle of wills that developed between servant and master began one Sunday when Allen sent the boy to the watch-house for refusing to attend prayers. It was aggravated another Sunday when he sent Robert a second time for drunkenness. In the following months, Robert protested mutely, but in a way calculated to distress his master intensely. Deeply upset, Allen confided in his diary, '[He] makes a point of going to sleep every time we have service. I have spoken to him over and over again. Where it will end I know not but it is really awful to see such depravity in a mere child. If he could not help it, it would be different but to see a lad compose himself to sleep as soon as the sermon or prayer be commenced is really *awful*.'[70]

Those convicts who found an employer with whom they were content received quite a different press. A settler writing home from Hobart in 1822 told his friend:

> You know that the greater part of servants and others, in this country, is composed of convicts, sent out for crimes committed. This it may be imagined would be the greatest evil the settler has to encounter. I have invariably found that where the master was wise, and kind, the servants have been good and faithful; and vice versa. The easiness of their condition—the removal of temptation—the certainty of subsistence; and, above all the habit of honesty, causes a transformation as surprising as complete. The lot of the labourer in England is not to be compared with the condition of the labourer here.[71]

In Britain in 1837, the Select Committee on Transportation known as the Molesworth Committee concluded that assignment was an unacceptable punishment because it was 'a mere lottery'. Like others before them, the Committee wanted punishment in New South Wales to fit the crime. This was a goal that was never reached. The crimes committed in Britain were utterly immaterial once the prisoners stepped onto the boat. Punishment in the penal colonies fitted behaviour in the penal colonies. Frustrated by the inconsistencies in the system, the Committee complained that 'no single case can be looked upon as a type of the whole system', which in the Committee's opinion was plainly a failure. The possibility its inconsistency was a strength never occurred to anyone. Despite condemning the system, the Committee failed to abolish it (although transportation to New South Wales ended shortly after, in 1841).

In one respect, however, the Molesworth Committee did succeed in creating yet another stereotype about the penal colonies. Assignment as 'a lottery' entered the lexicon of almost all subsequent commentators, and of several generations of professional historians. Never mind that everyone over-looked the impact of the desires, will and street-smart manoeuvres of the objects under discussion, the convicts themselves. They could manipulate the system by ingratiation, by insolence, by passive disobedience, by bad work-manship and, sometimes, by outright defiance. If they wished to change assignment, the women prisoners got themselves returned to the government as 'useless' with relative ease. They would then be sent to the Female Factory, where the circuitous process of reassignment would begin again until the women found a place that suited them. It was much harder for the men. Like the women, they soon learned that the way to change assignment was to make your employer so dissatisfied that he would return you to government. But not all of them realised that fine judgement was required about how to do it. Misjudge the degree to which you upset your master and the retribution could be terrible. Also, the men were disadvantaged in a way the women were not. Employers would persevere with their male labour force far more than they would with women. However resistant and unsatisfactory they were as workers, male convicts supplied the essential labour that the settlers needed. They would not part with them easily.

A.G.L. Shaw assessed private assignment as 'a remarkably successful attempt to arrange for basically a civilian population to supervise criminals'.[72] From the prisoners' point of view, the alternative was gaol in England in the dungeons of a castle or on the hulks. For all the rigours apparent to 21st-century eyes, to the prisoners private assignment in the penal colonies was easy by comparison. Even the Quaker visitors Backhouse and Walker, whose scrutiny of the penal colonies was sceptical and critical, commented that assignment was 'superior to that of the Jail system in England'.[73]

G.F. Davidson spent three years on the land at Paterson in the Hunter Valley. He gave a master's view of the benefit of the lash. 'The convict servant soon finds out what sort of a master he has to deal with and, to use their own slang, after trying it on for a bit, in nine cases out of ten, he yields to circum-stances. Two of mine tried a few of their old pranks at starting; but a timely, though moderate application of "the cat" put an entire stop to them.'[74] But a 'moderate application' was not always the case. Reading details of floggings, often for trivial offences, particularly when following individual cases, creates revulsion and anger on the prisoners' behalf. However, it is necessary to remember that this was a time when flogging was common. It was not peculiar to Australia. As we saw in Chapter 3, soldiers and sailors were frequently flogged nearly to death. Adults and children, too, were whipped as criminals in Britain, and in the case of the children, in workhouses and in schools. Australia was unique because its vast wilderness was a gaol without walls, through which the prisoners roamed widely, and often alone. As John Hirst pointed out, 'the lash had to do the work of the walls, the warders and the punishment cells'.[75]

In any event, analysis of the prisoners on the *John* suggests that the great majority survived their sentence with minimal encounters with the lash or indeed a bench of magistrates. They are notable more by their absence from the records than by frequent transgressions and floggings. In this, their experience is consistent with the findings of Norma Townsend and David Kent for the men from the *Eleanor* and, more recently, those of Brian Walsh in his study of the Tocal estate. Many stayed with their original master for years. The pattern evident among these men is similar to that found by Brian Walsh, who concluded that 32 per cent of the men assigned to James Webber at Tocal served their full sentences with him, and that the 55 per cent of his total sample who did change masters only did so once or twice. Walsh's material also suggested that only a minority of the Tocal group were punished by official judicial process and that rewards and incentives operated as an effective alternative. The prisoners of the *John* provide similar evidence. As with the Tocal group, the turnover in assignments and the punishments were concentrated in a small group.[76]

Some observers gave the penal system the credit for reform rather than the men. French naturalist, M. Peron, said, 'All these unfortunate wretches, the disgrace of their country, have become, by the most inconceivable metamorphosis, laborious cultivators, and happy and peaceful members of their community.' Charles Darwin was more sceptical when he visited in 1836. Despite his belief that 'any moral reform [appeared] to be quite out of the question', he nevertheless felt that transportation was 'a means of making men outwardly honest'. Darwin's doubts notwithstanding, the story of assignment in New South Wales, which is also the story of assignment in Van Diemen's Land for the first 40 years, is the story of the world's largest rehabilitation program. Its elements of abrupt change to a new environment mixed with personal challenge make it the nineteenth-century equivalent of Outward Bound. It had flaws. Floggings and bullying and vindictiveness frequently occurred. The prisoners were never saints. Nevertheless, it is overwhelmingly a sufficiently positive story to be a source of pride not shame.

Of course there is an opposing story. While transportation lasted, the division between those who believed one version or the other was for many years generally a division between, on the one hand, the colonists of all classes and status, including their officials and their governors, and on the other hand the observers, whether distant or just passing through. John Hirst called the latter group 'enemies' of convict society.[77] Around the middle of the nineteenth century, the contest between the two versions reached a peak in which the idea of the convict stain would play a major part in deciding the victor. Before turning to that subject, the negative version of the transportation experience must be explored.

CHAPTER 6
the bathurst road

'Your money, or your life.' Patrick Quigley came out of the creek bed in a rush, yelling the traditional demand of the legendary highwayman. Nothing else was traditional or in any way romantic. No cloak or black mask. Just the ragged slop clothing marked with the broad arrow that designated a serving convict. No finely crafted pistol either, nor a display of courtesy. Quigley carried a large thick stick, which he used to beat his prey so violently about the head that he brought him to the ground. His victim, whose name was Joseph Ashford, lived about thirteen miles further down the dusty track known as the Bathurst Road, not far from a large pastoral station named Bilong. In the bush tradition, Mr Lee, who owned the station, had offered Ashford hospitality the night before. That morning, Ashford had walked nearly two miles of the final stretch of his journey when Quigley sprang at him. 'Through bodily fear I gave him fifteen shillings and sixpence,' Ashford told the magistrate. But Quigley was not satisfied. According to Ashford, he insisted there was more. Quigley was as desperate as Ashford was frightened. The confrontation turned into a fierce hand-to-hand struggle. Quigley extracted Ashford's pocketbook, which contained memorandum and receipts. But Ashford meanwhile had been able to draw his knife, and as the two men wrestled he plunged it into the bushranger's side. 'After I wounded him, he ran away. I tried to follow but I was too weak,' Ashford reported. Nevertheless, he dragged himself to another station nearby, where information was sent to the police.

After hearing from Mr Ashford, Mounted Police Sergeant John Trantor went looking for a bushranger. Word reached him there was a man lying injured at Bilong. Trantor told the magistrate he was carrying the latest copy of the *Government Gazette* and it helped him identify the injured man as Patrick Quigley, who had absconded from the Hassan's Walls stockade about five weeks before. When he confronted Quigley, 'He first refused to tell me his name but subsequently admitted himself to be the man.'[1]

Identified by both Ashford and the police sergeant, Quigley was well and truly lagged. He was committed for trial before the Supreme Court in Sydney, and the local authorities asked for him back if he was found not guilty of bushranging—'to be dealt with for absconding for the 5th time', wrote police magistrate John Kinchella.[2] In fact, all parties knew he would be lucky to escape with his life.

It was April 1838. Quigley had been in the colony six years. When last seen, he held a supervisory position on the *John* that brought him the small privileges so essential to a prisoner's life. Now he was facing the ultimate penalty, and this despite having the advantage of being a convict soldier rather than a common criminal, which was a significant difference to the colonial authorities. After all, the reasoning went, they had 'only' been court-martialled. And 'only' for something like desertion, which was not a crime outside the military. On this basis, convict soldiers were often chosen to act as overseers or in other roles that gave them privileges and power.[3] Of course, civilians under-estimated both what it took to disobey the army and the effect military service could have on a man's character, if not his soul. At that time, taking the King's shilling was for life. There was no escape—except by death or, as it turned out, by transportation. Many soldiers had been flogged many times before they ever set foot in the penal colonies, and for many more lashes than was permit-ted in New South Wales in the 1830s. Fifty lashes was nothing compared with the 150 Patrick Quigley had already received in London. The long recital of escape and retribution that brought Quigley to the point of highway robbery in New South Wales revealed the tyrannical determination of the government to bend prisoners to its will, a refusal to be 'bested', as the notorious com-mandant John Price described it. Equally apparent was Patrick Quigley's determination not to succumb. He would go his own way, regardless. The result was a profound battle of wills with all the cards stacked against the prisoner.

When he landed four years earlier, in June 1832, Quigley had been assigned to John Hall in Sydney. Master and servant appear to have tolerated one another for about nine months before Quigley got drunk and Hall resorted to the magistrate at Hyde Park Barracks, who ordered Quigley flogged. An alter-native punishment option for those convicts assigned in Sydney was a sentence to the treadmill. Housed in Carters' Barracks along with the boys' trade school, it was used for punishing serving soldiers and civilians as well as prisoners. Barely two months after his flogging, another clash with his master resulted in a charge of insolence, for which the Hyde Park Bench ordered Quigley to the revolving steps. He absconded soon after, and by August was in a road party for the first time. Then the pattern of absconding, flogging, absconding, flogging began.

Patrick Quigley's record

1832	June	Assigned to John Hall, Sydney
1833	May 6	30 lashes, drunkenness
	July 1	21 days treadmill—insolence
	August 19	Absconded
	August 24	50 lashes, absconding
	November 7	Absconded 2nd time from No. 10 Road Party
1834	March 19	50 lashes, pilfering from a fellow prisoner
	March	Absconded from Bathurst Road
	March	Arrested on Bathurst Road
	May 20	Absconded
	June 9	12 months in irons for absconding
	June 26	40 lashes—feigning sickness
1835		No record, presumably labouring in irons
	November	Wangles visit to Sydney as witness at a trial
1836	September 30	12 months irons for absconding
	October 8	35 lashes for exchanging clothes
	October 12	Arrested—had absconded from W. Calf, Bathurst
	December 3	50 lashes—smoaking [*sic*] in stockade and telling a lie
1837		Muster at Hassan's Walls, Vale of Clwydd (Bathurst Road)
1838	March 2	Absconded from Hassan's Walls (Bathurst Road)
	April 6	Highway robbery of Joseph Ashford[4]

When he attacked Joseph Ashford, Quigley was an escapee from the worst punishment that could then be inflicted, short of transportation to a secondary penal settlement at Moreton Bay or Norfolk Island. It took a record of previous offences before a man was sentenced to labour on the construction of the Bathurst Road. To the authorities it had the advantage of being well away from the increasingly populated Cumberland Plain, for once the road began to climb the Blue Mountains it was almost entirely remote. Except for a handful of inn-keepers, no one had yet settled in the mountains. Beautiful to someone with a full belly and warm shelter, they were rocky and inhospitable and freezing to a man on the run. On the other side of the main escarpment it was little better if you were a bolter. Freezing in winter, scorching in summer, only slightly less difficult country to penetrate than the mountains, it was a largely dry, vast wilderness, with only scattered pastoral stations until you reached the settlement of Bathurst, 130 miles west of Sydney. Building the Great Western Highway, as it came to be called, was the biggest project under way in Sydney at the time. Busby's Bore might match it for engineering challenges, but in scale, the western road predominated. Its importance in both practical terms and as a symbol of early achievement is reflected in the appellation 'Great'.

Construction of the road was at its height during the 1830s, expanding, repairing and improving the first version driven through by William Cox and a party of convicts in 1814–15. Stockades and makeshift camps were based along the road to house the workers and their military guards. Nothing was static about the arrangement. Stockades opened and closed. Small road parties moved from camp to camp, according to the site of the current works. Regiments came and went almost as frequently as the changing population of prisoners. The major stockade actually on the mountains, which was known as 20 Mile Hollow, remained operative through most of the roadbuilding era. Situated near modern-day Woodford and distant enough from the base camp at Emu Plains to deter absconders, it was set in an area where the rocky ridges levelled briefly into something resembling a plateau. The ridges rose steeply

Convicts building the road over the Blue Mountains

again in this area, presenting the engineers with a series of tricky challenges as well as back-breaking work for the prisoners. Some kind of camp had existed at 20 Mile Hollow since the roadworks began, but by the 1830s there was housing for convicts, soldiers, stores and the local commandant spread over a two-mile site.[5] Seventy miles further, among the rolling, comparatively gentle hills below the steep western escarpment, was No. 2 stockade, at Cox's River. Nearby was its outstation, the Hassan's Walls stockade. Further back along the road was a second outstation at the foot of Mount Victoria. Established in 1832, accommodation at Cox's River included a fully fenced stockade for the several hundred prisoners based there, a commissariat store, plus barracks and accommodation for officials. Most welcome of all from the prisoners' point of view, there was a hospital with a resident surgeon who was attached to whatever regiment was currently in the vicinity.[6]

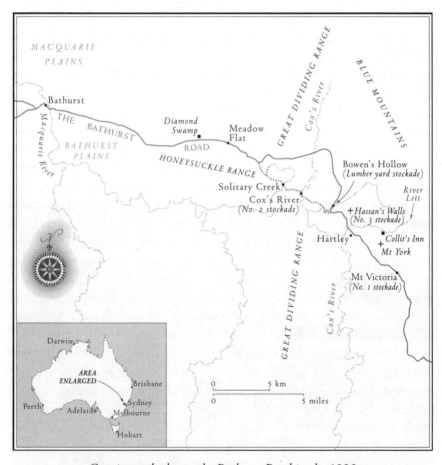

Convict stockades on the Bathurst Road in the 1830s

The number of convicts working in and around this area must have amounted to at least 500 men. In 1832, there were 219 men working in irons at the Mount Victoria stockade alone. Most of them transferred to Cox's River when it opened that year, but prisoners continued to be based at Mount Victoria or at Hassan's Walls, as well as 20 Mile Hollow, and the numbers would have risen as the number of convicts rose during the decade. Those working closer to the stockades were usually in irons, but others further afield in smaller road parties were not shackled. In addition there were jobs around the stockades—watchmen, cooks, hospital assistants, clerks.[7]

When the *Sir William Bensley* men were distributed in 1817, some of them were held back by the government to be used in clearing parties and bridge building, not to mention the specialised trade gangs used to build specific government projects in Sydney. If they required serious punishment, they were sent to Newcastle. Following a policy established by Governor Darling, sentence to the gangs had become a calculated punishment by the 1830s, but it remained the way in which the government mobilised the prisoners' labour for large-scale projects.

One of the convict clerks, Thomas Cook, left a record of his time on the Bathurst Road. In England, his life's experience had been a middle-class childhood culminating in apprenticeship to a solicitor when he was fourteen. Transported in 1831 on the *Surrey* for sending a threatening letter, he spent some years as a clerk in Sydney before running foul of the superintendent of Hyde Park Barracks. This unfortunate clash with power resulted not long after in a colonial sentence to labour on the mountain road, from which even the intervention of the Superintendent of Convicts was unable to save him. Mentally prepared to some extent by the tales he had heard, the reality of life in a road gang still overwhelmed Cook. Without detracting from the misery experienced by all the convicts who worked in gangs, Cook's background has to be borne in mind when reading his descriptions. Most of the men transported had been less fortunate and sheltered than he. They were used to harsh conditions, to being cold, to having no warm clothes or blankets and not enough food. They had experienced all these things in Britain. To Thomas Cook, their absence was a shock. His imagination, he said as he recounted his arrival at Honeysuckle Flat, had not prepared him for one-tenth of what he must endure: 'The dismal appearance, and still more dilapidated state of the habitation, which exposed its inmates to the inclemency of the weather—the wretched and haggard countenances of the men, the severity of the cold and the want of a second or even one good blanket to save the half frozen man from perishing.'[8]

Cook was also shocked by the society of the gangs, where all the brutality of hard men trying to survive hard conditions was on display. A hierarchy of power operated within them in which brute strength, ruthlessness, bravado and corruption were prized. The corruption of power was not limited to the gangs. According to Cook, it went right up to the Sub-Inspector of Roads and, under him, the overseers, an allegation that has been confirmed by the recent doctoral research into the western road by Sue Rosen and earlier investigation by Peter MacFie of the Grass Hill Road Gang in Van Diemen's Land.[9] It made complaining about something like the unfair distribution of rations imposs-ible. It was not just a matter of officials 'turning a blind eye'. With or without the compliance of the overseers, but frequently at their behest, men from the gangs supplemented their rations by preying on the stock and goods of farms in the vicinity.[10] Violence was endemic. Language crude. Occasionally, anger would explode into rage and prisoners murdered each other with a shovel or a pick. Sometimes, as we shall see, a man's rage was directed to one of the guards who, like the overseers, had the power to torment and harass the prisoners.

It would be misleading, however, to cast the society of the gangs as an example of class or race discrimination. This was not a simple structure of 'Us' versus 'Them'. Examples exist not only of prisoners and overseers cooperating to their mutual benefit, but even more significantly of soldiers and convicts collaborating and absconding together. For instance, Rosen describes a mixed group of four convicts and four privates from the 4th Kings Own Regiment who, having run away together, went on to become bushrangers. Furthermore, when violent crimes such as murder or rape were committed, the perpetrator could be one of the guards rather than a prisoner. Knowledge of the soldier convicts who feature in this book explains how easily this blurring of distinc-tion between guard and prisoners could occur.[11]

Sex between men in the gang was apparently common, although it is hard to be sure how common. Reading Cook's manuscript creates a suspi-cion that some extremes of behaviour and language were displayed just for the benefit of the young Mr Cook. Wide-eyed with horror, he contemplated 'the horrible propensities which the coarse and brutish language of my gang-mates in calamity, coupled with their assignations one towards the other, shortly told me the greater number of them had imbibed. So far advanced were these wretched men in depravity, that they appeared to have entirely lost the feelings of men and had imbibed those that would render them execrable to all mankind.'[12] While there is no doubt sex was being used as a means of corruption and intimidation in the gangs, it should also be noted that Thomas Cook, who was himself the subject of sexual approaches, never-theless survived several years on the Bathurst Road unmolested. If his fellow gang members had been as overwhelmingly depraved as he claims, this would surely not have been possible.

When Patrick Quigley first arrived on the Bathurst Road in 1834, the numbers of prisoners were at their peak. In one of those extraordinary twists, which occur so frequently in what Mark Twain described as Australia's 'picturesque' history, the commandant of Cox's River was Captain George Deedes of the 17th Regiment of Foot. Quigley's old regiment served in the colony from 1828 to 1836 and had in fact been in the process of transferring to the colony, in batches, when Quigley deserted in London in 1831 (which is also why there were several of them, as guards, on board the *John*). Among the guard on this stretch of the Bathurst Road were about 73 soldiers from the 17th, a number of whom Quigley would have known well from his nine years among their ranks. Some may have borne old grudges. Many would have sympathised with his situation. It can be no coincidence that Quigley's attempts to abscond from the Bathurst Road that year matched the time when his regiment pulled out at the end of its term at Cox's River (in June 1834).[13] Quigley's feelings when they left must have been bleak enough without the punishment he then endured for trying to go with them. For the first time, he was ironed round the ankles. Then, two weeks later, he was flogged 40 times for a charge of 'feigning sickness'.[14]

Prisoners under escort to Bathurst Gaol

While Quigley endured the Bathurst Road, some of his shipmates were in equal strife elsewhere in the colony. At Cox's River, he had just missed the London burglar, Tom Stacey, who had been there throughout 1833. Assigned initially to the architect John Verge, Stacey had either been returned or absconded immediately because they were chasing him as a bolter within two months of the *John* docking. Sentenced to a gang on the northern road, Stacey absconded again from his escort to the stockade at Wollombi. Around November, he was sent to Cox's River in the hope that distance would stop him absconding. His record for 1833 shows this plan failed almost immediately.

Thomas Stacey's record at Cox's River

1833	January 26	Absconded 50 lashes, and 50 lashes for [illegible]
	January 30	Theft—12 months in irons
	May 1	Absconded from No. 2 Stockade (Cox's River)
	May 9	Arrested
	June 6	Concealing Kagte—50 lashes
	October 8	Absconded from No. 2 Stockade 'second time run'
	November 11	Arrested—12 months irons. Gambling—25 lashes
	December 28	Refusing to answer the guards at night—50 lashes
	Dec 30	Absconded[15]

Like Quigley four years later, Stacey took to the bush. Unlike Quigley, he had company. He had been working with six men, all in irons, when they hatched a plot to escape. Three of them—George Bramner, William Johnson and John Whelan—overpowered their sentry and stole his musket and bayonet before fleeing. Stacey, Peter Thompson and 15-year-old John Ritchie followed hard on their heels. Now officially termed 'bushrangers', they trudged miles through the unforgiving country until they reached the outskirts of Bathurst. Musket and bayonet enforced their commands as they invaded the house of a settler named David Ramsay. Finding he was away, they held up his servants instead, at least one of whom was convinced they would kill him. Despite his terror, he was unharmed when they left laden with Ramsay's supplies.

They were caught, of course. Taken before the Supreme Court in February 1834 on charges of highway robbery (the musket and bayonet) and housebreaking, their case was to be heard by a military jury, a remnant of the martial law of the original penal settlement. Not surprisingly, the soldiers found Bramner, Johnson and Whelan guilty of overpowering the guard. All six men were found guilty of housebreaking and Mr Justice Burton sentenced them to transportation for life to Norfolk Island.[16]

A satellite settlement established in the earliest days of the colony and abandoned later, Norfolk Island was re-settled in 1825 at the same time as the establishment of Moreton Bay. Both were chosen in accordance with recommendations from Commissioner Bigge that secondary punishment sites should be far away from population centres. Norfolk Island was always intended as a place where 'the worst description of prisoners' could be incarcerated. Of course 'desperate' or 'troublesome' or 'rebellious' could be substituted for 'worst', depending on your point of view. Since most men there were sentenced to very long sentences, some for life, and since the smallest infringement could add time to that sentence, for many the island became not just a brutal place but a place without hope. Whatever their attitude on arrival, some men imprisoned there became so maddened by the regime that controlled them they would stop at nothing to escape. Some did get away, but by no means all. Tom Stacey arrived on the island only months after a large-scale 'mutiny', as it was termed by the authorities. 'Revolt' might have been the word chosen by the prisoners. Thirteen of them were executed, some grateful for the respite from a life of despair. By the time the *John* arrived, the island had a fearsome reputation.

For six months, Stacey was held on board the *Phoenix* hulk in Sydney Harbour. Moored in Lavender Bay since 1825, the hulk was used as a holding pen for prisoners in transit.[17] On board, Stacey, George Bramner and John Ritchie managed to stay together, sharing a cell with three others. With the prospect of Norfolk Island ahead, an attempt to escape must have seemed worthwhile. Painstakingly, this group collected an assortment of implements to remove the irons that chained them in the cell at night. Somehow they hid a saw and an auger that they used to start work on the timbers. But on the night air, every sound was magnified by the still water. Too soon, the noise attracted the attention of the sentry pacing above, who raised the alarm that prisoners were trying to cut their way out of the ship. Gathering his guard, Superintendent Thomas McKeg rushed the cell. Inside, they found all the men with their irons off. They had successfully cut away about three feet of the inner lining and pierced the outer planks. Only a short time was needed before they could have dropped through into the dark waters below, where the boatswain from a vessel in port was circling the hulk in a rowboat waiting to pick up passengers. Reporting to the Colonial Secretary, the Sheriff described it as an escape that 'very nearly succeeded'.

The boatswain was taken into custody and two magistrates were despatched to investigate what happened. The prisoners stayed loyal to one another. Each spoke only of his own actions and his own intentions. Each avoided implicating any other. All refused to implicate the boatswain. And all tried to protect young Ritchie who, at fifteen, was being consigned to a penal settlement designed for the most hardened and serial offenders. They were partially successful. The boatswain was allowed to go free for lack of proof, and when the magistrates ordered a punishment of 100 lashes for each man they reduced the number for Ritchie to 50.[18]

John Ritchie was one of the boys at Carters' Barracks who had been sentenced directly to an iron gang in 1833.[19] As we have seen, Samuel Rowney was also ordered to a gang at that time, and if Ritchie did not escape that fate it seems unlikely that Samuel would have done so. He was not in the gang long, however. By January 1834 he was assigned in Bathurst where he was sent to help two small-scale farmers with their harvest. But Samuel was determined to flout authority at every turn. According to the resident farmhand John Brady, the boy had been with him three days but 'did no work'. On the other hand, he was fascinated by a stack of wheat near the hut, so tall a ladder was needed to climb to the top. Twice he climbed up, and twice Brady ordered him down. Shortly after the second reprimand, Samuel came to Brady and announced coolly, 'I'm off now Jack'. As he walked away, Brady caught sight of the smoke and flames coming from the top of the stack. 'You young dog,' he yelled. 'You've set the stack on fire.' Samuel just kept walking.

In the Supreme Court with the boy on a charge of arson, the lawyers teased out every tiny detail of what happened. As an ex-convict, Brady was himself at risk of being accused of arson and was cross-examined very closely. But the shepherd, Henry Hazlett, supported what Brady had told the court. He too had ordered Samuel off the stack twice that day, but earlier in the morning. Questioned why he did it, Hazlett was specific. 'Because I saw him pulling large pieces of wheat out of it.' According to Hazlett, when Brady learned what Samuel was doing, he went outside and ticked him off, yelling, 'You young rascal. If I catch you at the stack any more, I'll give you a sound beating.' But Hazlett did not stay around to hear any more. He had his breakfast and went to look after his sheep. Meanwhile, Samuel sought out one of the owners, George Schofield, and told him, no doubt with glee, 'The old man has news for you.'

Everyone was puzzled about his motive. Brady testified that he had never beaten the boy, adding, 'I don't know whether his master had used him ill', but he said that Samuel had never complained to him about his master. George Schofield was a ticket-of-leave holder and owned the farm in part-nership with James Parker, who had been born in the colony, probably of convict parents. Schofield could shed no light on Samuel's motives either. 'I know of no ground of malice or revenge that the prisoner had against me,' he testified. 'I never knew of him doing anything malicious on the farm. He was idle . . . [but] the boy is sharp enough . . . he is quite aware of what is right and wrong, I am satisfied of that.' But malice was lurking in Samuel towards someone and it appears to have been the farmhand Brady, even if it was never explicitly stated. Perhaps, unknowingly, Brady shared characteristics with the father who had Samuel transported for 'stealing' his coat. Walking Samuel to gaol, Constable Taylor warned him of dire consequences for burning down the stack. He later reported that the boy replied, 'I don't care. There will be someone down along with me.'[20]

The jury found Samuel guilty and, as the law required, Justice Burton recorded a sentence of death. From his experience around other prisoners, Samuel would have known—and the judge explained—that 'death recorded' did not mean he would die. However, the law still required a death sentence for destruction of property to this value (over 200 bushels of wheat). The judge was more concerned with trying to make Samuel understand the impact on his victims. 'By destroying this wheat you have deprived two poor men, in all probability of their whole support till another harvest. At all events, you have scattered to the winds a very considerable portion of their property.' He told Samuel that because of his age he would send the papers to the Governor for consideration about a fitting punishment, but that he would recommend that frequent whipping form part of it.[21] Samuel was sent to Carters' Barracks, now renamed the House of Correction, in Sydney.

Samuel was not frightened into submission. In August that same year he was the key witness (and possible victim) in the trial of two men on a charge of 'abominable offences'. It was nothing unusual in New South Wales, any more than in England, for men to be tried for homosexual acts. And they were frequently hanged. In fact Michael Carey (or Carney) was hanged for just that reason at Sydney gaol only two months before Samuel's case was heard. It is even possible that the publicity about his case had some bearing on Samuel's allegations. What really happened is impossible to tell, but both the men he accused were acquitted and Samuel was charged with perjury. His punishment was a sentence to the No. 2 road gang, from where he absconded a few months later. Twelve months after that, he absconded from the House of Correction again. Recaptured, four years then passed before he was again recorded as absconding from the House of Correction in 1839. Assigned next to the Town Surveyor in Sydney, he absconded within the year, so they sent him to the Grose Farm stockade. Two years passed without a sign of him, but he absconded again in July–August 1842. Picked up within a week, he was convicted this time of larceny and sent to an iron gang. Finally, in 1846, now aged 28, Samuel Rowney obtained his certificate of freedom. It had taken him fourteen years to serve the seven imposed in England.[22] He is difficult to track after he was free. His brother George, using the name Rowney under which Samuel was convicted, married and produced two children. He was living in Taree when he died aged 79 in 1888. No similar trace of Samuel has been found. It would not be surprising to learn that he took off for the goldfields in California soon after he was free.[23]

While young Samuel was doing battle in Sydney, William Crooks was staging a protest of his own. Like so many of the soldier convicts, he had been assigned on arrival to a high-ranking official of the colony, in his case Dr James Bowman, the senior medical practitioner. Sydney residents were looking for good house servants or good tradesmen when they applied for a convict, and Bowman probably considered himself lucky to get Crooks—a military man, literate, who had travelled to India. As one medical man to another, he would probably have heard about Crooks from Surgeon Lawrence, who no doubt praised him as a reliable offsider on the voyage. Indeed, although by the 1830s convicts were assigned by a specially constituted board, arrangements could still be made by a wink and a nod. Bowman may well have asked his colleague which convict he would recommend from the current batch. Then a word in Mr Hely's ear, or a nod to a member of the Assignment Board, and Crooks was his. As a bonus, Crooks was also a painter and glazier. For a servant with these talents, there was plenty of work on Bowman's estate overlooking the harbour at Woolloomooloo.

It took Crooks only a few months to disabuse him. Some time in the first year, Dr Bowman sent his new man up country to the service of his son George, who managed their pastoral station in the Hunter Valley. The exact point at which Dr Bowman gave up on Crooks is unknown but it was probably when

A chain gang

'neglect of duty' changed to 'neglect of sheep'. Before Bowman passed the soldier on to the younger generation, he lashed him good and plenty in an attempt to put him straight. Unlike so many convict soldiers, Crooks had never been flogged. He would have seen many others flogged. He would have seen death and injury but his own skin had never been broken by the lash and, like Francis Bodenham so many years before, the shock must have been profound. As the cat's tails bit into his flesh, he must have writhed with anger as well as pain. Nevertheless, his shipboard behaviour suggested that Crooks was tough-minded and he could be mean. Even allowing a ready resort to flogging on Bowman's part, it seems likely that the soldier was provoking him with a finely judged indifference similar to that of the boy who pretended to sleep knowing how it incensed George Wigram Allen. His record was not created by a passive prisoner.

William Crooks' record		
1833	January 4	20 lashes, neglect of duty
	March 25	50 lashes, neglect of duty
	July 1	50 lashes, neglect of duty
1834	February 28	25 lashes, neglecting sheep
	March 18	12 lashes, neglecting sheep
	July 1	28 days cells—losing a sheep
	October 28	50 lashes—losing a sheep
	November 11	Returned to Government—'an ill conducted, troublesome character' [probably assigned to a road gang on the Northern Road at Wollombi]
1835	January 18	Absconded from Wollombi Bridge Party
	June 27	Absconded from Wollombi Bridge Party
	September 28	Before Singleton Bench—charge absconding: 'Prisoner says he absconded on account of the ill treatment he received in the Gang from the men.' Second time absconding—12 months labour in irons
	December 8	50 lashes—gross contempt of court 50 lashes—making a false charge against superintendent 12 months (irons?) misdemeanour
	December 15	Clash with Sergeant McKeon at Green Hills Stockade, Maitland[24]

The incident at Green Hills in December 1835 began when Crooks was locked up for the night in his individual stockade box (the invention of Sir Thomas Mitchell who thought portable boxes for individual convicts was a useful way of housing road gangs). Crooks was in a resentful and angry mood.[25] With doors on the boxes similar to stable doors but higher, it was the custom for the prisoners to pass out the knives given them to eat their dinner through the opening at the top of the locked door. Each prisoner was visible from about shoulder height. According to one version of what happened, as his *bête noire* Sergeant Francis McKeon locked Crooks' door, the soldier used his knife to tip off the sergeant's cap. According to the sergeant, he was raising his head to see who did that when he felt a heavy blow on the head. It was believed to be struck with a knife. The result was a charge against Crooks of assaulting Sergeant Francis McKeon of His Majesty's 28th Regiment of Foot with intent to kill and murder him, accompanied by a second count of having struck, cut and wounded him with intent to do grievous bodily harm.[26]

In the Supreme Court before the Chief Justice, Crooks defended himself and did it so ably that, after consideration, the jury could not reach a verdict. Crooks had made it a trying day, helped by his mate, Samuel Clay, who had denied earlier statements he had made to the magistrates. The Chief Justice was testy. 'All I can say is that you must go back and try to agree,' he told the jurors. Time passed. As was customary, the jury was locked up for the night, while Crooks and Clay were returned to the gaol. The next day the jury told the Chief Justice they could not agree. Once again, they were sent off with instructions to reach a decision, and again they were locked up. The following morning the foreman of the jury informed the judge they still could not reach a verdict. 'We wish to re-examine some of the witnesses.' Forewarned of this request, the judge had the witnesses ready in the courtroom. 'You must confine your examination to facts already elicited from the witnesses,' he told the jury sternly. 'No fresh evidence can be adduced.'

They stuck to the issues, but everyone had a go at the cross-examination. A juror wanted to clarify whether it was physically possible for Crooks to have struck the soldier. 'The prisoner could have easily put his arm out the window. The bars are up and down and about six inches apart,' the sergeant responded. Pushed by Crooks about this point, the sergeant dug in. 'I am between 5 feet and 5 feet 10 inches. I said the bars were between 4 and 5 feet [up the door]. You could rise yourself up to the bars. I went in and tried the experiment and I could put my arm out and strike down easily.'

George Morgan, a convict who worked in the stockade hospital, was sitting on the verandah edge watching as the sergeant locked the prisoners in for the night. The jury had a number of questions for him. Yes, he said, he had seen Crooks' arm through the bars. 'I did not see the prisoner knock the sergeant's hat off [but] I saw him strike the sergeant. He had a knife in his hand then.' Questioned about how Crooks had knocked off the hat and stabbed him in one seamless movement, Morgan could only say, 'He must have drawn his hand in to get the knife.' But he did admit that the bars only started at the prisoner's chest and he, Morgan, could only see Crooks' head and shoulders.

There were questions about whether Crooks had a knife at all. To the jury, the sergeant explained, 'I always allow a knife to the prisoners to cut up their bread. He must have concealed it.' But he had to admit that no one had asked for the knives back at the end of the meal that night. That was because the lock-up was late, he told them. Knowing the sergeant was on shaky ground, Crooks grilled him hard about why he had not searched them after dinner, wrong-footing him so successfully that the sergeant stuttered and stumbled until the Chief Justice intervened, saying, 'Sergeant McKeon you must answer distinctly every question put to you by the prisoner.'

Lastly there was the question of whether Crooks had threatened the sergeant. Some exchange had taken place between them during the lock-up. Possibly Crooks was forcibly pushed into his cell so that he fell against his raw back, flogged as the record shows only the week before. Witness for the defence Samuel Clay said Crooks was 'in a great passion' and told the court he heard Crooks say, 'This is the second time you have shoved me on my back since I was flogged.' In other respects, Clay backtracked on everything. He was positive that Crooks did not strike a blow, but he saw him knock the sergeant's hat off with the tip of a knife then throw the knife into the courtyard. 'I am quite sure I did not state to the magistrates that I heard the prisoner say, "You bloody false . . ." There was something said by the prisoner about false swearing and getting him flogged but I cannot say what it was.'

When the jury once again retired to consider its verdict, Clay was returned to the Hunter River to be dealt with by the magistrates, where no doubt he received a flogging for his pains. Nevertheless, he and Crooks had successfully cast doubt on the sergeant's truthfulness, possibly even in the mind of the Chief Justice. Found guilty by the jury, death was recorded against Crooks, as required by law. The sentence was commuted not to life but to fourteen years transportation to Norfolk Island. Crooks took with him, at least, the satisfaction of having made the sergeant squirm.[27]

At the island, Crooks would have met up with George Wheeler, the former marine and convicted burglar from Gloucestershire. Wheeler's record in the colony was much like that of the others who experienced the penal system at its worst, a cycle of continuous escape and recapture and punishment. He was assigned on arrival in 1832 to Mr John Carey at Appin in the south-west, and six months silence followed, during which master and servant appraised each other. Then in quick succession over the next six months Wheeler received 50 lashes for idleness, 25 for insolence, and 50 for disobedience and falsely accusing his master. From July, he spent six months in the Georges River iron gang for selling goods and stores at Berrima. From there he must have been reassigned because in 1834 another employer took him before the Liverpool Bench. This time he received another 25 lashes for 'being out after hours' and was sent to a gang again.

Absconding once more in March 1834, Wheeler avoided capture until July when John Buckland found him hiding in an outbuilding on his farm. Two half-crowns, two dollars and a silk handkerchief were discovered on him. 'It matches one that was stolen [from me] the previous Sunday,' Mr Buckland told the magistrates. 'It was offered for sale to one of my men.' Wheeler claimed he had bought the handkerchief. Before the committing magistrate, he cross-examined Buckland about the possibility there were other handkerchiefs like it, but Buckland was not going to be deterred by that. 'There were no others left after I bought it,' he insisted. By November, Wheeler was on trial at the Campbelltown Quarter Sessions for stealing the handkerchief. Found guilty by the magistrates, he was sent to labour at No. 1 stockade at Emu Plains. Two months later, he absconded from there.

Again, Wheeler succeeded in staying at large for several months until, in June 1835, he made the mistake of going to the Macarthurs' store at Camden. A farm constable, Michael Casey, spotted him carrying a bundle and asked the storekeeper, James Hilliard, who he was. Casey was himself a prisoner assigned to the Colonial Secretary, Alexander McLeay, but it made no difference to his attitude. When the storekeeper said he did not know, Casey took Wheeler into custody anyway. Walking beside the constable to the lock-up, with the store-keeper following behind, Wheeler's anger got the better of him. Or perhaps he tried to buy his freedom from Casey. Suddenly the constable called out to Hilliard, 'This man wants to cut my throat.' As Hilliard ran to help, Casey wrestled Wheeler to the ground, forcing him to drop the knife in his hand. Casey's own hand was bleeding. On trial in the Supreme Court on the serious charge of unlawfully and maliciously stabbing Casey, with a second charge for larceny, Wheeler cross-examined Casey and suggested that the constable was stabbed because he struck his hand against the knife in the struggle. Casey denied it vehemently. 'You attempted to stab me with the clasp knife,' he insisted. 'I put up my arm to save the blow.' Then he set about trying to make the evidence against Wheeler even worse. Appealing directly to the judge, he claimed, 'The prisoner struck at me violently as if he intended to do me an injury. The blow appeared to be aimed at my face.' But the jury was not convinced. They found Wheeler not guilty on the charge of stabbing but guilty of larceny, for which he was sentenced to seven years on Norfolk Island.[28]

Four years later they brought Wheeler back from the island but made the mistake of putting him to work on Cockatoo Island to serve the remainder of his commuted sentence. Plainly unable to endure any more of the authorities' 'petty tyranny', and despite the fact he had barely a year left, he absconded in June 1839. More adept than most at living on the run, Wheeler had learned from his past experiences. Deciding not to attempt escape by sea from Sydney, he headed west over the mountains into the wilderness beyond. Unquestioned, probably undistinguishable from the settlers now streaming into the area, he squatted on some land beyond the escarpment and established a small farm. An ostler, he would have been comfortable around cattle. Certainly he managed to collect a few.

This time Wheeler succeeded in staying at large for five years. Meanwhile the government kept publicising his details as a runaway. Year after year, they placed notices in the *Government Gazette*—the same details, just an update on the age each time, like this one in 1844: 'George Wheeler, per John (3), age 28, from Worcestershire, ostler, 5'6", ruddy, freckled complexion, dark brown hair, dark grey eyes, scar first joint of little finger of right hand, small scar on underlip, absconded from Cockatoo Island since June 17 1839.' In May, a sharp-eyed constable at Hartley near the now disbanded Hassan's Walls stockade read his *Gazette* carefully and something triggered recognition. Was it the scar on Wheeler's little finger? Or the one on his underlip? Or his freckled face? In New South Wales, they never advertised the scars on his back that had seemed such an important distinguishing feature to the gaoler in Gloucestershire. Perhaps an unexpected glimpse of those wounds had made the constable wonder about this local farmer's history. At any rate, Wheeler was brought in and sent down to Sydney. Meanwhile, the police seized his cattle and put them up for auction, first advertising their details in case they were stolen property. At the time he was caught, Wheeler had 'One dark-red cow, branded HC on off thigh; one poley heifer, branded (J) on off rump; one white cow, branded EL on off rump; one red sided cow, white back and belly, branded EL on off rump; one white heifer, unbranded; one red and white heifer, unbranded.' Whether HC or EL or (J) came forward to claim them is unrecorded. Wheeler gave the police some information, probably about other absconders. Combined with the fact he had been making a (relatively) honest livelihood for five years, it was enough for Governor Gipps to forgive, as Wheeler later described it, his being 'absent'. He was simply ordered back to a gang to complete the time outstanding from his commuted colonial conviction.

The 'smoko'

Wheeler was, above all, a survivor. Eighteen months later, in December 1845, he applied in the normal way through the nearest Bench at Berrima for a ticket-of-leave. Six months later, being somehow led to believe that it was refused because of his long 'absence', he petitioned Governor Gipps directly. In his clear, firm hand, he set out his arguments about 'forgiveness' and 'honest livelihood'. He claimed that, despite the foregoing, he understood the application had been refused because of his long 'absence', but just what he knew and didn't know is not clear. The truth was closely guarded in Wheeler's brain. He may have been trying to hurry them up. He may have been double-guessing the local magistrate in an attempt to ensure he got his ticket. Closing the petition obsequiously while strategically flying the kite of illegality, he told the Governor that 'no time being specified after which it was your Excellency's pleasure that he might again apply, your Petitioner, now, most humbly prays that your Excellency will allot to him the shortest period of probation allowed by law'.[29] On the receiving end of this missive there was a flurry of paperwork, which was exactly what Wheeler intended. The Superintendent of Convicts was ordered to provide details of Wheeler's history. Memos flew back and forth between His Excellency, the Colonial Secretary, the Superintendent and the magistrate in Berrima until it finally became clear what had happened. The ticket had been granted. 'It is probable that the above answer had not reached Wheeler before he forwarded this Petition,' wrote the Colonial Secretary for the Governor's benefit. He did not pursue the issue of why the answer had been despatched (hastily no doubt) only a few days before the Governor read Wheeler's petition. Cross about the time wasted, Gipps instructed his officials, 'Let this be put under care of the police magistrate of Berrima, who will inform Wheeler that if he gives any more trouble he will be immediately sent to Cockatoo Island.' His note was dated 15 May 1846.

Three days later, the police magistrate despatched confirmation to the Colonial Secretary that Wheeler had been told about his ticket 'and admonished not to give any more trouble'.[30] Wheeler was smart enough to recognise when silence was golden. They heard no more of him. Ticket in hand and still only 36, he married Elizabeth Ringwood the following year and settled in Goulburn. No doubt he met Isaac Fisher in the local pub and the two old hands swapped stories about their battles with the system. They may have shared their tales with the young men gathered round. And why not? It is unlikely they felt they had done anything of which to feel ashamed and in that town, where so many ex-prisoners settled, it was no secret who had been a government man. George Wheeler died in Goulburn in 1870, just short of his 60th birthday.[31] As we have seen, Isaac Fisher lived on to 1887, a year before the centenary celebrations of European settlement.

Edward Gill had no old age in which to reminisce. On arrival, the 27-year-old soldier had been assigned to Donald McIntyre at his station in Invermein. Their relationship functioned well enough to last over a year without incident, although we do not know what role Gill was playing initially. On the ship's indent he described himself as 'an officer's servant', so he may have been employed in the house when he started. Around October 1833, McIntyre changed Gill's duties to that of a shepherd. Suddenly the former soldier was expected to mind 300 sheep as well as take part in the shearing. Reading the depositions creates a suspicion that the change was designed to take him down a peg. McIntyre and his overseer, with the collaboration of other station hands, were riding Gill, perhaps because his difference challenged them. Intelligent and self-possessed, he obviously had a mind of his own. Taken before the Invermein Bench for 'refusing to work and insolence', Gill explained to William Dumaresq, Esq., 'I had been working all week like the rest of the men and took out the sheep on Sunday to oblige my master. On Monday when I told Mr Free (the overseer) I would not work, I thought I had a right to half of that day having been at work (also) all day Saturday.' Joseph Free's version was all sweet reason. 'On Sunday morning last, I ordered the prisoner to take out a flock of sheep which had just been shorn,' he told Dumaresq. 'And also the following morning.' He explained that one of the shearers was ill on the Monday and could not shear, so McIntyre sent him to take over Gill's flock as light duties. Gill handed over the sheep obediently but then he retired to his hut. Shortly after, Free ordered him to take the vacant place in the shearing shed, at which point Gill refused to work until Tuesday. Within 24 hours, the overseer and McIntyre got their own back. 'When he was assisting in shearing he dragged his sheep into the shed in a careless manner,' the overseer testified. 'When my master spoke to him about it he told him "not to be *at* him but to take him to court at once if that was his intention".' Dumaresq found the charges proved and sentenced Gill to 35 lashes. Flogging was not new to the former soldier. In the past, the British army had dealt him 200 lashes.[32]

One month later, Gill was before the Bench again, with Dumaresq again in the magistrate's chair but this time with H.C. Semphill, Esq., beside him. McIntyre's watchman, whose name was Kingsley, relayed the complaint. 'On Friday last, my master sent me to look after the prisoner and his flock of sheep because it was the first time he had been out with sheep.' Kingsley said he discovered later that he went in the opposite direction to the route Gill had taken. Nevertheless, 'I picked up fourteen sheep and four lambs which the prisoner had lost out of his flock.' On hearing about the wandering sheep, McIntyre ordered Kingsley to take four other men with him and find Gill. 'The prisoner was not again left with sheep,' Kingsley informed Dumaresq helpfully. In reply Gill explained what he thought happened. In the morning when the main flock was divided into groups for the shepherds, some of them headed into the bushes. With the overseer's permission, he first took his group to the overseer's hut where he had his breakfast, then he shepherded them over the range to feed. He did not believe he had lost any. In fact he felt that he had kept his eye over them all and the sheep that the men found must have been left behind when the flock was divided. Because of evidence that he 'was unaccustomed to sheep' and that McIntyre knew he might lose some, the Bench gave Gill the benefit of the doubt about wilful neglect and discharged him, telling him to be more cautious.[33]

At this point—and Gill would later allege that it was because the charge about the sheep had been dismissed—a Mr Thurlow, who was a guest of Donald McIntyre, rose to his feet to make a far more serious complaint. Early that morning he had seen Mr McIntyre walking back from his sheepfolds and saw Gill come out of his hut to walk with him. Thurlow went into the kitchen for a glass of water. When he came out, Gill was walking away down the track but there was no sign of McIntyre. Expecting to meet him, Thurlow walked down and asked Gill where he was. Pointing to the spot where Thurlow had last seen them both, Gill replied, 'You'll find him lying there. I've just been knocking down the damned rascal.' Thurlow found McIntyre sitting on a log with his head in his hands. His face was contused as if it had been hit and, according to Thurlow, his head 'was covered with blood'. Also according to Thurlow, 'The wound behind the ear was a very severe blow which must have been inflicted by some weapon. It could not have been given by hand.' With that evidence, Thurlow set in train events with tragic consequences for Edward Gill. Questioned by Gill, who denied he ever had a weapon, Thurlow responded, 'I saw you going to the hut. I saw you coming from the hut . . . I did not notice any weapon in your hand. Not supposing any violence to have been committed, it did not occur to me to look.' With that the case was stood over until Mr McIntyre could give evidence.[34]

A week later, Donald McIntyre told them how he went to the sheepfold in order to give Gill's flock to someone else. On the way back to the house, Gill joined him. McIntyre said, 'As he approached I observed his left hand was concealed in his trousers. He began by saying that he could not help losing the sheep, which he had lost a few days before. I told him, "You might as well tell me not to keep sheep as say a man could not look after 300 ewes."' According to McIntyre, that was all that was said, but as he kept walking he suddenly received a blow behind the ear. 'I was so much stunned that I could hardly recognise the prisoner Gill when he came round in front of me. Then calling me "a dammed rascal" excited my attention so much, I did recognise him as he struck me in the face.'

If it had been left at that, perhaps Gill would have been tried at Quarter Sessions for assault. But Donald McPhee, a Scot like his master, had something extra to contribute. Joining the overseer on the way to the courthouse, he asked where McIntyre was. Walking beside Gill, the overseer replied that his master was unavailable, at which Gill remarked that it was because of him. McPhee replied to that, 'It was the more shame to you then.' At which, according to McPhee, Gill then uttered the comment that surely hanged him: 'You may praise the bridge that carries you safe over but were all of the prisoners of my mind, many of them [meaning the settlers and overseers] would be put to one side [for] tyrannising over them.' Gill was a soldier of course, used to assessing the odds. He would have seen very clearly that the prisoners had the numbers in the colony if they chose to use them. He made no reference to the events, close to insurrection, which had occurred only one month before at Major James Mudie's property in the Hunter when six assigned servants had stolen guns, robbed the household and threatened both Mudie and his son-in-law John Lanarch with death. These men were hanged less than three weeks after Gill was committed for trial. When McPhee recounted what he had said, the events at Mudie's would have been in the minds of everyone in the room. The evidence was a death warrant.

Gill's words would also have been in the mind of those in the Supreme Court when he was tried in February 1834. Gill was represented by a leading Sydney barrister, Roger Therry, later a judge of the court. The Solicitor General prosecuted. Mr Justice Dowling, soon to be Chief Justice, presided. The case excited considerable media interest, except in the case of the *Sydney Morning Herald*, whose brevity was notable. It published a short note of the sentence with the crime described simply as 'cutting and maiming with intent to murder'. There was no mention of who was assaulted.[35]

The *Australian's* coverage included the four counts, although the reporter got the names wrong:

> Edward Hills [*sic*] was indicted for assaulting Donald MacIntyre [*sic*], with a piece of iron, with intent to kill and murder him . . .
>
> The second count laid the offence to have been committed with some sharp instrument to the Attorney-General unknown
>
> The third count laid the offence to have been committed with intent to maim and the fourth, with intent to do some grievous bodily harm.[36]

So many charges left the jury plenty of choices. As did the evidence. Gill always denied he had hit McIntyre with anything other than his fists. And he insisted his motive was only because he wanted to be assigned to another master. No instrument, let alone a piece of iron, was ever found. The evidence that the wound behind McIntyre's ear was made by a weapon was given by a local surgeon, who attended him the day after it happened. Unlike the *Herald*, the *Australian* reported the evidence, particularly the testimony of Mr Thurlow. The paper also reported one aspect of Gill's defence that no one else did, namely that Mr McIntyre had seized him by the throat during their struggle when Gill came round in front of him. In its follow-up coverage, the paper came closer than any other in explicitly reporting the reason for the sentence when it said, 'It is to be hoped that the continual examples made of unhappy men for similar offences will have effect in deterring them from the commission of these enormous crimes.'[37]

The *Sydney Gazette's* coverage was similar in space and content to the *Australian's*, except that it made reference to a conversation 'on the road, to which he [Gill] said in the hearing of several [people] . . . that he would be well satisfied to go to the gallows if he had taken the prosecutor's life'. This must have been courtroom evidence from McPhee, because it is not in the magistrates' depositions. The *Gazette* reported Mr Therry's submission that there was no case to go to the jury because there was no proof any weapon was used. According to the *Gazette*, the judge began his summing-up by saying it was a question of evidence, which was for the jury to determine. However, he added that *he* should put the case on its merits upon the second count, which alleged the offence to have been committed with an unknown sharp instrument. He then went on to summarise the evidence.[38] In other words, the judge believed the surgeon. McIntyre was never specific about the weapon. He told the magistrates that he was so hazy he could barely recognise Gill. His only evidence about a weapon was that he thought Gill was hiding something in his pocket.

The *Monitor,* generally supportive of prisoners, reported the trial in about the same detail as the *Australian* and the *Gazette* but its follow-up was greater. It was the only paper to report the broader threat and it did so in detail, describing an unnamed watch-house keeper who testified that Gill had said 'that he would not mind going to the drop, so that he had satisfaction on his master; and that if all the men were of his mind, they would soon put the Settlers and overseers out of the way and do away with the tyranny and oppression that was used on the farm'. Edward Gill's defence was also reported in more detail in the *Monitor,* which repeated the fact that his master had seized him round the throat, but included Gill's claim that McIntyre had called him 'a convict wretch' as he did so. The *Monitor* also revealed that the two men physically struggled (evidence that Thurlow supported by saying there were signs of a struggle). It also reported Gill's claim that it was falling over a tree that landed them on the ground.[39] Gill suggested some sharp branch was responsible for the wound behind Mr McIntyre's ear and continued to insist that he only used his fists.

The jury had listened to the judge and they found Edward Gill guilty on the second count. Mr Justice Dowling ordered him to be hanged by the neck until he was dead. On 28 February, the *Monitor* published a startling suggestion. The paper had initially accepted the verdict was fair because of the surgeon's testimony, but now it reported that the magistrate Mr Semphill had informed the newspaper that another surgeon who examined the wound believed it could have been caused either by fists or falling on something sharp. Why, asked the newspaper, would Gill use an iron instrument at first but not again when he and McIntyre confronted each other?[40] In these circumstances, why did he beat McIntyre with his fists? Diplomatically, but sensationally, the paper continued:

> Now, while we believe Mr McIntyre, yet we also think that transportation for life, (if not for fourteen years) would be sufficient to satisfy offended justice and that to hang Gill will be an unnecessary sacrifice of life . . . We must say that death is not merited in this case . . . Again, compare Gill's case and the soldier who stabbed the serjeant and who, after being sentenced to death, was let off for *three months imprisonment.*

Is it fair, is it decent, to make such a great difference between
soldiers and convicts?[41]

It is impossible to know whether the paper already knew that Gill was a
soldier. It certainly found out subsequently. On 6 March, Edward Gill led the
way up the scaffold in the yard of the Sydney gaol. He was followed by two
other men, William Elliott who had shot and wounded a mounted policeman,
and William Johnson, who had been the leader of a band of seven bushrangers
near Bathurst. Although leading the way up the steps, Gill was between them
when the noose was put around their necks. Before the trap opened, Elliott
shouted that he shot the policeman in self-defence, and Johnson warned the
prisoners gathered in the next yard to beware of going bush, but if they did
then go only with someone they trusted. Gill contented himself simply with
repeating that he had no intention of killing his master. 'It was just a common
assault,' he said. His appearance and his demeanour impressed the observers,
the reporter for the *Monitor* writing:

> Gill was a different man from his two companions and he
> had a much better countenance. He had served in the army
> ten years and knew the duties of a good citizen. He told Mr
> Weston [the gaoler] that he had lived eighteen months with
> his master before they began to quarrel. Gill was a man fit to
> live in civilised society. His untimely end is to be lamented.[42]

Hunter River magistrate H.C. Semphill had been actively trying to save
Edward Gill, which suggests that he, and possibly Dumaresq, were concerned
about the way the case had mushroomed since the parties appeared before them.
Semphill organised the second surgeon, whose opinion the *Monitor* had reported,
to send a statement to Governor Bourke. According to the newspaper, the
surgeon, whose name was Macready, deposed that he went to see McIntyre a few
hours after the attack and met him walking outside the house. '[O]n examining
his head, he found a small cut behind the left ear which, in his opinion, might
have been inflicted by the knuckles of a man's fist, or by the head having come in
contact with any hard substance in falling . . . but that no part of McIntyre's
head or face appeared to him, to have been injured by any iron weapon.'

It was too late of course. Gill was executed the day before the statement
reached the Governor. Injustice or not, he was doomed from the moment he
put into words the most deep-seated, always present fears of the free settlers,
the gaolers and administrators. Their numbers were very small. They were
outnumbered and they knew it. The prisoners were not fools. They knew it

too, even if Gill was one of the few to say so. Nor were the prisoners cowards. All kinds of reasons can be advanced to explain why wave after wave of transported men failed to act on their superior numbers, but at bottom it reveals something profound about their reaction to life in the penal colonies. It is yet another ramification of a distorted history that no one has ever considered its significance apart from assuming the men were subservient, cowed beasts ground down by a cruel system—a theory to which the evidence of Norfolk Island also gives the lie. There, where the prospects were different from the mainland, where the system was often remorselessly cruel, men threw their lives away in mutinies or escapes. Why didn't they do the same on the mainland in New South Wales or Van Diemen's Land?

Four years after Gill's execution, Patrick Quigley received his death sentence. 'Prepare yourself to make the most of the short time allotted to you,' said the judge. 'The sentence of death will be passed upon you.' In fact, there was mercy, of a sort, for Quigley. His was the 'fate worse than death', a sentence to life imprisonment on Norfolk Island. In June 1838, he sailed to join the men from the *John* who were already there.[43]

Quigley's conduct record on the island has survived. It reveals many tribulations, but there is no obvious or spectacular difference from his record on the mainland. If anything, it is more benign.

Patrick Quigley's record on Norfolk Island		
1838	June 23	Arrived on Norfolk Island
	July 17	Neglect of work. Reprimanded being first offence
	August 31	Malingering—Recorded only
	November 23	Applying and [illegible] to his foot in place of that ordered by the medical officer—10 days bread and water in jail
1839	February 19	Refusing to go to work and lingering at the ... Mill for [illegible]
	March 5	Making use of disrespectful language in front of the gang—50 lashes
	February 16 [*sic*]	Going to hospital on false pretences—reprimanded and to bring up this week
	October 19	Leaving his work and going to Hospital on false pretences—gaol on bread and water ...
1840	September 19	Cutting up a tin dish and having ... [soap?] in his possession—3 months at Longridge
1843	February 7	Having a teapot in Govt. House—14 days in irons[44]

Unfortunately, it is impossible to judge from the surviving records how much Quigley was helped or hindered by the presence on the island of Sergeant John Hiney, who had resigned from the 17th Regiment when it sailed for India and who held the role of chief overseer at Norfolk Island for nine years. One way or the other, Quigley managed to wangle an improvement in his situation, to the point where prison reformer Alexander Maconochie recommended him to Governor Gipps as a man whose good conduct warranted removing his irons.[45] On the island, Quigley overlapped with George Wheeler by about six months before Wheeler returned to New South Wales and with Stacey and Crooks.

Thomas Stacey was flogged twice at Norfolk Island. The first time was six months after he arrived, when he received 25 lashes for 'disobedience'. The second, two and a half years later, was a massive flogging of 300 lashes as punishment for being 'absent'. Prisoners on Norfolk frequently absconded into the bush, even though the island was small, and given the severity of his punishment, Stacey was probably involved in an attempt to escape. Between these events, he was punished a number of times by incarceration in a cell for several days. Stacey's record reveals glimpses of the petty feuds and tyrannical brutality between overseers and prisoners, as well as the corruption of the officials and military on Norfolk Island. This regime deprived the prisoners of rations and privileges to which they were entitled. It also created an active black market in which prisoners as well as overseers and military participated. The degree to which these practices flourished was very much influenced by the type of man acting as commandant, which varied significantly over the years. Most studies to date have been based on documents produced by people who were not prisoners, supplemented by memoirs from Martin Cash and Thomas Cook. No one has yet analysed the penal settlement from the prisoners' records, or individually examined the men who were sent there. The horror stories that describe life on the island cannot be dismissed as exaggeration. Much of what they depicted was undoubtedly accurate. But was it typical? Did all men sent there have similar experiences? The definitive examination of Norfolk Island remains to be written.

After the massive flogging in September 1837, Stacey continued to attract regular punishment, although it diminished noticeably during the more benign management by Alexander Maconochie as commandant from 1839 to 1844. Patrick Quigley and William Crooks both took advantage of the opportunities offered during this period.

Regardless of their sentences, none of the men from the *John* spent the rest of their lives on Norfolk Island. Crooks succeeded in getting himself back to New South Wales when that government was handing over the island to Van

Diemen's Land. Quigley and Stacey were not so lucky, their life sentences probably the deciding factor on where they were to go.[46] In November 1845, Quigley sailed for Hobart on the *Governor Phillip*.[47] However, Stacey, who had been due to leave on the *Lady Franklin* the previous year, was again tried for armed robbery and sentenced to death. The sentence was commuted to 'transportation' for life but the effect was a decision that he must stay at Norfolk Island indefinitely. During the regime of the commandant, John Price, he was subjected to almost monthly persecution around the provision of tea or sugar or tobacco and occasionally for insolence.[48] Stacey remained on the island until 1854, finally leaving in the closing months of the notorious penal settlement after twenty years there.[49]

The description in the Sydney *Monitor* of William Johnson, who was hanged with Edward Gill, could apply to all of the men featured in this chapter. At the time of his execution, the Sydney *Monitor* summed up Johnson as 'one of those men who, in bondage, is ever restless, and ready for anything desperate, loving danger and delighting in enterprise'.[50] Less romantically, Martin Cash explained his horrendous career as a convict as resulting from 'the daily annoyances and petty tyranny, which at that time men of my class were generally subjected to and which has ever been the bane of my existence'.[51] Another convict in Western Australia described men such as these as having 'a mania for running away'.[52] Together, these descriptions seem to explain the motivations of many of the convicts who refused to be either sensible or submissive and thus attracted the worst of the penal punishment. Age made no difference, as Samuel Rowney's career demonstrates. It was character that determined the route the prisoners took. And the fact that so many of 'the worst description of prisoners' were or had been soldiers may well be significant. Only a more specific study will reveal to what extent.

In 1985, Norma Townsend summed up the men who went to Norfolk Island as, 'These unfortunate men, the unbalanced, the brutalised, the psychopaths, the last surviving winnowings of Britain's system of punishment, [who] were for the good, even of a penal society, removed from it.'[53] Townsend was not a historian who usually fell for stereotypes, but in this instance it would appear she did so. Her description does not fit the men whose careers as prisoners are examined here. Rather, it conforms to the stereotypes created in the nineteenth century that were still distorting Australian history in the twentieth. No researcher has yet tested the stereotypes against the reality at Norfolk Island, using the archival material about the prisoners rather than opinionated reminiscences and diaries and some overused trial records that have provided the source material to date. Juxtaposing Townsend's comments with what we know of Patrick Quigley, George Wheeler, the boy John Ritchie, even with

Thomas Stacey's record on Norfolk Island

1834	September 18	Arrived Norfolk Island
1835	March 12	Dishonest conduct—25 lashes
1835	October 25	Disobedience—10 days cells
1835	November 11	Disobedience—10 days cells
1835	December 29	Absent and Disobedience—6 months cells
1836	July 27	Neglect—10 days cells
1836	August 27	Disobedience—21 days cells
1836	October	Neglect—14 days cells
1837	September 27	Absent—300 lashes
1837	October 14	Disobedience—2 months gaol
1838	January 8	Disobedience and Insubordination—6 weeks gaol
1838	April 11	Disobedience—14 days cells
1838	August 3	Assault—4 months gaol
1838	November 1	Insolence and Disobedience—100 lashes
1838	December 13	Insolence—20 days imprisonment
1839	March 25	Disobedience—1 months imprisonment
1839	August 8	Refusing to work—50 lashes
1839	September 14	Going to . . . hospital—25 lashes
1841	March 23	Absent—14 days cells
1842	March 8	Robbery—12 months' imprisonment
1843	March 24	Insolence—one week imprisonment
1843	June 9	Making away with clothing—6 months cells
1844		TO VDL per *Lady Franklin*—cancelled—Stacey charged with robbery
1845	May 20	Verdict Guilty as Principal to Robbery armed—Death recorded—Commuted to Transportation for Life and to be detained at Norfolk Island beyond his present term of detention
1845	September 12	Absconded—3 months H of C
1846	June 22	Having cards—14 days cells Same date—insolence 36 lashes Same date insolence—one month H & C
1846	September 12	To remain five years from 26 May 1845 at LGD
1846	September 16	Endeavouring to cause to be conveyed to a prisoner confined in the new gaol, a Bible containing two saws—9 months solitary
1846	December 12	Having tobacco—4 days sl (solitary)
1847	February 12	Having tobacco—14 days solitary
1847	July 1	Having tea and sugar—1 month H C

1847	July 19	Having tea and sugar—2 months H C extended
1847	August 2	Using obscene language to the Overseer H of C
		Same date: having tobacco—14 days solitary confinement (sc)
1847	August 25	Disobedience—10 days sc
1847	August 28	Disobedience—14 days sc
1847	September 21	Disobedience—7 days sc
1848	January 5	Disobedience—7 days sc
1848	February 1	Disobedience—7 days HC
1848	February 3	Insolence—10 days sc
1848	July 24	Working for . . . p..pr 7 days HC
1848	September 25	Fighting—1 month HC
1848	October 9	Receiving tea—1 month HC
1848	November 9	Having tobacco—2 months HC
1848	October 17 [*sic*]	Having bootlaces—14 days sol. confinement (vide Superintendent)
Note:		
18/5/53		Record in this man's favour having found a watch value 4 pounds property of John Townly in the Box and delivering it to Police CCO
1854	25 August	Arrived Van Diemen's Land from Norfolk Island

William Crooks, reveals that such a study is overdue. Tom Stacey comes closest to the much promoted stereotype by which Australians identify all convicts. His brutalisation began from the moment he absconded barely a month after he landed from the *John*. It continued on the roads in New South Wales and was completed during his long incarceration on Norfolk Island—and beyond. The extended promotion of Stacey's experience as typical has not been sufficiently challenged to give us any idea of the real figure for men who were brutalised in this way.

Under a policy of private assignment (which was most of the transportation era) many convicts never experienced a penal settlement or a gang of any kind. According to A.G.L. Shaw, based on figures for 1836 it appears that the gangs plus Norfolk Island contained about 8 per cent of all convicts at any one time. Shaw further calculated that about 18 per cent of all male convicts transported had been in an iron gang during the decade after they were established for punishment. Rounding up this percentage to allow for the penal settlements at Moreton Bay and Norfolk Island, Shaw estimated a total of between 20 and 25 per cent of all convicts experienced either the leg irons and/ or transportation to a secondary penal colony.[54] Nicholas and Shergold and John Hirst have reached similar conclusions.[55] Even allowing for error, the percentage is a far cry from the enduring stereotype of the shackled convict.

The debate about penal labour and the role of punishment continues. In 1992, Evans and Thorpe challenged the interpretation of figures for flogging, particularly those of Nicholas and Shergold. They claimed the numbers can be reappraised to conclude that only 23.7 per cent *escaped* flogging.[56] In reply, Hamish Maxwell-Stewart pointed out that a total of only 2259 men and 148 women experienced the secondary punishment settlement of Moreton Bay between 1822 and 1834, and that 1153 men experienced the dreaded Macquarie Harbour in Van Diemen's Land. Therefore Evans and Thorpe's sample of men at Moreton Bay was not a yardstick for convict experience as a whole. Allowing for figures for Port Arthur and Norfolk Island, which remain to be finally calculated and must be added to those of Macquarie Harbour and Moreton Bay, it is nevertheless a small percentage of the total transported. For Maxwell-Stewart the distinction by punishment was less relevant than the condition of being a convict, which applied to all prisoners regardless of where they worked, but he made his point using a description by Reverend John West—'a contemporary anti-transportationist' who, as we shall see, was a man with an agenda in everything he said about convicts.[57]

Regardless of the fate of individuals, the events that occurred on the Bathurst Road, in the stockades all over the colonies, at Moreton Bay and at Norfolk Island provided fodder for the enemies of the convict society. Much theoretical compassion was showered on them. Much hand-wringing took place in the cause of their morals, their depravity and the evils of their situation—as well as the inadequacy of their punishment. In the process, the men we have met here were reduced to ciphers, becoming abstractions in a political battle which interred their personal humanity every bit as much as the alleged evils of the system the debaters were determined to end. Chief among the contemporary offenders who buried the prisoners in this way was a young priest, a boy wet behind the ears, whose opinions shaped the paradigm about Norfolk Island long beyond his death.

After first trying the sea as a cabin boy, Father William Ullathorne chose the church, graduating from the seminary in 1831 at the age of 25. Dignified beyond his years with the title of Vicar General, he was promptly despatched on his first mission—to administer to the souls of the convicts in New South Wales. After a short stay in the Cape of Good Hope, he reached Sydney in February 1833. A little over a year later, still in his twenties, he was on Norfolk Island hearing confession from thirteen men about to face execution for mutiny.[58] Of course, he was shocked to the core. Indeed, on the return voyage to Sydney he was ill from the shock.[59] Barely recovered from this feverish state, if indeed he ever did recover, he wrote a pamphlet entitled *The Catholic Mission in Australia*, which was widely disseminated in Britain and throughout Europe. It was also the basis of Ullathorne's submission to the Select Committee on Transportation in London, to which he later gave oral evidence. 'Highly coloured' was how his superior, Archbishop Polding, described it. And, in a somewhat embarrassed tone, he felt obliged to justify its obvious hyperbole by emphasising its usefulness as a deterrent. 'It is highly coloured in some parts and I fear will give offence in some quarters,' wrote Polding to one of his flock, who he had just learned had been given a copy of Ullathorne's epistle. 'In Ireland, it has produced already, in Liverpool and Manchester also, the best effects in removing delusions spread abroad respecting the life of a convict in this Country.'[60] The consequences of giving Ullathorne a platform to 'spread abroad' his opinions, and their role in creating a convict stain that finally triggered shame in Australians who had previously rejected it, will be explored in the next chapter.

CHAPTER 7
an unclean thing

As Father Ullathorne's pamphlet was being distributed around Britain and Ireland, another very young man, Sir William Molesworth, was elected Chairman of the Select Committee on Transportation in London. It was a position of influence well beyond his years and experience. It did, however, reflect the political power he wielded as leader of a minority group called the Philosophical Radicals whose support in the House of Commons was essential to the Whig government. And in the land where class still ruled despite the Reform Act of 1832, it was also of course a reflection of his aristocratic birth. Molesworth was 27 years old in 1837 when he became Chairman of the Transportation Committee. He had been a member of parliament since 1832 and was known for his support for causes such as the abolition of slavery, further parliamentary reform, abolition of the Corn Laws as well as his belief that Britain and her colonies would benefit if the colonies achieved self-government but retained constitutional ties to the 'mother country'. One of his parliamentary colleagues, T.P. O'Connor, amused himself by observing Molesworth in 1837, noting in his diary:

> Of all the groups in the House, the one that strikes you as containing the youngest and best-dressed men is the Radical Group. At their head sits Sir William Molesworth, who does not look more than twenty-eight, a dandy in dress and somewhat Dundrearyish in delivery; fair in complexion, and with hair approaching in colour red; eye-glassed, and

altogether like a Radical leader who has a rent-roll of £12,000 or £14,000 a year.[1]

It was an anomaly of Molesworth's entire career that he lived richly and well within aristocratic circles in London and the counties, while passionately advocating the rights of the poor with whom he had no personal acquaintance. His was an intellectual passion, humanitarian in abstract rather than practice. Even his biographer was forced to admit that 'Sir William had no desire to obtain any grass-root knowledge of the people for whose rights he fought.'[2] To many of his contemporaries, Molesworth was 'a revolutionary and a traitor to his class'.[3] For this very reason, he is an attractive figure to 21st-century observers, almost modern in his concern for social justice. But an examination of his influence rather than the causes he championed gives pause for thought about whether the 'radical aristocrat' would have been better muzzled.

Sir William Molesworth in 1838, when he was
Chairman of the Select Committee on Transportation

Becoming chairman of the Transportation Committee was a step towards Molesworth's long-term ambition of becoming Secretary of State for the Colonies. In the short term, however, his aim was to achieve the abolition of transportation to New South Wales and Van Diemen's Land, which he believed was nothing more than a variation of Negro slavery, whose abolition he had long supported. Now he would make a name for himself by ridding the earth of a similar abomination in the southern hemisphere. It suited the government to keep Molesworth occupied. While always keeping abreast of what the Committee was doing, the Cabinet essentially let him get on with it. Within days of the House voting to establish the Committee, Molesworth set about organising witnesses who were likely to help him make his case.[4] Three of them were readily to hand.

Analogies between transportation and slavery were not new. The long campaign to abolish slavery in the British Empire placed much weight on how slavery corrupted not only the slave, but also the master and the whole society in which the practice occurred. During the 1830s, the same argument was increasingly applied to the convict system in New South Wales.[5] In this climate, three authors were particularly influential because of their experience in the penal colonies. In *New South Wales; its Present State and Future Prospects; Being a Statement and Documentary Evidence submitted in support of Petitions to His Majesty and Parliament*, James Macarthur, one of the largest landholders in the colony, argued among other things that the colony's prosperity was now so established that it would continue even without convict labour.[6] Reverend Dr J.D. Lang published a second edition of *An Historical and Statistical Account of New South Wales; its Present State and Future Prospects; Being a Statement with Documentary Evidence* and also a pamphlet titled *Transportation and Colonisation*. His passion was the cause of free immigration to the colony, with the aim that immigrants would soon outnumber the convict element. In making his argument, Lang drew parallels with slavery and its pervasive corruption. He also made much of the immorality of convict society, calling New South Wales nothing more than 'a human dunghill'.[7] *The Felonry of New South Wales* was written by 'Major' James Mudie, a landowner from the Hunter Valley. As we saw in the last chapter, Mudie and his son-in-law John Lanarch were the targets of revolt by his assigned servants, incensed by the harsh treatment they received. Not long after that incident, Governor Bourke had removed Mudie and several others from their positions as magistrates. In retaliation, Mudie was intensely critical of Bourke's administration and conditions in the colony generally. In the quest for revenge, Mudie in conjunction with Ernest Slade, former superintendent of the Sydney Barracks who had also been dismissed by Bourke, created a lobby group in London that trampled heedlessly on the reputation of the colony. It suited the Molesworth Committee to provide them with a platform. Before 1837 drew to a close, the three authors, and Ernest Slade, had made personal appearances before the Molesworth Committee.[8]

None of these three works was read discreetly or discussed behind closed doors by a few parliamentarians. They were extensively reviewed and debated in the press throughout Britain. For instance, in September 1837 the *Times* said of Dr Lang's two-volume work that: 'the most instructive part of the Doctor's volumes is the account which he gives of the fatal inadequacy of the system at present adopted for transported felons, the dreadful state of moral depravity in which the class is plunged and the absurdity of a punishment which is so administered as to be no punishment at all and often actually betters the condition of the convict'.[9] All three authors' views were disseminated even more widely in late 1837, when Molesworth published the evidence the Committee had received so far. On the strength of it, he ensured that his committee would be empowered to continue its investigation.

In Britain, public debate about Botany Bay had a long history. It was fuelled not only by conditions, or supposed conditions, in the colony but also by issues, such as penal reform or the abolition of slavery, that were advocated by one section or another of English society. The arena for these debates was parliament and the press.

Public controversy about Botany Bay began as soon as the Pitt Government announced that it was sending prisoners to found a colony on the other side of the world. Fiery words were exchanged in parliament. Prison reformers condemned the decision as 'a regressive step and an inhumane solution to the nation's penal problems'. The topic was enmeshed in political point-scoring between Whigs and Tories, between parliament and the monarchy, the latter personified by the unpopular Prince of Wales, later Prince Regent. Criticism frequently took the form of mockery and scorn, a deadly combination from Australia's point of view because they last longer than earnestness. The colony of thieves was a gift to the cartoonist's pen. Even before the First Fleet had sailed, the Prince of Wales and some of the Whig politicians were depicted being 'transported' along with the convicts. Jonathan King, author of *The Cartoon History of Australia*, concluded: 'Before long the concept of a convict settlement at Botany Bay became a popular vehicle for political satire and the butt of many English jokes. Having acquired this ridiculous image at the outset, it was some time before the new colony was taken seriously.'[10] It is questionable, however, whether the colony was ever taken seriously. Instead, as John Hirst pointed out, over time New South Wales changed from being a passive target to playing 'straight man' in the comedy. When, with due solemnity, the colony petitioned the House of Commons for its own parliament the request was greeted with howls of amusement: 'A precious tale the sage Australian weaves—A House of Commons for a Den of Thieves!' Such wit could bear recycling. It was picked up and publicised further by John Dunmore Lang in his *Account of New South Wales*.[11]

By no means did the jokes evaporate just because the young settlement stabilised and showed signs of prosperity. In the British mind, even the increasing number of free emigrants, most of them somewhat doubtful rather than enthusiastic about their destination, did not dent the image of a society of criminals. In any event, cartoonists made sure that anyone contemplating emigration to New South Wales was aware of the nature of their destination. 'Do you wish to go to hell or Botany Bay, sir?' asks the shipping clerk in one cartoon. There were games with the name, with the class of emigrants, with their suspect background. 'I want to go to Bottomy bay,' says a young man, drawn with the black-rimmed eyes and rough features with which cartoonists denoted criminals. Huddled nearby is a trio of over-dressed women in very large hats, giggling. 'I'd like to see the naughty place better than any thing,' says one to another.[12] Political satire alone would have ensured that Botany Bay remained in the public eye. Politicians continued to be 'transported' there in cartoons well after the Prince Regent had become George IV in 1820 and for years after he was dead. In the late 1820s and 1830s, when English politics was dominated by the question of parliamentary reform, the Duke of Wellington was 'transported' pictorially for 'oppressing the common people'. Slightly later, another cartoon showed the Tolpuddle Martyrs returning to England with their pardons, while in the foreground the Earl Grey Ministry, who transported them, is embarking for Botany Bay.[13] Cartoonists kept Botany Bay alive in the British consciousness for a very long time. The ingredients were simply too good to abandon and no high-flown sentiments or idealistic hopes for the colony managed to deflect their glee. The colony continued to endure a barrage of jokes to a level unmatched by anything thrown at others such as South Africa, America or Canada.

In the early days, one of the native-born sons, W.C. Wentworth, tried hard to combat the endless ridicule by placing some facts and figures before the British public. In 1819, he published *A Statistical, Historical, and Political Description of the Colony of New South Wales, and its Dependent Settlements in Van Diemen's Land*.[14] In England to study law, Wentworth was nevertheless involved in the politics of New South Wales which were then, as so often, being fought out in London. The book was published in the context of a petition from New South Wales to the Prince Regent seeking trial by jury and the abolition of certain trade and other restrictions that arose from being a penal colony. As always the colony and its affairs were a useful political football, kicked around in the interests of British goals. When these matched the interests of a faction of the leading colonists, they would feed their allies with ammunition for their attack on the British government. In the short term, colonial lobbyists might win or lose an issue, but in the longer term the reputation of Botany Bay was damaged. When Wentworth was in London, the political focus was on bringing down Governor Macquarie and, through him, Lord Bathurst—a tactic used by parliamentarian H.G. Bennet, who was an opponent both of transportation and of the Tories. In 1819 he published a strident criticism of Governor Macquarie's administration of New South Wales called *A Letter to Lord Sidmouth*. Intent on demolishing the colony, Bennet had no qualms about demolishing its young advocate as well. Listening from the Public Gallery, Wentworth was shocked to learn from Bennet's speech to the House of Commons that his father, D'Arcy Wentworth, had fled to Botany Bay to avoid conviction for highway robbery. Proud of his father, who was one of the colony's leading citizens, Wentworth had no idea of his past misdeeds until that moment.[15]

In addition to the jokers and the parliamentarians, many serious public commentators had pretensions to judgement about the morality of Botany Bay and the principle of transportation as a penalty. Frequently, what they said dripped with contempt for Britain's newest colony, or if not contempt then mockery. One of the most assiduous was Reverend Sydney Smith, editor of the influential *Edinburgh Review*, who wrote columns on the subject over many years. Reviewing Wentworth's book and particularly his call for democratic institutions to be established in New South Wales, Smith opined that it was far too early for such a suggestion and anticipated the response which would in fact be delivered later on this subject. 'At present,' Smith wrote, 'we are afraid that a Botany Bay parliament would give rise to jokes; and jokes at present have a great agency in human affairs.'[16] While allowing that 'this land of convicts and kangaroos is beginning to rise into a very fine and flourishing settlement', Smith criticised Botany Bay as a failed 'experiment in criminal justice', claiming its failure was demonstrated by 'the extreme profligacy of manners' in the colony and the lack of reformation of the convicts.[17] At the same time, just as free emigration to New South Wales began to attract significant numbers of Scots, he let fly with a coruscating opinion:

> New South Wales is a sink of wickedness, in which the majority of convicts of both sexes become infinitely more depraved than at the period of their arrival . . . As a mere colony, it is too distant and too expensive . . . a marsh, to be sure, may be drained and cultivated; but no man who has his choice would select it in the mean-time for his dwelling place.[18]

Smith reviewed Wentworth's book within the framework of H.G. Bennet's *Letter to Lord Sidmouth*. And it was Bennet's opinions—and Smith's own—that lasted, indeed gave substance to the yardstick against which later judgements would be measured.

The decision to send convicts out of Britain to a purpose-created colony displaced a scheme for purpose-built penitentiaries within Britain that had been first proposed in 1777 by the evangelical Christian John Howard.[19] Then, the foundation of the settlement at Sydney Cove virtually coincided with the publication of Jeremy Bentham's *Principles of Penal Law*, in which he argued against transportation and in favour of penitentiaries. Incorporating Howard's ideas in his plan, Bentham proposed separate confinement, strict discipline and time for moral reflection. He submitted the design for a model prison called a panopticon. A canny strategist, Bentham recognised that cost was an issue so he also made a strong case that penitentiaries would be cheaper than a convict colony. He even published the pamphlet *Panopticon Versus New South Wales*.[20] Supporting Bentham's ideas involved criticising the penal colony as part of the argument. The first debate in the English parliament about actual conditions at Botany Bay was prompted by a Benthamite who made much of 'the sterility of the soil' and general unsuitability of Botany Bay as a site for a convict settlement. Amid rumours that it was an unfit location, Pitt denied calls for an enquiry and refused to delay the sailing of the Third Fleet.[21]

The decision to found a convict colony would always have been controversial, but it was Botany Bay's misfortune to be juxtaposed not only with the rise of penal reform as a major issue but with the start of William Wilberforce's campaign to abolish slavery. The first anti-slavery organisation was established as the First Fleet sailed with its cargo of convict workers.[22] As Hirst points out, Botany Bay's image slowly changed during this wider debate from that of a penal colony with concern about the reform of the criminals to that of a slave colony where corruption was not confined to the criminals but to master as well as slave and all inhabitants of such a place. Wilberforce came to oppose slavery through his conversion to evangelical Christianity with its emphasis on morals both in thought and in action. A member of the Church of England, he was a rich and well-connected member of the English establishment, so well positioned in fact that it was Wilberforce who ensured the choice of an evangelical chaplain, Reverend Richard Johnson, to travel with the First Fleet.[23]

This appointment set the precedent for the later arrival of the equally evangelical Reverend Samuel Marsden, whose campaign to reform the morals of the women convicts in particular played such a significant role in creating their bad reputation. It would have done far less harm to the women's reputation—and that of the colony generally—if the early chaplains at Botany Bay had been Tory clergymen like Reverend Robert Knopwood in early Van Diemen's Land, who was worldly enough not to be shocked by the convicts. By comparison, the evangelicals Wilberforce introduced to the convict colony tended to alienate the convicts by their proselytising, although they were motivated by a deep religious commitment to reforming sinners. Johnson sailed for Botany Bay convinced of his mission. Even his later lamentations of failure were prefaced by commitment to the cause. 'Happy would I be were I to live upon bread and water [and undergo] severe hardships, did I but see some of those poor souls begin to think about their latter end.'[24]

The issues of penal reform, the abolition of slavery and the goals of evangelical Christianity were played out publicly in Britain. Caught in their spotlight was Botany Bay. Many of the leading proponents of one view or another, such as William Wilberforce, were members of parliament. The politicians' favourite tactic, then as now, was to establish a select committee. By that means, the character of the convicts and the nature of Botany Bay could be examined in minute detail, and to great public effect, while sensational accusations were given a platform as evidence to a committee. The press, of course, reported it all in detail.

In 1812, a select committee was established to enquire into transportation. Prompted in no small part by Reverend Samuel Marsden's crusade for the moral reformation of the women prisoners to his standards, it spent much time discussing whether the women were prostitutes. Were they capable of reform? Did their management as prisoners make them vulnerable to abuse and encourage prostitution? While exploring these questions, every possible complaint about the women's morals, their drinking, their language, and what was said to be their corrupting effect on their children as well as the male prisoners was widely publicised. These views were not new. They had been expressed from the time the First Fleet sailed. Books published by the officers on board those vessels contained derogatory descriptions, such as the now infamous passage where Lieutenant Ralph Clark described his reaction at Botany Bay to the sight of more female convicts arriving on the *Lady Juliana* in 1790. 'No, no—surely not! My God—not more of those damned whores! Never have I known worse women!'[25] From that moment, few claimed that they were anything but prostitutes. From the First Fleet to the end of transportation in Van Diemen's Land in 1853 and beyond, 'universal condemnation' describes the opinion of most observers. Even though it apportioned blame to the women's management in the colony, the vehicle for institutionalising this stereotype was the 1812 Select Committee in its final report:

> Your Committee feel . . . that the women sent out are of the most abandoned description, and that in many instances they are likely to whet and encourage the vices of men . . . much misery and vice are likely to prevail in a society in which the women bear no proportion to the men; in the colony at present, the number of men compared to that of women is as 2 to 1; to this, in great measure, the prevalence of pros-titution is reasonably to be attributed; but increase that proportion, and the temptation to abandoned vices will also be increased, and the hopes of establishing feelings of decency and morality amongst the lower classes will be still farther removed.[26]

The main preoccupation of the 1812 Select Committee, however, was whether the punishment of exile to Botany Bay fitted the crime better than could be achieved in penitentiaries in England. The investigation did not settle the argument to anyone's satisfaction. It only intensified matters. John Ritchie concluded: 'By 1818 New South Wales provided staple fare for politicians who clamoured for investigations into the state of the gaols, the criminal laws, and transport vessels. The antipodean outpost gave rise to books and pamphlets, and later to their reviewers' barbs. In its explosive propensity, Botany Bay furnished lobbyists with a cause.'[27]

In 1819, beset with complaints from all sides about the struggle between free settlers to the colony on the one hand and emancipists on the other, and from penal reformers and parliamentarians about the failure of Botany Bay as punishment, the British government sent Commissioner John Bigge to inves-tigate on the spot. Bigge's visit was the only time an official enquiry took place in the colony. They were usually carried out at a great distance, by people who had never visited the place they were discussing, with all the misconceptions that ignorance generated. The investigations of 1812 and 1819 specifically focused on Botany Bay. However, there were other enquiries into the state of British gaols, the amount of crime, the type of crime and the nature of punish-ment. Even though the situation in Britain was the issue, Botany Bay and its inhabitants came up for discussion in every one of them. The 1832 Select Committee on Secondary Punishment focused on the effectiveness of flogging, and information about the practice in New South Wales was closely scru-tinised. Reinforcing the criminal horrors of Botany Bay in the public mind, this committee concluded confidently that those flogged were 'criminals whose morals are so depraved that their reformation can hardly be expected'.[28] By the 1830s, arguments about convict transportation had reached a crescendo and a new voice was among the chorus. Promoting his own scheme for the establishment of an ideal colony in South Australia, Edward Gibbon Wakefield told the House of Commons Select Committee in 1836, 'I consider that in Australia at present there are no colonies; I look upon the settlements in New South Wales and Van Diemen's Land as mere gaols of a peculiar kind. They call the keeper "His Excellency" and the Chaplain "Right Reverend", but the real truth is that they are nothing else but gaols.'[29] The following year, Wakefield was appointed private secretary to Molesworth in his role as Chairman of the Transportation Committee.

After such a litany of select committees, it might be assumed that the Molesworth Committee was just one more in a long line. What could it possibly say about the colonies of New South Wales and Van Diemen's Land that had not already been aired in Britain? What could it add to the colonies' already disreputable image?

Like previous investigations, the Molesworth Committee focused on the system of managing the convicts, in particular the deployment of their labour. Everywhere they turned, they managed to discover the 'contamination' resulting from private assignment. 'In the evidence taken before Your Committee several horrible cases were stated of the corruption of the young children of settlers by convict servants; which cases presented a fearful picture of the social evils of the assignment system, and of the depravity of the persons whom it introduces into the midst of respectable families.'[30] The ambiguity about 'ownership' of the convict assigned to private employers was a boon to their abolitionist agenda and comparisons with slavery were repeatedly drawn. But the Committee struck an immoveable object in the form of Sir Francis Forbes, first Chief Justice of New South Wales, who would have none of it. He resisted the opportunity offered him to agree that assignment was analogous to slavery, telling the Committee instead that the extent to which an employer had right of property in the services of a convict assigned to him was similar to the extent a master had rights over his apprentice and definitely not similar to a master and slave relationship.[31]

Forbes' learned disclaimer cut no ice. The Committee simply turned to evidence from former governors, George Arthur and Richard Bourke. To some extent, both drew comparisons with slavery in their evidence, even though both believed in the benefits of transportation. Arthur argued his position in person, but Molesworth had been given permission to draw on Bourke's despatches to London since the former governor was still on the voyage home. When he read the published report, Bourke was horrified at the representation of his views as much as its general tenor. In December 1839, the nub of what had been taken as Bourke's evidence was published in the *Times*, but with additional comments that he had submitted since arriving home in late 1838. Bourke, or someone else

from the government, very likely arranged its publication. Outraged by the
Committee's conclusions, he was forthright in the colony's defence. 'A picture of
horrors has lately been drawn in the [Molesworth] report,' he wrote. However,
'the unfavourable representations are manifestly great exaggerations'. Pointing
out that the 'vices' nominated by the Committee of 'drunkenness and brutal
coarseness of speech and manner' had also been described by a recent traveller in
Upper Canada, Bourke argued that they were characteristics of any newly formed
settlement and not evidence of some extraordinary depravity in Botany Bay.
Furthermore, he continued, 'I give it as my deliberate opinion, that not only has
transportation administered efficaciously to the wants of the settlers, and raised
up a magnificent colony, but has led to the moral improvement of the convicts,
to the full as much as . . . [penitentiary] discipline in Great Britain and Ireland.'
Bourke went on to concede that he was aware transportation was a mixed benefit
and that he would favour gradually discontinuing it, and he did not resile from
his opinions of the effect of assigned convict labour on the colony's inhabitants
and the benefit that would arise from the end of transportation.

> The chief evils which will thus be avoided, besides the intro-
> duction of so many persons convicted of crime, are the
> pernicious effects of the use of convicts, which is slave labour,
> upon the character of the masters and the jealousy created and
> continued by the difference of caste between bond and free.[32]

Forced by Forbes to accept that assignment was not slavery 'in law', the
Committee nevertheless felt emboldened by references such as Bourke's,
quoted above, to conclude that assignment was slavery in practice. To do so, it
had to ignore the convicts' rights under the Master and Servant Act, which was
similar to that operating in Britain. It also disregarded the Summary Jurisdiction Act introduced by Bourke in 1832, which covered the discipline,
treatment and rights of convicts and limited the powers of a single magistrate
to impose punishment.[33] The Committee report even referred to 'the convict
slave'. Having given the slavery allegations a good airing, however, the Committee officially concluded that assignment was a 'mere lottery', which could never
guarantee the punishment would fit the crime.[34] They went on to justify their
recommendation to replace assignment with another system as follows:

> All these descriptions of punishment i.e. chain gangs, road
> parties and penal settlement, though differing in degrees of
> severity, nearly resemble each other in their main features; all
> the criminals under punishment are herded together, mutually

corrupting each other, and are constrained by fear alone to the performance of labour; and consequently the moral reformation of an offender is seldom or never effected.[35]

Despite this reasoning, the Molesworth Report then recommended replacing a system in which convicts were distributed widely across vast spaces, frequently labouring on their own or with one or two companions, or where they lived something approximating the life of a normal domestic servant, with the very aspects they criticise. Rather than newly arrived convicts being assigned to private service in towns or pastoral properties, they would be herded into gangs for at least two years. Working in gangs would become the norm rather than an exceptional punishment for colonial offenders. In this way, it was anticipated that management of the convicts would become predictable and orderly and fitting. New South Wales escaped this tidy but, as it turned out, terrible solution because the British government, increasingly concerned with the discrepancy between a free society and a gaol, ended transportation to that colony in 1841. Van Diemen's Land and Norfolk Island, however, felt the full force of Molesworth's recommendation.

In some instances the Committee had absolutely nothing new to add. The subject of the women prisoners was examined yet again and the same conclusions recycled with the same exclamations of horror as had occurred at intervals since Botany Bay was established. Molesworth's report was utterly predictable about the women. In 1837 the parliamentarians were still focused on prostitution, just as they had been in 1812. Sir Francis Forbes was one of those quizzed on the subject. 'You said there were many houses of ill-fame in Sydney; is prostitution common?' Forbes replied, 'It is common.' Pressed about how he knew, Forbes told the Committee that he had researched the subject because he was going to write a book about the colony; however, he had abandoned the project because someone, he doesn't say who, persuaded him not to publish it.[36] The verdict delivered in the Committee's report was a devastating condemnation, described by one historian as 'prurient, almost voyeuristic'.[37] According to the Report the female convicts:

> are all of them, with scarcely an exception, drunken, abandoned prostitutes; and even were any of them inclined to be well-conducted, the disproportion of sexes in the penal colonies is so great, that they are exposed to irresistible temptations . . . they are not uncommonly employed as public prostitutes . . . marriages among convicts rarely . . . turn out well.[38]

Having disposed of the female convicts in the usual terms, the Molesworth Committee then turned to the sexual lives of the men. This subject had not been canvassed by previous committees. Here, Molesworth discovered a goldmine of fresh, startling information that could be deployed in the cause of abolishing transportation and he exploited it to the full. The Committee's source was predominantly men of the cloth. In their evidence, 'depravity' was a term they used frequently. Exactly what constituted 'depravity' was not always articulated. Depravity could be more in the eye of the beholder than in reality. To some people, gambling or drunkenness or profanity constituted depravity. Most commentators agreed that all three were rife in Botany Bay. However, in talking about moral filth and depravity to Molesworth, the commentators were implying something that worried them, as men as well as clergymen, far more than prostitution amongst the women. It was homosexuality that pre-occupied the Molesworth Committee. When 'depravity' is mentioned, it is 'unnatural crime', sometimes 'nameless crime', that is meant.

Ministers of religion had been to the fore with opinions about the colony since the beginning of settlement. From 1788, the clergymen's views ranged from despair at the task before them to a later determination to abolish the evil of transportation altogether. A chronological selection of their opinions, however, reveals that their hyperbole increased and the content changed the further removed they were from personal acquaintance with the prisoners. At the small settlement beside Sydney Cove in 1788, where prisoners and gaolers were personally known to one another, the chaplain to the First Fleet, Reverend Richard Johnson, despaired. 'They neither see nor will be persuaded to seek the Lord of Mercy and Compassion of God,' he cried. 'They prefer their lust before their souls, yea, most of them will sell their souls for a glass of grog, so blind, so foolish, so hardened are they.'[39] Johnson, of course, was trying to save the souls of people on his terms, when they were enjoying themselves on their terms. As with Reverend Samuel Marsden who followed him as chaplain to the colony, it was the clergyman's view that went into the mix of opinions that made up the reputation of the convicts. They were the source that so many subsequent writers drew on. In 1799, Reverend William Henry enumerated the prisoners' sins as 'avarice, extortion, pride, theft, blasphemy, drunkenness, sabbath breaking, fornication and adultery'—a condemnation certainly, but one so specific that it was plainly based on personal encounters with its subjects.[40] In 1819, Reverend Robert Knopwood, the earliest chaplain in Van Diemen's Land, gave an equally personal but quite different opinion in evidence to Commissioner Bigge. His acquaintance with convicts was wide-ranging and direct. Asked whether transportation had caused them to reform, he replied, 'I do not think they would attempt now to do anything wrong and the Term they use is when speaking of such occasions "I will not throw a Chance away".'[41]

Before the Molesworth Committee, the clergymen outdid all previous efforts. In fact, the clerics reached such a paroxysm of alarm about the evils of transportation that their rhetoric shaped Australia's reputation for generations.

A primary witness was the Anglican Archbishop of Dublin, Richard Whateley, who had been campaigning against transportation since 1832.[42] Whateley had never been to New South Wales, nor met the convicts he condemned, but nevertheless felt free to express what A.G.L. Shaw described as 'passionate but singularly inaccurate' opinions. In a series of pamphlets culminating in submissions to the Molesworth Committee, Whateley denigrated all things Botany Bay from every possible angle, including for example the risk posed for Britons if the convicts returned there. 'If only five out of every fifty should come back, those five would bring home with them a mass of depravity great, and of a more infectious kind, than the whole fifty took out with them.'

By publishing a further letter from the Archbishop in the same volume as the Committee's report, Molesworth ensured that his views reached a wide audience, including not only parliamentarians and the press but legions of clergymen, priests and missionaries of all description. In his letter Whateley commented on the evidence the Committee had heard. In an attempt to rationalise how 'an enlightened and civilised country' such as Britain operated the penal colonies for so many decades, he argued that the details were so horrible that nobody could bring themself to look closely enough.

> Such facts as have been now established, men might be excused for refusing to credit without investigation. And then the investigation was not only troublesome, but so painful and revolting—the details were not only so horrible, but so nauseous and disgusting and unutterably indecent—so unredeemed by the excitement of any of those sublimer feelings which make men listen with avidity even to the horrors of war—that they turned aside and shut their eyes, with a vague hope that things were not so bad as had been represented. And thus the very enormity and loathsomeness of the evil helped to perpetuate it.[43]

This was New South Wales and Van Diemen's Land he was talking about, a place where many disadvantaged people had made good, a place they were intensely proud of. Whateley's views were not a re-run of old issues and similar conclusions. This was new indeed. The choice of words alone—'loathsome', 'nauseous', 'disgusting', 'unutterably indecent', 'revolting'—had not been applied before to the penal colonies.

Whateley's rhetoric was given substance by the later testimony to the Molesworth Committee of various religious visitors to Norfolk Island, such as the Quaker missionary James Backhouse, who gave evidence about his visit to the island in 1835, shortly after the execution of the mutineers who were visited by Father Ullathorne. Backhouse later published his impressions in a widely read book, *Narrative of a Visit to the Australian Colonies*. The trial of the mutineers revealed much about the brutal life on the island and the despair of the prisoners, he said. 'This island, beautiful by nature and comparable to the Garden of Eden,' reported Backhouse, 'is rendered not only a moral wilderness, but a place of torment to these men, not so much by the punishments of the law, as by their conduct to one another.' The Reverend W.T. Stiles, who accompanied Ullathorne, was more explicit. On Norfolk Island, he found 'blasphemy, rage, mutual hatred, and the unrestrained indulgence of unnatural lusts'.[44] Former Governor Sir George Arthur attempted to counter Whateley and the others. A genuine believer in transportation as an effective means of punishing crime, in 1833 he wrote a pamphlet entitled *Observations upon Secondary Punishment* and then, in 1835, *A Defence of Transportation*, which was in direct response to 'another effusion', as Shaw calls it, from Whateley. Unfortunately for the penal colonies, Archbishop Whateley's occupation gave his hyperbole credibility.[45]

And then there was Father Ullathorne. Having read his pamphlet, *The Catholic Mission in Australia*, which was circulated in Britain from late 1837, Molesworth sought him out with an invitation to appear as a witness before the Committee. Since the evidence taken so far had already been published, Ullathorne was able to read it in advance. While not disagreeing with any of it, he felt he had something to add. 'I can see clearly that they have not yet got hold of the right thread of ideas,' he wrote to a friend, 'viz. the effect of the system upon the mind and feelings of the prisoner and the specific result in his moral habit; nor have they got anything satisfactory about Norfolk Island.'[46] He appeared before the Committee on 8 and 12 February 1838,[47] his evidence consolidating vague allegations into solid accusations that transportation spread homosexuality, that homosexuality was rife among the prisoners, particularly on Norfolk Island, that men already homosexuals 'contaminated' others who were not, and that the community at large was at risk from this stain. For Molesworth, Ullathorne's evidence was a gift.

The young Vicar General gained enormous credibility from the fact he resided in the penal colonies. His personal acquaintance with the prisoners was something he emphasised at great length, yet what he had to say in *The Catholic Mission* gave the lie to that claim. His descriptions had none of the vivid immediacy of personal acquaintance. Instead, they depersonalised the men and women in the most emotive terms: 'for five years I have conversed and almost lived with the convict . . . I have attended him in his barracks; I have followed him through every district of the country . . . the daughter of crime has burdened my ear with her tale of folly and of woe; the dark-faced man has come to me, in his dress of shame and clanking fetters, from the degraded iron-gang . . . he has poured his whole soul into my breast ...' Like Molesworth's compassion, Ullathorne's was intellectual. For all his first-hand acquaintance with 'evil', his evidence was that of a man distant from his subject. Determination that transportation should be abolished because it was evil in principle won out over the reality he lived among in Sydney. In any event, he had not lived long enough in the colony to develop any affection for it. In both *The Catholic Mission in Australia* and in evidence to the Molesworth Committee, Ullathorne damned New South Wales and Van Diemen's Land to a global audience, the shock of his encounter with Norfolk Island raising his eloquence to transcendent heights:

*Father William Ullathorne was in his mid-twenties
during his time in New South Wales*

Sixty thousand souls are festering in bondage. The iron which cankers their heal [*sic*] corrodes their heart; the scourge which drinks the blood their flesh, devours the spirit of their manhood . . . they are infinitely worse than when their country threw them away . . . We have taken a vast portion of God's earth, and have made it a cesspool; we have taken the oceans, which with their wonders, gird the globe and have made them the channels of a sink; we have poured scum upon scum, and dregs upon dregs, of the off scourings of mankind, and as these harden and become consistent together we are building up with them a nation of crime, to be, unless something be speedily done, a curse and plague, and a by-word to all the people of the earth.[48]

Highly coloured indeed. Well might Archbishop Polding attempt to explain it away. But it fitted too readily the long-standing British image of scandalous, naughty Botany Bay, that 'sink of wickedness' as Sydney Smith termed it in 1819. After Molesworth, the penal colonies were no longer a fascinating curiosity, a 'land of contrarieties' where everything from animals to landscape to society confounded expectations.[49] The allegations about widespread homosexuality took the Bay's image to new regions. This did not titillate while it delightfully scandalised. This turned men's stomachs in a very basic masculine way.

When the Molesworth Report was tabled in parliament, Edward Gibbon Wakefield congratulated his young patron, Sir William, on having dealt the death blow to 'an unclean thing'.[50] In describing transportation this way, Wakefield encapsulated the revulsion of feeling that had occurred in people's minds. As a result of the Molesworth investigations, the analogies with slavery and most particularly the emphasis at every turn on 'depravity', the image of the penal colonies had been transformed. According to John Ritchie, the Committee had created a picture of New South Wales 'as a place in which drunkenness, prostitution, licentiousness and dissipation thrived, and where sodomy and buggery were not uncommon . . . the moral quagmire of the Empire'.[51] Humour about Botany Bay, some of it almost affectionate, was no longer acceptable. The 50-year debate about crime and punishment had been subsumed by something repulsive.

Those with first-hand knowledge of the colonies were horrified. As we have seen, the former governor, Bourke, hastened to get some contradictory opinions into print as soon as possible. For those who knew the colony, what hurt most was the way, to quote Ritchie, 'any advances and improvements which had occurred in New South Wales and in the social and moral conditions of its inhabitants were largely by-passed in the examinations and then suppressed in the report'.[52] The blow was that much harder because in Sydney they had been expecting praise for the transformation of their society. Moving to a fully fledged constitutional democracy was a major issue of the day in New South Wales. Most of the inhabitants were proudly confident that the Mother Country would recognise that they were ready for this responsibility. This eager but as it turned out naive expectation was obvious in the *Sydney Morning Herald* twelve months before Molesworth reported, when it noted the publication in London of works by James Macarthur, Dr J.D. Lang and James Mudie.

> Three books issuing from the presses almost simultaneously cannot but arouse interest in the capabilities of the Colony and in its political and social advancement. They must at least have the effect (whatever differences of opinion the respective works of these gentlemen give rise to) of exciting public attention to this Colony to a very considerable degree.[53]

As mentioned, Molesworth had arranged for the evidence heard by the Committee to be published in advance of its report, which was not tabled until August of 1838. By May, the colony knew what had been said, and by whom. Extracts of evidence were quoted in the colonial press. It caused, as Governor Gipps put it to Lord Glenelg, 'a very considerable sensation'.[54]

'Consternation' might have been more accurate. Hurt pride inflamed alarm at the damage that had been done to the colony's reputation. Fears were expressed about the economic and political impact. As might be expected, there was no discussion about the psychological damage to the local society and its inhabitants. Public meetings were held in New South Wales and Van Diemen's Land. In Sydney, Governor Gipps was asked for a committee of the local (appointed) Legislative Council to investigate how the system really worked to counteract 'the evil impressions which may have been produced in England in respect to the social and moral condition of the Colony'. The Council thought this idea unhelpful and instead added its collective voice by a series of resolutions that, one by one, countered the charges laid against the colony including, 'That the character of this colony . . . has unjustly suffered by the misrepresentation put forth in certain recent publications in the mother country; and especially in portions of the evidence taken before a Committee of the House of Commons'.[55] The members of Council were predominantly men with an economic interest in the supply of free labour that convicts provided. They were also the proprietors who had been described in evidence

to the Molesworth Committee as corrupt slave owners who cared nothing for
the reformation of their 'convict slaves'. The Council's testimony to convict
rehabilitation, therefore, was more self-defence than support for their ex-
prisoner fellow citizens. Nevertheless, they expressed the view that there had
been a widespread transformation in the behaviour of the former criminals:

> in the opinion of this Council, many men who previous to
> their conviction had been brought up in habits of idleness
> and vice, have acquired, by means of assignment, not only
> habits of industry and labour, but the knowledge of remu-
> nerative employment, which, on becoming free forms a
> strong inducement to continue in an honest course of life.

As requested, Gipps sent the Council's resolutions to London at the same
time as the petition from the public meeting.[56]

In Van Diemen's Land the reaction was slower than in New South Wales,
but by September 1838 that colony too had held public meetings. At Campbell
Town, the citizens recorded that they had 'read with serious and heartfelt grief,
mixed with honest indignation, the statements that have been propagated and
afterward disseminated through the press of the mother country'. Those who
came free to the country felt particularly threatened. They asked Sir John
Franklin, then Governor of Van Diemen's Land, if he would express his own
opinion of their social, moral and religious character as a community. Sir
John responded sympathetically to the wounded colonists, describing the
judgements of the Molesworth Committee as having 'absolute inapplicability'.
He countered the points raised in the report one by one, including the
charge that the convict gangs were so depraved that regiments stationed in
the colony were 'demoralised' by guarding them, then ended by reassuring the
colonists that:

> I should but imperfectly respond to your appeal did I confine
> myself a mere negative evidence in your favour, without
> giving my direct and ready testimony to your general regard
> to morality, decency and order; to the humanity and benevo-
> lence which mark all your efforts for the relief of suffering
> and of evil and to the desire which so universally prevails
> for improved means of education and more abundant minis-
> tration of religion . . . our free community need not shrink
> from a comparison with any corresponding population in
> Great Britain.

It may have been due to Franklin that the whole correspondence and the text of petitions and resolutions was published in the London press six months later.[57]

In the colonies, some indignation was expressed directly. Major Mudie had the temerity to return, apparently expecting to take up where he left off as a landholder in the Hunter Valley. He was confronted instead by the very angry son of John Kinchela, who whipped Mudie in the streets of Sydney for slandering his father in *The Felonry of New South Wales*.[58] Shortly after, Mudie quit the colony, never to return. Father Ullathorne was also confronted with the consequences of his claims. Returning to Sydney late in 1838, he faced harsh personal criticism for the evidence he had given. The colonists would have been even angrier had they known of his assiduous efforts to spread news of their 'pollution' by preaching from pulpits in Ireland and northern England and by conversation at the highest level at Dublin Castle, where a request was made for yet another pamphlet designed to correct the 'erroneous' impression held by the poor classes that transportation would place a man 'in a better state than fell to the lot of honest labourers at home'. Entitled *The Horrors of Transportation*, it essentially recycled the material from his *Catholic Mission,* but in this case 20,000 copies were printed and distributed to the parish clergy of Ireland.[59]

In Sydney, Ullathorne took the snubs and brickbats with equanimity, buoyed up, as his autobiography reveals, by his self-image as a martyr to a higher cause. 'Alone I endured the biting tempest. Not one friend had courage to stand by my side or near me. Should anyone look through the files of Sydney papers for the years 1838 and 1839, he will be astonished at the bitterness and the perseverance of that onslaught.'[60] In 1840, Father Ullathorne left Australia, also for the last time. His later career in Britain was star-studded, culminating in his appointment as Catholic Bishop of Birmingham.[61]

It is unlikely that most of the emancipists, let alone serving convicts, paid the furore much attention. What was said in Britain meant little to them now. In the far reaches of the bush, it was particularly irrelevant. In any event, illiteracy was still widespread. Even among those within reach of newspapers, only a few would have gathered to exclaim about reports in the *Gazette* or the *Monitor*. Undoubtedly, the horsewhipping of Major Mudie was passed along the bush telegraph amidst chuckles of delight, but outcries about 'depravity' and 'pollution' and 'unnatural crimes' would, if they reached the workingman's ears, have been greeted in most cases by the same indifferent shrug they gave a clergyman's proselytising. In New South Wales and Van Diemen's Land, the *Bensley* men continued to run their small business or drink or gamble the profits away, to raise their children, and to live and in some cases die unconcerned by such esoteric debates. Only a few of them were still caught in the penal system. The convicts from the *John* had reached ticket-of-leave status, and in some cases freedom. They had better things to do than worry about what the nobs in Macquarie Street were discussing, let alone the ones they left behind in London. On the Bathurst Road, the prisoners' work was nearing completion and in 1838 the large stockade at Cox's River closed, the smaller one at Hassan's Walls sufficient now to service the iron gangs.[62] When Ullathorne returned to Sydney, Patrick Quigley was waiting on the hulk for his despatch to Norfolk Island, and Francis Bodenham was in trouble again.

Two years earlier, Francis and Sarah had been charged at the Sydney Quarter Sessions with stealing nine jewelled pins including one of crystal and another of 'oriental amethyst'. Apparently in dire financial circumstances, they were living separately, Francis with his employer Lewis Joseph from whom he stole the pins and Sarah with Jane Ryan of Harrington Street. 'I took in the female prisoner for charity when her things were sold off,' Mrs Ryan told the court. Sarah had shown her and her daughter a collection of the pins and invited them to choose one each for themselves. Later, suspecting they might be stolen, Mrs Ryan sent word to Mr Joseph. He described how he had questioned Sarah at the Ryans' house and she had told him that Francis gave them to her to pay her board and lodging. Both Sarah and Francis cross-examined him, trying to save themselves from retribution. Sarah may have succeeded but Francis did not. As the Molesworth Committee was hearing its final witnesses, he was trying to recover his life after ten months on the roads in an iron gang.[63]

Within five years of its report, the Molesworth Committee was exposed as a failure. In December 1843, James Stephen at the Colonial Office declared assignment had been abolished 'inadvisedly'. A year later he wrote that the decision was taken 'rashly, hastily and ignorantly' and he was trenchantly critical of the Molesworth Report. 'Every fresh report seems to me more and more strongly to show how little the Transportation Committee understood the subject.'[64] Of course, no newspaper printed this criticism. No one published a book that reassessed the Report. Unlike the colonies and the prisoners concerning whom so many violent, extreme and excitable opinions had been publicised far and wide, criticism of Molesworth and his fellow committee members was expressed *sotto voce* and remained private.

When the activities of the Molesworth Committee are covered by Australian historians, which is infrequently, they are invariably illustrated by a photograph of the Chairman in middle age. Portly, sober, wearing a dark suit, Sir William Molesworth exactly fits the image of someone who would chair an important committee, a worthy figure for one so influential that he would fundamentally shape the culture of the Australian people. An alternative illustration exists in a portrait painted at the time he was chairing the

Transportation Committee, which tells a very different story about the age and social milieu of the man whose political ambitions had such influence on Australia. A few Australian historians, notably John Ritchie and Norma Townsend, have examined the politics and hypocrisy surrounding the Molesworth Committee, but it is usually treated as a 'dividing line'—for instance, it ended Volume II of Clark's *History of Australia*.[65] No one has examined it as part of a continuum. Consequently, no one has discussed the ramifications of sending a radical boy to do a man's job and the psychological havoc Molesworth wreaked on the colonies, whose citizens he deplored from the comfortable confines of Belgravia.

Historians argue about whether the Molesworth Report ended transportation to New South Wales or whether the British cabinet had anyway decided it was incompatible with the democratic institutions that colony was now demanding. There can be no argument about the sociological and psychological impact. Any Australians who examine the Molesworth Committee and the subsequent decade in detail find themselves moved to deep anger at the damage inflicted on their community. In 1976, that rage was apparent in John Ritchie's conclusion about Molesworth's activities. 'A people who had struggled to their feet and who were taking their first halting steps towards self-respect, permanent stability and independence were placed in the position of the mute accused and had slurs heaped upon them.'[66] But the damage did not end with those slurs. The seeds sown by Molesworth were harvested by others, with profound ramifications for the country they claimed to be saving.

Unlike previous select committees, Molesworth's influence was not confined to a couple of years of bad publicity in the British press, followed by indignant but futile responses from the colonies that petered out because the accusations had little local relevance. Molesworth's version of the convict stain was long-lasting. It crossed the seas to infect the colonists themselves. And his messengers, hastening to take ship in the years following the publicity about Molesworth's investigation, were battalions of clergymen.

CHAPTER 8
a pervading stain

By every account, the Reverend John West was a man of immense intelligence, energy and scope, 'a man of rare intellectual power, genial and warm-hearted, who quickly secured admirers who developed into attached and lasting friends'.[1] In 21st-century terms, West had charisma. Such a man would never have been content to spend his life as an Independent (Congregational) preacher in small British parishes such as Thetford in Norfolk where he spent four months, or Great Wakering in Essex where he spent two years, or Southam or Coleshill, both in Warwickshire, the latter his last and longest settling place. West needed to find a bigger challenge, the biggest possible challenge available for a man of his calling. After four years in Coleshill, he was ready for something more. In June 1838 he offered himself to the Independents' Colonial Missionary Society. In August, he sailed to Van Diemen's Land.[2]

West's decision to emigrate was sudden and it is not clear what prompted it. After four years of 'a vigorous achieving ministry', he suddenly became unsettled.[3] The Society's records reveal that he 'became available' after they had been looking for someone to 'hold the fort' in Hobart for over a year. Something happened at Coleshill, but exactly what cannot be discovered even by West's assiduous biographer, because the church Day Book for the period 'disappeared in the late nineteenth century'.[4] Nevertheless, West's friend and colleague, Reverend John Sibree, who preached at another chapel only a few miles away, felt it necessary to tell the well-wishers at West's farewell that he was 'not leaving because he is not beloved' and 'he is not leaving because of any moral

The Reverend John West

delinquency'.[5] Only two months earlier, and following heavy financial losses, John Fairfax, known to West as a prominent member of the Warwickshire network of Independents, had emigrated to New South Wales. His example might have set West thinking. Troubles with the congregation at Coleshill might have prompted him to metaphorically throw his hands in the air and resolve to leave it all behind. But this still begs the question of why Van Diemen's Land? Was it only because there was a temporary vacancy while Reverend Frederick Miller took a holiday?[6] Certainly, that 'living' would cushion the first shock of emigration for a man with a wife and five children. It would give them time to get established. But on the face of it, the recently 'free' New South Wales or the young 'always free' settlement of South Australia would have seemed far more attractive to an emigrant family. In 1852, when West was being severely criticised for his role in the anti-transportation campaign, a testimonial in the *Colonial Times* claimed that, 'When he left England he expected Van Diemen's

Land would hereafter be free. He did not mean to say that his ideas were very definite, but he knew that transportation was condemned and its abolition intended . . . it was not until 1843–4 that his sympathies were strongly engaged.'[7] There is sophistry in play around this point. Molesworth did not report until August 1838, after West had made the decision to go, and despite Molesworth's personal inclinations, the majority decision of the Committee did not recommend that transportation be abolished.[8]

The motive for West's emigration is important because of both the anti-transportation crusade he mounted in the decade following his arrival and its legacy. Where did that passion, verging at times on hysteria, come from? It is not drawing too long a bow to argue that in reading reports of the Molesworth Committee in the newspapers, as he would have done, and perhaps also reading Ullathorne's book or even more likely the opinions of the Anglican Archbishop, Richard Whateley, West saw a challenge that matched his own sense of destiny. West had plenty of opportunity and every reason to read the public debate in Britain about the state of the penal colonies. Indeed, this was just what the colonists feared potential migrants would do, read that their society was a cesspool and then decide that Canada or the United States would suit them better. For West—and it can be argued, for other clerics—the appalling picture of the colonies offered a mission in life, one they took up with vigour. Some support for this comes from the eulogist at West's funeral who recounted, 'In 1838, there was awakened in him [that] interest in the future and the fortunes of the Australian colonies.' According to the eulogist, he *then* sought information from John Fairfax, who was about to leave for Sydney.[9] Additional support that it was missionary zeal that made him choose Van Diemen's Land is evident from his friend Reverend John Sibree, who wrote on 30 August 1838 about the nobility of leaving England for 'that isthmus between heaven and hell, that receptacle of the felony and filth, the ignorance, hardihood, impudence and crime swept from the parent land, Van Diemen's Land'.[10] Ultimately, the greatest proof that West was influenced by Molesworth is the way he cast his crusade in Molesworth's terms, using his phrases and ideas and information.

It can be no accident that the most virulent anti-transportation campaigners were clergymen. The evidence of clergy to the Molesworth Committee was, in effect, a call to arms; there was work to be done in the southern hemisphere, battles to be fought by Christian soldiers. As we have seen, Ullathorne presented any clergymen looking for a cause with the perfect challenge: 'We are building a nation of crime to be, unless something be speedily done, a curse and a plague and a by-word to all the people of the earth.'[11] Want of religious instruction was often given as the cause of the depravity that Ullathorne and others deplored. In fact Lord Stanley had reacted to this concern by arranging for the employment (by government) of religious instructors to the convicts, who were civil employees because sufficient ordained clergymen were not available. Conflict erupted with the Church of England in Van Diemen's Land when Bishop Nixon refused to ordain them. The upshot was the creation of an ecclesiastical position of Superintendent of Convict Chaplains, to which position the colonial-based Archdeacon Marriott was appointed in 1845. He returned from visiting England in late 1846 accompanied by six ordained clergy and two lay religious teachers specially allocated for the convict service.[12] As we have seen, however, Ullathorne's message was widely distributed among the general religious community. Its impact can be judged by what followed.

In late 1838, five Sisters of Charity arrived to minister to the women convicts in the Female Factory at Parramatta. In 1843, the Roman Catholic Church responded to the challenge by elevating John Bede Polding to Archbishop in Sydney and sending him eighteen priests, students and brothers, including the first three Christian Brothers. It was the largest ecclesiastical group ever to land in Australia.[13] A similar surge in activity was noticeable in other denominations. In 1836 there were eighteen Anglican chaplains in New South Wales, which encompassed Port Phillip and Moreton Bay at the time. In 1847 there were 64, yet the population had only doubled.[14] Van Diemen's Land acquired its own Church of England bishop, with the appointment of Francis Nixon, in 1842.[15] In the same year R.W. Willson was appointed Roman Catholic Bishop of Hobart.[16]

It is not enough to explain the expansion of the churches by the 1836 Church Act (1837 in Van Diemen's Land). Introduced in New South Wales by Governor Richard Bourke, the Act 'irrevocably altered' the position of the Church of England by making financial assistance available to all denominations. Subsidies were provided to attract clergy from overseas, to help pay their stipends and to match parishioners' funds for the building of churches.[17] Thanks to the Governor's insistence that the subsidies apply equally, Roman Catholics, Wesleyans, Presbyterians and other smaller denominations flourished too. Only those groups, such as John West's Congregationalists, that adhered to the 'voluntary principle' did not accept state aid.[18] This was the period for which Michael Roe concluded, 'Despite many stresses, the Church [of England] probably had greater energy and inspiration in the forties than at any other period of her Australian history.'[19] He explained the religious energy during this period as a zeal for moral enlightenment, noting that this movement, although not exclusive to Australia, nevertheless established particularly deep roots here. While not examining the context created by the Molesworth Report and the subsequent anti-transportation campaign, Alan Atkinson nevertheless recognised that the evident moral zeal was a reaction to what went before. 'The great hope of reformers in this period . . . was to impose on the country something unlike its old self . . . there was to be a moral and self-respecting workforce to replace the convicts. There was to be temperance instead of drunkenness. There was to be settled family life instead of the old pre-dominance of single men.'[20] The Church Acts alone did not create this overwhelming drive to reform the population. If the work of the Molesworth Committee is examined not in isolation but as part of the whole, the role it played in creating the wider Australian context becomes obvious.

In 1838, when the West family landed in Van Diemen's Land, the popula-tion was divided almost equally between free and bond. The population was 41,562, of whom 23,244 were designated free but most of whom were eman-cipist families.[21] Transportation to New South Wales was soon to end, but Van Diemen's Land had no prospect of freedom to boost its confidence. Instead, the new system recommended by Molesworth was imposed increasingly from 1840. Private assignment was finished. Prisoners were to serve a probationary term of labour in public work gangs, during which time they would be care-fully graded. Eventually they would 'graduate' and receive a ticket-of-leave. But it was now that Van Diemen's Land actually fulfilled Governor Arthur's dream that it become 'the gaol of the Empire'. New South Wales was now a free society. Other colonies had refused to take convicts. With nowhere else to send its prisoners, the British government stepped up the numbers sent to the only remaining penal colony. By 1846 the total white population of Van Diemen's Land was 66,000, of whom 30,300 were convicts.[22]

The prisoners came from all corners of the globe: thieves, arsonists, burglars, forgers, poachers, protesters, rapists and murderers were from Britain gener-ally, but also court-martialled soldiers from India and China and all parts east and west, Hottentot bushmen from the Cape, rebels from Canada (and more soldiers), and Fenians, Ribbon men and Whiteboys from Ireland. The result for Van Diemen's Land was an influx of convicts in numbers the colony could not absorb. The probation system became grossly overloaded. Prisoners released with tickets-of-leave could not find work because of competition from their fellows—a situation made even worse by the economic depression of the 1840s. The Anglican Bishop of Van Diemen's Land called the island 'the lazar house of the British dominions'. In a private letter home, another resident described how the island, once 'a quiet, tranquil home for industrious man . . . is becoming the plague-spot of the south'.[23] By 1846, the probation system began to collapse under sheer weight of numbers. Finally convinced that the scheme had failed, the British government suspended transportation to Van Diemen's Land for two years while it reassessed the situation. Having also been assailed by reports from the colony that 'unnatural crime' was rife among the prisoners, it appointed Acting Governor Charles La Trobe to investigate.

Meanwhile, John West had settled in Launceston, where by 1841 he had established a new Congregational church. Barely a year after that, in conjunction with local businessman Richard Aikenhead, he had also founded and begun writing regularly for the *Launceston Examiner*, its editor in fact if not in name.[24] In effect, his congregation were his foot soldiers in the fight against transportation and the *Examiner* was his pulpit. The newspaper was described not as a religious paper but as a paper for the religious man. Writing with hindsight, West described his intention 'to create a new moral ground upon which the substance and true relevance of the fate of the colony could be promoted'.[25] Initially he trod very carefully on the subject of transportation, having been taken aback to discover when he first arrived that the assignment of prisoners was well regarded, as were the prisoners themselves in many cases.[26] A major source of this information was probably Edward Lord, a colonist of many years who was a fellow passenger on West's voyage to Hobart.[27] As the overloaded probation system increasingly created new political and economic attitudes to transportation, West was able to develop his moral attack against it. In pursuit of this high-minded goal, any weapon would do. Led by West—in fact inflamed by West—the colonists took up the rhetoric that their enemies had supplied to the Molesworth Committee. Even more destructively, they took to heart the allegations that a 'dreadful state of moral depravity' existed among the convicts.[28] People who had lived or worked beside such men for years, some who had been prisoners themselves, suddenly acted as though there was 'the unrestrained indulgence of unnatural lusts' in every barracks, behind every bush.[29]

The failure of the probation system was the factor used to justify the passionate opposition that developed to transportation. It was useful to explain changes in the attitude of leading colonists who had defended the convicts against Molesworth's criticisms in 1839 but were now making strident speeches against them. But there was a subterranean campaign at work, too. The clergy, West among them, were on the trail of the 'unnatural crime' described by Molesworth. As word spread of their views on this subject, particularly those described to La Trobe, the *Examiner* hastened to defend them against allegations of betrayal.

> When the free population were calumniated by the British press some years ago, the clergy belonging to every denomination came forward to vindicate our character from unjust reproach. But circumstances have changed; and these gentlemen possessing the same confidence in the colonists bear

testimony that they—that no class of men, however virtuous can resist the torrent of vice and contamination directed by the Imperial Government to this land.[30]

Public and private pressure on the subject of unnatural crime, as much as the actual breakdown of the probation system, caused the British government to call a halt to transportation while it established the truth of the situation. La Trobe was in the colony from September 1846 until late January 1847, during which time he toured every probation station. In the small, close networks of the colony, it soon became known that in addition to establishing the practical ramifications of the probation system, such as its cost, its inefficiency and its infrastructure, he was also looking for evidence of 'unnatural crime'. No doubt concerned that the government would simply blame the former governor Sir John Eardley-Wilmot for mismanagement and then continue as before, the *Examiner* stepped up its allegations of corrupt practices among the convicts to such a level of intensity that they provoked a reply.[31]

West's campaign against transportation can be dated publicly from a meeting of the Congregational Union in December 1843, and for some time he and his anti-transportation supporters were left to proselytise without vocal opposition. William Goodwin, proprietor of the *Cornwall Chronicle*, also published in Launceston, and a former captain of convict transports was probably the first to challenge them publicly. In November 1846, like West conscious that La Trobe would read what he said, Goodwin devoted his entire front page to attacking West's campaign. Under the heading 'Van Diemen's Land Grossly and Falsely libelled—the Miscreant Libellers—Their Motives and the Results', he began, 'We are compelled, in justice to this Colony, to allude to the disgusting subject, which for the past eighteen months or two years has been semi-weekly dwelt upon by a contemporary, who is self-styled, the organ of the religious public.' Goodwin blamed the *Examiner* for starting the panic over behaviour in the barracks.

It is we think, now, about two years, since the professed religious paper *discovered* the commission, at the chain gangs and penal stations, of crimes, the result of the association of depraved men; with a fiendish appetite for the beastly and the brutal, and a taste for the unnatural, the disgusting subject has been constantly dwelt upon ever since, and latterly in plain English the Colony at large has been described by the Organ of Religion as a Sodom and Gomorrah. [emphasis in original]

John West's opponent, William Goodwin,
editor of the Cornwall Chronicle

Knowing how much the emigrant population feared damage was being done to Van Diemen's Land's reputation at home, Goodwin emphasised the effect the *Examiner's* campaign was having in London by quoting an exchange between a visiting colonist and the 'head of a mercantile house' there. The colonist had been dumbfounded at the weight put on articles that had appeared in the *Examiner*. But when he tried to disabuse the businessman of their accuracy, he was silenced by the retort 'people do not usually degrade themselves'.[32] Over and above his rebuttals of West's charges, Goodwin was also a voice of commonsense. Sarcasm dripping from every word, he declared, 'The occasional commission of crime no doubt occurs in the large associations of felons in this Colony, as it does in England and in every country, but the common practice of the particular crime alluded to is most positively denied by the public authorities, by whom, in consequence of the reports circulated by the organ of the touch-me-nots, the most searching investigation has been conducted at every penal station and hiring depot in the Colony.' Pointing out that the gangs of men were well away from the community anyway, he concluded they 'could not have injured the colonists let their conduct be ever so bad . . . even allowing for the existence of the utmost depravity amongst them, and that it was dangerous to admit any of them into the service of the colonists, *the remedy for the evil was simply—not to hire them*' [emphasis added].[33]

Battle was joined. West did not take kindly to this public criticism and the extent of his resentment was revealed two years later when the reconstituted Anti-Transportation League included in its articles a resolution not to hire convicts. Whether from self-justification or the adrenalin of moral zeal, Goodwin's intervention spurred West to intensify his campaign during the following year.[34] In fact opposition was always a spur to West. Six months later, hearing that Governor Denison had described the anti-transportation group as 'fanatics', he responded in the *Examiner*, 'So much the better. Were never a great cause carried but by men of this character . . . The first advocates of religious liberty were all "fanatics". The first abolitionists of slavery were all "fanatics" . . . and now to this noble array of "fanatics", we have a small Tasmanian battalion added.'[35]

Strategically, West needed to ensure that the informal group of like-minded people he gathered around him expanded into an anti-transportation movement with wide support. In 1847, the Launceston Association for the Promotion of Cessation of Transportation was formed as an organising vehicle and a rallying point. Under its auspices, petitions were drawn up and meetings organised. West sometimes spoke at the meetings, but significantly, they were usually chaired and organised by others while West confined himself to the role of reporter. Some of the leading anti-transportationists came from his own Congregational flock, others were leading Launceston citizens. One of the most prominent was the wealthy landowner Richard Dry, himself the son of a political convict. Lloyd Robson is the only historian who has critically examined some of the movement's supporters. He looked closely for instance at a Dr Gaunt, whose gruesome ideas and appalling images carried weight because of his social and professional standing. Robson concluded that these stories, although accepted unquestioningly by historians, were 'dangerously close to crazed'.[36]

A major tactical goal of the anti-transportationists was to ensure that opposition extended beyond the middle class. The tactics for rallying the working class behind the movement began in Van Diemen's Land, although they would subsequently be taken up in other colonies. On 21 April 1847, a 'meeting of mechanics, tradesmen and others' was held in Launceston attended, according to the *Examiner*, by about 400 working-class persons. 'The higher classes might know and hear of the evils, but the lower classes, the working population, feel them,' Mr John Denny told the audience. He proposed a resolution that would put the opposition of the 'tradesmen, mechanics and other inhabitants' on the record.[37] Meetings like this were reported in detail in the *Examiner*. The texts of resolutions and petitions were reproduced. Each speaker's name and their comments were fully transcribed, with descriptions of how they were received by the audience.

When Governor Denison invited private comment from the magistrates on the subject of transportation, West drafted 'Thirty-Nine Articles Against Transportation' and ran them in a major splash over two days in the newspaper. The debate about the Articles that followed contains a demonstration of the tactics used to intimidate people into supporting the movement by making it a point of morality that they align themselves with it. To do otherwise was to risk contamination by association, as John West made very clear when demolishing a Mr Williamson who had dared to challenge his Thirty-Nine Articles. In the *Examiner*, West said about Williamson 'a man must have sunk very low in his own estimation if he preferred the society of the degraded felon to that of the lowest upright emigrant'.[38] At an individual level, particularly among the middle class, but in larger public gatherings as well, this was the pressure that converted people to support for the movement.

John West needed to be careful that he could not be undermined by complaints that he was neglecting his religious duties. This may be one reason why, as his biographer explained, it was 'his custom, to promote ideas, facilitate their life from his knowledge and remain *at the margins of the fray*' (emphasis in original).[39] Obviously, his superb tactical skills were often deployed verbally at planning meetings, in personal conversations which left no enduring trace. And many of the articles he wrote for the *Examiner* did not bear his name. Another example of the extent to which he was running the anti-transportation movement from under cover was the publication in 1847 of a passionate anti-transportation pamphlet entitled *Common Sense: An Enquiry Into the Influence of Transportation on the Colony of Van Diemen's Land*. It bore the by-line of Jacob Lackland, which was later revealed to be a pseudonym for John West.[40]

Throughout 1847, the *Examiner* relentlessly pursued the subject of depravity among the convicts and the contamination of the surrounding community. Barely an issue of the newspaper passed without some article on the subject. The activities of the prisoners in their barracks, for instance, was a recurring topic which veered from speculation to outright condemnation based on supposition. In response to the newspaper's constant attacks, the Superintendent of Convicts reorganised the Launceston hiring depot into three dormitories that held 250 men on principles of 'separation and surveillance'. The *Examiner* immediately shifted its focus to the potential for (sexual) corruption arising from overcrowding. Having forced an investigation by local magistrates, it was partially vindicated by the revelation that there was indeed overcrowding. In addition to 250 men sleeping in separated berths in the new dormitories, there were a further 208 men sleeping between them on the floor. Presumably these men, too, were separated—by the berths rising on either side.[41]

In 1847 the anti-transportationists established a London Agency Association to lobby the British parliament on their behalf. The attraction of mixing with the aristocratic political class around the Houses of Parliament must have been appealing and, according to Robson, West had hopes of becoming the Agency representative in London on a salary of £600 per year.[42] It came to nothing, however. Although not named on the committee that managed the association from Launceston, it was John West who drafted the instructions to John Alexander Jackson, who was appointed as the London-based representative.[43] In particular, Jackson liaised with Sir William Molesworth, who they had invited to chair the Agency board and who remained fully engaged by the subject.[44] As late as 1852, the 'radical aristocrat' was described by the London *Times* as the 'advocate of the cause of the oppressed and ruined colony'.[45]

In 1846 transportation had been suspended to Van Diemen's Land for two years only, although this fine detail was misinterpreted by Governor Denison, who told the colonists it had ended completely. However, the rejection during the 1840s by other colonies of British Colonial Secretary Lord Grey's offer to send them 'exiles' left the British government with nowhere else to send their prisoners. In 1848, over the outcry of 'betrayal' from the colonists, Grey resumed transportation to Van Diemen's Land and sent boatloads of men also to Victoria, New South Wales and Moreton Bay. He justified its continuance on the grounds that the prisoners had been rehabilitated by their period of separate confinement at home followed by public labour, all in accordance with the most modern penal principles. Abandoning his first idea that they should be transported with conditional pardons, he made a virtue of the fact they would arrive with tickets-of-leave, which meant their distribution through the colonies could be controlled. In fact, the discussion became very pedantic in its fine distinctions about what constituted transportation. In 1850, Grey insisted to Governor Denison, 'The penal system known as transportation will not be renewed. The diffusion of men instead of concentrating them in Penal and Probation Gangs totally changes its character.'[46]

John West's response to the arrival of more convicts was not long in coming. Another large and passionate meeting was held in Launceston, at which West spoke forcefully and persuasively. It was agreed that another petition should be sent to the Queen in England and to the British parliament. Through the mouthpiece of the *Examiner*, the formal constitution of an anti-transportation league was proposed whose members would agree not to employ convicts. In January 1849 the proposal became reality, first at Launceston and three months later at Hobart.[47] But West's ambition had outgrown the confines of Van Diemen's Land. He was aware of protests during 1849 in Victoria, New South Wales and Moreton Bay about the arrival of ships carrying Lord Grey's exiles, which created a more favourable climate for a movement against transportation.[48] In New Zealand, in 1849, even two petitions from Maori were forwarded to England, although according to Gregory Picker they had been 'craftily conceived and written' by European hands.[49] The *Sydney Morning Herald*, the *Moreton Bay Courier* and the *Southern Cross* in Auckland were writing supportive articles, even though Bathurst and its newspaper the *Bathurst Free Press* refused to cooperate.[50] West described the *Sydney Morning Herald* as 'the chief organ of the abolition cause', but the extent to which he, alone or with John Fairfax and the other newspaper proprietors, deliberately coordinated their coverage will require research in its own right.[51] Aware of all these activities, in August 1850 West proposed that the Vandemonians should appeal to the other colonies for support in their anti-transportation crusade. He even drafted the invitations to a meeting.[52]

In January 1851 a meeting of anti-transportation associations from other colonies, including New Zealand, was held in Melbourne.[53] Only New South Wales refused to take part. As the publicly acknowledged leader of the movement, West headed the delegation from Van Diemen's Land. His powerful oratory conjured up a frightening prospect for the other settlements. It was in their self-interest, he argued, to help Van Diemen's Land. If they did not, even New Zealand would not be free of the convict taint.

> In twenty years . . . convicted persons will have passed through Van Diemen's Land into the neighbouring colonies. They will consist of men not only originally depraved: all will have gone through the demoralising probation of public gangs; they will have dwelt, for several years in exclusively convict society, where every prevailing sympathy must be tainted with the habits of crime. This island will not be a filter; but the accumulation of moral wretchedness will unavoidably contaminate every mind and stamp on every character the impression of its peculiar constitution. The sacrifice of this colony will not, therefore, exempt the neighbouring settlements from any portion of

the mischief incident to direct transportation. They will receive the prisoners later in life, but deteriorated in character. Evil associations and evil men become worse and worse.[54]

In the face of such scaremongering, it is not surprising that the meeting resolved to band the individual bodies into one Australasian League dedicated to ridding their shores of convicts. Nor is it surprising that eighteen months later Victoria legislated to keep Vandemonians from crossing Bass Strait into the colony. They were followed not long after by South Australia. In the following decade, both colonies led the campaign to end transportation to Western Australia.[55]

In April 1851, a follow-up conference was held in New South Wales to persuade that colony to join the Australasian League.[56] After the Sydney meeting, the *Sydney Morning Herald*, established by his old friend from Warwickshire, John Fairfax, hailed West as a great man. 'His memory will ultimately be associated with a peaceful triumph which it belongs alone to a philanthropist who united earnestness and enthusiasm with vigour of mind and deep moral and religious feelings to achieve.'[57]

Despite this high praise, West worried about his reputation, as missing documents from both Coleshill and Launceston attest.[58] In the closing years of the anti-transportation campaign he was the target of much criticism, and in 1851 he was attacked so vehemently by the *Hobart Town Advertiser* that he threatened libel action. The matter was settled out of court when the paper paid him £50, which he gave to charity. Behind the scenes, some influential men were scathing. In 1851, Governor Denison described West to the Colonial Secretary of New South Wales as 'a dirty dog with whom no gentleman would associate . . . a man of some talent, but certainly unscrupulous as to the means he employs to gain his object' and one who 'pushed his hatred of transportation to the verge of disloyalty'.[59] Denison erred in one glaring respect. West's moral certitude that transportation was an evil may well have been genuine, but the basis on which he conducted the anti-transportation campaign revealed that he cared little for the colony. And the subsequent publication of his *History of Tasmania* ensured that he had the last—and lasting—word. Having conferred on the governor the kind of 'measured praise' he accorded other governors and which helped create his reputation for being 'judicious', West evened the score, saying about Denison, 'But even then it will not be forgotten, that in perpetuating the convict cause, he adopted any argument, however false, and tolerated any ally, however abject.'[60]

West wrote his two-volume *History* in what can be seen as a defensive move against the criticisms that he knew existed. Published in 1852, it was so well received that it became a primary source for historians until the present day.

Although highly praised for its literary qualities as well as its judicious tone, the *History* was also described by A.G.L. Shaw as 'propaganda' in the anti-transportation battle.[61] This is undeniable, given that the book was written while the anti-transportation campaign still raged and the space allocated to the cause far outweighed any examination of the prior history of the penal colonies. Beautifully written it may be, but in section 27 particularly, any attempt at balance is abandoned and West systematically demolishes any claim that a colonist could make in favour of transportation.[62] Unremarked to date is the extent to which the *History* distances West personally from the campaign, bringing forward colonist after colonist, naming them, describing their actions, giving them credit . . . and blaming others for anything that offended emancipists. From the *History*, you get little idea of the catalytic role that West himself played, and no idea at all of the tone and the language he used during the campaign. West was no fool. By 1850–51, when he was writing the *History,* he knew there were many people who would cast his role in a bad light. He used the book to dissociate himself from some of the extreme sentiments which he, more than most, had been responsible for stirring up. Noting that 'respectable expirees were disposed to murmur', he wrote: 'The caution and discrimination of the leaders of the movement could not always restrain the oratory of their friends and many offensive metaphors dropped in the warmth of speaking, not in any circumstances to be justified.'[63] Written virtually simultaneously with his own speech at the formation of the Australasian League in Melbourne, it is a mark of West's strategic skills that he prepared his cover so well. *The History of Tasmania* not only ensured his own view would dominate for years to come, it was his self-defence.

On the strength of his *History of Tasmania*, West has been categorised as a 'liberal'. It is an assessment based on the objects of his sympathy (the Aborigines, for instance) and his appraisal of the issues and characters that made up the story of the penal colony. For example, he was seen as 'cautious' and 'balanced' in dealing with the various governors.[64] Emphasis on the liberal aspect of his attitudes ignores the religious commitment that made West a Congregational minister in the first place. Presumably it is this that explains the virulence of his anti-transportation campaign. He made no secret that it was a moral crusade. He said so, again and again. 'As men and as Christians, we should declare in the presence of God that we are opposed to transportation and that no bribe shall induce us to seek its continuance . . . Let us all in the presence of God declare that we shall leave no measure unemployed to save our children from ruin and our fellow-colonists from destruction.'[65]

The subject of the anti-transportation movement and West himself warrant careful studies from several different angles. Beyond the occasional journal article, this has not so far been done. In their absence, a researcher can only agree with environmentalist Richard Flanagan that 'The myth they helped form as a weapon in their moral crusades against . . . transportation has survived to the present day.'[66]

Underlying all the liberal and logical reasoning, all the moral justification and the outpouring of compassion for the 'sinners', the real impetus for the anti-transportation movement was surely homophobia. Middle-class men in particular passed the message from one to another in muttered asides, evidence for which occasionally surfaced in public. At the inaugural meeting of the Australasian League, for instance, William Weston told the audience, 'Even I have been shocked some few days ago by a few simple details that had been related to me by my colleague [John West] which with all my knowledge of the wickedness of the system, I had never before dreamt.'[67] West's modern-day defenders argue that his homosexual scare campaign was 'just' a tactic designed to influence the British—a strange point if the goal is to preserve his self-defined reputation as a man of principle. Better, surely, to accept that his reaction to homosexuality was simply that of a man of his times and religion, and was genuinely felt.

When he died in 1873 the *Sydney Morning Herald*, of which West had been editor for nineteen years, ran an extravagant obituary which also purported to analyse his character. His *History of Tasmania*, the paper claimed, revealed a man with patience, who could master detail but see the bigger picture, a man with a philosophical mind, a certain judicial quality of mind that could discriminate and weigh evidence, a mind quick to find the salient points of attack, good at argument, without personal bitterness, a man with an enlarged tolerance of opinion.[68] If West possessed all these qualities—and it is true that his *History* and journalism reveal many of them—why were they not evident in his leadership of the anti-transportation campaign? So virulent were his allegations about the convicts, so hysterical his scaremongering about their contamination, that they betray some profound personal revulsion. They are incompatible with the man presented in the obituary. In normal circumstances, such a man would have found a balance between his determination to end transportation and concern for the good reputation and welfare of the colony. The fact that West proved incapable of achieving such equipoise on this subject is revealing in itself.

The hunt for evidence of homosexuality intensified with the operation of the probation system in Van Diemen's Land. When not labouring in gangs, the men slept in barracks together. Rumour was rife. Anxious settlers wrote letters to governors or colonial officials in London. Gentlemen passed confidential complaints from one to another and onwards to London. Ministers of religion were active in forwarding evidence directly to ministers in London. For instance, Reverend Philip Palmer, Minister of the Holy Trinity Church in

Hobart, wrote to the Secretary of State for the Colonies William Gladstone in April 1846, enclosing a letter from Robert Officer in which he described 'the awful extent of unnatural crime which exists among all the probation and other convict gangs'.[69] In a private letter to the Secretary of State Lord Stanley, Governor Sir Eardley-Wilmot confided his misgivings about 'unnatural vice' in the gangs, although he insisted in his official correspondence that he had 'no doubt of the moral and religious improvement' of the prisoners.[70] A report to the Comptroller General of Convicts in Van Diemen's Land on the probation system at Norfolk Island in 1845 was laid before the British parliament. Much of the writer's investigation focused on potential for and incidents of homosexuality beginning with the muster before the men went to bed, where he criticised the failure to personally identify each man.

> Under this lax numeral rather than personal muster, men in fact change from ward to ward with impunity, attracted by a vile all-pervading motive hereafter referred to . . . I am informed . . . that atrocities of the most shocking, odious character are there perpetrated, and that **** [asterisks in original] is indulged in to excess; that the young have no chance of escaping from abuse and that even forcible violation is resorted to.[71]

To support his findings, the writer, Robert Pringle Stewart, enclosed a letter from the medical officer about the cases of sexually transmitted disease he had treated.[72] As noted earlier, in 1846 Charles La Trobe, who was administering Van Diemen's Land in a gap between Eardley-Wilmot's dismissal and the arrival of Sir William Denison, was asked by the British government to investigate.

After a comprehensive tour of all the probation stations in the colony, including extensive discussions with officials of every kind, La Trobe's report was forwarded to London. It was published as a British parliamentary paper in 1848, but his findings on homosexuality, which were contained in Section Five of the Report, were considered so shocking that the section was omitted from the published version.[73] Now available for examination, that section reveals how the evidence before the Molesworth Committee had really set the hares running on the subject of homosexuality. By the mid-1840s, the citizenry of Van Diemen's Land were in a fever of anxiety. Some people 'open their ears to every tale or statement often promulgated by interested parties conscious of the difficulty of proof or disproof', wrote La Trobe. Some other people, he reported, would not concede any truth to the suggestion about 'the wide prevalence of such fearful pollution'. They simply refused to believe that arrangements 'devised and sanctioned by a Christian people' could give rise to it.[74] Others, however, were agitated and anxious, never doubting the rumours were true, speculating and whispering behind their hands about every sleazy possibility. Those most alarmed, La Trobe said, were the upper and supervisory classes. 'A very general impression of the existence and increased prevalence of the crime : . . appears at the present time to be entertained amongst the better class of Colonists,' he reported. 'And among those whose professional functions brings them more or less in contact with prisoners of certain classes, or with those directly placed in charge of them.' To this he added, 'It is also believed the [British] government is unwilling to do anything about it.'[75] These claims about the prevalence of 'unnatural crime', said La Trobe, were made 'by men whose personal character and intentions, were beyond question'. On further enquiry, however, he found that their whispered confidences were no more than suspicion or second-hand reports. His requests for details of names and places were met with denial or evasion. It became obvious he would find no individual prepared publicly and definitely to give substance to the rumours.[76] Cases brought to court were not definitive, either. In the main they failed to result in conviction. At the same time the number of committals demonstrate the mania that had gripped the colony.

1836	one	1842	none
1837	two	1843	two
1838	none	1844	three
1839	one	1845	four
1840	one	1846	nineteen[77]
1841	none		

Commenting on the steep increase in the twelve months during which he conducted his enquiry, La Trobe explained that few convictions had resulted from these charges. He added that sometimes the charges were trumped-up accusations by convicts against their fellows, either born of malice or because they thought it would do them some good.[78]

Deprived of hard evidence from the courts, La Trobe turned to the medical staff. Based at the various probation stations, they had direct and intimate knowledge of the prisoners. Some produced evidence of venereal disease, while warning it was not necessarily proof of sodomy. At Port Arthur there were two men categorised as homosexuals and fourteen diseased, but about whom no conclusions could be drawn. The boys at nearby Point Puer were found to be disease-free.[79] One forthright assistant surgeon, who had been at the Broadmarsh station for five years, declared with what seems to be impatience at the questioning, 'I have never had professionally the slightest reason to suspect the existence of unnatural crime amongst the men.' He was forced to admit, however, that he could not conclusively disprove its existence.[80] In fact, few medical men confirmed that the crime was widespread. Summarising their collective views, La Trobe reported, 'it is the opinion of the Medical Officers that unnatural crime does exist, but not to the same extent that common rumour would lead one to suppose'.[81]

The reaction of the clergymen was quite different to that of the medical men. La Trobe reported that they had 'no hesitation' in believing the wild rumours to be true, but their views were not based on vast personal acquaintance with the men. According to La Trobe, their impressions were gathered 'chiefly from the confessions of prisoners awaiting trial for capital offences or already under sentence of death', who had told the clergy that homosexuality was common. Told them what they wanted or expected to hear is the suspicion that arises. La Trobe questioned the clergymen in some detail and his scepticism is obvious when he adds, 'These revelations have been generally made either by those who denied being personally participators or youths averring their being unwilling, but passive instruments.'[82]

La Trobe examined the women's stations too. He reported that unnatural practices were definitely to be found at the Brickfields Hiring Depot in Hobart. 'To what extent the evil exists, it is however difficult to say,' he wrote, adding that the information was obtained by observation of the women rather than their confession. 'One absconds the other follows immediately; one receives punishment for misconduct the other commits some offence with the hope of rejoining her companion.' He relied on the matron for information and complimented her for 'the utmost care and vigilance'. It is not clear whether she told him that the women prisoners themselves reported the existence of homosexuality or whether he asked them directly.[83]

Essentially, La Trobe, for all his cautions about rumour-mongering and lack of proof, concluded that unnatural crime 'had taken a certain root among the convicts'. In his opinion, this alone was reason to change the system of managing convict labour. In making this recommendation he was as conscious of Britain's reputation as he was of the welfare of the colony and its population. 'The credit of the Government and of the Mother Country; the future welfare of both the Convict and the free population of the Colony, admits of no other alternative.'[84] Many respectable men had forcibly argued that 'this detestable vice' had a demoralising effect on the whole character of the colony. Allowing for their self-interest in returning to a system of private assignment, La Trobe admitted that it is 'a stigma upon the Colony; and that there are classes upon which it does exercise an influence, and that, undoubtedly, a most degrading one, even at this day'.

Knowledge that unnatural crime existed in various forms and the abominable details connected with it were not confined to the prisoners' barracks, but could be found in a village watch-house or a tavern.[85] La Trobe reported that it had become common talk with the lower classes. Whenever the Quarter Sessions included some poor benighted men accused of unnatural crime, the courthouse filled with spectators. 'There can be no doubt that to a certain extent, the public mind has become familiarised to the idea and [to] mention of it and consequently tainted.'[86]

The upshot of this prurient witch-hunt was to make it impossible for many people to support transportation, let alone admit to having been a convict or having a convict ancestor. Worse, the convict colony then set about shooting itself in the foot. Lacking the confidence to rebut the charges of depravity, the colonists took on the allegations of their enemies as if they were true. The large landholders could justify their support for the supply of free labour through transportation on economic grounds, but other citizens needed to prove their morality by opposing it.

It is impossible to gauge the extent of homosexuality in the colony—if it even matters. The perception alone that Botany Bay and Van Diemen's Land could be compared to Sodom and Gomorrah was damaging. There had always been concerns about the imbalance between the sexes in the colony, and this anxiety informed some of the inquisition at the 1812 Select Committee. Gradually, however, this focus on the lack of women was subsumed by something that was regarded as much more alarming. Writing in 1819, the gentleman convict James Hardy Vaux put sodomy on the record. He claimed that among his fellow prisoners 'robbery from each other . . . is as common as cursing and swearing . . . and unnatural crimes are openly committed'.[87] By the 1830s there were rumours that it was prevalent among the road gangs in New South Wales, at Moreton Bay and also at Norfolk Island. The Molesworth Committee asked, among others, Ernest Slade, Superintendent of the Hyde Park Barracks in Sydney before his dismissal by Governor Bourke, whether sodomy was common. He replied, 'Yes, but it was always impossible to establish it.' Quizzed further about where or among which convicts it occurred, he informed the Committee that complaints were made by young boys that the older men were taking liberties with them. The Committee then asked him: 'Amongst the convict population, would the suspicion of a person having been guilty of an unnatural crime excite abhorrence and detestation?' To which Slade answered, 'Only among the gentlemen convicts.' And there lies the nub of it. Class differences were crucial to judgement and no assertions of 'depravity' should be accepted at face value.

In the 1830s, young Thomas Cook could never quite bring himself to be explicit about what he saw along the Blue Mountains road. For the 21st-century reader, it is hard to be sure whether his sensibilities were being offended by foul language, rough manners, gambling, violence, corruption by the overseers, masturbation, or homosexual acts. Probably all of them, but to what degree is impossible to tell. Cook was appalled that there was some sympathy for the offenders. 'Several individuals were punished for the heinous offence, and although it may appear incredible it is nevertheless true that these wretches were generally viewed with feelings of sympathy and those who had brought such cases forward were looked upon with contempt and very few would afterwards associate with them.'[88]

Like prostitution, homosexuality could be in the eye, or the suspicious mind, of the beholder, but there is no doubt it existed. After his return from Norfolk Island William Crooks was involved in a case that sheds some light on what could happen in convict barracks. It confirms the loathing of informers but also reveals the heterosexual pressures operating in the prisoners' barracks.

Working in a gang out of the Newcastle stockade in 1845, Crooks turned Crown witness in the trial of James Fitzpatrick (known as Towzer) and John Fitzgerald for the murder of Peter McCormick, also a prisoner. The prisoners in the stockade slept four abed and this group was together. According to Crooks, he was sleeping peacefully on a Sunday night when his bedmate, McCormick, woke him up to point out what Fitzgerald and Fitzpatrick were doing alongside them. 'I'll report them,' McCormick told Crooks in a voice loud enough for the other two to hear, and he did. The next morning, Sergeant John Wilson, who was in charge of the stockade, cross-questioned Fitzpatrick. When Fitzpatrick returned to the barracks, other prisoners gathered round asking what it was about. Committing an unnatural crime, he told them, adding, 'That bloody wretch McCormick was trying to take away my character.' Michael Mulligan fired up, 'If he'd done that to me, I'd knock his brains out.' Other men echoed him. Now Fitzpatrick's manhood was at stake among the group. Shortly after, he demanded Mulligan let him have a knife. Despite his earlier incitement, Mulligan tried to dissuade Fitzpatrick but without success. 'Let me have it,' he insisted.

That night the whole barracks waited for the repercussions. McCormick was afraid. Crooks, ever the opportunistic old soldier, cast himself in a noble light, later telling the court, 'I took care to lay down next to McCormick. Neither of us were liked in the prison.' He noticed that Fitzpatrick was fully dressed. Despite the danger, Crooks left McCormick, ostensibly to urinate. Did he do a deal to save his own skin? Providentially, he was absent when Fitzpatrick yelled, 'You bloody wretch, I'll learn you to inform against me.' McCormick screamed, 'Murder! Murder!' Crooks said he rushed back to see

Fitzpatrick on his knees leaning over McCormick and stabbing him. Crooks called for help but none came. He said he tried to pull Fitzpatrick off but had to fall back because he was threatened too. McCormick staggered from the bed with his entrails hanging out. In the darkness, Fitzpatrick lunged after him calling out, 'Where is he?' Three voices from the other side called, 'here he is'. Fitzpatrick stabbed McCormick again, at which there was a general cry from the men, 'The bloody wretch!' and 'It serves him right.' The watchman, John Bateman, gazed out the door but called no one to help. He later told the court he was too frightened of the men to do anything. John Smith, another watchman, claimed his eyes were so bad at the time that 'I could not see a man two yards off. I did hear a general cry of "Give it him Towzer".' McCormick lived long enough to make a statement, which implicated Fitzgerald as well as Fitzpatrick.

The two young men endured the eight-hour trial each in his own way, Fitzpatrick highly emotional throughout; Fitzgerald, described by the *Maitland Mercury* as 'a remarkably little man', remaining impassive at all times. As the judge pronounced the sentence of death with no hope of mercy, Fitzpatrick erupted in an emotional frenzy. Face flushed, temples throbbing, he flourished his cap in the air, shouting vehemently, 'Hurrah! Hurrah! Hurrah!' They removed him hurriedly. Once outside, he fainted.

Crooks made the most of the limelight. Without him, a conviction would have been difficult. Other witnesses debated his claim that he had already left the bunk when Fitzpatrick attacked McCormick. Despite these doubts about his credibility, his demeanour and clarity impressed the *Maitland Mercury*. His evidence 'was given with great clearness', the newspaper commented, and when he had finished his testimony he told the court, 'in the most solemn manner' that 'although I am not liked in the gang, I have no malice against the other men'.[89] Nine months later, by then removed to the Woolloomooloo stockade at Sydney, Crooks tried hard to turn this cooperation with the court to his advantage. In June 1846, he petitioned Governor Sir George Gipps for mitigation of his colonial sentence, claiming, 'His Honour Mr Justice Dickenson was pleased to say that he would recommend me to the favourable consideration of your Excellency for the manner in which I gave my evidence.' The local magistrate duly forwarded the petition to the Governor but penned an indignant note on the flap: 'Mr Justice Dickenson merely recommended Crooks on having given good evidence and in a proper manner.' Then the magistrate added, 'Another witness says that he heard Crooks recommend Fitzpatrick to have satisfaction out of McCormick on account of what he had told of him.' Sir George called for Crooks' police record. After taking one look at the long recital of transgressions culminating in a sentence to Norfolk Island, he denied the request.[90]

The Crooks matter confirms, as might be expected, that there were homosexual incidents among the prisoners. Significantly, it also reveals that it was the homosexuals who suffered rather than the other way round. 'Contamination' was not an issue. Confronted by incidents of 'unnatural crime', the heterosexual criminal class was likely to make common cause with the aristocrats, the clergymen and the bourgeoisie. Even greater than their group dislike of homosexuals, however, was their hatred of informers. McCormick paid the penalty for running to the authorities. Crooks incurred the odium of his fellow prisoners for siding with them. It is a case such as this one, displayed for all to read in both the *Maitland Mercury* and the *Sydney Herald*, which informed people such as Chief Justice Forbes that sodomy existed among the convicts. However, similar cases could be found reported in the British press (although in far less detail) throughout the transportation period. In 1811, on the strength of one complaint, an investigation was carried out into sodomy on the *Captivity* hulk. No one condemned every Briton as 'depraved' on the strength of such an example.[91]

The section of La Trobe's report relating to homosexuality did not see the light of day until published by Ian Brand in 1990. Unofficially, however, a select circle in Hobart and Sydney and London was no doubt made aware of its contents. Outside that circle, speculation continued to run rife. Condemning the probation system as 'a fatal experiment', La Trobe reported that it had indeed contaminated Van Diemen's Land and that 'vice of every description is to be met with on every hand, not as isolated spots, but as a pervading stain'.[92]

Of course the prisoners did not take this nonsense passively. Beneath the effusions of morality, the anxious officialdom, the self-serving allegations, they had their own view. Some destroyed the bed boards erected to keep them apart. The superintendent of the Oatlands Probation Station reported that these were regularly 'removed and destroyed by the men in whom a general spirit of destructiveness exists and which it would be impossible to prevent'.[93] Reminiscent of a boarding school, suspicious superintendents reported men scrambling for cover when they entered barracks without warning, incidents which were solemnly put forward as proof that unnatural crime was occurring.[94] Surveillance was regularly thwarted. At the Colonial Hospital in Westbury, Mr Hall insisted that he placed lights in every ward at night, but confessed that 'they are seldom alight in the morning which they ought to be if no tricks were played with them'.[95] At Port Arthur, a prisoner poked a stick through the peephole, catching an officer on watch in the eye.[96]

Someone wrote a poem, which ran to ten verses, linking freedom from the pollution of unnatural crime with the end of transportation. Its scaremongering was explicit, as these extracts demonstrate:

Shall fathers weep and mourn
To see a lovely son
Debas'd, demoralis'd, deformed,
By *Britain's filth and scum?*

Shall mothers heave the sigh,
To see a daughter fair
Debauch'd, and sunk in infamy
By *those imported here?*

Shall Tasman's Isle so fam'd,
So lovely and so fair
From other nations be estrang'd
The *name of Sodom bear?*[97] [original emphases]

No one doubted this poem's serious nature at the time. It was published first in the *Launceston Examiner*, and not long after in Britain.[98] The poem could easily have been written by a despairing colonist or an anti-transportation campaigner. It could have been written by John West himself. Its publication certainly suited the campaign to end the flow of prisoners forever. Allegedly, the convict watchman for a probation gang kept a copy after finding it in a convict barracks.[99] However, it would be quite in character if the poem was, in fact, composed by a prisoner—and passed to a gullible official to the vast amusement of the entire barracks.

So if the prisoners at the time viewed the shenanigans of the officials with a mixture of contempt and humour, what were the feelings of ex-convicts? Dismay, mixed with fear for their descendants, most likely. Some of the *Bensley* men who were sent to Van Diemen's Land had moved away. William Brodribb and his family moved to Victoria about this time. But many had lived on the island now for more than 30 years.

In 1817, William Penny began his life in the colony ambitiously by renting a 50-acre farm at Herdsmans Cove. Sorell granted him an early ticket-of-leave and within eighteen months of his arrival he had ten acres of wheat and an acre of potatoes, with another 39 acres under pasture to feed his twelve cattle and 30 sheep. After his limited options in Gloucestershire, it must have seemed an amazing achievement. Back in the Vale of Berkeley, the Pennys did not have the community status or the experience that Collerton Farm gave his fellow poachers Thomas and William Collins. At any rate, it was all too hard for someone who had always been an employee and by the 1820 Muster Will Penny had returned to working as a servant, employed by Mr H. Thrupp, who was a landholder at

Old Beach. In December 1820, Will married Sarah Ring, but was still with Thrupp at the following muster in 1821. His convict record remained entirely unblemished. In May 1830, perhaps as a legacy from Governor Sorell's good offices, he received a free pardon. He could have chosen to return to England. Not long after, however, there are signs he was in financial difficulty. Someone took him before the magistrates over a debt of £3 6s. The verdict went against him even though the Bench reduced the sum he owed by half. Two years later he had another dispute over money, this time with his servant, J. Walker, who claimed he had not been paid for 'husbandry'. They settled the matter with Walker agreeing to return to Penny's service. By the time he died in 1860 at the very old age of 75, Will Penny was living in Campbell Town, the site of an emotional public meeting about Molesworth's comments on the colony. In death, he no longer had the status of a farmer. The register described him simply as a 'labourer'.[100]

Another Berkeley poacher, Jack Reeves, was also in Van Diemen's Land at this time. Like Will Penny he had received a ticket-of-leave in 1819. Also like Penny, he took up farming in his new home. Initially he rented a farm at Brown's River, which was about ten miles out of Hobart and could only be reached by water. In 1824 he moved closer to town and rented a farm at Crayfish Point, Sandy Bay. By 1828, the scope of his ambition had increased and he was renting 300 acres of land in Kingsboro parish. Granted a free pardon in 1831, he too could have returned to England. Instead he stayed and changed direction. By 1834 Reeves was a publican in Hobart. His wife, Elizabeth, died the following year, her illness perhaps the reason they gave up the farm. Over the next ten years, Reeves held the licence for the Stag and Hounds Hotel in Harrington Street, becoming something of a Hobart identity. In his entire career as a convict, Jack Reeves transgressed only twice. In April 1817, very soon after he arrived, the authorities solemnly recorded 'Absent from Divine Service', followed by the note 'acquitted'. Three years later, some equally officious clerk recorded 'Absent from Sunday muster', followed by the note 'reprimanded'. Both these absences occurred while he was farming at Brown's River. During the last decade of his life—and at the height of the slurs cast on all who were or had been convicts—Reeves lived in Patrick Street, at the corner of Lansdowne Street in Hobart. Thomas, the eldest of his three children, lived with him for at least part of that time. Reeves died painfully in 1859, aged 68, of what sounds like prostate cancer. His death certificate recorded his occupation as 'yeoman', a class category reminiscent of the land of his birth. After his death, his son and family moved to South Australia.[101]

The long voyage to Van Diemen's Land must have given Berkeley farmer Daniel Long a taste for the sea. Despite the attractions of his land grant in Sorell and the pub in the village that he ran as an extra source of income, he became caught up in the excitement of chasing whales. In 1832 the *Hobart Town Gazette* noted that he had killed '16 fine whales'. This distraction from his traditional occupation was only short-term. He was described as a 'farmer' when he died in December 1853, just as the colony was celebrating the end of transportation.[102]

The Scottish burglar whose name varied in the records from Charles to James to Henry Clephane was also in Van Diemen's Land during the anti-transportation debates. The tricks with his name had confused the convict officials so much that in at least two musters he was written off firstly as 'missing' and secondly as 'ran'.[103] A sailor by training, it appears he spent most of his penal servitude at sea. In 1822, as Charles Clephane, he prevailed upon his skipper, the captain of the colonial brig *Nereus*, to support his application to bring his father Andrew—a convict in New South Wales—to Van Diemen's Land.[104] He must have slipped away for a sea voyage or two after that, but he comes to light again in 1827, when a period of sustained harassment by the police begins. In Launceston, Clephane father and son skated on the edge of the law. They were 'known to police'. To what extent, however, the various charges laid against them were harassment rather than lawbreaking, it is impossible to tell. The number of absconding convict women whom Charles was accused of harbouring suggests he might have been running what was then called 'a bawdy house'. On the other hand, he might simply have been so sympathetic to absconding prisoners that he operated a safe house. The charges between 1827 and 1832 included illegally retailing wine in his dwelling-house (charge dismissed), illegally harbouring John Murray (fined), assaulting Elizabeth Hughes (charge dismissed), harbouring and concealing Mary Ann Scaley, wife of Odeland, a convict illegally at large (fined), illegally retailing gin (charge dismissed) and harbouring a convict (fined). Although accused many times, Charles avoided serious punishment.[105]

The nearest the police came to convicting Charles Clephane of serious charges was an allegation of stealing wheat from his employer, Joseph Gellibrand, who was the colony's Attorney-General and a large landholder. Gellibrand was out of the colony when the charge was made. By the time he returned, Charles had already been committed for trial in the Supreme Court. Fortunately, Gellibrand protested so vigorously that Charles was discharged with the comment 'case dismissed'.[106] Andrew Clephane was not so lucky. After he had served his sentence in New South Wales he was given permission to join his son and it was he who apparently established the pub in Launceston. In January 1827 he was charged with receiving a fowling piece (or gun) knowing it to have been stolen. The fact that the person who stole it was the bushranger Matthew Brady ensured that the police would pursue every avenue to secure a conviction against someone who had helped him. They assembled two charges and succeeded on the second. Despite being represented by Mr Gellibrand, who argued fiercely with the Chief Justice about the nature of the charge, Andrew Clephane was sentenced to twelve months in an iron gang. If word reached Charles that his father was in trouble it may explain why he suddenly reappears in the convict records. After serving his twelve months, Andrew returned to the pub, which he and Charles ran together from that time. In 1832, Charles married Sarah Beaven at St John's Church, Launceston. They had two sons and called the first one Andrew after his grand-father. Charles Clephane died in Launceston in March 1852 just as John West's history was being published. He was 57.[107]

The *Bensley* man with probably the most to lose by exposure that he was once a convict was Joseph Barrett, the former highway robber from Gloucester-shire. By the 1840s he had created a substantial stake for his family in the Launceston community. Like many another, he began by running a pub. Granted a conditional pardon in 1827,[108] Joseph applied for a liquor licence which he held for some years. As a publican he too had his share of confrontations with the police, although they were infrequent. In December 1829 he was fined for 'ille-gally harbouring in his public house James Trimming and Joseph Counsell, convicts, for the purpose of tippling'. He was fined again, in January 1832, 'for allowing Edward Thomas and others to remain on his licensed premises for the tippling and drinking'.[109] Meanwhile Joseph bought an allotment of land opposite the pub, on which he built a two-storey brick building.

Ex-convict Joseph Barrett made a stake for himself in the Launceston community

In 1836 he used this capital improvement in support of his application for a grant of ten acres in the heart of the town, which was approved by Sir John Franklin the following year.[110]

In March 1831, Joseph married Mary Dodd, a young nursery girl from Shropshire who had been convicted with her cousin Maria of stealing two pounds of bacon from a house.[111] After a turbulent couple of years in the colony, Mary came to the Launceston district as an assigned servant to the landowner, Richard Dry. He took her before the magistrates in June 1829, where she was sentenced to one month in the Launceston gaol, fourteen days of it on bread and water, for 'secreting a man in a bedroom in her master's house'.[112] Her son, Abraham, was born around the time of her marriage, which suggests the relationship began while Mary was working for Dry and that Joseph Barrett may have been the man hidden in her bedroom. What happened to their marriage is unclear. Mary liked to tipple, in fact she was frequently drunk. They had a second child, who did not survive. It is possible they struck a bargain. Joseph would pay for Mary to return to her family in England, but she must leave the boy with him.

Mary returned to Shropshire, but conditions were no better there than they had ever been. In November 1836 she was caught stealing potatoes from a garden in Shrewsbury. At her trial at the Salop Quarter Sessions in January 1837, Constable William Davies described how, suspecting she had stolen them, he took her shoe and returned to the garden to measure it against the footprints left in the potato patch: 'When I told her that her shoe fitted the track round the potatoes, she acknowledged that she had been there and she stole the potatoes.'[113] Sentenced to seven years transportation, Mary smiled and said to the judge, 'Thank you Sir. Thank you for the next' (the paper did not explain what 'the next' meant).[114] This time Mary sailed on the *Platina*. When she arrived in Hobart, she confessed everything. 'I committed this offence in order to get transported,' she told the Superintendent of Convicts, 'I was discharged once before to marry. My husband Joseph Barrett is in Launceston. He's a publican worth two or three thousand pounds.'[115] It is difficult to establish whether she and Joseph ever resumed their relationship. Over the next five years, Mary's conduct record suggests she was in assigned service to other employers, during which time she was constantly charged with being drunk and disorderly or absent without leave. Near the end of her seven-year sentence, it appears that Joseph took her in. When she was found drunk either in a pub or on the street, she was convicted of being 'drunk and absent from her husband's residence', for which she was sentenced to three calendar months hard labour. What happened after that is even more uncertain. There are no family records to suggest that Mary remained part of the family. The only likely trace of her is the death of a Mary Barrett, aged 69, at the New Town Pauper Establishment in August 1879.[116]

Abraham Barrett was the proverbial apple of his father's eye. The boy was bright, high-minded, energetic and public-spirited. Originally considering the church (he attended St John's Church of England), he decided to become a schoolmaster instead. In that role, he achieved eminence in Launceston and, later, as headmaster of a school in Dunedin before returning from New Zealand to become head of the Middle District School in Launceston around 1890.[117] As a young man, his erudition was well known in the town of his birth. His love of Shakespeare extended to acting in Shakespearian roles. Over his lifetime, he was also a frequent contributor to the *Launceston Examiner* on a range of subjects, some of them literary. Abraham was a member of the Mechanics' Institute and he and Joseph would have attended the meeting held there by the anti-transportationists in 1847. Abraham subsequently served on the institute's board of management several times.[118] During the virulent anti-transportation debates, Joseph must have feared deeply for his boy's future. Whether from collusion between them or not, in the longer term Joseph was eliminated from the family history. By the twentieth century, his descendants thought 'the family started at Abraham Barrett'. They believed that the family 'came from New Zealand'. It may well be that Abraham's decision to take his family across the Tasman was similar to that of others—a strategic move to blur the convict connection. By the time that happened, however, Joseph no longer cared. He lived long enough to see his son elected to the Launceston Town Council in 1861. Two years later, he saw Abraham crown that achievement by becoming Mayor of Launceston. In 1865, the former highway robber now described as a 'gentleman' must have died contented.[119]

Initially, the anti-transportation movement found it hard to attract support in New South Wales. The senior colony, and the largest in terms of population, was much distracted by other issues during the period 1840–53 when the campaign against convicts occurred. Most significant was the transformation of the notorious Botany Bay into a free society. The end of transportation in 1841 presaged the arrival of democracy. Not one but two elections had to be scheduled, the first in 1842 for a Sydney Municipal Council, and the second, a year later, to elect for the first time members of the New South Wales Legislative Council. The Council had previously consisted entirely of appointed members but would now include two-thirds who were elected.[120] Issues concerning the franchise and the size and population weighting of electorates, let alone the drafting of a constitution for responsible government which was also now in prospect, were engrossing topics for the Sydney establishment, both conservative and radical. And there were other momentous events. In 1850, the Australian Colonies Act enabled the separation of Victoria into a colony in its own right, requiring more elections in both colonies.

Even in 1849, when the ground was fertile with the resumption of ships carrying convicts, resistance to the anti-transportationists among community leaders was apparent. Charles Cowper, the son of an early clergyman and later premier of the colony, founded a New South Wales anti-transportation league. Supported by newspapers like the *Sydney Morning Herald*, he called a public meeting in March 1849, but it was poorly attended and some of the newspaper coverage was at first ambivalent. As Michael Sturma has noted, the *People's Advocate*, edited by the Chartist Edward Hawkesley, 'initially scorned talk "about contamination and pollution" as "the very weakest kind of argument" against transportation. A short time later it was referring to convictism as the "ugly foulness rooted in our blood" which made the colony a "dunghill".[121] That proud old native son, William Wentworth, was among those who withheld his approval for the campaign against convicts. It was the discovery of gold in May 1851, not the disparagement of the convicts, which convinced him that transportation must end.[122] The pastoralist Nicholas Bayley, who employed several of the *John* men, was another who challenged the ugly rhetoric about the convicts. Dismissed by the opponents of transportation as speaking only from self-interest, he said in a forthright letter to the *Sydney Morning Herald*:

> To talk of [the prisoners] demoralising the community is all humbug, from fifteen years experience in the bush and having had hundreds of immigrants and prisoners in my service, I am enabled to form a tolerable opinion as to the conduct of both, and the only difference I have been able to discover is, that the prisoner has invariably shown more gratitude for an indulgence than the immigrant. With regard to their moral conduct, they are on a par, many of the immigrants that I have questioned have admitted that they had several convictions recorded against them at home, for offences that would a few years ago have sent them here. I have now some of the last importation of exiles in my service, and find them as well-behaved as any men I ever had.[123]

Despite some prevarication by landholders in the late 1840s, the larger colony was more confident in its resistance to renewal of transportation in any form. The then Secretary of State for the Colonies, William Gladstone's attempt to renew transportation outright, although debated, was rejected and so, after some argument among the Legislative Councillors, was Lord Grey's proposal in 1847 to send 'exiles'. Grey sweetened his proposition by promising to fund immigrants as well. Believing the colonists had accepted his plan, Grey revoked the Order in Council that abolished transportation to New South Wales and despatched two boatloads of exiles. They were not, however, accompanied by immigrants. Swamped by ever-increasing numbers of prisoners, exacerbated by famine in Ireland, Grey apparently had no funds for the free settlers.[124]

Before the exiles arrived, Grey's delight at the resumption of a form of transportation was reported fully in the Sydney press.[125] Three months later, in June 1849, the ship *Hashemy* with a cargo of 236 men docked in Sydney. To the astonishment of a British Army officer who was based in the colony, its arrival was greeted with the largest, noisiest protest Sydney had ever seen.

'The usually drowsy, well-fed and politically apathetic Sydney broke into a perfect fever of excitement,' he wrote, adding, 'The demagogues and mob orators took care to whip up the [crowd].'[126] Between 4000 and 5000 people gathered at Circular Quay. They were said to be predominantly working class, 'a rabble of Sydney's worst elements', as police reports described them. This, of course, increases the likelihood they included convicts and ex-convicts. At this, and particularly at a second meeting later, the speakers concentrated on the moral and political evils of convicts. At neither gathering were the economic benefits of their labour, nor the timeliness of the transition from penal colony to democratic society, even mentioned. Their aim was to unite the working class to the anti-transportation cause, and to do so they had to eradicate residual loyalty to the prisoners so many present knew personally. Convicts were cast as a threat to jobs as well as an unspeakable contamination.[127]

At the first protest meeting, the English aristocrat Robert Lowe, who had emigrated to the colony for his health and had become a member of the New

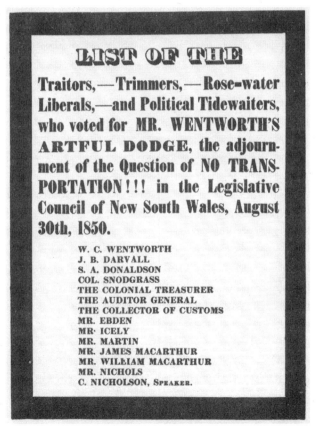

Anyone who disagreed was shamed: an anti-transportation handbill distributed in New South Wales

South Wales Legislative Council, shared the platform with Reverend Dr J.D. Lang, whose book so influenced Molesworth, and a young immigrant named Henry Parkes. Like Parkes, Lowe had only arrived in the colony in 1838, a few months earlier than John West. Their views of the convict era were influenced by what they had read of the Molesworth debates in the British newspapers. As newcomers, they also had no investment in the past. Shaping the future was their concern. Lowe spoke confidently to the crowd, revealing no conflict of loyalties about mixing political issues with the idea of convicts as 'pollution'. 'The threat of degradation has been fulfilled,' he told them. 'The stately presence of our city, the beautiful waters of our harbour, has this day again been polluted with the presence of that floating hell—a convict ship.' The *Sydney Morning Herald* reported there were 'immense cheers' at this point. Referring to 'a cargo of crime borne across the waves', Lowe continued to ramp up the rhetoric:

> You behold a ship freighted not with the comforts of life . . . but with the moral degradation of a community—the picked and selected criminals of Great Britain . . . New South Wales must be the university in which these scholars in vice and iniquity must finish their instructions. New South Wales must alone supply the college where these doctors in crime can take their last degrees . . . (Cheers) Let us send across the Pacific our emphatic declaration that we will not be slaves— that we will be free. Let us exercise the right that every English subject has—to assert his freedom. (Cheers)[128]

It was in these terms and at this moment that Australians denied the first six decades of their history.

The success of the anti-transportationists ensured that their version not only of events but of the ethos of the convict colony became the authoritative one. Little is known of those who tried to oppose them. Anne McLaughlin is virtually the only historian to have investigated this, and she found some evidence of deeply rooted anger. As a brawl threatened at an election meeting addressed by Richard Dry, the son of a (political) convict who was prominent in the anti-transportation campaign, a voice rang out from the crowd: 'Go it you bloody old lags, go it—hit the bastards! We've all been convicted . . . and thank God, some of us have been two or three times convicted! . . . we're all convicted here.' Sometimes commonsense—and more than commonsense— surfaced through the hysteria of the anti-transportationists. At one meeting in Van Diemen's Land, Mr Richard Lewis thanked the convicts who had worked for him, telling the meeting he was 'indebted' to those servants. 'If people would speak truthfully, they would speak of their men as I do, and candidly acknowledge their obligations to their services.'[129] In Britain, too, sanity occasionally surfaced. In April 1850, in a speech to the House of Lords, Lord Grey attempted to allay the hysteria about moral pollution that had been confected around the subject of convicts. He could have been describing Joseph Barrett and many of the prisoners studied in this work when he said:

> I am not prepared to deny that much moral evil has arisen from sending large numbers of convicts to penal colonies; but I must express my belief that these evils have been exaggerated . . . there are at this moment at large in the Australian colonies no less than 48,000 persons who have undergone transportation, the great majority of whom are now earning an honest livelihood, but who, had they remained in this country would in all probability have been almost compelled, by the force of circumstances, to continue to live as criminals.[130]

It was too late for the British to admit that the prisoners they sent to Australia had been 'almost compelled, by force of circumstances' to become criminals. The damage had been done in the colonies. The anti-transportation campaign was the vehicle for transferring the convict stain from the minds of the middle-class free settlers, where it had always existed, to that of the working class, including ex-convicts. How many of those who supported the anti-transportationists realised that words like 'pollute' and 'contamination' or 'contagion' did not simply refer to crime, but were homophobic in origin, is not clear. Publicly, the leaders often adjusted their rhetoric to their audience to emphasise crime, or the need to protect wives and children, and in Sydney particularly where they had to tread delicately, to argue that newly arrived convicts would take work from the free man. Whatever the emphasis, there could be no misunderstanding in anyone's mind that convicts had gone from being the objects of proud rehabilitation to something repulsive and dirty. For the protection of their families, if not for themselves, it became necessary for the ex-prisoners to hide their past.

CHAPTER 9
best forgotten

The transference of the contact stain was not just from one class to another, it was also geographic. It did not stop at the eastern half of the continent but impacted on the Western Australians who, coinciding with the easterners' campaign against convicts, were making the momentous decision to accept them. Conscious of the allegations being made about prisoners, the colonists were extremely reluctant to make the change—even more so because the Swan River settlement had been established by free immigrants in 1829 with a pledge never to include convicts among their numbers.[1] In the intervening years, however, the colony had so failed to attract a critical mass of population that, by the late 1840s, its very existence was threatened. The settlers were therefore unexpectedly receptive when Lord Grey, having suspended transportation to Van Diemen's Land for two years in 1846, wrote to every colony in the Empire trying to find one that would accept the contents of the overflowing British gaols. After a battle between principle and pragmatism similar to that of those anti-transportationists who broke their own rule against employing convicts, Western Australians decided they were prepared to risk the taint for the influx of labour and finance that would result from it.[2] Despite this justification, they were ashamed of becoming a penal colony. And fearful.

Officially, Western Australia began taking convicts in 1850. But for all the fanfare about the start of transportation, the colony had already received convicts, though not by that name, for a number of years. Euphemistically termed 'juvenile government immigrants', boatloads of boys from Parkhurst prison were despatched to the colony between 1842 and 1851. They were no different in any material way from the boys on the *John* who went to New South Wales in 1832 as fully fledged convicts. Nor was their status any different from that of the adult 'exiles' later despatched to various eastern colonies. Allocated to an employer on arrival, the Parkhurst boys were described as 'apprentices', but they were in fact Western Australia's first convicts. The pretence was finally dropped for two boats that arrived carrying Parkhurst boys in 1850 and 1851, after transportation to the colony had begun. These youths arrived like other convicts, complete with tickets-of-leave.[3] In July 1850, the first group of 75 adult prisoners arrived on the *Scindian*, with another 100 following three months later. In all, nearly 10,000 adult males were transported to Western Australia in 37 ships between 1850 and 1868. The last boatload arrived on 9 January 1868.[4]

Dismayed by Western Australia's decision, the eastern colonies were initially busy fighting their own battles to abolish transportation to Van Diemen's Land. It was not until success had been achieved there that they turned their full attention to the west. Ten years after the anti-transportation campaign led by Reverend John West, the colonists in eastern Australia remained anxious about the risk of contamination from convicts on the far side of the Nullarbor Plain. Determined to drive the pervading stain from the entire continent, representatives from the Australasian League sent a heartfelt petition to the Queen in 1863. Frightened that a Royal Commission into transportation might recommend its resumption in their part of the Empire, delegates from New South Wales, South Australia, Victoria and Tasmania entreated 'that your Majesty will be pleased to direct that as early as possible, the transportation of convicts from the United Kingdom to Western Australia should cease, as daily experience proves that the existence of a penal settlement there inflicts much injury upon these colonies . . . we humbly beseech your Majesty to prevent the infliction of so deadly a blow to the welfare and happiness of these colonies, and to their moral and social progress.'[5]

By now, amnesia about the extent of public allegations of the incidence of unnatural crime had begun to take hold in many quarters. But not all. In 1861, the British parliament set up yet another select committee, this time to investigate whether the east coast colonies had sound reasons for objecting to the penal colony in Western Australia. The usual suspects such as James Macarthur and the Reverend Dr J.D. Lang were among those who gave evidence. Macarthur prevaricated uncomfortably when the Committee tried to establish the nature of the moral issue that he said was the main objection to importing prisoners. Without specifying details, he told them the opposition was 'particularly of persons in the humbler classes of life . . . [who] obtained a very strong objection to it on that ground'. They never did elicit a straight answer from Macarthur. Instead, he produced a tortured echo of a middle-class speaker in Launceston at the meeting at the Mechanics' Institute in 1847, namely 'that the upper classes might not feel the evil consequences of an influx . . . so sensibly as the working classes, because the working classes and their families come into direct and immediate contact with such persons'. Attempts by the British Committee members to suggest the colonists' objections were based on the workers' fear of competition for jobs met with only grudging assent from Macarthur, who insisted this was a minor reason.[6]

James Youl, Esq., who followed Macarthur as a witness, had been an active participant in the anti-transportation movement from the beginning.[7] In the 1840s he had been a member of a committee in Launceston whose task it was to gather evidence on the subject of unnatural crime. He told the parliamentarians, 'the vices of the convicts themselves, as brought out before [our] committee were of such a character that we were simultaneously compelled to say we would hear no more evidence of that character for it was too much for our feelings'. Sympathetic towards such delicacy, the Committee let him off the hook. 'You now allude to vices too horrible to specify?' asked one of the members. 'Yes,' said Youl. In the decade since the hyperbole of the anti-transportation campaign, it is plain from the evidence to this committee that those who supported it had become somewhat embarrassed and were trying to shift responsibility elsewhere. Like Macarthur, Youl claimed at first that the entire impetus against transportation arose from the working class. He continued to avoid specifically stating the nature of the objections but in common with other witnesses denied they were prompted by fear of unemployment. Pressed by a member of the Committee who could not understand why witnesses were denying the simple proposition that objections from the working class were caused by fear of competition for their jobs, Youl contradicted himself about the origins of the movement.

> Q. And didn't the opinion against the admission of convicts originate with that class of men?
>
> A. No, it originated entirely from the upper classes; from the employers of labour.
>
> Q. I thought you said the feeling amongst the poorer classes was very strong against the introduction of convicts?
>
> A. Yes, but before that [it] was exhibited by a number of the larger proprietors, by notice in the papers, [who] showed a strong disinclination to receive them.

Desperately groping for some reason that would explain why the working class subsequently became opposed to transportation, Youl added, 'And I recollect one reason, which may have operated on the poorer class, namely, that there would be no free institutions in the colony so long as it was a convict colony' (by which he meant no democratic parliament). More confused than ever, the Committee persisted:

> Q. Then you would say that the opinion against the introduction of convicts originated with the upper classes?
>
> A. Yes, in the first instance; that is to say, the first public exhibition of it.
>
> Q. And that the opinion went downwards and permeated the labouring classes after it had permeated the capitalist?
>
> A. Yes.
>
> Q. So if we are told that it originated in the other way, we have been misled?
>
> A. I think so. So far as the public attention was drawn to it, it was drawn by the upper classes who were employers of convicts.

Poor Youl then had his attention drawn to his signature on a petition in 1835 supporting continued transportation. Asked what had changed his mind, he fell back on suggesting that the English had changed their criminal law and the colonies were now receiving worse convicts.

> Q. Can you show any connexion between those two facts?
>
> A. Yes, formerly we got men sent to us for political offences, for poaching, machine breaking, and so on. There was always a very large body of convicts who prided themselves that they were not thieves and rogues. But since the alteration in the laws in this country, it seems to be that every man who comes out has committed some very grave offence.

This explanation was first used by John West in his *History* when he wrote, 'The abolition of capital punishments and the erection of penitentiaries at home, left the penalty of transportation chiefly to more serious offences.'[8] Thus were stereotypes created on which countless later assumptions were based.

Even more entertaining, indeed startling in the light of historiography that describes Australians as racist towards Chinese, were claims made by the subsequent witness, Lauchlan Mackinnon, Esq. After arriving in New South Wales in 1838, he served in the Legislature of that colony and subsequently of Victoria. In his early years as a squatter, Mackinnon had convict servants and at a public meeting in Melbourne in 1849 he leapt to his feet to protest at the idea of giving them up, sufficiently antagonised to accuse the previous speaker in favour of this motion as making 'a windy and humbugging speech'.[9] However, someone found the right words to convert him to the anti-transportation cause. Not long after that he bought the leading Victorian newspaper, the *Argus*, and from that platform he stirred the Victorians to paroxysms of fear and loathing towards the convicts during the anti-transportation campaign.[10] In 1861, Mackinnon spent much time telling the Select Committee about the atrocious crimes the men committed and the frequency with which all convicts resorted to crime. Much discussion also concerned laws passed by the various colonies to keep the convicts out. In this respect the Committee, which was well informed, drew parallels with laws designed to keep the Chinese out. 'Was that done to keep up the price of labour?' they asked. 'No,' replied Mackinnon. 'It was to exclude people who were believed to be extraordinarily vicious in their habits . . . I think there were two or three women amongst 35,000 men.' Q: 'And it was in that direction that the evil was apprehended?' A: 'Yes.' Introducing the Chinese to the inquisition was a tactical manoeuvre by the British parliamentarians. They already knew that the New South Wales legislature had investigated claims that unnatural crime was flourishing among the Chinese. They also knew that no grounds had been found for the allegation. Despite their challenges, Mr Mackinnon remained resolute in his opinions, but in light of his and other evidence they heard, it is not surprising that this particular Select Committee decided there was no reason to interfere in the existing transportation of prisoners to Western Australia.[11]

Meanwhile, back in the antipodes the citizens continued to assert that prisoners from Western Australia were infiltrating the eastern colonies in great numbers with a consequent increase in crime. News that members of the British parliament in 1863 had described their alarm as 'wild and unreasonable' resulted in an indignant letter to the Adelaide *Daily News* quoting two prominent South Australian magistrates as the source of the information:

> over one thousand conditionally-pardoned and ticket-of-
> leave men found their way from that colony [of Western
> Australia] to Adelaide . . . the result was a rapid increase of

violent assaults, robberies and burglarious crimes. We have it also upon good authority that forty similar scoundrels found their way to Sydney in one vessel, who had scarcely landed when they commenced operations.[12]

In Victoria, the *Argus* sent a journalist to Western Australia to report back on the state of the penal colony and the risk it posed to the east.[13]

In their turn, Western Australians were furious at the slurs, not in defence of their convicts but at the suggestion they could not control them. They challenged the easterners to prove their case, and when they received no specific reply they were scathing in their denunciation. 'They merely assert but never prove,' wrote H. Grellet in 1864, 'and I have not yet found a single well authenticated instance of a convict from Western Australia committing a crime of a heinous nature in the other Colonies. We need not doubt that had there been any, it would most certainly have been brought forward . . . let them produce a list of the crimes committed within their boundaries by escaped convicts.'[14]

Over a decade earlier John West's frightening picture of the convict stain crossing Bass Strait and permeating the mainland colonies had resulted in legislation in both Victoria and South Australia to stop such contamination. For their part Vandemonians had instituted a checklist at the island's ports which tracked who was leaving their colony and where they were going. After they began receiving convicts, Western Australia put a similar system in place. An employer from that colony described how 'no man can disembark from a vessel arriving from Western Australia without showing a passport, stating he is untainted by crime. Should he be unable so to do, he is detained in prison until the sailing of the vessel, and the master of the ship conveying him to the Colony is fined £100 for each passenger so brought, and obliged to convey him away at his own expense.'[15]

The practice of travellers having to prove they were not and had never been a prisoner of the Crown was well established by the 1860s. And it was long-lasting, as a famous traveller discovered in 1872. About to embark at Albany, the novelist Anthony Trollope found it hard to decide whether he was more aggrieved at the need for a certificate to prove he had not been a convict or the requirement that he pay one shilling to obtain it. He was sympathetic towards the Western Australians. 'So many have been convicts, that the certificate is demanded from all!', but nevertheless felt they would do better to hand out the passport discreetly rather than 'raise a revenue out of their own ill fame. It is not my fault that South Australia demanded the certificate.' Just as he was about to leave, a policeman handed Trollope the essential document, which read:

I hereby certify that the bearer, A. Trollope, about to proceed to Adelaide per A.S.N. Co's steamer, is not and never has been a prisoner of the Crown in Western Australia.[16]

There had been negotiations between the colonists and the British government over the conditions under which the colony would take convicts. In effect, both sides sought to avoid errors made in the eastern penal colonies. Western Australians were particularly concerned not to be swamped by an influx of prisoners as the Vandemonians had been during the probation system. Their capacity to absorb new arrivals was monitored closely by the colonists.[17] Experience in Van Diemen's Land also shaped the structure for managing the convicts. There were to be no more probation gangs. In keeping with Lord Grey's idea of 'exiles', only those reformed by their experience of the penal system in Britain and now eligible for a ticket-of-leave would be transported. Depots were to be established where the ticketers, as they were known locally, could be accommodated and fed and allocated to work on public projects between private employment, the expense for this to be covered by the British government. The rule that only ticket-of-leave men should be transported was modified after the colony became familiar with having prisoners in their community. Men with some time still to serve before obtaining a ticket were later preferred. It allowed the colony to get greater use from them on public works rather than having their valuable labour swallowed up immediately by private employers.[18] From the beginning, the colonists refused to accept female convicts. Instead, a plan was devised for boatloads of immigrant women to be sent out at regular intervals. Unlike similar undertakings to the eastern colonies, this was a promise that the British government kept. Known locally as 'Bride Ships', they eventually delivered nearly 2000 single women to the fledgling settlement, many of whom married former convicts.[19]

The *Lord Dalhousie* arrived in Western Australia in December 1863, by which time the colony had been receiving adult convicts for thirteen years. Like most of the ships chartered for the Western Australian convict service, the *Dalhousie* was a sleek, modern frigate built at the Sunderland yards as recently as 1847. She landed her prisoners at Fremantle on 28 December 1863 after a voyage of 90 days direct from England, half the time it took the *Sir William Bensley* in 1817.[20] Two hundred and seventy men had embarked from Portland Prison for the uneventful voyage. They included 43 convict soldiers from all over the Empire. The arsonist Henry Sherry had been joined by the poacher Caleb Stapley, embezzler/solicitor Joseph Shaw, and the burglars George Rawlinson and Joseph Sowden Ledger. Little Dick Reeves was also on board. So were the Liverpool con men William Simpson and William (aka Edward)

Hillier, who ended up sailing for Australia themselves leaving the Galway Grecian behind, presumably too poor to make the passage after they fleeced him. The two men would have very different fortunes in the colony. William Simpson was 43 when he landed. He died the following year in Perth prison. Hillier was younger. Married with two children, he left for Singapore in 1873 as soon as he was free, very likely going home to organise his family because he returned to Western Australia and departed from there to Victoria in January 1878 under the name of Edward Hillier.[21]

The guards on the *Dalhousie*, as with all the Western Australian ships, were military pensioners. Known as Enrolled Pensioner Guards, these men were part of a settlement scheme for the people-starved colony. They contracted to serve as guards on the voyage and had a choice of staying in the service on arrival. Once discharged as settlers, they were in any event a reserve force which could be called on in a civilian emergency. If they stayed in the guards for seven years, they became eligible for a small land grant which in practice often consolidated a leasehold taken earlier. As an extra incentive to settle permanently, they received a gratuity of £10 and were promised the use of convict labour to help clear their land. It was a popular policy, which most accepted. Accompanied by their wives and children, they were a significant contribution to the Western Australian population.[22]

The mantra that the convicts who were sent to Western Australia were worse than men sent to the eastern colonies had become accepted wisdom by the 1860s, propagated particularly by eastern colonists seeking to justify their opposition to transportation. Their campaign made the western settlers defensive and shaped their attitude to their convict workers. By the 1870s, Western Australians felt compelled to justify their compliance in what was said to be a 'great evil' that 'pervades the colony', and they frequently claimed that the convicts sent there were not the ones promised to them. Anthony Trollope reported sceptically, 'There was,—so goes the allegation,—a condition made and accepted that the convicts for Western Australia should be convicts of a very peculiar kind, respectable, well-grown, moral, healthy convicts, who had been perhaps model ploughmen at home,—and men of that class.' Somewhat acerbically he added, 'I have always replied . . . that I should like to see the stipulation in print, or at least in writing. I presume the convicts were sent as they came to hand.'[23]

It is true the prisoners sent to the west included some who would have been hanged in an earlier period. Rapists, for instance, and some of those who committed murder, although the case of the Berkeley poachers who were convicted of murder reveals that clemency was always a possibility. In the circumstances of his case, Dick Reeves may well have been spared in 1816 as he was in 1861. Superficially, the type of crimes sounded far worse in the 1850s and '60s but a closer look reveals that crimes which, for example, now bore the alarming designation of 'assault and robbery' or 'robbery with violence' were usually no different in detail from those described as 'highway robbery' in earlier years. 'Shooting and wounding' could hide a poaching clash, as it did in the case of Caleb Stapley. And thieves and burglars were still stealing the same things they stole in 1816 and 1832 and 1853. Tom Tomlinson, aged twenty, was transported on the *Dalhousie* for stealing a handkerchief, just as so many others on the *Bensley* and the *John* and the *St Vincent* had done. Tomlinson's transportation for six years was justified by a claim that he had seven previous convictions. But multiple prior offences do not necessarily mean he was a hardened criminal who had already served lengthy sentences. More likely his priors were a string of juvenile thefts that resulted in a whipping or a few months in the House of Correction; they were quite possibly offences that in an earlier time would have escaped prosecution because there was no police force. The theory that Tomlinson was not a confirmed villain is supported by his track record in the colony. He had a ticket by March 1865. Settled in the York area, in 1876 he married Sarah Ann Hicks, by whom he had four children before she died in childbirth in 1881. Tomlinson himself died in 1891 at the age of 50, without having transgressed again. His story of a youthful offender turning into a respectable citizen is no different from many that occurred in the eastern colonies.[24]

The *Dalhousie* group did include some professionals for whom crime was a regular occupation, particularly among the burglars, but prior offences did not always indicate the character of the man. Superficially, arsonist Josiah Brown who arrived in the colony with a fourteen-year sentence and two previous convictions sounds a serious, potentially dangerous criminal. But an examination of the detail of his case reveals a different picture. At the age of seventeen in Bedfordshire, he was first charged with stealing a drake, for which he was 'bailed out' and discharged. Three years later, he was sentenced to five calendar months hard labour for stealing ten fowls valued at fifteen shillings. Later that same year, he served three calendar months hard labour in lieu of paying a fine for unlawfully using a gun to kill game. Three years later he burnt down Farmer Goosey's barn because he was hungry. The circumstances and nature of his prior convictions are almost identical with those of Daniel Deacon, one of the men on the *John* in 1832. And it is worth noting that, in both cases, most of the committing magistrates were clergymen.[25] By comparison, the forgery of Russian bank notes which would have seemed a far less threatening crime to the nervous colonists, was in fact a major offence on a grand scale. None of the perpetrators of this scam had previous convictions.

Compared with earlier periods, the most notable difference in the convicts carried by the *Dalhousie* was the presence of nine men guilty of rape. Case papers were not preserved and newspaper reports were brief, making it impossible to form a considered judgement of their character. Generally, it seems that the men sentenced for sexual crimes were a mixed bag and cannot be uniformly condemned. In the colony, some can be tracked working hard as ticketers. Some were married in Britain and remained alone in Western Australia, but at least two married locally and integrated into colonial society with no further offence.

The belief that the Western Australian convicts were worse than others would repay a specific investigation. As would the percentage who were court-martialled soldiers. If the figures for the *Dalhousie* are any guide, it could be as high as 17 per cent. The explanation for transporting such a large number of soldiers may lie in the colonists' demand for a better class of convict, the choice of soldiers probably reflecting the belief that they were not 'real' criminals and would therefore settle more easily. If this was the reasoning, then it must be said that the soldiers had the last laugh.

The idea that the Western Australian convicts were older than earlier convicts has contributed to the negative image of them. It implies 'more hardened in crime'. True, on average, the Western Australians were older than those in the east, but the relevant question is, 'older than whom?' They would want to be older than the boatloads of teenagers transported in the 1830s. Or the boys sent to Point Puer in Van Diemen's Land. In fact, the Western Australian convicts were far from being old men. Of the 270 on the *Dalhousie*, 140 were only in their twenties. Another 61 were in their early thirties. The youngest, William Wood, was a 17-year-old burglar from the Manchester area. At 57 years, Abraham Rosenberg, who was part of the Russian bank note scam, was the oldest. Most importantly, the average age for Western Australian convicts would be transformed if the Parkhurst juveniles were acknowledged as convicts and included in the calculation like the youths sent to the eastern colonies.

The image of older, hardened and brutal implies that, compared with earlier convicts, the Western Australian prisoners were different in character as well as crime. This too is a topic that would repay further investigation. Unlike earlier convicts, they had avoided captivity on the hulks. As explained in Chapter 7, the issue of penal reform propounded by Jeremy Bentham had dogged the Australian penal colonies from the beginning, sensationalising and distorting their reality as the Benthamites tried to win the debate in Britain. By mid-century, when Western Australia decided to take convicts, the system Bentham advocated as the best means for moral rehabilitation was well on the way to full implementation in Britain. It was accepted penal philosophy that prisoners should spend time in solitude reflecting on their sins, followed by a period of hard physical labour.

Bentham's panopticon or model prison—Pentonville—had been built in the early 1840s, and his theories were implemented there undiluted. The men who were sent to the west, as well as those who arrived in the final years in Van Diemen's Land, were subjected to the exquisite torture devised by these middle-class reformers who seriously believed that months, years even, of silence and solitude would rehabilitate uneducated men. Apparently no thought was given as to whether they would possess the intellectual or emotional resources to cope with it. As one convict explained, prisoners preferred the lash any day to imprisonment in a dark solitary cell. 'Offenders dreaded this as infinitely worse than any brief corporeal suffering—thirty, sixty, and ninety days being the ordinary terms—though individuals have been thus entombed for years. Of course the brain is the seat of pain—very dreadful.'[26] In Pentonville the silent treatment was not just limited to solitary confinement and forbidding conversation, it included slippers to prevent any sound as well, and masks to prevent eye contact between the men. It sent some men mad, but it was some time before the reformers were forced to accept the incontrovertible negative effect and agree that the masks, at least, should be abandoned.[27]

In 1853, two ships, the *Robert Small* and the *Phoebe Dunbar*, arrived at Fremantle from Mountjoy Prison, Dublin, where the silent system was practised. The convicts they delivered were found on arrival to be not only physically debilitated from long solitary incarceration, but suffering great mental depression as well.[28] Fortunately, this was the exception rather than the rule, and most prisoners arrived in good health after the sea voyage from Britain. Generally, the Western Australian men revealed the same resilience, independence, anti-authoritarian, hard-drinking characteristics of the thousands who had preceded them in the east. The same sardonic humour would surface in moments of stress or defiance. The same devil-may-care attitude. In 1853, a road gang of men who had been reconvicted after they arrived were labouring in irons on a public project about a mile from the prison where they lodged each night. Guarded by a solitary drunken warder, the temptation proved irresistible. Spur-of-the-moment escapes in the small, remote colony were impossible, particularly wearing irons, but there was always a chance for a drink and a smoke and a bit of a laugh. As a contemporary observer put it, 'At 4 o'clock, six of them shouldered their picks, bid the warder good afternoon and walked away.' They were returned to the gaol the next morning, probably agreed among themselves that the break from monotony had been worth it.[29]

The silent system in operation at Pentonville

By the time the *Dalhousie* delivered her men to Western Australia in December 1863, it was established practice for the colony to utilise their convict labour on public works before distributing tickets-of-leave. An analysis of the tickets given to the *Dalhousie* men indicates that by the end of 1865, 152 men were ticketers, including some who received their tickets within months of their arrival. Most who received their tickets in the first two years were men with sentences of ten years or less, plus a couple with fourteen years who had already served ten years in English gaols. Also included in this early batch of tickets was Thomas Gorman, last seen attacking a warder in Millbank prison after such a history of disruption at other gaols that the staff were relieved to move him on. Convicted for that offence at the Central Criminal Court for the common law crime of 'wounding with intent', Gorman turned out to be a soldier. Sentenced to transportation for life at his original court-martial in September 1857, he had served eight years when he received his ticket-of-leave in Western Australia in 1865. If asked, he may have replied that it was a price worth paying to extricate himself from the British Army.[30] Tickets handed out the following year, in 1866, appear to bear little relation to sentence and may have been influenced mainly by good behaviour. Joseph Shaw, the solicitor from Derbyshire, had been sentenced to fifteen years but received a ticket in 1866. Richard Reeves, with a life sentence for murder, also received a ticket that year. By 1870, most men had their tickets.[31]

The system for managing convicts in Western Australia was designed to be an improvement on the versions that had existed in the eastern colonies. Assignment to private employers had been discredited by the Molesworth Committee, and despite its financial attraction to the British government there was no attempt to reproduce it. More recently, the difficulties of ticket-of-leave holders in Van Diemen's Land, fresh from the probation gangs, had revealed the uncertainties of their employment prospects in times of economic stress or between peak seasons. This background shaped the system in the west. After their short period of public labour, the Western Australian ticketers became independent contractors, encouraged to travel around the colony engaging in whatever employment they could find. As in the east before 1840, they were controlled through dividing the colony into districts for which a man must register to work and obtain a pass before he could move to another. The major difference was the creation of a network of hiring depots that operated simultaneously as an employment bureau and a control point and accommodation for the men between jobs. And there were broader points of difference. In 1863 Governor Hampton noted of the convicts in his colony that they 'possess in almost every important point the privileges of free men. They are eligible to engage in business, to hold personal property, and in hired service they are generally treated in the same manner as those who have never been in bondage, the chief exception being that all ticket-of-leave men are liable to vigilant police supervision.'[32] All jobs and the wages paid had to be reported to the depot. Wages sometimes included board.

Jobs were often obtained at the local depot, since employers quickly developed the habit of picking up their extra labour from there . . . and just as swiftly returning the man when the work ran out. In this respect, the employers in the west had it much easier than those in the east. They could take on an extra pair of hands when they needed it, or for piecework such as chopping firewood, which was common, but they had no longer-term responsibility for their employee. Few men lingered long in the depot if they could avoid it. According to one prisoner, their reaction was quite different to Governor Hampton's glowing description of the depots. 'They differ in nothing from the prison—neither in discipline, garb, food, or society; in some respects, they are even more comfortless.'[33] For minor infringements that did not warrant returning a man to the Convict Establishment in Fremantle, a ticketer could be confined to the depot for, say, a month. In addition to a resident magistrate who made summary decisions about punishment, there was a small number of pensioner guards based near each depot for security purposes. Many of these men took up land nearby and became settlers in the area.[34]

Toodyay Depot

One of the busiest hiring depots was Toodyay. Located over the Darling Range approximately 60 miles east of Perth, it was in the middle of some of the best farming land in the colony. Until convict labour became available, the lack of roads and bridges to this area had hampered the ability of the colonists to take full advantage of the opportunities it offered. But by the 1860s, convicts had built infrastructure that made travel to the coast easier and the district was flourishing.

Among those who worked out of the Toodyay Depot was Richard Farrell. At 22, he was the youngest of the soldiers on the *Dalhousie*, with a hot temper that caused him to shoot at a sergeant while he was stationed on St Helena and created just as much trouble for him in the colony. His character on arrival was described as 'indifferent', but his conduct on the voyage had been sufficiently good to earn him some remission. His first year working for the government on probation passed without incident and he should have been on course for a ticket. But Farrell was one of those men who could not stand being controlled by others, and he was free with his fists. Working on a government project in 1864, he punched Surveyor Carey and was sentenced to work for twelve months in irons. At the end of that year, he was in trouble again for twice assaulting another prisoner, then six months after that for assaulting a prison constable. The punishments were minor—seven days in his cell, three days on bread and water—but his ticket receded further and further. Nevertheless,

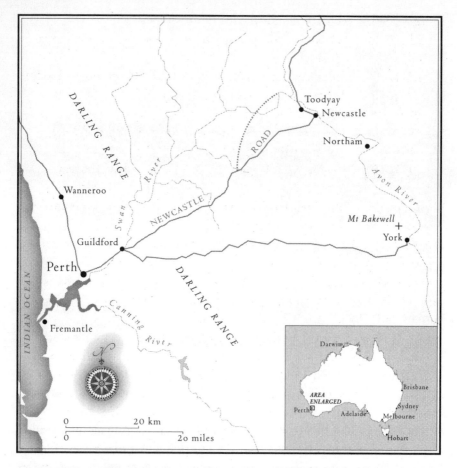

Western Australia, with places mentioned in this book

Farrell refused to submit. Over the next eighteen months, the pattern continued with offences of insolence, insubordination, threats, assaulting another
prisoner and refusing to obey orders.

Finally, in September 1869 he was issued with a ticket-of-leave. Once
relatively free of the 'petty annoyances and daily tyrannies' that beset a
prisoner, Farrell's demeanour and his behaviour changed radically. A horsebreaker in the army, he had a range of skills that were useful in the colony.
During his time as a ticketer, he worked variously as a groom, shepherd,
teamster, labourer, at threshing and as a general servant. Unlike some of
his shipmates, who moved frequently and ranged widely between districts,
Farrell stayed around the Northam, Toodyay and Newcastle area where he
was consistently hardworking, with minimal down time in the depot, as his
record reveals:

23–10–69	Perth to Toodyay
23–10–69	Grooom— 40/- per month to V. Garrido at New Norcia Mission
25–12–69	Alexander Fagan, general servant, £2.5.0. per month Toodyay
29–1–70	Thomas Jones, threshing 6d per bushel
9–3–70	J. Cooke threshing £2.0.0 at Northam
19–4–70	Teamster for Michael Bowen, 20/- per month at Toodyay
30–6–70	Pass from Toodyay to Newcastle
21–7–70	George West, labourer £2.0.0. per month at Toodyay

In August 1870, Farrell was given a ticket-of-leave to work for himself, but he stayed in the district taking whatever jobs were available, including one as a shepherd and another as a general servant. In June 1872, he began horsebreaking at 50 shillings per month for James Drummond of Toodyay. Over the next two years this became his regular occupation, although in future he worked on his own account rather than for an employer. He did not receive a conditional pardon until 1874,[35] and it was around that time that the purpose of his hard work was revealed. Farrell was an unusual soldier because he was both married and the father of a child. The year before his pardon, he applied through the government for his wife Mary and son Robert, aged ten, to be brought to the colony. In what must have felt like a heartbreaking rebuff, when the answer came back from the government it said, 'Letter returned. Not known.'[36] But Farrell was a determined man. Two years after receiving his pardon he was on a boat for Singapore. The island was a major market for the export of horses reared in Western Australia and he may have gone there to sell stock on his own behalf or for others. It is also possible he caught a ship for England. Secrecy was necessary if he did return home. As a lifer, he would never receive a certificate of freedom that marked the end of his sentence and his pardon was conditional on not returning to Britain. Whether he found his wife and child and whether they were willing to come back to Western Australia with him has unfortunately proved impossible to establish. Richard Farrell did return to the colony. As late as 1889, he was known to be working at Dandaragan.[37]

Other soldiers from the *Dalhousie* passed through Toodyay, but few spent more than a year there. Former Private John Jinks arrived in September 1869. Described by his superiors in Bermuda as 'a habitual drunkard', a condition which was no doubt behind his rash decision to strike one of them, Jinks picked up a job with an employer at Victoria Plains at 30 shillings for the month, followed by another sawing wood for 25 shillings per ton. Early in November he was engaged to work for a Mr J. Watts, which involved transferring to the district of Swan.[38]

John Conway was court-martialled for threatening his commanding officer in Malta. In Britain, he had been much trouble to prison officials, to the point where he hit one. They moved him around from Millbank (after twelve lashes for filthy and insubordinate conduct) to Portsmouth (where they gave him 36 lashes for hitting the warder), then back to Millbank and further 'corporal punishment for shouting, singing, cursing and using filthy disgusting language' before being returned to Portsmouth a second time. Twelve thousand miles away, at Toodyay, he did a week's work for George Hayes at a rate of 25 shillings per month before he was returned to the depot. He was soon hired by P.W. Paisley, but that relationship quickly failed too. Conway was returned to the depot charged with insolence to Mr Paisley plus having money in his possession supposed to be stolen. For good measure, the depot superintendent charged him also with breaking prison rules. Transported with a sentence of fourteen years, Conway had already received a ticket-of-leave when he came to Toodyay in 1866. He lost it as a result of his behaviour there. On 4 August, barely two months after he arrived in the area, Conway was ordered back to the Convict Establishment at Fremantle for two years.[39]

Unlike the volatile record of the soldier convicts, the young London coiner Henry Milford was so well behaved during his probation that he was issued with a ticket only nine months after he arrived. Sentenced to six years penal servitude at the Central Criminal Court in 1861, he had spent less than two years in British prisons before arriving in the colony. In Britain, as he was circulated from Newgate to Millbank, to Pentonville, to Portland, he always recorded his next of kin as 'Emma Milford, 8 Frederick Place, Balls Pond'. Wife or sister, this Emma was probably 22-year-old Emma Theobald, who was one of the two girls caught with Henry in the act of making coins. Both of the girls were sentenced to eighteen months in prison. Emma's term expired just before Henry sailed, timing that makes it very likely she was the person who visited him at Portland three weeks before he embarked on the *Dalhousie*. That farewell marked the end of their relationship. Henry never applied for a wife to join him in Western Australia. As a ticketer, he found employment around the Perth and Fremantle area, sometimes working as a labourer, sawyer or general servant, and sometimes using experience gained in Britain as an ostler. He must have liked the opportunities the colony offered because, unlike many others, he did not move on once he was free. Abandoning his coining talents forever, he settled in the Canning Hills district outside Perth and developed a business for himself as a carrier. In 1872 he married Alice Bayliff (or Bayliss) at Guildford. Together they produced nine children before Henry died at the age of 52 in 1892.[40]

Poacher Caleb Stapley was another who received an early ticket-of-leave. One year after he arrived, he was free to organise his own future. After the privations of trying to earn a living as an agricultural labourer in Sussex, the choices in Western Australia were enough to make a man optimistic about his future. His literacy skills, described in the official records as 'imperfect', were probably too uncertain to allow him to write home to his many siblings in the village of Sedlescombe, but he must have often longed to do so. His older brother's child, his niece Elizabeth Necklen, was planning to emigrate, but she and her husband chose the freely settled land of New Zealand rather than a penal colony. On gaining his ticket, Caleb worked as a sawyer, but his experience as an agricultural labourer would have been much in demand and he headed for the farming district of the Swan Valley north-east of Perth. Once he had adjusted to the difference in climate and soils in the colony, he had the requisite knowledge to farm himself rather than continue as someone's employee. When he received his certificate of freedom he was in Guildford, then a small village approximately nine miles from Perth, which functioned as a gateway to the lower Swan Valley. At some time within the next two years, Caleb moved further north to the Upper Swan. It was here that he married Jane Murray in 1870. But Caleb was already 33 when he was transported and he ran out of time to establish a new life for himself. Less than four years after marrying Jane, he died aged 43.[41]

Joseph Sowden Ledger was one of the more professional burglars delivered to Western Australia by the *Dalhousie*. His criminal experience showed not only in a record of prior convictions but in the adept way he reversed his names from document to document and in varying circumstances. He was convicted as Joseph Sowden, which appears to have been two christian names. Elsewhere Joseph remained constant, but sometimes he was known as Sowden Ledger, sometimes as Ledger Sowden. To his nephews and niece, he was just 'Uncle Sowden'. Most of the prisoners on the *Dalhousie* arrived with nothing but a hymn book distributed by the ship's chaplain, but Joseph Sowden was carrying a photo whose date and place suggests it was his mother, Sarah Ledger.[42]

Sowden spent six years caught in the penal system of Western Australia, three of them for a colonial sentence in Perth when he was charged for 'endeavouring to obtain goods under false pretences'—a harsh setback for a man already 37 years of age, which delayed his ticket. Being forced to remain under the control of the Convict Establishment meant he continued to be subject to the petty charges of prison, like 'having cooked provisions improperly in his possession' for which he endured three days on bread and water and, the following year, 'having his cell and his cell utensils in a very dirty state', which also resulted in three days on bread and water. Finally, in January 1869, Joseph Sowden Ledger became a ticketer allowed to work on his own account. A blacksmith and tinsmith, he could also make nails, and his skills were much in demand among the colonists, who would pay seven shillings per day for them. At a personal level, he wasted no time. On arrival he had declared that he had a wife in England, although there were apparently no children. In any event, in Perth in 1869 Sowden Ledger married Mary Ann Hart, who was the daughter of a policeman. Having a father-in-law in the force may explain why, in December 1871, Sowden was drinking in a police station. Perhaps he was celebrating something with his father-in-law. It does not explain how he came to be charged with 'being drunk at the police station'. Faced with fourteen days in the cells or a fine of ten shillings, he paid up. It was his last brush with the authorities. In July 1872, he received his conditional pardon, ten years to the day since he was sentenced.

The Ledger brothers, Edson (standing) and young Joseph, expanded their uncle Joseph Sowden's business

In the following years, Sowden Ledger used his blacksmith's skill to lay the foundations of what would become a significant business. Between 1885 and 1889 he employed 29 ticketers. Like his first marriage, his union with Mary Ann produced no children. Instead, in 1880 he was joined in the colony by his nephew, Joseph Edson Ledger. As a free immigrant, after two years in the colony young Joseph was eligible for a land grant, which he duly acquired in Perth and shortly after sold to his uncle, whose expiree status prevented him obtaining free grants. Not long after, they were joined by Sowden's younger brother, David, who was Joseph's father. David Ledger brought his entire family with him, including his 14-year-old second son, Edson. The Ledger family had long been involved in the metal trades, and over time young Joseph and Edson enlarged Joseph Sowden's business, which was then expanded further by Edson's son, Frank, into a large industrial engineering company, J.&E. Ledger Pty Ltd. After Mary Ann's death, old Joseph visited Melbourne in 1892 and found himself another wife, typically using yet another reversal of his name on the marriage certificate. When he died three years later, he left the significant estate of £600, half to his siblings and nephews and half to his wife. His story reveals how a family that had struggled on the edge of the law in Yorkshire—and in Sowden's case outside it—prospered in Western Australia, where their brains and hard work could be applied in a law-abiding way.[43]

Jennifer Cook, the grand-daughter of Edson Ledger, reported that all knowledge of Joseph's career in crime and his transportation to Western Australia had been lost by the family. 'It was only about twenty years ago [*c.* 1985] that we discovered Joseph was a convict. Some records show him as Joseph Sowden Ledger who arrived with an "assisted passage", a good alternative description of how he got here! At that time some of my aunts and uncles were quite shocked when I told them of the discovery. My own father had no idea of the convict connection. Possibly his father [Edson] may not have known either. My dad was quite fascinated when I told him about it.'[44]

The various schemes to bring free immigrants to the colony, particularly women, benefited several *Dalhousie* men, one of whom was the shoemaker George Rawlinson. In Hertfordshire, he had pleaded guilty on two counts of breaking and entering and stealing five watches and a pair of boot trees, for which he received a sentence of six years penal servitude.[45] There is no record of any previous offences, and none in the colony. In many ways Rawlinson's transportation could more fittingly be described as 'forced migration'. He received his ticket-of-leave barely nine months after he arrived in Western Australia. Six months later, in 1865, when they were both working as servants, he met a young Irish immigrant named Margaret Coghlan who had arrived on one of the Bride Ships, the *West Australia*, in 1859. In April 1865 they married and the first of their five children was born later that year. Rawlinson received a conditional pardon in 1866 and his certificate of freedom in 1868. Some time shortly after that, he did exactly what the eastern colonists dreaded and successfully transferred his family to South Australia. In the process, he was equally successful in breaking the connection to his convict past.[46]

George Rawlinson's descendant Lorraine Clarke uncovered his background in 1989. She reported that Rawlinson's grand-daughter, who was her own grandmother, was horrified at the news he was a convict. 'How dare you look into my family. Look into your grandfather's!' she told Lorraine, who did just that, only to discover yet another convict. 'I have spoken to various members of the family in Western Australia and, just recently, to a branch of the South Australian family,' Lorraine wrote in March 2007. 'Nobody knew that George Rawlinson was a convict.' In 1895, George and Margaret's son, George William, moved to Western Australia to work on the railway and settled at Narrogin. The other children remained in South Australia, where many descendants live today. Some of the family thought the Rawlinsons came from Germany. Others in the South Australian branch had been told they were Irish and had come direct from England to South Australia. This version of the family history was embellished further with the information that 'all of the records were destroyed in the Irish Rebellion'.[47]

Little Dick Reeves was another who fared well in the colony, particularly through his marriage. A Londoner with no experience of agricultural labour but a conviction for the serious crime of murder, on the face of it he was everything the colonists did not want in their prisoners. Nevertheless, he arrived bearing a character report of 'Very Good' and continued well behaved in the colony. The only blemish on his probationary record was a sentence of three months hard labour for 'being out after hours and loitering about in Perth without employment'. Little did the local gaolers know that he was repeating the pattern of wandering the streets and alleys which had made him so well known around the Covent Garden area in London. Once he received his ticket-of-leave in November 1866, Dick Reeves worked around Perth as a servant or labourer for various employers. During one of these jobs he had the great good fortune to meet Agnes Atkinson. Eighteen years old at the time they met, Agnes was the daughter of John Atkinson who, with his wife Ann and two children, had been one of the first to take up the chance to emigrate under the prisoner guard scheme. The family arrived on the convict ship *Scindian* in 1850. At the time she met Reeves in 1869, Agnes was living with her parents in Claremont but probably working as a servant elsewhere in Perth. Very likely their relationship upset the family dreadfully when it was revealed that she was pregnant. Agnes and Dick may even have kept it secret until the very last moment. They were not married until three months after the baby was born. A year later, Dick Reeves transferred south to the Murray district, where Agnes' brother James was a prosperous landowner near Chittering. James Atkinson employed ticketers as labourers on the property and Dick Reeves joined his workforce. Later the couple settled in Perth, at Wembley.[48]

Dick never lost his habit of wandering off. He could be difficult and moody and unpredictable, a temperament that towards the end of his life was exacerbated when he lost his sight. But the couple had nine children together. With fortitude and commonsense and energy, Agnes organised their life and managed the family and provided Little Dick, as he was called by his many relations and descendants, with the kind of stability he had never known in his tormented childhood. As parents, they shared the tragedy of losing children including their eldest boy, Richard, who died aged eleven years from tetanus, and their son William who enlisted in the AIF in 1916 and was killed in action in France in October 1917. When the war ended, Richard Reeves was in his seventies. He died in 1923 at the age of 81. Agnes lived on for many years. In 1936, a journalist who met her reported, 'Now 84 years of age, Mrs Reeves is in many ways a remarkable personality. Apart from occasional turns she is particularly happy and bright and, even from these bad turns, she recovered with a rapidity that suggests a sturdy constitution.' Agnes was celebrated in the paper as the 'Lady With the Red Flag', the last of many women gatekeepers who had once been employed at railway crossings around Perth. She died in August 1942. Nearly 25 years after her death, her name was inscribed on the Pioneer Women's Memorial in King's Park overlooking the city of Perth.[49]

Richard Reeves   *Agnes Reeves (née Atkinson)*

The careers of the 24 arsonists who arrived on the *Dalhousie* were peaceful compared with the turbulence created by the soldier convicts. Four arsonists served their time without incident and are recorded as leaving the colony soon after they were free. Others may have done the same but avoided the attention of the authorities. The eastern colonies attracted some of them, but not all. Thomas Dunn, convicted in Chester, chose New South Wales. William Young, one of several men convicted at the Maidstone Assizes in Kent, went to Victoria.

Welshman John Robinson, from Cardiff, left for South Australia, but George Davis who was also convicted in Cardiff was probably heading home to Wales when he sailed on a P&O coal ship for Port Callao. Two arsonists died while they were still prisoners. Charles Wormsley, aged 38, died at Fremantle prison three months after he arrived in Western Australia. William Gibson, who was 29 when he was convicted at Oxford, was found dead in the bush in 1867 after disappearing from the service of a Mr Parker at Dargin the previous year. Several can be traced settling in Western Australia and producing many children for the population-starved colony. One of these was William Mason, who was 23 when he was convicted at Oxford. As a ticketer he worked out of the Toodyay Depot, where he established a good relationship with the land-owner Donald McPherson, for whom he worked almost continuously over the next three and a half years. He was still with McPherson when he received his conditional pardon in December 1868. Mason married Mary Ann Larwood in 1871 at Gingin, then settled at Victoria Plains where they had seven children. He died aged 61 in 1900.

Henry Sherry, who had attempted to burn down the family home after a fight with his father, spent his nearly eight years as a ticketer working in the Murray district, initially as a groom or a labourer and later as foreman for Captain Fawcett at Pinjarrah. His conduct as a prisoner would later be described as 'exemplary', with no convictions for misconduct after he arrived in the colony. In January 1874 he received his conditional pardon but before that, in 1870, he had married Ann Elizabeth Hains who also worked as a domestic servant for Fawcett. The couple settled in the Williams area, where Henry took up farming in his own right. Over the next fifteen years they had seven children. In 1878, Henry left the colony for Colombo. His reason for the visit is uncertain. He may have gone home to England or, in view of what followed, he may have been checking whether it was possible to make a living in Ceylon. He was back in Western Australia by 1882 because the following year Annie Elizabeth gave birth to a daughter who they called Alice Melinda.

Eighteen months later, an explosion of deadly rage from Henry brought their family life to a tragic end. At some time in the past, he had fallen in love with a neighbour's wife, whose name was Catherine Waldock. Sixteen years younger than Henry, who was now 47, she lived on a nearby farm with her husband John and their two boys. In Henry's own words, he 'doted on the ground she walked on'. Despite that devotion, he spent two years quarrelling with her for refusing to elope with him and leave the colony. Finally, he resolved to kill her and himself. At dusk on 16 September 1885 he confronted Catherine as she walked with her children in the bush near their house. When she saw Henry, she drew him out of earshot of her sons. Waiting while the two adults talked, the boys saw Henry point a gun at their mother and say loudly, 'Here goes' as he did so. When she turned to run, he shot her in the back.[50]

Henry did not kill himself and gave different people different reasons why he did not. He never attempted to deny the murder and when the case came before the Supreme Court he was sentenced to death. In the two weeks that followed the sentence, he was calm and composed and apparently penitent. He made his will. According to a newspaper report, he wrote to Annie Elizabeth acknowledging the great sin he had committed and the great wrong he had done to her and his six surviving children. He even managed to sleep for a few hours on the night before his execution. Shortly before 8 a.m., with the death bell tolling relentlessly, he was escorted by the Bishop of Perth down the gaol corridor. In stockinged feet, he was dressed only in moleskin trousers and a cotton shirt opened by the executioner to bare his neck. His hands were tied behind him. A watching reporter described the scene in detail.

> He was a tall, rather spare built man, with prominent nose and sharp, intelligent features. He walked erect without any assist-ance, and indeed, he seemed quite as composed as any one present. He scarcely seemed to change colour, and his eye was as steady as if nothing of consequence were happening . . . When he came in view of the black painted machine of the law, the condemned man never faltered but quietly and with steady step followed the executioner up a flight of stone steps on to the platform . . . he walked on to the trapdoors, looked up at the rope dangling above so as to place himself in the right position and then stood firm as a post ready for his fate. In a trice, the executioner had placed the noose round the criminal's neck and drawn the cap over his head . . .

With everything in place, the executioner moved instantly to the lever that operated the trapdoor. But the Bishop of Perth, who had been reading the burial service aloud throughout the preparations, had not finished. Henry Sherry stood motionless with the noose round his neck until the Bishop reached the end. Overcome with admiration, the watching reporter described Henry's extraordi-nary calm during the interminable wait—'the only emotion he evinced being once or twice a hard drawn breath'. The moment the clergyman said 'Amen', the executioner opened the trapdoor. Mercifully, death was instantaneous. Blotted out in that moment, along with memories of Catherine, of Annie Elizabeth and the children, were the traumatic events he experienced in the army during the Crimean War which sent him home to his father and sister damaged beyond repair.[51] In a sad postscript, Annie Elizabeth, who was pregnant at the time Henry was executed, married Catherine's widower, John Waldock.[52]

Henry Sherry's terrible crime was not typical of the men who arrived on the *Dalhousie*. An analysis of their records after arrival suggests that most were law-abiding, with 166 out of the 270 having totally clean sheets, free of any offence. A further 62 recorded one or two minor transgressions, which were mainly master and servant issues, but 41 of them also included a conviction for drunkenness. The following were typical of their offences for this law-abiding or nearly law-abiding group: 'out after hours' (fine ten shillings), 'creating a disturbance and calling his late employer a liar' (one month in the Toodyay Depot), 'being absent from his permanent place of abode' (fourteen days hard labour), 'absent from chapel without leave' (three days bread and water), 'assaulting a fellow prisoner' (three days bread and water), 'refusing to work and gross insolence' (cautioned and sent back to Road Party), 'assault and loitering about town' (fine ten shillings and four days in lock-up), 'riding on team without permissions and being absent from team in his charge' (fine five shillings for each count), 'furious riding in town' (fine ten shillings). In addition to the men detailed above, fourteen men could be classified as serious drunks—one died from delirium tremens soon after he arrived. Six men had colonial convictions of twelve months or more. They ranged from a year in Fremantle prison for stealing clothes to three years with hard labour for receiving stolen property. James Kelly was convicted of breaking and entering and stealing in the house of William Brown at Fremantle, for which he was sentenced to three years hard labour in the prison, six months of it in irons.

Anthony Trollope, who was travelling systematically from colony to colony, recording the 'past history', 'present condition' and 'future prospects' of each one, thought the Western Australian colonists were unrealistic in expecting each prisoner to exhibit obvious signs of reform by upright, sober and industrious behaviour. He was sympathetic towards ticketers like those from the *Dalhousie*.

> Men were daily committed for bad language, drunkenness, absconding, late hours and offences of like nature. For men holding tickets-of-leave are subjected to laws, which make it criminal for a man to leave his master's employ or to be absent from his master's house after certain hours, or to allude in an improper manner in his master's eyes. And for these offences, sentences of punishment are given which seem to be heavy.[53]

A prisoner in Fremantle Gaol who described the Western Australian penal system as 'on the whole, judicious and has good results', nevertheless agreed with Trollope that punishment could be disproportionate to the crime. Writing to his brother in England, he commented: 'society may one day think that so natural and harmless a thing as an attempt to get out of prison called for a punishment somewhat less severe than one to which death itself were leniency'. He described how the heaviest punishments were reserved for those who tried to escape. In an attempt by the authorities to avoid flogging, the bolters were confined in a separate, dark cell for 50 to 100 days, with a diet of water and one pound of bread. They were forced to wear exceptionally heavy irons, which could not be removed day or night. When they emerged from their long confinement, they were 'weak, sickly, famine-stricken men, looking much as persons do who are in a consumption'. Despite this condition, the next stage of their punishment was to work on the roads, still heavily ironed. The letter writer estimated that 'nine-tenths of the attempts to escape are now from this very chain gang'. As a last resort, flogging would then be added to their misery. To no effect. 'The men who form this gang are by no means the worst in the prison; but they are under a mania for running away and the more heavily they are ironed the more will they try to get free. In the meantime, the effect on the poor fellows is ruinous; every day does something towards making them hard, fierce, savage. Break them down you never can. And when they come to their liberty, it will be found that they have been made very dangerous.'[54]

In Western Australia, the colonists did not distinguish between one type of convict or the other. They were all members of 'the criminal class', and that was enough to cause alarm. Changes in the context through which convicts were viewed was the major difference between the penal colonies in the east as compared with the west. For more than 40 years in New South Wales and Van Diemen's Land, residents and travellers alike marvelled at the reformation of the convicts. Despite the many criticisms, doubts and investigations, both colonies and their emancipists benefited from a fundamentally optimistic environment. Sir William Molesworth's committee and the anti-transportation campaign changed the paradigm. Free settlers in Western Australia disbelieved the prospects of reform and they were always frightened about their safety. A clergyman's wife expressed the fear they shared when she wrote, 'The colony has been saturated with professors of crime and, if by the withdrawal of home supplies [funding], the dangerous classes within it should ever want bread, the position of the free settlers would be very terrible.'

Despite the colonists' fears, there was in reality little crime in the colony, a fact confirmed in 1860 by Governor Kennedy, who reported to the Duke of Newcastle, 'The absence of all serious crime is remarkable and satisfactory.'[55] Twelve months later the Comptroller General reported, 'The general conduct of the convict population throughout has been as satisfactory as could well be hoped. I believe the chaplain is right when he says that the majority of them are sincere in their wish to amend, so long as they are not assailed by temptation.'[56] And again, in 1863, Governor Hampton told Newcastle that 'few crimes of violence have been committed by the convicts . . . and that life and property are generally very safe throughout the colony'.[57] Nonetheless, the absence of crime in Western Australia did not reassure the locals. According to Trollope, they insisted that it was simply due to the convicts' fear of each other and was no proof of reformation. They told Trollope that 'the physiognomy and gait, and general idleness of the men, their habits of drinking when they can get drink, and general low tendencies' were proof that the men had not reformed.[58]

The fears of the colonists were magnified and in some cases endorsed by a variety of global developments. The first, chronologically, was the novels of Charles Dickens, which were serialised in popular magazines in Britain, many of which were read in the colonies at the time or in book form later. One of the most influential was *Oliver Twist*, which was published monthly in *Bentley's Miscellany* from February 1837 through to its last chapter in the April 1839 issue.[59] In the character of his villain, Bill Sykes, Dickens simultaneously personalised and stereotyped criminals transported to the colonies. In 1872, like many visitors to Australia, Trollope had Dickens' image in mind and was looking for similarities among the convicts. On the assumption his readers would know exactly what he meant, he referred several times to 'the Bill Sykes physiognomy'.[60] He titillated their curiosity even further with the following observation, even if his comments were intended to defend convicts against what Trollope thought were the unreasonable expectations of the colonists. 'The Bill Sykes look of which I have spoken is produced by the gaol rather than by crime. The men are not beautiful to look at. They do spend their money in drink, filling the bars of the public-houses, till the hour comes at which they must retire. But it is much in such a community that they should not return to crimes of violence.'[61]

The second influence on colonists' perceptions (and this applied across the continent) were developments in science and pseudo science. In November 1859, Darwin's *Origin of Species* was published. In 1866, Darwin's supporter Herbert Spencer popularised his friend's theories by coining the term 'survival of the fittest', which in the mind of the public quickly replaced Darwin's more genteel phrase 'natural selection'.[62] The controversial debate that Darwin's theories triggered raged throughout Western Australia's final decade as a penal colony and continued in the decades following, when the convicts were working through their sentences. Existing ideas of criminals as a distinct species were reinforced by the philosophy of eugenics, which was systematised by Francis Galton, a cousin of Darwin who was influenced by his work. Galton viewed his theory as a moral philosophy to improve humanity by breeding from the healthiest and most intelligent people. It was not until 1883 that he coined the term 'eugenics' to describe it. Like the idea of 'survival of the fittest', eugenics crossed the boundary between scientific and philosophical theory into popular culture. In the first half of the twentieth century, supporters of eugenics often equated 'improving' humanity with 'purifying' it, with consequent implications for issues such as sterilisation, immigration and race segregation.[63]

During the early decades of the Australian colonies, phrenology—'reading' character through the shape of the head—had been seen as a way to understand the nature of man in general and criminal man in particular. It was believed that if unfavourable propensities could be detected early, they could be remedied by education. Historian Michael Roe discovered an example of its application to Australia among the Colonial Office records in London where, in 1836, a Scottish baronet suggested that all convicts should be phrenologically examined to see if they were suitable to become colonial pioneers.[64] In the latter part of the nineteenth century, Italian criminologist Cesare Lombroso was far less optimistic than the phrenologists. Performing an autopsy on an Italian bandit in 1872, he found an anomaly in the man's cranial structure that he called a fossette. From this experience, Lombroso developed a theory that a man could be born a criminal and his nature would be revealed by defective cranial structure. In 1876 his groundbreaking book, *Criminal Man*, popularised the idea of an innate criminal type that was thought to be a reversion or atavism of an ancestor of all humanity.[65] His theories gave rise to research in 'criminal anthropology', with devastating consequences for Australia's indigenous people and disquieting implications for convicts and their descendants.

These interlocking, overlapping strands of science and sociology and philosophy created a new and threatening context for the Australian colonies, which helped frame the attitudes of residents and visitors alike. Their influence could be seen in comments by the wife of novelist Robert Louis Stevenson in 1892 when she wrote to a friend from Sydney, 'The criminal stamp is very obvious on the faces of the passers-by.'[66]

Given the history of the birthstain, it is not surprising that Australians did everything they could to counter the argument that heredity determined an individual's characteristics and propensities. They found reassurance in arguments about the influence of environment that developed to counter the theories of the hereditarians. Australians were not alone in emphasising one aspect to suit their own context. In class-based Britain, for instance, heredity was the dominant theory. In the United States, where both race and immigration were controversial issues, opinion also favoured hereditary determinism. By contrast, Australia put its faith in the 'purging effect' of the environment. But in Australia it was argued by some that the 'environment could transform the British raw material and create a new man, physically healthier and mentally more stable'.[67] The eugenics debate was at its height from the turn of the nineteenth century through to the mid-twentieth. Australia's exultation during World War I in the sheer physicality of its young soldiers as well as their performance on the battlefield must be understood in this context. They were not only purifying a nation stained by convictism, they were confirming the victory of environment over heredity, demonstrating that the stain had not been passed down. As local eugenicist Meredith Atkinson passionately explained in 1920, 'Whatever hereditarian dogmatism may say about the laws of natural selection and survival of the fittest, Australia has demonstrated beyond question the supreme and infinite potentialities of social environment and she is but on the threshold of the new order.'[68]

In the second half of the nineteenth century, the idea of a genetic inheritance or predetermined tendency to crime was added to the shame of depravity that had been associated with convicts since the mid-century campaigns to end transportation. It is not surprising that the former prisoners and their descendants increasingly felt it necessary to hide their convict connections from society at large and from their own children.

In Western Australia this wider context was intensified by the specific social structure of the colony. Unlike the convicts in eastern Australia, the Western Australian expirees did not find themselves trying to make a new life in a community dominated by their fellow emancipists, many of them employers. Those egalitarian forces were not operating in the west. In the first place, the former convicts were called 'expirees', a more negative term than 'emancipists'. Secondly, expirees did not predominate as emancipists had done for so many years. In Western Australia the population was always fairly evenly divided between the two classes. Even after the arrival of 10,000 convicts, the population was approximately 25,000. Even more significantly, the western colony was shaped by a far more distinct class structure than in the east, and the distinctions dated back to the foundation of the colony by free settlers who were accompanied by their servants.

Fear and distaste towards convicts among the genteel class reinforced these differences. Like the exclusive class in early New South Wales, polite society protected its status by drawing up strong demarcation lines. They differentiated between doing business with expirees and inviting them into their private lives. To some extent this behaviour was emulated by free immigrants too, although the tendency was reduced by intermarriage between the two lower-class groups. The extent to which they interacted could not be publicised, however, for fear of deterring prospective immigrants to the colony. With this in mind, the Registrar General of Western Australia explained reassuringly in 1870, 'However moral their lives and however unimpeachable their conduct in every social relation, they have hitherto been unable to remove the barrier that separates them from that class from which they have fallen.'[69] There were in fact enough former convicts and their families to provide society for themselves, but they also faced direct discrimination that affected their quality of life. Expirees could not join the Mechanics' Institutes, the agricultural societies, town trusts and race clubs. They could not serve as jurors, or attend the Assembly Balls.[70] Discrimination limited their employment options and constrained the social mobility that had been such a hallmark of the Australian colonies. John Purcell, a former soldier on the *Dalhousie*, had ambitions to be a schoolmaster but there were limits to where he could be employed. Ex-convicts were not accepted as teachers in government schools in the more populated areas of Perth and Fremantle and Guildford because the parents would not accept them. In the rural areas, where the need for teachers of any kind was desperate, people were not so choosy. Some convicts and ex-convicts were even employed as private tutors in rural districts.[71] Two *Dalhousie* men found work as teachers: architect Thomas H.J. Brown and solicitor George Newby Wardell, both of whom were transported for forgery.[72] Generally, the experience of former convicts in Western Australia bears out a suggestion made by Jenny Gregory in 1986 that further research is needed into the limited social mobility in Western Australia.[73]

Joseph Shaw   *Maria Shaw*

Nowhere was the convict stain felt more acutely than by the wives of professional men who had been transported.[74] Maria Shaw, wife of the former solicitor Joseph Shaw, lost her social status entirely when she joined her husband in Western Australia. When Joseph arrived in the colony, he served two years probation without incident, his clerical skills ensuring that he was spared the road gangs and instead put to use by the Convict Establishment. Educated convicts were employed on the desk in the department, in the store-keeper's office, in the prison school and at the hospital.[75] In March 1866 Joseph became eligible for a ticket-of-leave. Of course, Joseph was a lawyer who, like William Brodribb 40 years earlier, could no longer practise the profession for which he was trained, a disadvantage not shared by an agricultural labourer, or a carpenter, or a blacksmith. On the other hand, Joseph had capital. Shortly after he received his ticket, he bought land which he farmed himself for eighteen months before returning briefly to employment as a clerk for the Comptroller General of Convicts. In December 1868 he began working as a clerk for police magistrate G.W. Leeke in Perth, which involved travelling between Perth and Fremantle and Guildford. He was still with Leeke when he obtained his conditional pardon in March 1872.[76]

Maria Shaw arrived six months after Joseph received his pardon. She was accompanied by their three children, Joseph Thomas aged fourteen, John Francis aged twelve and Alice, now ten, who was barely a year old when her father was convicted. In preparation for their arrival, Joseph had rented a house in St George's Terrace which became the family's home for the next four years. They were comfortably situated, but Maria must have been shocked by the small range of local society and the barriers it erected against her. After the wealth and social standing she enjoyed in Derbyshire, the taint would have been hard to bear. Western Australian historian Rica Erikson, who has researched the topic in detail, concluded, 'These gentlewomen needed excep-tional strength of character to give moral support to their husbands and to bear the snubs of society.'[77] In 1873, Maria gave birth to their third son, Charles, and three years later to Phillip. Shortly after Phillip's birth, the family moved to a property owned by Joseph at Claisebrook. Joseph developed several business interests. He owned other properties in the Claisebrook area and was involved also in timber at the Canning. However, Joseph and Maria's relation-ship was faltering. In 1888, she left him, taking the two youngest boys and their daughter Alice with her. The reason Maria gave up on their marriage after travelling so far to maintain it remains a mystery to her descendants. Theories range from the suggestion that she came into money left by a relative in England which facilitated the move, to the suspicion that Joseph had a drinking problem. Both could be accurate. The deciding factor could also have been anxiety for her children's future. In Melbourne, where they settled, Maria posed as a widowed immigrant. The two boys attended Wesley College, one of the best schools available. Later, Charles married the daughter of the publisher

George Robertson. After her daughter Alice died young and unmarried, Maria moved to Sydney to be near the Robertsons. She died there in 1913. Joseph Shaw remained in Perth working as a law clerk. He died there in 1906, aged 70. His eldest son, Joseph Thomas, who followed his father into the profession of law, developed a practice at Kalgoorlie.[78]

Within a very short time, the Shaw family's knowledge of their complicated history was obliterated. In the early 1980s, Maria and Joseph's granddaughter, Kath Francis, became interested in family history and joined the Victorian Genealogical Society. She had vivid memories of Maria from her childhood, but all she knew was that Joseph and Maria had emigrated to Western Australia, where he had died. Wandering around the Society's library, she came to the Western Australian section and picked up Rica Erikson's *Dictionary of Western Australians*. 'Of course, I looked for Shaw and that was when I discovered that he was a convict. I knew he had to be my grandfather because it mentioned his wife and three children. On my way home, I called on my son who was a master at Scotch College. "How would you like a convict ancestor?" I asked him. He said, "Who?" And I replied, "My grandfather." His reaction was "By gee, that's mighty close." My older sister was terribly shocked. She always thought we were very uppercrust.'[79]

The convict era in Western Australia is close to 21st-century Australia. The last boatload of prisoners arrived in 1868. The last six convicts were pardoned in 1906 at the instigation of the Prime Minister, Alfred Deakin.[80] Many of the former prisoners lived well into the twentieth century, two of the last being Samuel Speed, who arrived on the *Belgravia* in 1866 and died in November 1939 aged 95, and Frederick Bicknell, who died in 1936 at 96 years after arriving in 1868 on the *Hougoumont*. The convicts' children and grandchildren, many of whom knew them well, were part of the Australian community throughout that century and in some cases into the 21st. At present, descendants who have revealed—and in some cases, uncovered—their ancestor's story are few in number. With time, more descendants will emerge and it will be possible to gain a fuller, more three-dimensional picture of the prisoners who were transported to Western Australia. The process is complicated by the enormous number who left the colony once they were free. Some went home. Some went to America or New Zealand. Despite the restrictions on travel, many moved to the colonies of South Australia, Victoria and New South Wales. Convict records in Western Australia noted that 49 men from the *Dalhousie* left the colony but this figure is not accurate. It does not, for instance, include George Rawlinson, who family history reveals went to South Australia in the 1870s.

Fundamentally, the eastern colonies were no more successful than the convict authorities at preventing a determined man from doing what he wanted. Travelling to Melbourne in 1863 in order to catch a ship home to Britain, expiree John Mortlock was accompanied by eight or ten other 'pardoned law-breakers'. After they left port, a ticket-of-leave holder emerged from hiding. The sympathetic captain put him to work among the crew and 'when the anchor dropped, and many boats surrounded us, he and his friends stepped into one of them, was pulled to the wharf' and vanished.[81]

Mortlock himself had a last tilt at the system before he departed. While he was waiting in Melbourne for his ship to sail, Victorian parliamentarians were debating the vexed question of an invasion of convicts from the west. Such was their agitation that a Mr Kyte went so far as to propose the government meet the cost of sending expirees back to Britain. With the cheek so typical of the convicts, Mortlock wrote a letter to the editor of the *Argus* mocking their deliberations. Published in May 1864, it suggested that a private company be organised 'with a particular agent at Swan River, ready to furnish a passage to England to any expiree willing to accept it'. Public moneys to cover the expense could be solicited from Victoria and the adjoining colonies. He concluded the letter, 'I fear he [Mr Kyte] may deem me rather intrusive for, I am, your very humble servant AN EXPIREE—anxious enough to return home and rather wishing to be transported—gratis—back again.'[82]

Close examination of individuals suggests that convicts sent to Western Australia were little different from those sent to the eastern colonies. Assertions they were 'worse', older or less likely to reform prove to be inaccurate because they were based on false or misleading data (for example, the elimination of Parkhurst boys from the count) or exaggerated as part of the argument about abolishing transportation. The terms of the anti-transportation debate fundamentally affected the convict era in Western Australia. Many of the prisoners hid their background. Institutionally, the shame of becoming a convict colony became entrenched in Western Australia, just as it did over time in the east, creating a reluctance to commemorate or preserve the transportation era of the colony's history. As we have seen in Chapter 2, in relation to convict letters given to the Western Australian Historical Society in the 1930s, people tended to agree that the convict period was 'best forgotten'.[83]

CHAPTER 10
distinctions of moral breed

The anti-transportationists' focus on Western Australia was only possible because they had won their battle in the east. In June 1853, Governor Sir William Denison received news that the British government would send no more prisoners to Van Diemen's Land.[1] Transportation to the colony was finished.

Crucial impetus to Britain's decision had been the defeat of Governor Denison, who supported its continuance, in the colony's newly constituted Legislative Council. In a prelude to eventual self-government, the elected membership of the Council had been increased in 1851, and in the fiercely fought ballot that followed many anti-transportationists won seats. Prominent among them were Richard Dry and T. Gregson from Launceston. In fact Dry became President of the Council. After the election, although Denison could still have prevailed with support from appointed members who held civil office in the colony, adroit tactics by the Anti-Transportation League carried the day for a motion supporting the end of transportation. This official resolution gave weight in the eyes of the British government to the torrent of petitions, letters, personal advocacy and press articles which formed part of the League's campaign to bring about abolition. Combined with the recent discovery of vast fields of gold in close proximity to the convict colony, as well as the increasing cost of transportation to the British government, it was decisive.[2]

The celebrations that followed the news reflected mixed local feelings about the issue. In Hobart, the elected municipal council was concerned that a class division had been created in the colony between anti-transportationists and those who opposed them. Conscious of this opinion, Governor Denison refused to declare a public holiday even though 10 August 1853, the date chosen to celebrate, also marked the 50th anniversary of the settlement of Van Diemen's Land. In Hobart, ceremonies were muted. By contrast, in Launceston, joy was unrestrained. Government offices remained open but everything else shut, including banks and shops. A celebratory arch was erected at the intersection of St John Street and Elizabeth Street. Services were held in all the churches, followed by an official lunch presided over by the Mayor and the Member for Launceston, Richard Dry. Afterwards Dry addressed a large crowd in St John's Square. The ceremony ended with a jubilee anthem in which they all joined. A procession, led by a band, then paraded through the town before returning to the square, where every child was given a ticket entitling them to a commemorative medal. As a symbolic gesture the municipal authorities pulled down the gallows, even though capital punishment remained on the statute books.[3]

The convicts on the *St Vincent* arrived two months before these celebrations but they acted as though they too had something to celebrate, treating the voyage as a holiday from the beginning. 'Their behaviour was tolerably good during the passage, but they were excessively indolent,' the surgeon Thomas Somerville recorded crossly in his journal. His charges had resisted all his attempts at 'instruction', whether religious or literacy. Nor did they show the slightest inclination to dance or sing or take part in any of the 'amusements' deemed appropriate for passing the time. 'Especially those that were embarked at Gibraltar,' added the surgeon. And why not? The 99 men taken on board at Gibraltar had been labouring two, three years or more on the fortifications for the British naval base. They felt entitled to take it easy. For them, the voyage on the *St Vincent* was rest and recreation. All they wanted to do was lie about and smoke. Their addiction to their pipes made the surgeon even crosser. 'I had much trouble in trying to stop them smoking,' he recorded. 'It was impossible particularly because the Guard and the Blue Jackets persisted in giving the prisoners tobacco.' But the one relief to the labourers at Gibraltar had been the smoko. As a matter of routine, they had been allowed to down tools every three hours for a smoke. On the ship, the surgeon's attempts to stop their favourite pastime generated such a torrent of complaints that in the end he backed down, even recommending in his report 'a modest allowance of tobacco' for prisoners in future.[4] It was a wise concession. The threat of mutiny on convict transports had become a rarity but the men were not in a mood to be coerced. In their minds, they were sailing to freedom. Half of them had been issued with tickets-of-leave 'for Van Diemen's Land' when they left their gaols in England.[5] Those embarked at Gibraltar were expecting a ticket-of-leave on arrival or soon after. The worst of their servitude was over. They would not have known they were the last group transported to Van Diemen's Land because the decision was taken after the *St Vincent* sailed, but the crew would have told them about the gold rush. Ahead lay unlimited prospects for a working man.

The St Vincent *landed 207 men in Van Diemen's Land*

John Hobbs had been stuck in Gibraltar since 1849. Once on the *St Vincent*, he must have been buoyed by optimism that, at last, his spectacular gamble to change his life would pay off. The young pickpocket Patrick Brian had been with Hobbs in Gibraltar. So had four of the six soldier convicts.[6] The other two soldiers, William Loder who was tried at Woolwich, and William Scheal, who was court-martialled in Barbados in mid-1850, went through the prison system in England, including public labour, before boarding the *St Vincent* in November 1852.[7] The Scottish shepherd Angus McKay, Captain William Kidd and Henry Taperell, the attorney's clerk from Exeter, had the good fortune to miss transportation to Gibraltar.[8] So had John O'Neil. After his sentence at Preston, he was sent down to Leicester Gaol, where he served a year. This was followed by nearly two years at Portland Prison.[9] While John—or Jemmy as his young wife Ellen called him—was following Jeremy Bentham's prescribed route to reformation, Ellen was already in Van Diemen's Land.

Moving to Millbank not long after their trial in February 1850, she sailed on the *Emma Eugenia* for Hobart in October that year. When she left, there was no certainty that John would follow her to Van Diemen's Land.[10]

The *St Vincent* delivered 207 men at Hobart on 27 May 1853. They had lost five en route: one by suicide when he jumped overboard, one who fell overboard, a third from 'diseased bladder and old age', and two who drank themselves to death when they got into 'the spirit room'. The surgeon reported that there was no epidemic on board but many of the prisoners had spent so long in prison that they were very susceptible to changes in the weather.[11] As usual, the great majority (158) were single men. They were also young, although not dominated by teenagers like those who sailed on the *John* twenty years earlier. Ninety on the *St Vincent* were aged 25 years or less, but only nine of those were teenagers. Altogether two-thirds of the men (144) were under 30 years.[12]

The authorities in Hobart took a cavalier attitude to the tickets-of-leave issued in Britain. Those men who held them were described locally as 'pass holders' and the 'authentic' ticket-of-leave was handed out according to judgements made after they arrived in the colony. Nevertheless, 120 men had been granted tickets by the end of 1853, and by 1860 approximately 200 local tickets-of-leave had been given to the men who arrived on the *St Vincent*.[13] Some of these were a re-issue because some men had their first ticket revoked for misconduct. Their offence was often trivial. John Mitchell, for instance, was charged with misconduct for playing skittles, for which he received an admonishment from the Bench. After several dry years, some men headed straight to the pub and swiftly found themselves before the magistrates charged with drunkenness. Most of the soldier convicts were punished in some way within the first six months, but by comparison with the soldiers on the *John* their transgressions were trivial and their punishments mild. Thanks to Jeremy Bentham, solitary confinement had replaced the lash for criminals, if not for soldiers, and the only iron gang was at Port Arthur. None of the soldiers was a long-term offender.[14]

Most conduct records for the *St Vincent* men are brief and end with a note 'absent' (which probably meant from a ticket-of-leave muster) or 'absconded'. While the Victorian Prevention Act was in force to stop convicts entering that colony, a list was kept of people departing the island, but it was by no means comprehensive. It seems that a large number of the *St Vincent* men managed to head across Bass Strait or in the direction of New Zealand within three to six years of their arrival.

When the men arrived in the early 1850s, there was plenty of work available, the Anti-Transportation League's resolution not to hire convicts being honoured in the breach rather than the observance. For instance, all 292 prisoners on the *Fairlee* which arrived the year before the *St Vincent* had been hired immediately at an average wage of £18 a year plus board and lodging. Employers wanted the men's labour regardless of their status and 1259 people applied for their services.[15] Conditions favoured men like Michael Nash, who stepped off the *St Vincent* obviously determined to start a new life. The leader of the group who assaulted Lord Monteagle's steward in County Limerick received a ticket-of-leave in December 1853 with the proviso that he must wait eighteen months before he was eligible for a pardon. After working without incident for employers in Westbury and Longford, intersected by a period in hospital, Nash received his conditional pardon in January 1855. Family information reveals that he then crossed Bass Strait to Victoria, where his wife and children joined him.[16] Ironically, as the Nash family reunited in Melbourne Lord Monteagle was acquiring a reputation as a great philanthropist for assisting the emigration to New South Wales and Victoria of families from the Shannagolden area. Their numbers included people called Nash but there is no evidence that the family of Michael Nash were among their numbers.[17]

Captain William Kidd took a job as a constable in Hobart when he landed, but a few months later he was contacted by the well-known local seafarer Captain James Kelly. As a young sea-dog in 1818, Kelly in his vessel the *Sophia* had enthusiastically chased the *Bensley* 'pirates', James Jenkins, Robert Dye and others, out the mouth of the Derwent and up the east coast. By the 1850s he was in charge of the port authorities at Hobart and it appears that he found a use for Captain Kidd.[18] Being away at sea would explain why, in April 1855, a note that Kidd's ticket-of-leave was revoked for 'absence' did not penalise his conditional pardon which he received in November that year. From that point, he vanishes from the convict records and from the colony. In fact no trace can be found of Captain Kidd in the genealogical records of any of the Australian colonies. He may have gone to New Zealand. He may have returned home to Scotland. His seafaring skills gave him many options.[19]

The young London thief Patrick Brian, or O'Brien as he became, had endured over three years labouring at Gibraltar. Born in the slums of St Giles, transported with a sentence of ten years for stealing a handkerchief plus similar prior offences, he was another whose determination to start afresh was evident. Required to serve a further twenty months after he landed in Van Diemen's Land, he did not jeopardise his standing by drunkenness or any other misconduct and received a ticket-of-leave in December 1853 followed by a conditional pardon in September 1856. The next May he applied to join the police force and at the same time married 17-year-old Catherine Morrissey, daughter of convict Bridget McMahon who had arrived on the *Earl Grey* in 1850. Patrick O'Brien was still a constable when the first of their twelve children, a son William, was born in 1858. Later, Patrick used his stonemason's skills to earn a living. When he died in February 1901, just after Federation, he was 72. Catherine died in 1916. Their many children lived far into the twentieth century, the youngest Martha still alive when the Whitlam Government came to power in Canberra in 1972. She died in October 1974. Some of the children may have known about their parents' convict origins but others did not. Carl O'Brien, who is descended from the O'Brien's third son, James, reported that the knowledge was lost entirely in his branch of the family.[20]

Patrick O'Brien stole the proverbial handkerchief

Catherine O'Brien (née Morrissey), wife of Patrick O'Brien, daughter of convict Bridget McMahon

Henry Taperell was 21 when he landed at Hobart. A short, stout young man with a round pale face, his skills as a clerk made him an attractive employee. Within days of arriving, he was employed by the *Hobarton Guardian* newspaper whose proprietor, John Moore, was a former convict. Henry obtained a ticket-of-leave in December 1853, then a conditional pardon in May 1855, but he waited for his certificate of freedom which completed his sentence before leaving Van Diemen's Land in January 1859. Eighteen months later at Wellington, New Zealand, he married Mary Ann Tompkins, the daughter of the pioneers John and Mary Tompkins who had settled there in 1841. Mary Ann gave birth to a son, Harry, in Wellington in January 1863, but despite his wife and child, Henry was not settled.[21] According to his descendant Sue Tooth, 'In November 1865, when he was working in a store in Queenstown in the South Island of New Zealand, Henry Taperell travelled to the junction of the Arnold and Grey Rivers on the west coast with money (said to have been given to him by his father-in-law) to buy land for goldmining. He crossed the Arnold River by ferry, but was never seen again. Despite long and careful searching, his body was never found. According to the *Grey River Argus,* he was feared murdered by one of the notoriously dangerous persons in the area.'[22] Intriguingly, his descendants discovered that one of Henry's brothers, Albert, and his two sisters Rosalie and Elizabeth all disappeared in England about the same time. None has ever been traced. In New Zealand, Henry kept his criminal past hidden and Mary Ann and their son Harry knew only that he once worked as a journalist. In later years, Harry tried to find his father but without success. In 1891, accompanied by his mother, Harry Taperell moved to Sydney where he became a respected leader writer, theatre critic and editor for several Sydney newspapers.

The older Henry's fate in New Zealand remained a puzzle for his relatives. Some accepted that he had been murdered but his grand-daughter and Sue Tooth, his great-granddaughter, were never satisfied. The discovery in 1988 that he had been a convict was both a surprise and something of a relief. At least it explained some of the mystery. But there was more to discover. In 1998, Sue Tooth met some Taperell relatives in England, one of whom told her a family story about two Taperell brothers who returned to England in the late nineteenth century with a large amount of money said to have been earned by goldmining in South America. With it, they purchased a large coaching business in 'the south of England'. And they changed their name. The rest of the Taperell family regarded the money as 'black money' and refused to have anything to do with them. Unfortunately, by 1998 the English relatives had forgotten the name chosen by the Taperell brothers to disguise their identity and their coaching company has yet to be tracked down.[23]

Arsonists John Hobbs and Eliza Morrison must have met in 1854 when both were working in Hobart as ticket-of-leave holders. Eliza had arrived in the colony in spring 1852 on the *Earl Grey*. In a burst of misplaced confidence, she told the muster clerk that she had burned down the Widow Cavanagh's house deliberately to be transported. Fatally, she also told him she was married. 'My husband, William, is in America,' she said and then gave him further details of her father and mother and four brothers and three sisters in Ireland. The clerk in turn assessed her appearance and thought it worth recording that she had a double chin and was much freckled. He agreed with the reporter in Kildare that her hair was red. Women prisoners were gathered after landing at the Female Factory while the men were sent to the Prisoners' Barracks. From the Factory, by that time called the House of Correction, Eliza was assigned as a housemaid to Mrs Cooke in Murray Street, with whom she stayed only a month. Returned to the Factory, she was assigned next to work at the hospital in Hobart where she continued nearly a year until returning to the Factory on 27 May 1853, one day after the *St Vincent* arrived. In an attempt to divert her from the bright lights of Hobart, the Factory sent her next to a Mrs Langley at Campbell Town in the midlands—which lasted three weeks. By now Eliza had learned how to work the system and she managed to get her next employer to return her to government, after which, in March 1854, she was assigned to George Burt, a publican in Liverpool Street.[24]

Apart from spending seven days in solitary for being 'out after hours and representing himself to be a ticket-of-leave holder', John Hobbs had no transgression on his record, but his long sentence of fifteen years delayed his freedom compared with some of his shipmates. A ticket-of-leave was issued in March 1854 with the notation that he must serve three years in that capacity before being eligible for a conditional pardon.[25] It is unlikely that he was bothered much in the interim. Work was plentiful and wages good, even for ticket-of-leave holders. He may even have found work at his trade as a french polisher. Very likely John and Eliza met in the pub where she was working. Perhaps he went there to celebrate receiving his ticket. At some point one must have asked the other, 'What did you do?' and the answer set off an enthusiastic conversation that created such a bond between them they decided a few months later to marry. In September 1854 their application was approved officially 'so long as the clergyman agrees'. But the clergyman checked the record and found Eliza's revelation about her husband. The application was refused, but Eliza now had her ticket and it is possible that she and John managed to keep their relationship alive in the following nine months without attracting the attention of the authorities. If discovered, they would have been condemned for immoral conduct and their tickets revoked. In any event, time was short. In the new year, Eliza fell ill with a 'disease of the lungs'—probably a chronic condition she brought from Ireland—and in the winter of that year it finally caught up with her. She died at His Majesty's Hospital, Hobart Town, on 1 July 1855, all her bright hopes, her courage and daring dying with her.[26] Six months after Eliza's death, John Hobbs was recommended for a pardon, which he received in January 1856. What happened to him after that will remain unknown until his descendants supply the rest of his story.

The tragic young mother Eliza Dore arrived on the *Duchess of Northumberland*, the last ship to bring female convicts to Van Diemen's Land, which reached Hobart the month before the *St Vincent* in 1853. Something of the guilt Eliza carried was evident when the Superintendent of Convicts asked her about her crime. She did not just reply 'murder' or 'my partner murdered my child'. Despite the evidence at the trial, she described the act as hers and assigned Abel a lesser role, giving the superintendent the full details as though relieving herself of a burden. 'Murdering my own child,' she told him, 'by throwing it into the Canal at Newport. I lived for ten months with Abel Ovans who assisted. He was hanged.' A year after her arrival, in May 1854, Eliza married a sailor named George Files and their first child John was born four months later. During their marriage, she gave birth thirteen times but, as often happened in the nineteenth century, only five children, all boys, survived past infancy. Eliza developed cancer when she was 47 and died at the 'Old Wharf', Hobart, on 15 May 1875.[27]

Ellen O'Neil's crime was far less significant than Eliza Dore's, but Ellen arrived in Hobart in March 1851 with a surgeon's report that described her succinctly as 'Bad'. Still only seventeen, she was clear about her goal at the muster. 'Married,' she told them firmly. But the Superintendent of Convicts looked at the document called a caption that travelled with her. 'It says "Single",' he pointed out. 'My husband was convicted with me. I am married,' she insisted. Because of the surgeon's negative report, Ellen was ordered to spend three months in separate confinement at the Factory before being assigned as a housemaid. On 24 June 1851 she was sent to work for Mr Fitzgerald in Elizabeth Street but, probably fretting with impatience to begin the search for John, she did not please her employer and was returned to government after only one week. On 3 July she was assigned again, but absconded three weeks later. Perhaps, assuming that John was still in prison in England, she headed out of Van Diemen's Land. Her disappearance was gazetted and a reward of £5 offered for information, but it was not until October 1852 that she was found in Victoria. Returned to Hobart, she served eighteen months probation before being assigned in January 1854 to Mr Dore in Barrack Street.[28]

Meanwhile, John O'Neil had been in the colony for six months, during which time he had been charged twice—for absconding and for being out after hours—after which his employer returned him to government. In December, after a charge in the gaol for 'disobedience of orders and being under the influence of liquor', he was sent to the Cascades probation station on the Tasman Peninsula. Discharged from there in April 1854, he made his own way back to Hobart where Ellen was now working. Somehow they met. On 10 May, Ellen was charged with 'being in bed with a man in her master's house', for which she was sentenced to nine weeks hard labour. A note on her file recorded that she was not to be assigned south of the midlands town of Ross. John escaped punishment, perhaps because Ellen would not reveal his identity. He is noted at the Prisoners' Barracks as returning from Cascades a few weeks later.

After working for a further six months for the Colonial Marine Department, John received a ticket-of-leave in January 1855. Meanwhile, Ellen lasted a few months in the midlands before absconding again. And again, the two of them found each other but this time it was John who was caught. Charged with misconduct for 'being with a female, absconding and representing her to be his wife', he lost his ticket-of-leave and was sentenced to two months hard labour on 1 June 1855. Another unexplained charge of misconduct shortly after suggests that somehow he and Ellen made contact again, but this time the authorities accepted the inevitable. John was reissued with a ticket-of-leave on 2 October 1855, and Ellen achieved her goal when she was assigned from the Factory 'to husband, John O'Neil, Macquarie Street'. In December, he received his conditional pardon.[29] Of course, they celebrated—for which John was fined for disturbing the peace—and their story should have ended at this point, with the couple together in a land of opportunity, both still young, healthy and sufficiently skilled to earn a living in a colony that needed servants and labourers. Instead, a strange, wild recklessness was carrying them inexorably to tragedy.

On Thursday 1 August 1856, John and Ellen and a ticket-of-leave convict named James King appeared before the Hobart magistrate on a charge of assaulting James Rowlands and robbing him of about £10. Rowlands testified that he was second mate on the *Emma Prescott* and the previous Saturday he had called at the Hope and Anchor to change a £10 note. John O'Neil saw him change the note but, according to Rowlands, he left the pub before him. No one else was present. 'I had nearly got back to the ship when a man came behind me and caught me by the neckcloth and nearly strangled me,' Rowlands testified. Although losing consciousness, he remembered O'Neil taking his purse from his pocket. 'I've known him for some time. He goes by the name of "Jemmy". He's always knocking around the wharf. I am quite positive it was him.' As he lay on the ground he was beaten or kicked about the head and when he came to he was covered in blood. The publican, Richard Wright, supported Rowlands' evidence. The testimony of Mr Louis Abrahams of Liverpool Street was also crucial. He described how John and Ellen bought some clothes at his shop later that evening. 'The woman paid me a £1 note and 5 shillings in silver. I saw other notes in her hand.' Their landlady, Johannah Guppy, said that she had asked Ellen for the rent on Saturday and Ellen had told her she didn't have it but would pay when her husband got home. It seems that Ellen may have found a way to sweeten what she said, because at this hearing Mrs Guppy added that they paid 25 shillings for the rent *before* they went out. The morning following the robbery, the pair tried to flee from Hobart but were caught on a barge that was leaving for Recherche Bay. Discharging Ellen and James King as nothing more than bystanders, the magistrate ordered Ellen to hard labour in the House of Correction and committed John for trial in the Supreme Court.[30]

John O'Neil's case was heard in September 1856. The witnesses all repeated what they had told the magistrate except Johannah Guppy, who this time told the court that when she asked John for the rent he said he had no money, 'until the skipper came on board'. Mrs Guppy testified that he returned in the evening and paid her the money. The *Hobart Mercury* noted that John made no defence, adding, 'Nor was there any legal gentleman present to watch the proceedings on his behalf.'[31] With the case unchallenged, the jury had no difficulty finding him guilty. In passing sentence, the judge said, 'At a time when robbery and violence stalks through the land, when even murder appears to be on the increase, when life and property are not safe, it seems that nothing but the strong arm of the law striking terrors through its executions, can put an end to such a fearful state. It is most painful to me to see a young man like you, in the vigour of life and who might by industry have earned a competence, perhaps independence, placing yourself by crime in a fatal position.' And he sentenced John O'Neil to death. As his words sank in, Ellen began to scream. And scream. Heart-rending screams, according to one newspaper report. When she would not stop, they led her out of the courtroom.[32]

They hanged John O'Neil two weeks later. His companion on the gallows was a man called George Langridge who had been convicted of the murder of his wife and it was he who attracted most attention from the press. By comparison, John was just an unimportant supporting player. His conviction was described by the *Mercury* as 'assault under arms'. The *Courier* had earlier referred to it as 'a garrotte robbery'. Most reports described it as 'assault and robbery'. There were no references to a weapon in the newspapers, and particularly nothing resembling a garrotte. At most was a suggestion that John used a stone or his boot to kick Rowlands when he was on the ground. In the circumstances, hanging him seems utterly disproportionate to his crime and by comparison with others who were hanged. In the 1850s, it was the practice for judges to provide the governor with the reasons for their sentence. Archival copies of these reports have survived for some years before and after 1856, but the file for that year is missing. There is no reason to think it was destroyed deliberately and it may yet be found, misplaced in the archives. Without the file, and with no surviving case papers, it is hard to understand how the judge reached his decision that John O'Neil must hang.

Ellen might never have seen John again after they removed her from the courtroom, but as long as he lived she would not have stopped fighting, weeping, screaming, writing letters, trying to persuade people to save him. Almost certainly, some sympathetic official or clergyman arranged for the couple to meet one last time, or at least carried a note for her. Seeking comfort from her family in England, Ellen wrote to tell them what happened. No doubt, she called regularly at the Convict Office to see if there was a reply, because they knew who and where she was in May 1860 when someone noted on her record, 'Letter for this woman from her father, John Clark, 92 Charter Street, Manchester' and a different hand recorded that the writer had given the letter to Ellen personally. Altogether, Ellen soldiered on in Hobart for nine years after John's death. In March 1857 she was fined five shillings for 'disturbing the peace', possibly in the House of Correction, but there were no details to reveal whether she had been weeping, or screaming or drunk. It did not prevent her receiving a ticket-of-leave three months later. But life was no longer a reckless adventure for Ellen. All her rebellious high energy had finally been crushed by the tragic death of her beloved Jemmy. In late February 1865, she entered the General Hospital in Hobart ill with pleurisy and on 3 March they noted in the records that Ellen O'Neil, widow, had died. She was 29 years of age.[33]

Although work was plentiful when the *St Vincent* arrived in 1853, it did not continue that way in Van Diemen's Land. The island colony did not share the prosperity of the 1860s and '70s that was experienced by the mainland colonies. Instead, Tasmania, as it was now called, slid steadily into depression. The sustained downturn was created by a combination of factors, including the undesirable reputation that resulted from the anti-transportation campaign. Reverend John West was among many people who left, taking up an offer in late 1854 to edit the *Sydney Morning Herald* for his old friend, John Fairfax. According to Manning Clark, in that role he was 'a man so swayed by success that the one-time radical turned his coat inside out and embraced a mawkish conservatism', an opinion at odds with those who eulogised West at his death.[34]

West's was not the only significant departure. In his book *Australian Squatter*, William Brodribb junior recounted how he returned to Tasmania in May 1851 for the first visit since he left after receiving a message from his youngest brother, Kenric, that their mother wanted to see him. At the time, Brodribb senior was in Gippsland visiting their daughter, Lavinia. In his absence, it is likely that Prudence took the opportunity to seek her eldest son's advice about whether they should move to Victoria. Realising that the proposal for legislation to prevent convicts and ex-convicts entering Victoria would, at the very least, inhibit Brodribb senior's ability to travel to and fro across Bass Strait, she must have been fearful of being cut off from Lavinia. To add to her worries, Kenric, who was a lawyer, was acting editor of the *Colonial Times*. Ignorant of the circumstances in which his father came to the colony, he was writing thundering editorials in support of the anti-transportationists. Prudence must have been apprehensive that one day someone who was opposed to his views would throw his father's conviction in his face. Shortly after Brodribb junior's visit, the Brodribb family left Tasmania after 36 years in the colony. Prudence died suddenly at Brighton, Victoria, in 1856. William senior died in 1861 at the age of 72. As previously mentioned, their eldest son became a member of the Victorian parliament. He died in 1886. The youngest son, Kenric, practised as a solicitor in Melbourne, initially on his own but later with a partner. Their practice eventually transmogrified through various stages into one of Australia's largest law firms, Allens Arthur Robinson.[35]

The quick dispersal of the *St Vincent*'s convicts was typical rather than exceptional. Between 1846 and 1854, 22,000 ex-convicts are estimated to have left the island, a figure which A.G.L. Shaw pointed out was 60 per cent of the number who arrived during the probation period and immediately after.[36] The exodus continued as the island sank into an economic decline. The steadily diminishing injection of British funds as convict numbers dropped impacted seriously on the colony's economy, a problem which was compounded by Tasmania's trade difficulties due to tariffs imposed on its exports by other colonies. In 1870, when the last British military forces were withdrawn, the colonists were alarmed as much by the economic effect as by fear of a breakdown in law and order. A traveller who visited Hobart in the 1860s commented, 'The streets are almost empty. Nobody looks busy. Nobody is in a hurry. Converse with anyone about the state of the Colony, and the word *depression* is one of the first you hear and it will come over and over again until you are weary of it.'[37] Visiting Tasmania in 1871, just as the novel *For the Term of His Natural Life* publicised the brutality of the penal colony, Anthony Trollope found the colonists lamenting the loss of their convicts and remembering their contribution nostalgically. 'Though one hears much of flogging in Van Diemen's Land, one hears still more of the excellence of the service rendered by convicts . . . Ladies especially are never weary of telling how good and how faithful were the females allotted to them and to their mothers . . . And, though the ladies are the loudest, men also tell of the convicts by whose labour they were enriched in the old days.'[38]

Western Australia was in a similar situation at the time. In 1870 the *Fremantle Express* described all classes as being in a state of 'gloomy despondency' adding, 'After having had the gratuitous labour of some fifteen hundred men, with an annual expenditure of £100,000, for nearly twenty years, we now awake from our normal state of apathetic indifference to find ourselves upon the verge of ruin.'[39]

The Tasmanian census taken in 1857, four years after the end of transportation, recorded that 50 per cent of all adults—and 60 per cent of adult males—were convicts or ex-convicts. In fact, former prisoners remained a significant proportion of the population until the final decades of the century when the native-born overtook them, rising from 37 per cent in 1857 to 73 per cent in 1881. Like New South Wales, however, most of the 'native born' were the children of convicts.[40] This predominantly emancipist community formed the backdrop to all the debates during the anti-transportation movement. When the success of the movement appeared to confirm the allegations made about the convicts, the shame hit hard. The reaction of many was to go to church. For approximately twenty years, piety prevailed in the formerly irreverent, blasphemous community to such an extent that visitors noticed it. Trollope commented in surprise at how many working-class families went to church, but as Alan Atkinson pointed out, 'Never were the Europeans in Australia so apparently devout as they were when Trollope saw them.' Such uncharacteristic behaviour had almost run its course. The old irreverence would shortly reassert itself. From the 1870s, the numbers going to church declined, as if the extraordinary moral zeal and reparation generated around the end of transportation had finally spent itself.[41]

Their confidence shaken by the pall of depravity cast over them, it is no surprise that the former prisoners and their families strove to prove their worth by conforming to the immigrants' standards. Collectively, these were embodied in ideas called 'moral enlightenment', which proposed, according to the colonial poet Charles Harpur, that 'A large faith in the capacity of human nature for good, is the root of all genuine morality.' To fulfil the moral imperatives of the time, the working class must achieve respectability, thus contributing to a society that would 'necessarily be wise and good and splendid' too. Education was believed to make people good as well as wise and also to promote social cohesion. Even more significantly, education would prepare them for the democratic power that it was increasingly apparent they would soon exercise. Fear of mob rule was a strong motivation for educating the populace. Temperance was also seen as a mark of an individual's progress towards the desired state of purity, as was self-help in the form of bank savings, involvement with voluntary associations, personal cleanliness and healthy living. The assiduous propagation of moral and physical purity may even have given rise to Australians' well-known devotion to showers and baths. Women were particularly responsive to the agenda of moral enlightenment—for instance, between 1846 and 1871 they were the predominant depositors in the Savings Bank of New South Wales. They were also to the fore in the Temperance movement, with the consequence, as Marilyn Lake has pointed out, that they were often seen as killjoys or 'wowsers'.[42]

The ideas of moral enlightenment originated in eighteenth-century Britain and their impact was by no means confined to Australia, but the movement was particularly successful in the former penal colonies, where it was facilitated by an anxious ex-convict class and chimed with the determination of so many clergy and community leaders to reform it.[43] Reflecting on the impact of the movement for moral enlightenment, Michael Roe concluded that 'In Australia, more than in most countries, propriety of behaviour has always won both respectability and respect', a conclusion that is hardly surprising when the motives of its proponents are examined.[44] From 1850, it may be an accurate description, but for the *laissez-faire* convict colonies this was a major change. The noticeable conformity of the mid-century period led Henry Reynolds in 1969 to challenge his fellow historian Russel Ward's thesis about the pervasive influence of convict values. Reynolds was surprised (and disappointed) at how the Tasmanian working class allowed ideas imported by free settlers to dictate their behaviour.

> the Tasmanians who grew to maturity between 1853–1870 do not appear to have been greatly influenced by 'pervasive social mores which derived . . . from convict origins' . . . In politics, as in morality, they were probably more receptive to the values of their social 'superiors' . . . Tasmania's largely emancipist working class . . . was probably the most dispirited proletariat in the Australian colonies and provided little concerted challenge to the free-settler oligarchy.[45]

In fact, almost no one in this ex-convict community could challenge the new paradigm, let alone defend the old. To do so risked being categorised as endorsing homosexuality and, worse, as someone who had participated in unnatural crime. In this context, hiding convict connections became essential, something that created a noticeable tension. According to Trollope. 'It is not only that men and women in Tasmania do not choose to herd with convicts, but that they are on their guard lest it might be supposed that their own existence in the island might be traced back to the career of some criminal relative.'[46]

In New South Wales in the 1840s, Governor Gipps noticed the same pattern.

> The ordinary proprieties of Society are observed amongst the better portion of the population of New South Wales, in as great and perhaps in a greater degree than amongst persons of the same class elsewhere. The fear indeed of being suspected of the taint of Convictism operates in a wholesome manner as a restraint upon those who are free from it.[47]

According to Reynolds, this legacy of moral enlightenment was still detectable a century later. Describing the behaviour he observed as 'pretence and snobbery', he blamed not the immigrants of the 1840s but 'Hobart's convict/

emancipist heritage', which he said flourished in the twentieth century 'with undiminished vigour'.[48]

Moral enlightenment can be construed positively as Michael Roe argued in his influential work, *The Quest for Authority in Eastern Australia, 1835–1851*. The *petit bourgeois* ideas it embodied were attractive in themselves, as well as a logical aspiration for families who had newly established themselves above subsistence level—every ex-convict mother wanted her children to be better educated than she was. But the zeal with which these ideas were proselytised was less constructive. The Molesworth Committee and the probation system it recommended gave newly arrived immigrants during this period a sense of entitlement to make over colonial society to their liking with almost no regard for what existed before they arrived. They had no qualms in removing all traces of the convict colony. In the name of moral enlightenment, they eradicated existing community attitudes, customs and ethos as surely as changing names and destroying buildings obliterated more noticeable reminders. As a consequence, the reality of convict society was lost in memory and almost lost in fact.

According to Roe, the ideas of moral enlightenment filled the vacuum created at the end of transportation by the loss of authority based on brute force.[49] But Roe's argument only holds if the functioning of colonial society before, say, 1850 was indeed reliant on brute force—a premise increasingly called into question by modern research. A very different picture emerges from this sample—a picture that is supported by population figures that document the preponderance of convicts, emancipists and emancipist families throughout the transportation era in Van Diemen's Land and New South Wales.[50] With the exception of the secondary punishment settlements, convict society was not controlled by the lash and the musket. For most of its existence, the authority of convict society derived from the de facto consent of the community, including serving convicts.

Angus McKay, the shepherd from the Isle of Lewis, lived through this climate in Tasmania, struggling to make a precarious living during the years of economic downturn. Aged 21 when he landed in Hobart, he was a passholder from Portsmouth prison. While waiting for his conditional pardon he worked for the large landholder Roderic O'Connor at Fingal and avoided any transgression apart from one incident when he was admonished by the local magistrate for 'absconding' into Avoca without the necessary (local) pass. He was still working for O'Connor when he received a ticket-of-leave in December 1853.[51] Soon after, he moved to Campbell Town, where in 1855 he obtained his pardon and applied almost simultaneously for permission to marry Sarah Hall, who had been born in the colony at the town of Ross. In the next eighteen years, Angus and Sarah had nine children. To support the family, Angus roamed widely through the midlands, working variously as a labourer, a vet and a shepherd, but family history records that he was frequently paid in potable kind. Life in one prison after another had not given young Angus many chances to drink, but now he developed a taste for alcohol. Grog was the traditional cure for the prisoners' miseries, but post-transportation colonial society had lost its tolerance for drunkenness. The pressure for temperance was very strong. Although drink did not apparently impair Angus McKay's ability to work, the family was financially struggling in 1878 when he briefly went to Victoria, leaving them in Tasmania.

Angus McKay wearing his
'hard hitter'

Then in 1881, Angus McKay, now aged 45, resorted to the crime for which he had been transported. In June he was convicted in the Supreme Court on three counts of stealing sheep from Mr Caleb Smith of Deloraine, who was his current employer and for whom he had worked frequently in previous years. Sentenced to four years in Hobart Gaol, he served three before returning to his family. This incident was a one-off return to crime, not the start of a regular pattern. The only subsequent charges against Angus were a couple for being drunk and disorderly. He spent the rest of his life farming at Osmaston with his son Francis, who died in 1909. After Francis' death, Angus and Sarah continued to live at Osmaston, but Angus applied for the recently introduced old age pension. His final years were spent living next to his youngest daughter Martha at Quamby Brook, outside Deloraine, where he died at the age of 93 in 1924.[52]

Angus McKay is vividly remembered in his family. Legend had it that he was 'as tough as nails', his daughter Sophie recalling that if he ever cut himself he would pour salt onto the open wound. His children also told the story of how he broke his leg by falling from a horse, but made a splint out of firm bark, strapped his leg, and rode home. Perhaps it was this badly healed break rather than the hills of the Isle of Lewis that gave him his distinctive lopsided gait. He was also remembered for his insistence on wearing a hat known as 'a hard hitter'. It was so glued to his head that there are no surviving photographs of him without it. Two of Angus' grandchildren were still alive in the 21st century, both of whom remembered him well from their childhood but had no idea of his past. Despite all the stories that survived about Angus, his trial in Scotland and his arrival as a convict were hidden until rediscovered in the 1980s.[53]

In October 1852, in response to allegations being made by the anti-transportationists, Governor Denison surveyed the conduct of men who arrived on one Irish and two English ships during the probation period in 1843 and 1844. The figures showed that 22 per cent committed no offence after arrival and 71 per cent committed breaches of discipline but no criminal offences. Only 7 per cent were sentenced for criminal activity, and of these 1.3 per cent were guilty of a crime similar to the one for which they were transported.[54] The pattern for the men on the *St Vincent* was very similar. Because so many left the colony, statistical analysis is not possible, but surviving archives make it possible to conclude that 45 men came to the attention of the police between 1861 and 1872, of whom fourteen were either invalids and paupers or convicted simply of being 'idle and disorderly'.[55] The offences for which they were charged varied greatly but were mostly trivial. Some were employment offences committed under the extremely punitive Master and Servant Act. Many were very petty crimes such as that of the coiner Thomas Feeney, who was sentenced to a month in gaol in 1867 for 'wilfully destroying personal property'. Several men, including the ex-soldier Matthew Maxwell, were sentenced to a few days in the cells for 'indecency', which almost certainly meant they were caught urinating in a public place. Many were charged with being 'idle and disorderly', which could have meant anything from playing cards somewhere a constable thought inappropriate to hanging round waiting for the pub to open.

Twenty-nine men were tried for larceny during this period, their sentences ranging from one month to six years. Typical of these was Thomas Fleming. A young, single man of twenty when he arrived, in 1848 he had been convicted in York of 'stealing from the person'. The gaoler in England described his conduct as 'indifferent', which is reflected in his behaviour in Van Diemen's

Land. With a seven-year sentence, he should have been immediately eligible for a ticket and in a position to make a new life for himself. Instead, his record suggests that he drifted from one minor infringement to another: misconduct for smoking (twice), misconduct for using improper language, disobedience of orders. A year after he arrived, he was charged with absconding, which resulted in his original transportation sentence being extended by eighteen months. In the 1860s his offences changed. Sentenced to three months for being idle and disorderly in September 1866, a year later he was before the Supreme Court on trial for housebreaking. He was found guilty and sentenced to six years penal servitude, a punishment which took him to Port Arthur.[56]

Thomas Fleming at Port Arthur, c.1874

At 28, William Whittaker or Baker was older than Thomas Fleming when he arrived and the behaviour that got him into trouble was much more spirited, at least initially. A pass-holder on arrival with eighteen months left to serve, his only transgression was to be out after hours within a few weeks of arriving, but that was an offence shared with many others. Two months later, he was sentenced to three months hard labour for 'making a false and vexatious complaint about his master', the details of which have not survived. A year later, Whittaker served ten days in solitary for assaulting a constable in an attempt to 'rescue' a prisoner. This was followed shortly after with four months hard labour for being absent without leave. In 1859 Whittaker married at

William Whittaker (aka Baker) at Port Arthur, c. 1874

Launceston, and for eight years there were no further charges against him. Then, in 1867, he was found guilty of larceny at Ross and sentenced to twelve months. Two years later, in September 1869, and this time using his alias Baker, he was convicted of burglary in Launceston and sentenced to Port Arthur for five years.[57] Whittaker and Thomas Fleming were among the last convicts at the infamous penal institution.

Twenty-nine men out of the 207 from the *St Vincent* went through Port Arthur, and if that is the measure of serious offences then it is less than the transportation average of 20–24 per cent calculated by A.G.L. Shaw in the 1960s and supported in the '90s by the calculations of historians at the Port Arthur Historic Site.[58] But as so many men from the *St Vincent* left the colony quickly, the number was bound to be lower.[59] Ducie Denholm, whose 1971 analysis of the men who went through Port Arthur is one of the few publications on this subject, was surprised to note that in her sample of men imprisoned there after 1840, 10 per cent were soldier convicts transported for desertion. Despite this timeframe, which coincides with the *St Vincent*, none of the soldiers who arrived on that ship were sentenced to the penal settlement.[60]

Ex-soldier Patrick Quigley, who arrived many years before the *St Vincent*, also avoided Port Arthur. Aged 46, the irrepressible Irish reprobate arrived in Van Diemen's Land from Norfolk Island in November 1845. At that date, he had served seven years six months of his colonial life sentence. The probation system was at its height when he landed and Quigley was assigned to a gang at Southport where he was required to serve one year. In fact he only stayed six months before he was granted an exemption from gang labour. Quigley's record is littered with examples of 'feigning sickness' and this may be another example of it. He was not assigned elsewhere, but in October was raised to 3rd Class status (in accordance with the classification layers that were part of the gang system), then issued with a ticket-of-leave in December 1846.

Quigley had not experienced so much freedom since he landed from the *John* 15 years earlier, and like so many others he immediately set about finding wine, women and song. In great quantities. Despite any celebrations, nothing was heard of him for a year until November 1847, when he was sentenced to a month's confinement and hard labour at Glenorchy for harbouring not one, but two, female passholders in his house. Someone was on his case. On 21 December he was charged at Hobart with larceny, an allegation that was dismissed by the magistrate. Ten days later he was before the Bench again charged with misconduct for being at large without a pass and for which he served seven days in solitary. This incident marked the end of Quigley's career as a prisoner apart from three reprimands for being drunk and disorderly over the next couple of years. In December 1849 he was recommended for a conditional pardon, which he received in April 1851.[61] Once free, Quigley arranged his life for maximum enjoyment. Having discovered the village of Westbury was a designated soldier settlement, he settled there in some capacity. No doubt he assumed the posture of an old soldier so adroitly that most people assumed he had simply been respectably discharged. The 17th Regiment of Foot had served in the colonies and it would have been easy to establish a fiction that he had chosen to stay behind when they left for India. But it may not have been necessary. The convict stain did not matter to the rank-and-file ex-soldiers with whom Quigley mixed. Although the officers would have reacted like any middle-class colonist, among the other ranks being court-martialled for desertion may well have been a badge of honour.

Next on Quigley's agenda was marriage, for which he chose a mature Irish woman named Mary Fay who was around 40 years of age when they met. She had been transported on the *Kinnear* with a sentence of seven years for stealing a coat, a handkerchief and a ring. On arrival from Dublin five years earlier she had taken the precaution of describing herself as 'Single', so there was no impediment to their marriage. Ominously, when asked at the muster about her prior offences, she told the Superintendent of Convicts that she had been convicted 'thirty or forty times for drunkenness'.[62] Mary and Patrick were married on 3 January 1853. Both signed their names on the register, Quigley describing himself by his old trade as 'a tinsmith'. The marriage lasted ten years, volatile no doubt but perhaps companionable when both were in their cups. In August 1863, Mary died suddenly, the coroner's certificate recording the cause as 'apoplexy accelerated by drink'. Although now aged 58, Quigley was not done yet. Within months he was married again, this time to a widow named Christina Green who was five years his junior. They, too, had ten years together before the old soldier's resilience finally ran out. Patrick Quigley, tinsmith, died of pneumonia at Westbury, Tasmania, on 5 November 1872.[63]

If Quigley had an epitaph, it might have read, 'He made his mark on the convict history of Australia'. But of course characters like Quigley are the very ones hidden by our inability to cope with our history since the anti-transportation campaign. To cover up a belief too gross to acknowledge—a belief that the colonies were incubators of homosexuality—we subscribed to a surreal myth which over the latter decades of the nineteenth century swelled to such proportions that it swept aside the reality of the convict society. The lasting distortion, which will be discussed further in the following chapter, began around the time of Quigley's death with the publication in 1870 of the first episodes of the novel *For the Term of his Natural Life*. Prompted by the widely read novel and by other books such as the memoirs of convict Martin Cash, Australians developed an appetite for sensational 'history' which extended to more than the written word.

As the convict system was converted to legend in literature, it was closing down in practice. Since 1853, the Tasmanian colonists had been arguing with the British government about who should bear the costs of the remaining 'imperial' convicts, and in what proportion. Port Arthur was part of this debate, its closure in fact delayed by the colonists' reluctance to take full responsibility for it.[64] However, the problem of Norfolk Island had been easily solved. Once the last prisoners were removed in 1854, the Pitcairn Islander descendants of the *Bounty* mutineers were re-settled there. Port Arthur was more difficult. Only sixty miles from Hobart, it was too close and too substantial to be ignored or left to crumble into ruin. But after the publicity created by Martin Cash's book and even more by *The Term of his Natural Life*, Tasmanians were more embarrassed than ever about this prominent reminder of their convict past. Their views were expressed by the *Mercury* in 1876:

> For years it has been the one desire of the people of Tasmania, the one object of legislation in connection with our penal and charitable institutions, to break up the establishment at Port Arthur, to erase, as it were, its sad history from our memories, and to remove the plague spot that disfigures fair Tasmania.[65]

In 1877, the penal settlement was finally closed. Quoting from the *Hobart Mercury*, David Young described how 'all the remaining convicts, paupers and lunatics were transferred to Hobart, leaving only a small work gang at the establishment. The sight of the hand-cuffed and leg-ironed old men being unloaded at Franklin wharf attracted a large crowd, kept back by police. As the carts containing the convicts rumbled their bizarre way to the Campbell Street Gaol, they were followed by "a large number of idlers".'[66]

Even before it closed, Port Arthur was attracting intense interest from the public, who sensed an opportunity to see the place for themselves. Interim ideas of making it a permanent institution for invalids, paupers and lunatics were fiercely criticised, but until the discussion about its future, few people understood the real nature of Port Arthur. It was not simply a gaol with a high wall and a few outbuildings that housed the guards and the commandant. Despite the visual dominance of the large prisoners' barracks, Port Arthur was a fully fledged village, complete with church and rows of cottages, with extensive and beautiful gardens, with a bakery, a blacksmith, general workshops and a boatbuilding yard. Finally, the Tasmanian government decided it must be recycled. In an attempt to bury its history, the name was changed to Carnarvon and, later in 1877, the government tried with limited success to auction off the land and buildings. At a cost of fifteen shillings, a two-day steamer trip was arranged for intending purchasers to inspect the site, the second day including an escorted viewing of the abandoned prison buildings, the church and the cemetery on the Isle of the Dead.[67] Shortly after, two-day steamer trips for members of the public were so popular that many who tried to buy tickets missed out.[68]

*Former prisoner
Bill Thompson, dressed
up in convict uniform to
act as a guide at Port Arthur
in the 1870s*

Since the end of transportation, tourism had increasingly become an important element in the colony's economy. Travellers were encouraged to visit the island for its healthy climate and beautiful scenery. Initially, most guidebooks avoided all mention of its history as a penal colony, even though reminders of the convict era confronted the traveller at every turn in the form of crumbling probation stations or beautifully crafted buildings, bridges and roads. Promoted so effectively by *The Term of His Natural Life*, Port Arthur became too important as a tourist attraction to ignore. Day trips to the site by steamer or extended summer holidays were popular with Tasmanians as well as visitors from the mainland. Many of the larger cottages became boarding houses for the visitors. Some buildings were recast as public institutions, such as the model prison, which became the Carnarvon Town Hall. Ex-convicts acted as guides, enthralling the holidaymakers with horror stories of the dreadful deeds and evil people in the old days. They were a major attraction in themselves, promoted for instance by J. W. Beattie in his guidebook *Port Arthur, Van Diemen's Land*, in which he advised visitors that 'for actual experiences relating to the convict days of Port Arthur, one of its old hands, still alive and residing in the township, can always be engaged, and will act as guide about the Settlement'.[69] Very likely, the enthusiastic tourists also included ex-convicts come to inspect the fate they escaped, or perhaps to take a look at areas which were forbidden during their time there as prisoners. Secret elation must have described their feelings at the freedom to climb on the steamer and chug back to Hobart when the visit was over.

Other convict sites such as Maria Island, along with stage plays, memoirs, guidebooks and striking photos by James Beattie, swelled convict tourism, at the same time distorting convict history. But Port Arthur was always the centrepiece. Two events in particular helped Tasmanians exorcise the ghosts of Port Arthur, even while they remained ashamed of both convict history and convict ancestry. Firstly, on 31 December 1897 a massive bushfire bore down on the settlement, destroying some smaller buildings and gutting both the penitentiary and the church. Few locals expressed regret, some regarding it as Divine providence, others as a symbol of the real end of the convict era.[70] But Port Arthur was a magnet for spectacular events. Given the history of the settlement as punishment site, functioning town, bonfire and holiday resort, the decision to make a film of its darkest days—on location—seems less bizarre than it does in isolation, but in 1920 that is what happened. It was not the first film of *The Term of His Natural Life*—an earlier one had been made in 1908 without protest—but using the actual locations added a new and as it proved controversial dimension. Objectors were led by the Royal Society, which thought it would be a bad advertisement for Tasmania, and the *Hobart Mercury* which worried that it would spread 'an outrageous lie' throughout the world. Nevertheless, the Tasmanian cabinet approved the project, after which excursions by sea and land were specially arranged for the crowds who flocked to watch the filming. In 1927, politicians' instincts were again proved right when performances of the film were packed out, night after night. According to David Young, 'The dark side of the novel was shirked only in the predictable avoidance of references to homosexuality; floggings, sadism and suicide were graphically presented.'[71]

By comparison with the woes—and woeful outlook—of Tasmania and Western Australia immediately after transportation ended, New South Wales appeared almost carefree about its past, and that despite sharing the economic depression that gripped all the colonies to varying degrees in the early 1840s. After an initial burst of outrage, the oldest colony had shrugged off the Molesworth Report, being far more absorbed by its transition to free institutions including democratic elections for the first municipal council in 1842 and for the enlarged Legislative Council in 1843. In a gesture of egalitarian defiance, Establishment candidates, such as Alexander McLeay and Dr Charles Nicholson, were defeated in the election for the city council, while citizens who were tradesmen or descended from convicts were elevated to the status of alderman.[72]

Despite increasing immigration, as late as 1851 there were almost as many emancipists and their descendants as there were newcomers.[73] Unlike Van Diemen's Land, in New South Wales new arrivals still adjusted to the existing culture rather than the other way round. Nevertheless, the colony was not immune to the impact of the moral enlightenment movement which arrived with the immigrants. It just took longer to spread. In the long term, education, temperance, financial savings and self-help through voluntary associations were as important in New South Wales as they were elsewhere. In this climate, convict connections became an increasing liability to those who needed to prove their respectability. From about 1851, when the community enlarged further by immigration and the gold rush, it was possible to hide such connections, which ordinary people began to do, but it was the 1860s before the effect was widespread.

By 1870, convicts were rarely mentioned, in public life or in private. Comparing the New South Wales attitude with that of Van Diemen's Land, Anthony Trollope put the difference down to New South Wales' 'enormous area', which allowed the idea that its former convicts 'have wandered away whither they would. Now and then good-natured reference is made, in regard to some lady or gentleman, to the fact that his or her father was "lagged", and occasionally up in the bush a shepherd may be found who will own to the soft impeachment of having been lagged himself—although always for some offence which is supposed to have in it more of nobility than depravity.'[74] In truth however, New South Wales was as sensitive as anywhere else about its convict past, although brazen rather than discreet in its reactions, as some visiting cricketers discovered in 1879.

In February that year the *Sydney Morning Herald* reported a riot at the cricket ground when the English team, who were repaying a similar visit to the 'mother country' by the colonists, found themselves 'in the middle of a surging, gesticulating and shouting mob . . . one rowdy struck Lord Harris across the body with a whip or a stick'. As officials tried to grab the offender, the crowd became equally determined to rescue him and 'a scene of confusion ensued and blows were received and returned' in what the *Herald* called 'a display of unbridled rowdyism'. The cause was first thought to be a decision by the English umpire that a member of the New South Wales team was run out. The crowd started hooting and groaning and demanding that the umpire be withdrawn, after which, according to the *Herald*, 'a large number of "larrikins" sitting at the bottom of the terrace . . . made a rush for the centre of the ground and were quickly followed by hundreds of roughs who took possession of the wicket'. Although play was resumed later that day, when the crowd realised the same umpire was taking the field the following morning they again rushed the wicket and held their ground until it was too dark to resume play.

Only later was the reason for the crowd's 'frenzied excitement' revealed. The *Herald* reported that either before or after Lord Harris was assaulted, 'one of the English professionals made use of a grossly insulting remark to the crowd about their being nothing but "sons of convicts"'. Of course, that clash was the start of a great tradition. In the 21st century, English spectators still greet Australian sporting teams with the chant, 'You all come from a convict colony, a convict colony, a convict colony . . .' Unlike the nineteenth-century crowd, today's Australians listen to them with amusement and wonder if the English will ever get over it.[75]

Meanwhile, polite society in New South Wales was as anxious to draw the same distinctions between free settlers and those tainted by convictism as their predecessors had attempted, but as the nineteenth century progressed it became harder. Government House remained the centre of social prestige and invitations were highly prized. In 1874, the Governor's wife, Lady Robinson, who was reared in Mayfair drawing rooms, was assiduous about enquiring into the antecedents of the colonial gentry. While she was the hostess at Government House, Sir James Martin, the Chief Justice and a former Premier of New South Wales, and his friend William Bede Dalley who was Attorney-General, were relegated to the sidelines, but she could not refuse to include them. In Martin's case, his crime was having poor Irish immigrant parents. Dalley was the son of two convicts.[76]

On the subject of convicts, Lady Robinson's concern reflected the opinion of many of her class, as expressed eloquently 40 years earlier by Reverend Thomas Arnold, principal of Rugby public school in England, to his friend Sir John Franklin, governor of Van Diemen's Land. As a clergyman, Arnold was obviously influenced by his Christian beliefs—he was writing before Lombroso's theory of 'the criminal type', for instance—but from whatever angle they arose, the views he expressed were shared by many down the generations while the penal colony operated and beyond.

> I am satisfied that the stain should last, not only for one whole life, but for more than one generation; that no convict or convict's child should ever be a free citizen; and that, even in the third generation, the offspring should be excluded from all offices of honour or authority in the colony. This would be complained of as unjust or invidious but I am sure that distinctions of moral breed are as natural and as just as those

of skin or of arbitrary caste are wrong and mischievous; it is a law of God's Providence which we cannot alter, that the sins of the father are really visited upon the child in the corruption of his breed.[77]

For many years, the convict stain was confined to the minds of people like Dr Arnold. Its impact on convicts and their families was minimal until the anti-transportation movement shamed the populace at large. By the 1860s the old toleration for people's background had given way under the pressure to prove moral purity. By then working people in New South Wales were 'sledging' one another with convict abuse, as we saw in Chapter 2 when former London pick-pocket John Yeates, now parish clerk for the Church of England in Braidwood, took his neighbour to court for calling his wife (who was an Irish immigrant) 'a damned convicted bitch'. Yeates was the father-in-law of Susannah Watson's son Charles, who married his daughter Eliza. At the time of this incident, they were all living in the gold-rush town of Braidwood, where Charles founded the first newspaper. Giving the lie to Dr Arnold's assertion about distinctions of moral breed, Susannah reared all her children, including her two Australian sons, Charles and his brother John Henry Clarke Watson, with a strong ethical base that included the maxim, 'Zeal in a good cause is commendable'.

As a journalist, Charles put this idea into practice, becoming a fierce advocate for the working man and jousting with the Establishment to such an extent that when he died in 1886, the *Bulletin* described him admiringly as 'top scorer' in libel actions. His mother's ethics were also detectable in the motto he chose for the *Shoalhaven News*, which he established in Nowra in the late 1860s promising his readers that it would be guided by the Shakespearian epithet, 'Let all the ends thy aimst at, be thy God's, thy country's, and Truth'. Susannah Watson herself died in 1877, aged 83. There is no evidence she was weighed down with guilt about her crimes. In fact, writing to her English daughter some years earlier, she reflected simply on her 'many ups and downs' since they last met. Most significantly of all, she recorded that except for the loss of her English children, transportation was the best thing that happened to her.[78]

As the nineteenth century progressed, the descendants' resort to secrecy was accompanied increasingly by a sensational public distortion of what happened during the transportation era, which is discussed in the next chapter. This version came to be accepted as a realistic picture. Australians' greatest misunderstanding was the idea that all convicts shared the brutal suffering depicted in convict literature when, in fact, only a minority did so.[79] That is not to deny the physical and emotional pain they endured but to make the point that for most it was limited in time and did not dominate their entire lives.

Out of the sample of close to 1100 convicts considered in this book, only a handful matched the version portrayed publicly, of men destroyed by relentless punishment, their lives wasted away under the lash at the penal settlements of Norfolk Island and Macquarie Harbour and Port Arthur, or by labouring on the roads. None of them were men from the *St Vincent* or the *Dalhousie*, but they included the bigamist Francis Bodenham and the young highway robber Thomas Smitherman from the *Bensley*, and the thief George McGiverall as well as Tom Stacey from the *John*. The two soldiers William Crooks and Patrick Quigley, both from the *John*, shared but survived the worst of the system, in Quigley's case sufficiently to reconstruct the last twenty years of his life. Crooks, as we saw in Chapter 8, was sent to the Newcastle stockade when he returned from Norfolk Island. After giving evidence against Fitzgerald and Fitzpatrick, he was removed from Newcastle to Woolloomooloo stockade but subsequently sent to labour at the last stockade on the Bathurst Road at Blackheath in the Blue Mountains. In 1847 he received a ticket-of-leave for the Yass district, but the following year it was revoked for 'absconding from the district' and 'riding on a dray'. In 1853 the police found him incoherently wandering the streets of Sydney and lodged him in Darlinghurst Gaol, where a doctor certified he was 'insane'. On the doctor's testimony, application was made for Crooks to be admitted to the lunatic asylum at Tarban Creek (now Gladesville) but he died before that occurred.[80]

Francis Bodenham was also in Sydney in 1853, his eyesight failing from years of close work with jewellery and watches. The previous year he had begun what became an annual visit to the Sydney Infirmary which sometimes, if he was lucky, resulted in admission to the Liverpool Hospital run by the Benevolent Society. Both institutions were increasingly overcrowded and no doubt he was often discharged when he would have preferred to stay in a shelter where he could rest. In April 1857, he approached the Infirmary again and was recommended to Liverpool because his bad eyes left him destitute. For a young man with no previous record of crime before he was convicted of bigamy, Bodenham displayed amazing resilience in his arduous life in the colony. With his education and his trade skills, he was well positioned to achieve a law-abiding and peaceful life, but either because of the influence of Sarah Franks or later because of his tendency to drink, he failed to make that transition. He died at the Liverpool Hospital on 2 December 1858 aged 65, leaving no descendants in the colony but several in England from his two marriages there, none of whom had any idea until the 1990s that they were descended from a convict.[81]

The most tragic person in the entire sample of prisoners was Tom Stacey, who was transported for burglary on the *John* aged approximately nineteen.

Yet he was not a simple victim of a brutal system. Time and again, he was agent of his own fate. As we saw in Chapter 6, Stacey tried to escape within weeks of landing and, consequently, was soon labouring in irons on the Bathurst Road. Escape from the iron gang and a robbery near Bathurst then resulted in a sentence for life to Norfolk Island. After an abortive attempt to escape from the *Phoenix* hulk, he reached the island in September 1834. Unlike Patrick Quigley who, despite his life sentence, left the island after six years, Stacey remained there for twenty, his record one of increasing torment and despair.[82] By the time he was transferred to Hobart in 1854, he was too old and ill to take advantage of the change. He was sent first to the invalid station at Impression Bay but the following years were interspersed with periods in hospital. At some time he had acquired skills as a cook and, when issued with a ticket-of-leave in January 1858, he may have worked in this capacity, but essentially, he was beyond coping with freedom. Receiving a conditional pardon in May 1860 had little impact. Barely three years later he entered hospital for the last time and died there in May 1864 after 32 years in the colony, all but three of them as a prisoner.[83]

Except that he died younger, Stacey's record almost equals that of Denis Doherty, a soldier convict made famous more by his recalcitrance and his constant attempts to escape than by his crimes. When Anthony Trollope spoke to him at Port Arthur a few years before it closed, Doherty had been a prisoner for 42 years. He was then in solitary confinement for yet another attempt to escape. Trollope described him as 'a large man—well to look at in spite of his eye, lost, as he told us through the misery of prison life . . . He had been always escaping, always rebelling, always fighting against authority—and always being flogged—a whole life of torment such as this; forty-two years of it; and there he stood, speaking softly, arguing his case well, and pleading while tears ran down his face for some kindness, for some mercy in his old age. "I have tried to escape—always to escape," he said, "as a bird does out of a cage. Is that unnatural—is that a great crime?"'[84]

Doherty, Stacey, the boy Samuel Rowney, Francis Bodenham and the soldier convicts we have met in this work are the human face of the stereotype that was created to hide from Australia's birthstain. Their characters are diverse, their stories tragic. But they were not typical. We will demolish the stereotype by understanding what happened to them and why, but we will never comprehend our transition from penal colony to democracy to nation if we concentrate on their experience alone. The foundation of modern Australia was laid by men like Joseph Barrett, Daniel Long, James Jaye, George Rawlinson, William Brodribb, Angus McKay, Patrick O'Brien, Joseph Sowden Ledger, James Wilde, Tom Vaughan, Richard Nicols, George Wheeler and Richard

Reeves to name just a few—and women like Susannah Watson, Ann Storrett and Eliza Dore. Studying their story, their crime and its circumstances, how they managed as prisoners of the Crown and the later construction of their families and businesses, explains to us the real trajectory of our history and the elements that underpin our national character. Studying the history of the birthstain explains why, for a while, we disowned them.

CHAPTER 11
the lost world

The acceptance of convict ancestry by descendants of the prisoners over the last 40 years has not been accompanied by a similar paradigm shift in public consciousness. In many areas, the interpretation of Australia's past still rests on a base laid by the anti-transportationists that was converted into stereotypes in the decades that followed. Fear of the birthstain has, in effect, resulted in a whole nation accepting a distorted version of its early years, with detrimental consequences for understanding and analysis of the present as well as the past.

The distortion of history began with the anti-transportationists who shamed convict society into silence. John Hirst pointed out 25 years ago that accepting at face value the movement's claim that its great moral crusade was making history disguised how it was also making history in another sense:

> It was proclaiming a view of what the colony had been like under the old convict system. In the speeches of the anti-transportation men, that age was symbolised by the triangle and the lash, fetters and chains, cruel task masters and slaves. The whole colony it was alleged, had been contaminated by the convicts and there had been bitter division between bond and free.

Unaware then of the depths to which homophobia was a motive in the anti-transportation campaign, Hirst concluded that the movement's behaviour was simply a case of the 'colonial cringe' and added, 'The anti-transportation league was following the dangerous course of seeking the world's respect by enthusiastically embracing its view of the colony's past.' This was true, of course. The movement's leaders were aligning themselves with Molesworth's view. But as we have seen, it was by no means the whole explanation. Indeed the concept of 'colonial cringe', as used here, is one that should now be reconsidered.[1]

After the success of the league in the east, silence descended on the nature of convict society while the movement directed its attention to fomenting opposition to the Western Australian penal colony. It was seventeen years, shortly after the final shipload of convicts to Fremantle relegated transportation to the past, before the silence was broken and the comprehensive victory of the league's point of view became apparent. Between 1870 and 1890, the version of history created in the 1840s and '50s consolidated into a sensational, distorted form that would have lasting consequences for Australians' understanding of the first century of European settlement.

Public discussion was triggered initially by writers in search of a profit. In 1870, the notorious ex-convict Martin Cash published the first edition of his popular *The Adventures of Martin Cash*.[2] Since the days of Michael Howe in 1816, the island colony had always responded to a 'gentleman' bushranger whose depredations combined audacity and quick wit with courtesy and honour. Cash embodied this tradition when he took to the bush during the 1840s. Newspapers breathlessly reported hair-raising encounters with his pursuers, a spectacular escape from Port Arthur by swimming across the notorious Eaglehawk Neck, capture while pursuing a faithless wife and the high drama of a death sentence that was commuted to life imprisonment on Norfolk Island. Publication of the Cash autobiography took the reader behind these headlines. It also satisfied enormous curiosity in the Australian colonies generally about what happened at Port Arthur and on Norfolk Island. No one had ever been there—except for a small percentage of prisoners and the officials who managed the settlements. What Cash had to tell was sensational at the time because it was new.

When checking the memoir against archival documents, a historian soon discovers that, generally speaking, the Cash memoirs are accurate. Furthermore, although the manuscript was edited by a fellow ex-convict named James Lester Burke, the 'voice' rings true. The distortion that occurred around the Martin Cash book was not in its content but in the marketing. As a convict, Cash served his seven-year sentence without incident in New South Wales, working in the bush of the Hunter Valley during the 1830s alongside the men from the *John*. He appears, free by servitude, in the Scone Bench Books of the period.[3] This experience, which was the only experience of the penal system for so many convicts, was fully and at times lyrically described in the original manuscript but heavily edited for publication. In some editions, the New South Wales section was virtually omitted altogether. For marketing purposes, Cash was always described as 'the Tasmanian bushranger' and the sensational exploits he committed, in fact as a recidivist, were the focus. It was the start of a myth that Port Arthur and Norfolk Island represented the entire penal system.

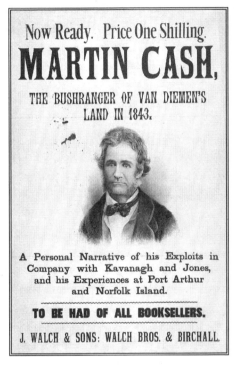

The marketing of Martin Cash's
book omitted NSW altogether

If convict literature had stopped with memoirs from the prisoners them-selves, little harm would have been done to Australia's historiography, but simultaneous with the Cash memoirs publication began of the most influential of all works of convict literature, the novel *For the Term of His Natural Life*. Serialised in the *Australasian Journal* over two years from 1870 to 1872 and then published in book form in 1874, the story reached a wide readership in Australia and overseas. Its author, Marcus Clarke, was a 23-year-old Melbourne journalist whose express intention was to write a great convict novel.[4] With this in mind, he visited Port Arthur early in 1870 to collect information. From the beginning, his material was highly selective. Although the settlement was fully operational with 574 men still imprisoned there, he was given ready access to the records. Registrar Joseph Maule later recounted: "'I don't want any of the ordinary prisoners' records, only those of the most notorious criminals," Clarke told me, so for two days I kept handing him volumes . . . They opened of themselves at the most used places, and Clarke put a slip of paper between the pages to keep the place. For two days he took notes, and wrote very fast and voluminously.'[5]

Unlike the former convicts, Clarke was writing within the conventions of the Victorian gothic novel and of Victorian morality. In these terms, his protagonist could not be an unrepentant rascal like the real convicts, such as Cash and others. Marcus Clarke's hero, Rufus Dawes, was middle class, a gentleman whose soul must be tested by suffering and degradation before he achieved redemption through death. Clarke justified his emphasis on 'tragic and terrible' events because they were 'needful to my purpose to record them, for they are events which have actually occurred, and which if the blunders which produced them be repeated, must infallibly occur again'. His research extended to reports and evidence and petitions contained in the British Parliamentary Papers, so it is not surprising that in an article written to mark the close of Port Arthur, he sounded remarkably similar to Molesworth and the anti-transportationists. He is also defensive about criticisms of his picture of the penal colonies.

> In the folio reports of the House of Commons can be read statements which make one sick with disgust, and flush hot with indignation. Officialdom, with its crew of parasites and lickspittles, may try to palliate the enormities committed in the years gone by; may revile with such powers of abuse as are given to it, the writers who record the facts that it blushes for; but the sad grim truth remains. For half a century the law allowed the vagabonds and criminals of England to be subject to a lingering torment, to a hideous debasement, to a monstrous system of punishment futile for good and horribly powerful for evil; and it is with feelings of the most profound delight that we record the abolition of the last memorial of an error fraught with so much misery.[6]

Reading this description in the light of conditions in the penal colonies when the *Sir William Bensley* arrived, or compared with the experience in New South Wales of most of the men from the *John*, starkly illustrates the extent to which the reality of the system had been lost by the second half of the nineteenth century. Nor do Clarke's comments resemble the experience of prisoners in Western Australia. More than any other example of convict literature, *For the Term of His Natural Life* created the stereotype of life as a convict. The book laid the template for approaching the subject and was influential for decades into the twentieth century in maintaining this image of the convicts' experience.[7]

The distortion continued during the 1880s and '90s as 'history' became not just the source of sensational stories for an avid public, but a political tool. A significant contributor to this development was another journalist, William Astley, who was better known by his byline of Price Warung. The son of an immigrant, Astley arrived in Victoria in 1859 at the age of four. Acquaintance with Henry Graham, a former medical officer at several penal stations in the 1840s, roused Astley's interest in transportation when he was very young. He began a lifelong collection of every piece of information he could find, from parliamentary papers and newspapers to diaries, letters and even convict records. Documentary material was supplemented by visits to sites in Tasmania and interviews with old lags who were still alive. From this variety of evidence, Astley constructed sensational stories. The convicts were presented as the scapegoats of the brutal English system, more sinned against than sinning but so degraded that they in turn reacted to their treatment with brutality, betrayal, murder and cannibalism. It was an approach that coalesced with Astley's radical nationalist beliefs that Australia should avoid being enmeshed 'in the gilded net of Imperial federation'—that is, the British Empire—but whatever his motives, Astley always insisted that his popular 'convict tales' were true, that he 'just wrote up the records'.[8]

The Bulletin *co-opted history to politics during the 1888 Centenary*

The radical nationalist movement, of which Astley was part, had come to prominence around 1880 with the foundation of the Sydney *Bulletin*. Not for the first time, nor by any means the last in Australia, it was a point when politics co-opted history. Led by the *Bulletin*, radical nationalists used the (by then notorious) brutality of the penal system as a weapon to support their argument that Australia should cut ties to Britain and become a republic. Their campaign reached fever pitch in 1888 as the Australian colonies celebrated the centenary of Governor Phillip's landing at Sydney Cove. Unavoidably, the celebrations required some appraisal of history and the *Bulletin* made full use of the occasion. In a three-part historical series entitled 'The History of Botany Bay', which was published in late January 1888, the lash and the leg-irons loomed large. No lurid details were spared.

> One man was sentenced to receive 300 lashes . . . the unfortunate man had his arms extended round a tree so that flinching from the blow was out of the question . . . Two men were appointed to flog, namely Richard Rice, a left-handed man and John Johnson, the hangman from Sydney . . . who was right-handed. They stood on either side and I never saw two threshers in a barn move their flails with more regularity than these two man-killers, unmoved by pity and rather enjoying their horrid employment than otherwise. The very first blow made the blood spout out from the man's shoulders . . . I could only compare those wretches to a pack of hounds at the death of a hare, or tigers that torment their victim before they put them to death.[9]

As we saw in Chapter 3, they flogged just as hard and frequently in the West End of London, but the *Bulletin* justified its gory coverage on the grounds that 'such a record explains the genesis of our own existing Australian customs'.[10] It was the explanation that Australians feared most—the stain passed down, not just genetically to individuals, but as a community birthmark.

In 1988, Lloyd Robson tried to explain to Australians how their history had been tainted: 'The convict experience was denied its voice as history as the result of a vast conspiracy of silence and shame . . . But it was not and could not be forgotten. The general public never lost its curiosity about those "dark" years . . . A popular history stuffed full of tales of horror sprang up to supply the demand of the history-starved Australian colonies.'[11] His words fell on deaf ears because the spadework had not been done to dismantle the distortion. In fact the publication of Robert Hughes' *The Fatal Shore*, also in 1988, appeared to confirm the distorted version since Hughes perpetuated the radical nation-alist version using traditional nineteenth-century sources rather than drawing on the convict archives. By these means, ignorance about the nature of convict society remained widespread in the twentieth century.

Immigrants who arrived in Australia after the anti-transportation campaign began knew only the melodramatic, brutal version of life in the penal colonies. Reluctance to discuss the subject in the decades that followed simply rein-forced the idea that it was unspeakably horrible. Unsurprisingly, newcomers adopted the existing practice of skipping over the first 60 years on the basis that nothing worth remembering happened before the gold rush of 1851 which, in any event, subsumed the last of the convicts. Transportation to Western Australia was rarely mentioned on either side of the continent, except as a threat to the east. And since there was no one to be heard proudly describ-ing how they arrived in the country as a prisoner and now had a successful business, or basking vicariously in the success of a son who had become a mayor, or a grazier, the newer arrivals never thought to question how the stereotypical suffering convict beaten down by a brutal system had nevertheless laid the foundations for a flourishing democratic society. Presumably, they believed the number of immigrants in the earlier years was much greater than it was in fact. And given the popular understanding, first publicised by John West in his history, that the convicts had few descendants, nor did later immigrants fully realise the extent to which convict families permeated the community at the end of the century.[12] Deprived of this information, newcom-ers could not hope to achieve a realistic understanding of the penal colony and the origins of Australian society. And indeed by the period of the greatest distortion, from 1870 to 1890, many children of convicts knew no more than the immigrants.

The practical effect of the distortions of the late nineteenth century can be illustrated readily by the subject of Australia Day. Emancipists and descendants of convicts developed the custom of celebrating the arrival of Governor Phillip and the First Fleet with unselfconscious if somewhat spasmodic enthusiasm (some years they skipped it altogether) from approximately 37 years after it occurred. Originally called Anniversary Day, as noted in Chapter 5 it was marked variously by a regatta on Sydney Harbour where boats sailed by convicts' children competed vigorously for the honour of winning, and by a ceremonial dinner at which emancipists and the sons of convicts predominated, boister-ously raising the proud toast to 'The land, boys, we live in'. The toast became a tradition. Nearly two decades later, in 1842, the sentiment remained undiluted, the dinner had expanded to 200 people and it included the native-born sons of free settlers. On this occasion, Governor Bligh's grandson, Captain

Maurice O'Connell, who was born in the colony, proposed the toast, 'Australia, the land we live in'. According to the *Sydney Gazette*, deafening shouts of applause followed as the musicians struck up 'Hail Australia'.[13]

In 1888, the *Bulletin* used Australia Day to make a political point. Before urging that Australia shake off 'the old fetters and the old superstitions of that dark era' by breaking the ties with Britain, it set about destroying the people's instinct to celebrate the day, using terms that had become easy currency since the anti-transportation campaigns.

> [T]he one [day] among all others which has been fixed upon as the natal-day of Australia is that which commemorates her shame and degradation, and reminds the world most emphatically of the hideous uncleanness from which she sprung. The day which gave to the New World her first gaol and her first gallows—the day when the festering vileness of England was first cast ashore to putrefy upon the coasts of New South Wales—the day which inaugurated a reign of slavery and loathsomeness and moral leprosy—is the occasion for which we had called upon to rejoin with an exceeding great joy.[14]

With that condemnation the *Bulletin* set in train an ambivalence about celebrating Australia Day which was evident at the Bicentenary in 1988, and which continues in the 21st century. Such an attitude could not have taken hold if the traditions established in the first half of the century had not been disrupted by the distortion of the second half. And twentieth-century historian Peter Spearritt would have remarked on the discontinuity rather than comment as he did in 1988 that 'European Australians have been uncertain about, and slow to develop, "indigenous" national rituals'.[15]

The federation of the Australian colonies in 1901 changed the conversation about the convicts once again. Blaming Britain was no longer acceptable to a nation that was also a dominion of the British Empire. Now discussion was forced to turn to what the prisoners had done that warranted their transportation. The fact they were convicted under the much-respected British law could not be overlooked. Excuses multiplied. Casting aside the traditional plea of 'just a handkerchief', Sir John See, Premier of New South Wales, told the Legislative Assembly in 1901 that it was wrong to brand as felons the men 'who were sent to this country, perhaps, for taking a halter or a lolly out of an old lady's lolly shop'.[16] Only two years earlier, Lord Beauchamp greeted the colonists with the news that they had overcome their 'birthstain'. Sadly, much as Australians wanted to believe him, in their heart of hearts they did not.

With Federation imminent, in this Bulletin *cartoon the Victorian Premier knocks the convict off his pedestal to symbolise Australia's new image. John West's stereotype is perpetuated by the drunken white (ex-convict) labourer who carouses below*

Generally, the distortions originating with the anti-transportationists remain uncontradicted today. As we have seen throughout this book, the historiography of the last 40 years is shot through with assumptions, conclusions or disregard arising from their arguments, or with attitudes that mirror their era, many of which may well be proved unsustainable after research in the convict archives. By default, the idea that the convict stain was all in the mind of pretentious descendants is equally prevalent. Most historians see that stain as a consequence of the desire to be respectable rather than the reality that the creation of the stain by the anti-transportationists drove people to seek cover in 'respectability'.

It need not have been so. In the late 1960s, with the archives fully accessible, one of Australia's brightest postgraduates took up A.G.L. Shaw's challenge to follow his empirical work with detailed local studies. In an article entitled 'That Hated Stain: The Aftermath of Transportation in Tasmania', Tasmanian-born Henry Reynolds researched the impact of the convict 'taint' on his home state. He set the parameters of his project from the end of transportation in 1853 until 1870. Among the authorities he relied on in reaching his conclusions was 'the judicious John West'.[17] Not surprisingly, given how this work has revealed that 1853 marked the point at which colonial

Tasmanians were finally shamed into piety, Reynolds decided there had been little impact in the years that followed. Despite West's insistence that penal colonisation had created 'a caste embittered by ignorance and revenge',[18] Reynolds found no evidence of a feisty working class fired by the resentments of the convict era. On the contrary, his disappointment as a Marxist was evident in his conclusion that:

> convict values failed to flourish in Tasmania . . . Although a
> local patriotism, 'a strong attachment' to the colony, emerged
> in the fifties it lacked the radical convict-derived temper
> apparent in the incipient nationalism of New South Wales.
> Tasmania's largely emancipist working class gave little impetus
> to social or political radicalism. It was probably the most
> dispirited proletariat in the Australian colonies and provided
> little concerted challenge to the free-settler oligarchy. In fact
> the large ex-convict component in the population probably
> retarded the growth of radical and working class politics.'[19]

With those words, Reynolds turned away from the convict era, taking with him the best chance of using the newly available archives to dismantle the myths and arrive at a more realistic assessment of transportation. In due course, he found a new and engrossing issue in the dispossession of the Aborigines, a topic through which he became the most eminent historian of his generation. 'That Hated Stain' was not only influential because it changed Reynolds' own direction. Through his publications about Aboriginal history, he also influenced a younger generation of historians to such an extent that convict history was sidelined for 30 years in what one of his followers described as 'a seismic shift in Australian history' from the 1970s.[20]

Reynolds also influenced those few who stayed with convict history. 'That Hated Stain' has been widely cited as an authority ever since its publication in 1969, perhaps reaching its broadest influence through Robert Hughes in his hugely successful work, *The Fatal Shore*. Hughes compounded the inadequate premise from which Reynolds drew his conclusion about the 'dispirited' emancipists who 'probably retarded the growth of radical and working class politics' by adding, 'Probably this was because so few Irish convicts were sent there'.[21] As a consequence of such historiography, John West's interpretation of events was left undisturbed.

It was not until the closing years of the twentieth century that a small but significant group of historians triggered a resurgence in convict studies. They included Lucy Frost and Hamish Maxwell-Stewart who vividly reconstructed details of individual convicts. Cassandra Pybus published on the American/ Canadian 'patriots' and the black convicts. Grace Karskens uncovered the vigorous life of colonial Sydney. Penal labour replaced convict criminality as the key debating issue, with a major investigation of Macquarie Harbour by Hamish Maxwell-Stewart now due for publication and similar work on Moreton Bay in progress by Ray Evans and William Thorpe. Other work which is part of this resurgence has been cited throughout the text.

There were certainly subjects other than convicts which were worthy of attention during the interregnum—Aborigines, of course, women, most definitely, but also Chinese and other immigrants from diverse ethnic backgrounds such as Greeks, Jews, Turks, Italians, Serbs and Afghans, to name just some. But the conclusion must surely be that all those topics would have benefited from greater understanding of the Australian context in which their own story took place—and from identifying the disjunction in the European narrative that occurred around 1850.

Those who would have benefited most strikingly from knowing the history of the birthstain were homosexuals, that other minority group who were part of the great liberation movements of the 1970s. Their struggle took place with no understanding of its Australian historical context, the source of the birthstain being as much unknown to them as anyone else. Author Robert Reynolds unconsciously revealed this ignorance in *From Camp to Queer* when it did not strike him as odd that, 'Unlike United States and Britain, Australia did not have a tradition of active and visible homophile organisations . . . until 1969.'[22] Tracing the history of the birthstain makes it very clear why Tasmania, in 1997, was the last Australian state to decriminalise homosexuality. Knowing that history could have provided gay liberationists with a persuasive argument to achieve change earlier.

The widely held belief that Australian heterosexual relationships are uniquely difficult has been blamed variously on the convict era or the harsh masculinity of a frontier society. Certainly qualities such as stoicism that are not helpful to relationships were essential to surviving the rigours of convict life, as one prisoner made clear when he recorded, 'In Australia, silent composure under suffering is strictly prescribed by convict etiquette (inability to bear pain without lamentation and fright being followed . . . with loss of caste).'[23] The formation of Australian masculinity, as well as relations between the sexes, gain an extra dimension with knowledge of the extreme homophobic pressure that was brought to bear on men in the mid-nineteenth century.

Due to the impetus of feminism, the experience and character of female convicts was one of the few topics from the transportation era that was closely examined in the late twentieth century. In the 1970s, the prisoners were co-opted by historians such as Beverley Kingston, Anne Summers and Miriam Dixson to help demonstrate the disadvantaged position of women in Australian society. These authors explained but did not challenge the nineteenth-century interpretation of the women. The first to challenge the traditional view was Portia Robinson, particularly in *The Women of Botany Bay*, a large-scale project that aimed 'to allow these women to speak for themselves after some two hundred years of neglect and misrepresentation'. Published almost simultaneously with Robinson's work, my book *A Cargo of Women: Susannah Watson and the Convicts of the Princess Royal* also challenged the tradition but, according to Hamish Maxwell-Stewart, was also 'the first to show that convicts had agency' and to reconstruct the lives of some convict women in three-dimensional detail.[24] In the 1990s Deborah Oxley's *Convict Maids* and Kay Daniels' *Convict Women* followed up *A Cargo of Women* with expanded studies of the female prisoners in New South Wales and Tasmania.[25] Notable throughout this process was the civility, intellectual rigour and professional generosity between the various authors whose works collectively established a new paradigm for the women convicts.

The colonial attitude to the Chinese is an important subject that would be worth re-examining to establish the role of the anti-transportationists, who believed the Chinese harboured 'the same vicious traits'—that is, a propensity for unnatural crime—as the convict men.[26] It may well be that the anti-Chinese riots in 1857–58 and 1861 owed as much to the anti-transportationists as they did to racist attitudes from the diggers.

Anti-transportationists were active during the anti-Chinese riots of this period. For instance, Captain John Lamb, who supported Charles Cowper in establishing the Anti-Transportation League in New South Wales, sat on the parliamentary select committee in 1858 which considered whether Chinese immigration should be restricted. Virtually the only question Lamb asked witnesses was whether they thought the Chinese had a proclivity for unnatural crime.[27] In the process, he revealed that the rumours were widespread even though most witnesses denied their accuracy. As we saw in Chapter 9, unnatural crime was a significant issue in the enquiry into Chinese immigration in 1861. At ground level, the Miners' Protection League copied the anti-transportation bodies in its name but may also have done so in its tactics. Tracing the activities and linkages between parliamentarians and miners could be illuminating, as would comparing the role of the press in reporting the anti-Chinese riots with its coverage of the campaign to end transportation. At the time, it was said that the trouble on the goldfields was inflamed by 'agitators' or 'outsiders' rather than originating with the miners. This allegation seems to have been given little weight by historians. It would be helpful to analyse the lives of these leaders, several of whom, for instance, later joined Captain Lamb and Charles Cowper as members of parliament.[28]

Analogies between opposition to the Chinese and the anti-transportation campaign were explicitly drawn in 1857 by the *Age* in Melbourne:

> [This] . . . community has always avowed itself ready to go to any lengths to prevent the introduction of British criminals into the country . . . But although it is not possible that individual Europeans of bad character should be singled out for exclusion from the country, it is quite possible to prevent the wholesale introduction of a *profoundly immoral* race of people.[29] [emphasis added]

Australian attempts to perpetuate the idea of a homosexual contagion were met with scepticism from British parliamentarians, as we saw in Chapter 9. By contrast, the less sophisticated populace in the colonies had been primed to swallow it. Descriptions of the Chinese as threatening to 'degrade' and 'pollute' colonial society were a familiar refrain. With the anti-transportation debates so inadequately examined, John Hirst was not unusual among historians in declaring, 'The hatred of the Chinese sprang from the hearts of the people without prompting from the politicians.' Describing the reaction to large numbers of Chinese who arrived at the time of the 1858 election, Hirst continued: 'The popular view of the Chinese was that they were dirty, cunning and thieving; they were molesters of white women or worse, they practised the abominations of homosexuality, offences which could not be named but only darkly hinted at.' It was the anti-transportation argument all over again. Even more striking is the way the leaders of that movement turned their coat. Charles Cowper was described by Hirst as 'completely free from crude prejudice against the Chinese, but as leader of the popular party he had to act against them'. This is the same Cowper who established the New South Wales Anti-Transportation League in 1849, then went on to become President of the Australasian League, having facilitated New South Wales' belated collaboration with the other colonies. Meanwhile John West, now the powerful editor of the *Sydney Morning Herald*, was writing 'well-sustained and passionate defences of the Chinese' and praising the achievements of Chinese civilisation compared to those of 'the drunken white labourer'. According to Hirst, West and the conservatives in parliament shared a view that the people's behaviour regarding the Chinese demonstrated that they were unfit for political rights.[30]

The legacy of the anti-transportation campaign did not end in 1861. Unaware that the contagion spoken about was fear of 'catching' homosexuality,

Andrew Markus nevertheless touched peripherally on the subject in 1979. In *Fear and Hatred: Purifying Australia and California, 1850–1901* he pointed out that the anti-transportation movement was cited as a precedent for the campaign against the Chinese as late as 1901. Markus also recognised why this underlying issue had never been dealt with. 'In many instances, historians have not been sensitised to the pursuit of certain lines of inquiry, yet their primary materials have provided cues to direct their investigations.'[31] Markus was concerned that links to Aborigines had been missed. The same can be said about the homophobic campaign against the convicts. On this topic, Dan Huon was explicit in 1992 when he discussed the anti-transportationists' reiteration of terms such as 'vice' and 'corruption'. In an address that waited five years to be published, Huon asserted: 'this language masks a taboo which helped engage emotions and support for their cause . . . but the same taboo by imposing self-censorship over what could be said publicly, has hidden some of the evidence from historians in the twentieth century'.[32]

Australian historians have been misled by more than the inability to deal with the allegations about homosexuality. Nevertheless, that aspect has been significant. Manning Clark chose to believe that Father Ullathorne had 'that grace and insight which had enabled him to see into the heart of the matter about transportation'.[33] In *Earl Grey and the Australian Colonies* John Ward wrote a whole chapter entitled 'The Anti-Felon Confederation' without mentioning unnatural crime once.[34] Shaw scrupulously mentioned the subject in passing and then moved on. Writing in the early 1980s, Lloyd Robson, John Hirst and Michael Sturma dealt with the subject more frankly but none had the benefit of La Trobe's report, which was not published until 1990 and which was necessary to decode the anti-transportationists' message.[35] La Trobe's report was responsible for turning the spotlight on the Tasmanian anti-transportationists in this book.

Even without the decoder, it seems extraordinary that the movement has attracted so little attention from historians.[36] John West's *History* is an important reason for this. It has acted as a roadblock to interpretation, too often being treated as a primary source in its own right rather than the secondary opinions of someone writing with an agenda. West created many lasting stereotypes which are in need of deconstruction. In 2001, one stereotype to which he contributed substantially was tackled by Jan Kociumbas, who analysed the extent to which the demonisation of convicts 'especially by John West' has skewed the analysis of black–white relationships. According to Kociumbas, 'the original Tasmanians, once relocated or dead, became ever more innocent and harmless, while the convicts were represented as their chief adversaries from whom missionary rescue had been mandatory'.[37]

Much work on indigenous history has been 'positioned' by casting the convicts as villains. Undoubtedly this was sometimes the case, but as we saw in Chapter 5 there were also examples of good relations between the two. Evidence exists that some convicts were interested in Aboriginal culture and in learning bush skills from the indigenous people.[38] In historical terms, Aborigines and convicts have much in common. They have often shared the silences, the exclusion, the denigration and even the stereotyping. As Henry Reynolds pointed out in 1999, Australians 'now want to know the truth about the past and to come to terms with it. They see this as an essential step along the way towards national maturity.'[39] If the wider Australian community was aware of the gross obsfucation when it comes to convict history, they would no doubt feel the same. At this point, recovering the individual humanity on both sides of the colonial race debate may do more to advance the cause of reconciliation than perpetuating a cast of stereotypical victims and villains.

Another factor in accounting for lack of attention to the anti-transportationists has been the presumed intellectual linkage between them and the radical nationalists two decades later. Traditionally, they have been described as 'liberals' or, as Jan Kociumbas put it, 'colonial liberal nationalists'.[40] This view was given substance by surprising conversions to their cause, such as the Chartist, Edward Hawkesley, editor of the *People's Advocate*, who as noted in Chapter 8 switched suddenly from condemning the League to supporting it. He was not the only example of an opponent being abruptly converted. Charles Cowper's switch surprised his biographer John Ward, who rationalised, 'Perhaps he had never liked convict labour; certainly his associations with the liberals [*sic*] in Sydney helped to decide him against it.'[41] Noting the way Robert Lowe changed from being pro-transportation to anti in March 1849, A.W. Martin commented, 'He was not of course the only man to change his mind about transportation.'[42] In 1996, Mark McKenna quoted Henry Parkes, who remarked at a meeting of the Anti-Transportation League 'that there was a "higher loyalty" than that to any earthly monarch'. McKenna concluded that Parkes' 'higher loyalty' was to English constitutionalism. In fact he may well have been referring to a 'higher loyalty' to God, bearing in mind the biblical injunction against 'unnatural crime'.[43] In *The Beginning of an Australian Intelligentsia*, Manning Clark was puzzled by what he described as 'a curious kink or quirk in the thinking of Australian intellectuals when they suddenly perceived the direction in which the river of life was flowing in Australia'. In particular, he was pondering the change in the poet Charles Harpur. By birth the son of convicts, by inclination an Australian patriot, Harpur became a fervent supporter of the anti-transportation movement and by 1847–48 despised the society he was reared in so much that he believed it would be best ruled from England.[44] This pattern suggests—and it would bear following up—that moral pressure was being applied behind the scenes in the form of confidential asides between gentlemen about the alleged prevalence of unnatural crime among the convicts.

Another factor that made the anti-transportation movement seem liberal was the co-option to their cause in New South Wales of the small number of radicals, of which Hawkesley was one. Some of this group were also republicans, an intellectual position that appealed to the radical nationalists twenty years later. In reality, the leaders of the anti-transportation movement were predominantly conservative.[45] A break with Britain was the last thing they wanted.[46] The long-lasting Australian practice of referring to England as 'home' began around this time. It was a way of conveying that you were not prohibited from returning there by a conditional pardon. Furthermore, many of the leaders in the 1850s, John West most publicly, despised and distrusted the white working class. To these men democracy meant mob rule, a situation to be avoided at all costs.[47] The strategically clever confusion by the anti-transportationists between freedom from Britain's right to impose more convicts on the one hand, and colonial self-government and democratic freedoms such as men's right to vote on the other, disguised the extent to which they held illiberal views.

This traditional configuration had the effect also of casting the squatter/grazier group as villainous conservatives, a designation that may bear re-examination in the light of the underlying homophobic issues. Men designated 'conservatives' like W.C. Wentworth, Nicholas and Henry Bayley (quoted in Chapter 8) and even James Macarthur had far more experience with convicts than the recent immigrants who led the anti-transportationists. As we saw in Chapter 9, Macarthur, who formed a view in the 1830s that New South Wales had developed to a point that transportation should end, was a most discomfited fellow traveller with the anti-transportationists in England in 1861.

A major factor in the neglect of the anti-transportation movement has been a Sydney-centric or mainland view of the issue. A widespread assumption exists that the whole matter—the individual anti-transportation leagues, the Australasian League, the virulence and the noisy protests—was just a response to the arrival of Earl Grey's exiles in the late 1840s.[48] From this perspective, historians have missed the origin of the campaign in Launceston, its connection to Molesworth, the importance of John West and the purposeful, strategic activities that took place between 1843 and 1853, most of which were orchestrated by West. The scale of his achievement with the movement is not understood at all.[49]

Australian social commentators have picked up the language of the anti-transportationists without understanding its source, as Adam Jamrozik demonstrated when he claimed, 'From the outset, or from the time of

Federation, Australians have been on the defensive, maintaining fear of *contamination* by people from other than the "British stock".'[50] Recognising the original source makes crying 'racist' on the subject of the Chinese suddenly far too simplistic. As indeed it does when applied to the penal colony generally. Convict society was always multi-racial, drawing its numbers from the far reaches of the British Empire as well as cosmopolitan London and the seaports of Liverpool and Glasgow. Hottentot bushmen from the Cape were convicts. So were Maori from New Zealand, Negroes from America and the West Indies, as well as men from India and Mauritius. Hezikiah Green and Charles Clifford on the *Lord Dalhousie*, and John Baptiste and Nicholas Battis on the *Sir William Bensley*, were all 'men of colour', sharing with the 'whites' the common denominator of a criminal conviction. Being populated by the absolute bottom layer of society—not just the poor, or the 'deserving' poor but the *desperately* poor—meant any concern about race and ethnicity and religion was overwhelmed by the need to survive. The shared struggle created fellowship between people of a different background.

The anti-transportation movement left a wound at the heart of the nation that has resonated for more than 150 years. Resonated because it has been unrecognised and neglected. Researchers with narrow projects or predetermined sympathies long ago declared a pivot in Australian history to be racism, a verdict which few have challenged and many have built on. Since 1961, Russel Ward has been almost alone in declaring, 'there is slight evidence of racist feelings in Australia during the period [1788–1851] and a good deal of evidence of the lack of them'.[51] By comparison, in 1974, after a compilation of evidence of racism towards Aborigines, Henry Reynolds concluded:

> Racism was far more deeply rooted in Australian historical experience than we have usually cared to admit. It was already an important force when gold was discovered, and Chinese and later Melanesian migrants fitted into a well-established pattern of race relations. Events of the early colonial period prepared the community for the ready acceptance of social Darwinism in the last part of the century and influenced the development of colonial attitudes to all non-European people.[52]

Reynolds extrapolated from racism towards the Aborigines to racist attitudes generally, while Ward did not initially distinguish between the two, only doing so in the late 1970s in the light of research on Aboriginal issues.[53] For a realistic appraisal to be achieved, a distinction must be drawn between the treatment of the Aborigines, which was frequently racist, and of those from different races or ethnic background—including, for example, Maori or Tahitians—which was usually not. For instance, many of the colonial sailing ships and whalers were crewed by a mixture of Britons and Pacific Islanders. Like Russel Ward, I found no evidence of racism towards non-European races generally and, on the contrary, some evidence of comradeship regardless of race. Two examples of conflict with Aborigines were found among this sample of convicts. One was William Brodribb's active participation in Governor Arthur's 'Black Line' in Van Diemen's Land which, it should be remembered, followed the killing of Richard Rutter and the spearing of one of Brodribb's children. The second involved Thomas Dickson Saunders, transported for forgery of £1 notes, who arrived on the *Bensley* in 1817. In November 1838, Saunders was tried in the Supreme Court for killing an Aborigine with whom he had been drinking while firing a rifle at a nearby stump. Reports of the trial suggest the judge thought the correct verdict was manslaughter, but with emotions running high about the pending trial of white stockmen for the massacre of Aborigines at Myall Creek earlier that year, the jury acquitted Saunders.[54]

Generally, the insistence that convict society was overwhelmingly racist is a conclusion that never meshed for those who understood the reality of the penal colony, where men and women of all races, all religions, backgrounds, education and experience were rendered equal—and tolerant of each other—by a criminal conviction. Nor did it sit well with the subsequent history of a country that successfully integrated so many immigrants. Greater knowledge of convict history illuminates the later nineteenth century and beyond. Combined with greater knowledge of the role of the anti-transportation movement, it calls into question many of the issues which are fundamental to analysis of Australian history and society.

Beyond the implications for specific groups is the impact on the community overall. Ever since the anti-transportation campaign, Australia has been searching, always searching, for a 'new' identity. Even the so-called 'radical nationalists' of the 1880s and '90s who built on the rhetoric of the anti-transportationists were part of the search. Two world wars quietened the unease for a while, but by the last 40 years of the twentieth century what some described as an 'obsessive search for identity' had recommenced. The corroding insecurity was clear to social commentators, but the cause was usually derided as a version of the 'cultural cringe', too often assumed to be the result of a community pretentiousness similar to that of convict descendants who supposedly created their own 'taint'. Analysis of the cause has been befuddled by other factors too, as sociologist Geoff Stokes pointed out. In the late twentieth century, he detected a sector of the community similar to those mid-nineteenth-century immigrants long dreaded by the emancipists, who felt entitled to make over society to their tastes. According to Stokes, 'the critics of Australian identity have seldom engaged in purely scholastic inquiries. They have frequently sought practical remedial outcomes. That is, the "quest" for identity has been as much about what Australians ought to be, as what they are.'[55] Professor of Cultural Studies at the University of Queensland, Graeme Turner said something similar about the Australia Bicentenary Authority, which he decided 'had an almost pedagogic objective'. It was, he said as if 'Australians were being *taught* [his emphasis] their bicentennial behaviours'.[56]

One social commentator, James Jupp, identified the nub of the problem when he wrote, 'The repeated claim that a sense of national identity is lacking suggests that once some common link was there which is no longer shared and which has not been replaced by other common links.'[57] Not surprisingly, given the general level of ignorance about convict society, he failed to detect the change, which amounted to loss, that occurred between 1838 and 1853. No doubt influenced by a multicultural perspective, he instead concluded: 'The only strong common link that has so disappeared was racial and cultural descent from the inhabitants of the British Isles. The idea that *all Australians once shared a sense of national identity, which they subsequently lost,* must be seriously questioned' (emphasis added).[58]

What might Australia have been like if the disjunction in history had not occurred? What if convict society had made a gradual, organic transition not only to political democracy, as was happening in New South Wales anyway, but to the social virtues of education and civility and ultimately to its own version of respectability—at its own pace? If the community pride and self-confidence, so evident in the first half-century of European settlement, had expanded slowly and steadily? Would it have made any difference to what we experience today?

Using New South Wales as the template, it can be seen that convict society had made a transition of its own accord towards freedom and responsible government. Progressing towards that goal, it had struggled and won issues such as the change from military to civil juries as well as freedom of the press. Socially, it had also evolved. The division in polite society between emancipists and exclusives closed in the early 1840s when John Macarthur's son James expressed the view that 'the time had arrived when the long agitated Emancipist question might be dropped'.[59] These achievements did not need impetus from the opponents of transportation, whose campaign in fact detracted from them.

The most profound difference would have been the level of national self-confidence. Rather than an enduring brash uncertainty, a noticeable anxiety about what others thought, Australians would have acquired a solidly based understanding of what we were and what we could do. Although hard to document, this greater confidence would have pervaded every debate and every issue in Australian life, from multiculturalism and immigration to constitutional and political topics, to race and gender relations. (For instance, greater knowledge of convict fears that their society would be destroyed illuminates the enduring Australian insistence that new arrivals conform to the existing mores of Australian society.) Greater confidence among Australians might have bridged the continuing gulf between an alienated intellectual class and the rest of the people, giving rise to mutual respect rather than a long-standing contempt that mirrors the attitude of the anti-transportationists. More specifically, it might have been a means of overcoming a detrimental Australian habit of disparaging achievement, a tendency to cut people down to size in what is known colloquially as the tall-poppy syndrome. Although not unknown in other nations, it is particularly virulent in Australia and usually ascribed to the egalitarian culture, perhaps increased by envy and acquisitiveness. In fact, the accentuated Australian version must owe much to the inability to look back that was created by the birthstain. At both individual and community level, we could not celebrate achievement if we had to ignore the first steps on the path forward.

Ignorance about the convict colony has facilitated some enduring theories about Australian history. They may not be sustainable if tested against pre-1850 reality rather than assuming that post-1850 was a continuous paradigm from the earlier years.

Knowledge of the convict colony makes a mockery of Robert Hughes' attempt to declare it Britain's gulag. As it does any attempt to cast it as oppression of the Irish by the English. Fundamental to refuting those who search for a class drama is understanding that there was no large body of free settlers to create a middle class through almost the entire duration of the convict colonies. Yet as late as the 1950s, Russel Ward was surprised to discover that 'George Boxall writing about bushrangers in 1890 claimed he could "find no evidence . . . that the highwaymen robbed the rich to give to the poor" and [Ward says] *he went on to bolster his claim by such extraordinary statements as that a wealthy class "did not exist in convict times, and is only just beginning to appear now"*'(emphasis added).[60] To those like Hughes who have written more recently on the assumption that class was always relevant to the era, John Hirst pleaded passionately in 1983, 'It is of the utmost importance to the understanding of this society and the nature of its politics to realise that there was no colonial ruling class.'[61] His comments fell on the same deaf ears as Lloyd Robson's a few years later about 'shame and a conspiracy of silence' denying 'convict society its voice as history'. By constantly mentioning the population figures, reinforcing in the reader's mind the preponderance of convicts and convict families at any given time, this book has tried to make the same point.

Record keepers have always confused the population issue by failing to distinguish convicts' children from free settlers, thus disguising the extent of convict allegiances. In 1820, 32 years after New South Wales was founded, a useful petition written by emancipists revealed the numbers of their children. It should be noted that this document does not include serving convicts, who if they were added would swell the emancipist column even further.

		Emancipists	Emigrants
Abstract of the Emigrant and Emancipist Population 1820 with a schedule of property belonging to them			
Population:	Adults	7556	1558
	Children	5859	878
Total		13,415	2436
Excess of emancipists		10,979[62]	

Mystified by Boxall's claim there was no wealthy class, Russel Ward analysed the colonial population for his book, *The Australian Legend*. His table, set out below, illustrates the dominance of 'the convict element' in the community of New South Wales until at least mid-century.[63]

	Convicts, Emancipists and Native Born	Free Immigrants
1828	31,925 (87%)	4673 (13%)
1841	73,367 (63%)	43,621 (37%)
1851	110,713 (59%)	76,530 (41%)

Unless these proportions are understood, the nature of the convict colony is missed. Many elements of convict society contributed to the egalitarian Australian ethos, including most significantly the criminal conviction. Equally important, however, is the fact that there was no 'Us' and 'Them'. It was evident for all to see in the police constables, the scourgers, the ships' crews and military guards, the clerks and employers, the pastoralists and squatters, the wealthy as well as the poor, that 'Them' was 'Us'. They were one and the same. And you could find Irish as well as English in any one of the roles. With the exception of Western Australia, the absence of class was one of the defining features of the transportation era. As a nation, we are the poorer for not understanding this.

Any discussion of Australia's birthstain must canvass the crimes that resulted in the convicts' transportation. A bonus is the discovery of an amazingly diverse and ingenious group of people. Hidden behind the wall of silence about the prisoners are stories to match the multi-faceted tragedy of the Berkeley poachers. That is not to say the convicts should be romanticised. Like the poachers, they were three-dimensional people who displayed the flaws of temperament and character shared by all humanity. For instance, their legacy too often includes contempt for the intellect. However, this is a trait whose source might repay further investigation, given that those who brought the benefits of education were those who shamed their society into disavowing their origins and giving up their traditional pleasures. Some have called the convicts cowards for not rebelling, a denigration that convict history counters with its revelations not only of extraordinary encounters in the bush and on the sea, but of the many face-to-face confrontations between male and female convict workers and their employers. Generally, whether conforming or rebelling in Australia, the convicts displayed qualities that had been honed by trying to survive in Britain—wit, daring, opportunism, the ability to keep your nerve, the courage not to weep, the stoicism to endure and the determination to find a way when everything is ranged against you.

These qualities are familiar to anyone who has studied the character and behaviour of Australian soldiers in twentieth-century wars. Disrupted by the taboos of the past, however, no connection is generally acknowledged between the convicts and their military heirs. A genealogical link between the convicts and the diggers is easily proved. For instance, Richard Reeves' son William died in France in 1917, as did Daniel Long's great-grandson. Patrick O'Brien's grandson fought in World War I, as did descendants of James Wilde, Susannah Watson and Joseph Barrett. The cultural connection is also strong. Apparent in the characteristics described above, it is revealed again in the reluctance of the World War I diggers to salute. Raised in an egalitarian community that emphasised respect for the person rather than the badge they wore, why would they? But behind the boys stood thousands of grandfathers, and in some cases fathers, who had too often been compelled to do so. Despite any number of immigrants since, this irreverent ethos has survived, although young Australians who congregate at Gallipoli each year have no idea of its origin. For too many of them, Australian history begins with World War I. They would be enriched by understanding the earlier links.

Understanding the development of the birthstain also explains a conundrum that has long puzzled historians. Sadly, it confirms the accuracy of those who have detected in the Australian reaction to the Great War a need for purification through battle, an almost palpable sense of the community seeking a blood sacrifice through the Diggers. What Lloyd Robson described as 'the great sigh of relief'. In Robson's opinion, it was 'the blood sacrifice necessary for a deep stirring of the unsophisticated unconscious' that clinched the Anzac tradition and crystallised a sense of nationality.[64] Unknowingly, it may have addressed more than an inferiority complex. World War I coincided with the growth of the eugenics movement which, as we saw in Chapter 9, along with Lombroso's theory of Criminal Man, might have been designed to make Australians feel anxious and inferior. Predating either philosophy, however, was a memory of being made to feel not just criminal but dirty and ashamed. If this gave rise to a need to be 'purified', it is hardly surprising.

George Arnold Wood was among those who detected something of the sort. Addressing this need underlay his lecture to the Royal Australian Historical Society in 1921 with its emphasis on the (almost innocent) poachers. Significantly, in the light of what we have discovered about the birthstain, he also told his audience that night, 'it would be wrong to believe that a consequence of convict origin was that the morality of New South Wales was of a lower standard than the morality of England . . . Each generation, more free from poverty and the moral consequences of poverty, more free also to reap those spiritual advantages that come from sense of independence and responsibility, rose to greater worth, until the day came when at Gallipoli, in Flanders, and in France, the Australian-born proved themselves to be among the greatest and noblest souls who have ever grown among the British race.'[65] Decades later, it should make us weep rather than condemn our forebears for needing such reassurance.

In 1912, approximately a decade after Lord Beauchamp shocked Australians with his public pronouncement that they had made good their 'birthstain', Sydney journalist Adam McCay satirised the community's anxieties in a poem called 'The Birthstain'.[66] Nearly one hundred years later, the satire may have faded but the humour endures.

> If only my great grandsire had been sent
> Out of his country for his country's good
> To help to people some new continent—
> If thus I traced my lineage, I would
> Face all the world with gallant hardihood,
> For my pedigree would be an entry
> Like that of the nobility or gentry.
>
> So I'd be glad if a pickpocket smart
> Had captured grandma with his loving smiles;

I wouldn't go around with careful art
Expunging records in the public files
(Criminal records of the British Isles),
But I would glory in the demonstration
Of genius in a previous generation.

Sometimes I dream myself of that good strain
Wherein there is no vile suburban smudge,
See my great-grandad in the dock again,
Taking his gruel from the thin-lipped judge,
Thus having dreamed, to work I gaily trudge
Rich in the ancestry which surely traces
My breed above the breed of commonplaces.

Alas, it is a fond and idle thought;
My veins contain no fluid so sublime;
My family always did the things they ought,
Sold socks, mixed drugs, preached sermons all the time
And never rose to one immortal crime.
But oh, if only happy fate could fall so
I wish I had a birthstain! Don't you also?

Being founded by criminals brought Australia some idiosyncratic benefits,
not least a mordant gallows humour. Descendants of convicts who have recovered their ancestors have recovered their sense of humour on the subject with
them. How could they not when those very forebears used laughter as one of
the few resources that no one could take from them whatever the circumstances? Whether standing in the dock, sailing into the unknown, or facing the
lash, laughter—often in the form of 'cheek'—was their best, indeed their only,
defence. Any number of Australia's criminal founders literally laughed in the
face of death.[67] So, with equal courage, did their heirs in two world wars. Their
humour, laced with bravado, dry, self-deprecating, face-saving, is still a defining
characteristic of the society they left behind.

Transcending race and culture, that legacy more than any other unites
Australians with an underlying bond which surfaced for all to see during
the 2000 Sydney Olympics, when humour permeated everything from the
Opening Ceremony to a television show with an unofficial mascot, to adver-
tisements, to crowd control on trains and buses and ferries. Humour counters
the convict 'taint' that continues to flourish in the minds of our detractors as
surely today as it has always done, most notably in its quick production by

people on the losing end of an argument with Australia. 'Bad stock,' declared the aristocratic eugenicist Winston Churchill in 1942 after Prime Minister Curtin insisted our troops return to defend their homeland. 'Everyone knows Australians are criminals,' riposted President Robert Mugabe, Prime Minister of Zimbabwe, in 2003 in the face of Australian criticism. Sadly, this defence can also come to the fore from one of our own. In 2007, seeking the ultimate insult but misjudging its impact in modern Australia, Sheik Taj al-Hilali said of Muslim Australians, 'We came as free people. We bought our own tickets. We are more entitled to Australia than they are.' The reaction was one of incredulous laughter. Despite the sheik's angst, he and other Australians of the Islamic faith will in due course discover, as so many immigrants before them have done, that humour, including the ability to laugh at yourself, is the passport to acceptance in Australian society.

Laughter aside, although anxiety about a birthstain has all but vanished at the family level, public and institutional ambivalence lingers. Even more apparent is the vast ignorance of a community with little historic reference beyond that of two world wars. Understanding the history of the birthstain, and through that route incorporating the first 60 years of Australia's European history into the community consciousness, would greatly enhance the calibre of our public discourse. It would allow us all—whether descended from convict or free settler, refugee or Aborigine—to better understand the multiple layers of people who make up the Australian nation and the society in which we live.

The condemnation of transportation ended the larrikin but confident ethos of the convict colony. It banished a state of mind that caused ex-convict James Jaye from the *John* to blazon his maxim 'Live and Let Live' on the wall of his business in Bathurst. This is the same James Jaye who, around 1870, set about disguising his convict background for the benefit of his descendants. The Molesworth Committee's definition of transportation as a variation of slavery, but most particularly as an instrument that created homosexuality, set in train events that made it impossible for individuals like Jaye to identify themselves as convicts. In turn, that reluctance permeated institutions and government. The mid-nineteenth century was a turning point in Australian history that marked the start of the national amnesia. We must ensure now that the 21st century marks the end. It is time to recover the lost world of convict society with all its ramifications.

acknowledgements

The dedication reflects the debt I owe Penelope Nelson, who is also a writer. Her personal encouragement and professional feedback during the writing of the book was essential to its completion.

Many other people were important, too many to list more than a few here. Among them were Michael and Phillida Preston who not only put me up in Perth, but in Michael's case made later sorties into the Battye Library on my behalf; Ziggy Sieradski, whose instruction to 'dig deep' was a demonstration of faith that was heartening; as was Jim Silkman's help and the enthusiasm of family historians Tony Harrison, Geoff Jaye and his late wife, Margaret.

Rhonwyn Cuningham and John White, Angela Compton, Jo Watson and Chris Woods punched the project into manageable shape by compiling the database of convicts. Without their initial help, I would never have reached anything like a deadline. Jo Watson is a descendant of William Brodribb and I thank her for suggesting the *Sir William Bensley* as one of 'my' ships. Many other descendants contributed information. Some are cited in the text but to all of them I wish to express my grateful thanks. This book is an acknowledgement of their hard and valuable and engrossing work.

Australian genealogical societies spread my request for information among family historians. In this regard I owe particular thanks to the Society of Australian Genealogists in Sydney and the Western Australia Genealogical Society. Generally, the work of genealogists in indexing archival records and of writing up family histories was of great benefit to my research, as it will be to many others. Among those who have moved to projects of a broader nature is Perry McIntyre, who generously supplied information from her doctoral thesis.

British family historians also contributed greatly to this book. In Britain, researchers Peter Curle and John Trevett not only supplied me with information about 'their' convicts but penetrated the archives in Gloucestershire and north London to track down some missing links. Jill Chambers is well known for her expertise on the Swing rioters as well as for her indexing of Home Office records in The National Archives at Kew. She was extremely generous in her help to me and I look forward to returning the favour.

In Britain I was fortunate to have personal support from Meredith Daneman and from Elizabeth and David Smith whose encouragement, company and accommodation made an intensive research trip a pleasure as well. The freedom to travel was made possible by my cousin Christina Lincoln who took care of Casey.

Throughout this project, I received great encouragement from academics at the University of Tasmania, particularly Lucy Frost and Hamish Maxwell-Stewart, both of whom have published in the area of convict studies. Diane Snowden and Philip Hilton were generous with information arising from their own research, as was Sue Hood at the Port Arthur Authority. Staff at the Archives Office of Tasmania went out of their way to help me, particularly Deborah Drinkel.

In New South Wales archivists past and present were of great help, particularly Christine Yeats, Gail Davis, Janette Pelosi, John Cross, Dawn Troy and Michael Saclier. So were foundation family historians Malcolm Sainty and Keith Johnson.

Academics Brian Fletcher, Miriam Dixson and Alison Alexander were good enough to read the uncompleted, draft manuscript and to give me the benefit of their professional, sometimes trenchant comments, not all of which I adopted. They were an invaluable sounding board. Any errors, of course, are mine.

Elizabeth Weiss was every writer's dream of a publisher, encouraging me to think big in the first place, then nurturing me through periods of self doubt. Angela Handley, Senior Editor at Allen & Unwin, was a pleasure to liaise with during the production. Carl Harrison-Ford edited the manuscript with his usual adroitness, for which I am very grateful.

The encouragement of my family, Robert and Nicole Macfarlan, Rosalinde and Bill Kearsley, Christina Lincoln and my son, Joshua, provided the essential motivation to persevere to the end for which I thank them all.

BABETTE SMITH

PHOTO ACKNOWLEDGEMENTS

Page

13   Supplied by Brodribb descendant, Jo Watson
23   Gloucestershire Archives SRDANCEY/DY1/36
33   Mitchell Library, State Library of NSW
52   Supplied by descendant, Geoff Jaye
53   Supplied by descendant, Geoff Jaye
59   Guildhall Library, City of London
67   From Henry Mayhew, 'London Underworld'
72   Dixson Library, State Library of New South Wales
77   C.T. Constantini, Allport Library and Museum of Fine Arts, State Library of Tasmania
84   From Mark Herber, 'Criminal London, A Pictorial History'
91   Archives Office of Tasmania PH30/1/1425
114   Tasmaniana Library, State Library of Tasmania
133   Thomas Bock, Dixson Library, State Library of New South Wales
134   Thomas Bock, Dixson Library, State Library of New South Wales
148   Thomas Bock, Dixson Library, State Library of New South Wales
150   Thomas Bock, Dixson Library, State Library of New South Wales
153   Thomas Bock, Dixson Library, State Library of New South Wales
159   Thomas Bock, Dixson Library, State Library of New South Wales
162   Thomas Bock, Dixson Library, State Library of New South Wales
171   Charles Rodius (1802–1860), Convicts building a road over the Blue Mountains, NSW, 1833 (watercolour 17.3 × 28.8 cm) National Library of Australia, nla.pic-an6332110
175   George Lacey (ca. 1816-1878?), Prisoners under escort for Bathurst Gaol (watercolour, 32.3 × 38.8 cm), National Library of Australia, nla.pic-an3103631
180   Mitchell Library, State Library of New South Wales
186   Allport Library and Museum of Fine Arts, State Library of Tasmania
201   With permission of Lady Molesworth of Pencarrow, Cornwall
218   Catholic Archives, St Mary's Cathedral
223   Lithograph by Robert Dowling, Queen Victoria Museum and Art Gallery, Hobart
229   From the collections of Launceston Library, State Library of Tasmania
247   Supplied by descendant, Pauline Connell
265   *London Illustrated News*
267   Courtesy Battye Library, State Library of Western Australia
272   Supplied by descendant, Jennifer Cook
275   Supplied by descendant, Kerry Allbeury
283   Supplied by descendant, Kath Francis
289   *London Illustrated News*, 13 April 1844
292   Supplied by descendant, Carl O'Brien
303   Supplied by descendant, Dr Christopher Riley
305   Archives Office of Tasmania PH30/1/3196
305   Archives Office of Tasmania PH30/1/3199
309   Archives Office of Tasmania PH30/1/634
319   Mitchell Library, State Library of NSW

notes

ABBREVIATIONS USED IN THE NOTES

ABGR	Australian Biographical and Genealogical Record
ADB	*Australian Dictionary of Biography*
AGCI	Australian Genealogical Computer Index
AJCP	Australian Joint Copying Project
ANU	Australian National University
AOTAS	Archives Office of Tasmania
BL	Battye Library, Western Australia
BPP	British Parliamentary Papers
CO	Colonial Office
CSIL	Colonial Secretary In Letters
GRO	Gloucester Record Office
HO	Home Office
HRA	*Historical Records of Australia*
JACH	*Journal of Australian Colonial History*
JRAHS	*Journal of the Royal Australian Historical Society*
LUP	Leicester University Press
ML	Mitchell Library
MUP	Melbourne University Press
NAS	National Archives of Scotland
NSWBDM	New South Wales Births Deaths and Marriages
NSWGG	*New South Wales Government Gazette*
OUP	Oxford University Press
PRO	Public Record Office of Great Britain (now TNA)
RAHS	Royal Australian Historical Society
RO	Record Office
SAG	Society of Australian Genealogists
SRNSW	State Records of New South Wales
SROWA	State Records Office of Western Australia
TASBDM	Tasmania Births Deaths and Marriages
THRA	Tasmanian Historical Research Association
THS	*Tasmanian Historical Studies*

TNAUK	The National Archives, United Kingdom
UNSW	University of New South Wales
UQP	University of Queensland Press
UWA	University of Western Australia
WABDM	Western Australia Births Deaths and Marriages
WAGS	Western Australia Genealogical Society
WO	War Office

INTRODUCTION

1   Brian H. Fletcher, *History in New South Wales, 1888–1938*, p. 437.
2   In 1955 Manning Clark also thought that the Eureka Stockade had been inflated as a historic event. See C.M.H. Clark, *Select Documents in Australian History, 1851–1900*, p. xi.
3   Rudyard Kipling, 'Song of the Cities', written after a brief visit to the Australian colonies in 1891.
4   Numbers are approximate. These figures are based on L.L. Robson's calculations, *The Convict Settlers of Australia*, p. 4.
5   B. Baskerville, 'Felon to Farmer—Thomas Harrison and his family', thesis, 1984.
6   Ronald D. Lambert, 'Reclaiming the Ancestral Past: Narrative Rhetoric and the "Convict Stain"'.
7   Seven hundred and thirty-six convicts and seventeen convicts' children landed at Port Jackson from the First Fleet, and 7035 arrived between 1788 and 1800. Manning Clark pointed out that this is only a fraction of the total number transported (around 160,000). It was not until after the war with France in 1815 that numbers increased sharply. The peak transportation year was 1834, when 4920 men and women arrived. See C.M.H. Clark, 'The Origin of the Convicts Transported to Eastern Australia 1787–1852, Part 1'.

CHAPTER 1 *Something to Hide*

1   John West, *The History of Tasmania*, pp. 518–19.
2   BPP, *Select Committee on Transportation,* Minutes of Evidence, 1861.
3   G.A. Wood, 'Convicts'.
4   J.L. and B. Hammond, *The Village Labourer, 1760–1832*.
5   Ibid., p. 242, quoted in Wood, 'Convicts', p. 183.
6   Wood, pp. 183–84.
7   Ibid pp. 200–01.
8   The details in this chapter are substantially drawn from the following document. Where necessary, it will be referred to as 'Transcript'. *The Trial at large of (the Poachers by name) for the Wilful Murder of Wm. Ingram . . . likewise the Trial of W.A. Brodribb, Gentleman for administering an Unlawful Oath, Gloucester Lent Assizes 1816 before the Hon. Mr Justice Holroyd, to which is prefixed an Introductory Narrative . . . and a Plan of the Ground*, printed and sold by D. Walker and Sons, Journal Office, Westgate Street, Gloucester 1816. Available at The National Archives of the United Kingdom and at libraries and record offices in Gloucester and Bristol.
9   Family information supplied by Brodribb descendants Jo Watson and Ruth Carter; professional information from W. John Lyes, 'William Adams Brodribb, a Transported Attorney', *Transactions of the Bristol and Gloucestershire Archaeological Society*, Vol. 122, 2004, pp. 161–68.
10 'The Poaching Affray of 1816', *Bulletin of The Society of Thornbury Folk*, Series 2. No. 22, January 1962.
11 Harry Hopkins, *The Long Affray*, pp. 8–9.
12 Ibid., p. 305.
13 The *Militia Act* 1757 created a force of local men in each county who could be called on to defend the county in time of invasion. They could not serve outside their own county.

Training and equipment were paid for by county rate. A ballot held in each parish decided who should serve. They had to be able-bodied men 18–45 years of age. Exemptions were made for professional men such as doctors and local officials. A man who did not want to serve could provide a substitute. They were only paid when away from home on a training exercise. www.lofthouse.com/history/JohnsonF.html.

14 Information from *Burke's Peerage*, online, consulted 2004.
15 *Gloucester Journal*, 21 August 1909; first published in the *Bristol Times and Mirror*, 8 January 1876. The unnamed poacher in this article is identified by this author on circumstantial evidence as William Collins. For clarity, the short citation will be 'William Collins interview'.
16 'The Poaching Affray of 1816'. The opinions of Greville and others are cited in this article, as well as the conclusions of twentieth-century local historians.
17 *Worcester Journal*, 18 April 1816.
18 William Collins interview.
19 Ibid.
20 Ibid.
21 Ibid.
22 Lyes, 'William Adams Brodribb'.
23 Occupations and physical descriptions from Gloucester Gaol Register 1816, Gloucester Record Office GRO Q/Gc 5/1.
24 William Collins interview.
25 Ibid.
26 Transcript; also *Worcester Journal*, 18 April 1816.
27 William Collins interview.
28 Ibid.
29 *Gloucester Journal*, 5 February 1816.
30 Transcript; plus Burley's deposition, GRO D1229/49.
31 *Worcester Journal*, 18 April 1816.
32 *Gloucester Journal*, 5 February 1816.
33 *Bristol Gazette*, 18 April 1816.
34 Lyes, 'William Adams Brodribb'.
35 GRO 1229/49.
36 Chaplain's Journal, GRO Q/Gc 31/1.
37 Copies of letters supplied by Jo Watson, descendant of William Brodribb. The originals are held at the Bristol Record Office.
38 Chaplain's Journal; Governor's Journal, 1814–16, GRO Q/Gc 3/8.
39 Chaplain's Journal.
40 Hopkins, *The Long Affray*, p. 10.
41 *Times*, 15 April 1816.
42 Hopkins, p. 10; William Collins interview.
43 Hopkins, p. 10.
44 R. Bransby Cooper to Lord Sidmouth, Home Secretary, Correspondence and Recommendations of Circuit Judges 1816, TNAUK HO6/1

CHAPTER 2 *Amnesia*

1 *Worcester Journal*, 18 April 1816.
2 *Gloucester Journal*, 5 February 1816.
3 K.A. Johnson, 'Rumsey, Herbert John (1866–1956), *ADB*, Vol. 11, MUP, Carlton 1988, pp. 479–80.
4 Peter Chinn, *The Thin Red and Blue Lines*, p. 99.
5 Tamsin O'Connor (citing Raymond Evans' unpublished manuscript), 'A Zone of Silence: Queensland's Convicts and the Historiography of Moreton Bay', pp. 124–25.
6 *Queensland 1900: A Narrative of her Past, Together with Biographies of her Leading Men*, 1900, cited in O'Connor, p. 126.

7   Brian H. Fletcher, *History in New South Wales, 1888–1938,* p. x.

8   Angus Mackay: AOTAS CON 33/115, CON 18/59 description, CON 14/49 indent.

9   Fletcher, *History in New South Wales,* p. 26.

10 Ibid., pp. 72, 74–75.

11 Source for the warning to Wood is Brian Fletcher in his talk at the Mitchell Library, 30 July 2007.

12 Ibid., p. 26.

13 Frank Crowley, *A Documentary History of Australia,* Vol. 3, p. 115.

14 George F.J. Bergman, 'John Davies 1813–1872: A Jewish Convict, Journalist, Actor, Policeman, Publican, Parliamentarian', THRA, *Papers and Proceedings,* Vol. 26, No. 3, September 1979, p. 85.

15 Press clipping in possession of the author, date missing. Interview published in a Sydney Sunday newspaper in the 1990s.

16 Fletcher, p. 158.

17 Alexandra Hasluck, *Unwilling Emigrants,* pp. 7–11.

18 Johnson, 'Rumsey'.

19 Information about Eleanor Dark's motivation from Tom Griffith, speaking at the Sydney Writer's Festival, 1 June 2007.

20 Recounted to the author by Bevan Carter, former president of WAGS, who was told this story by the workman concerned.

21 Robyn Eastley, 'Using the Records of the Tasmanian Convict Department', p. 139.

22 Ibid., p. 140.

23 Ibid., p. 141.

24 George Rudé, *Protest and Punishment.*

25 G.A. Wood, 'Convicts', pp. 181–82.

26 Eastley, p. 141.

27 *Hobart Mercury,* 27 October 1973.

28 Eastley, 'Using the Records', p. 141.

29 Interview with Keith Johnson and Malcolm Sainty, members of SAG, 13 January 2005.

30 Ibid.

31 Ibid.

32 Michael Saclier interview, 16 December 2005.

33 Phyllis Mander-Jones (ed.), *Manuscripts in the British Isles Relating to Australia, New Zealand and the Pacific,* ANU Press, Canberra 1972.

34 Guides to the AJCP documents can be purchased from the Australian National Library.

35 ML PRO Reel FM4007219, *Police Gazette; or, Hue and Cry,* 1831–32.

36 Dawn Troy interviews, 20 December 2005, 7 January 2006.

37 Eastley, p. 142.

38 Alison Alexander, 'The Legacy of the Convict System', p. 51.

39 Ronald D. Lambert, 'Reclaiming the Ancestral Past: Narrative Rhetoric and the "Convict Stain"'.

40 Interview with Keith Johnson and Malcolm Sainty.

41 Figures cited by John Spurway, 'The Growth of Family History in Australia', *The Push From the Bush,* No. 27, 1989, pp. 54–55.

42 Descendant's website, www.bestwick.info/besfam/beshist1.htm, consulted 2006.

43 W.A. Brodribb, *Recollections of an Australian Squatter, 1835–1883.*

44 Email between Brodribb descendants David Scott and Jo Watson, 19 November 2004.

45 Jo Watson to Babette Smith, email dated 17 November 2004.

46 Linda Forbes to Babette Smith, *c.* November 2004.

47 Ibid.

48 Information from descendant Lauris Crampton.

49 Alison Alexander, 'A Turbulent Career, Jane Hadden', pp. 60–61.

50 Jill Roy (with the assistance of descendants Jan Irving, Janice Jackson, Shirley Stone and Richard Stone), 'The Story of William Honeyman, 1792–1821'.

51 Ibid.
52 Information supplied to the author by Gwen Martin. Descendants of 'John Smith' who did the research are Val and Graham Davey.
53 Information supplied to the author by descendant Leonie Mickleborough, 2005.
54 Information supplied to the author by descendant Trevor Carey, 2005; information about William Gunn's reputation in Linus Miller, *Notes of an Exile in Van Diemen's Land* [1846], cited in Cassandra Pybus, *American Citizens, British Slaves: Yankee Political Prisoners in an Australian Penal Colony, 1839–1850*, MUP, Carlton 2002, pp. 65–69 and photograph at p. 80.
55 Author's family history. For further information see Babette Smith, *A Cargo of Women*.
56 Descendant Karen Macreadie to author, 2005.
57 Smith, *Cargo of Women*.
58 Letter supplied by descendant Geoff Jaye, 2004. Copy in possession of the author.
59 Author's family history. The neighbours' dispute is recorded in the Braidwood Bench Book.
60 Descendant Pauline Connell to author, 2005.
61 Descendant Brian Barrett to author 2005.
62 See Smith, *Cargo of Women*.
63 Spurway, 'The Growth of Family History', p. 53.
64 Michael Roe, Introduction to *Pros and Cons of Transportation*.
65 Alan Atkinson, 'The First Fleet Lives', *The Push From the Bush*, No. 27, 1989.
66 Mollie Gillen, *The Founders of Australia*.
67 Herbert John Rumsey, *Pioneers of Sydney Cove*, Sunnybrook Press, Sydney 1937; Alfred Rumsey entry in *ADB*, Vol. 11.
68 G.A. Wood, 'Convicts'.

CHAPTER 3 *An Amazing Cast of Characers*

1 W.K. Hancock, *Australia*, p. 24.
2 C.M.H. Clark, 'The Origins of the Convicts Transported to Eastern Australia, 1787–1852'.
3 A.G.L. Shaw, *Convicts and the Colonies*; L.L. Robson, *The Convict Settlers of Australia*.
4 George Rudé, *Protest and Punishment*.
5 Ibid.
6 Stephen Nicholas (ed.), *Convict Workers*.
7 *Sir William Bensley* indent, SRNSW 4/4005 Reel 393; *John 1(4)* indent, SRNSW 4/4017 Reel 905; *St Vincent (3)* indent, AOTAS CON 14/47 indent, AOTAS CON 18/59 description; *Lord Dalhousie* registers SROWA Acc. 128/Reg. 32, 43 and SROWA Acc. 1156/Reg. 29; *Lord Melville I (1)* indent, SRNSW 4/28267 Reel 393; *Maria I (1)* indent, SRNSW 4/4006 Reel 394; *Princess Royal (2)* indent, SRNSW 4/4014 Reel 398; *Duchess of Northumberland* (2), AOTAS CON 41/37, CON 15/8 indent, CON 19/11 description.
8 Gloucester Gaol Register, GRO Q/Gc 5/1; *Gloucester Journal*, August 1831; *John* indent.
9 *Sussex Advertiser*, special edition, 28 March 1862; *Surrey Gazette*, 1 April 1862; family information supply by Stapley descendants Marie Young, Neville Thomas and Brian Saunders.
10 John Andrew Lovell: *Bensley* indent; AOTAS CON 31/27 p. 3, CON 13/1 p. 73.
11 John Hobbs, Thomas Frederick Webster and Robert Lewer: AJCP ML Central Criminal Court, Seventh Session, 10 May 1847.
12 Eliza Morrison and Mary Nowlan: *Leinster Express*, 21 July 1849; personal details from AOT CON41/26, CON 15/6, Eliza Morrison *Earl Grey* 1850 No. 1093. The research on Eliza Morrison supplied by Diane Snowden, 'A White Rag Burning: Irish Women Who Committed Arson in Order to Be Transported to Van Diemen's Land', doctoral thesis, University of Tasmania, May 2005.
13 Snowden, 'A White Rag Burning'; *Jackson's Oxford Journal*, 8 March 1862.

14   Indent for the ship *Wanstead* 1814, plus information supplied by descendant Ron Norton.

15   *Princess Royal*: see Babette Smith, *A Cargo of Women*; *Duchess of Northumberland*: see Christine Woods, *The Last Ladies*—Mary Ann Hurren at p. 132 and Ann Jones or Johnson at p. 137.

16   Sherry: *Maidstone and Kentish Journal*, 30 July 1861.

17   Rudé, *Protest and Punishment*, pp. 230–31.

18   The prosecutor was William Evans of the parish of St Chad. Valentine Wood was tried at the Salop Assizes on 20 March 1816. *Salopian Journal*, 13 March 1816, 'Calendar of Prisoners for Trial at Shropshire Lent Assizes on March 20,1816'.

19   Staffordshire Adjourned Sessions, 7 March 1850, Criminal Registers, AJCP ML Reel 2830; Calendar of Prisoners, William Salt Library, Stafford; *Staffordshire Advertiser*, 9 March 1850.

20   Old Bailey Sessions, 3 April 1816, www.oldbaileyonline.org, Thomas Plows, 3 April 1816, t18160403–67.

21   *John* indent: 'Samuel Rowney, age 14, born County Longford, Occupation sweep, tried Surrey Quarter Sessions, 24 October 1831, for robbing father of coat. 7 years. Prior: 3 months.'

22   Old Bailey Sessions, 7 April 1831, www.oldbaileyonline.org, t18310407-218, consulted November 2006.

23   Richard Welsh: 3 July 1848, Central Criminal Court, Ninth Session, 1847–48; Patrick Brian: Clerkenwell Sessions, 11 April 1848, AOTAS CON 14/47; Thomas Tomlinson: Central Criminal Court, Seventh Session, 1861–62.

24   Calculation from an electronic search of www.oldbaileyonline.org, consulted June 2006.

25   Joseph Williams: AOTAS CON 31/45 p. 15, CON 13/1 p. 104.

26   Lindsey QS, 21 October 1831, Lincolnshire Record Office, LQS A/9/3 and LQS A/1/537/1–5, 163, 176, 182, 212.

27   The O'Neils: *Preston Chronicle*, 19 January 1850; Criminal Registers for Lancashire HO 27/92 AJCP PRO Reel 2829.

28   Fleming: *York Herald*, 8 January 1848.

29   Ann Storrett: TNAUK ASSI 41/14, Crown Minute Book for Northern Circuit Lent Assizes, 3 March 1828.

30   Henry James Taperell, convicted Exeter City Sessions 30 July 1850. *Woolmer's Exeter and Plymouth Gazette*, 3 July 1850: *Trewman's Exeter Flying Post*, 1 August 1850.

31   Liverpool Borough Sessions, Friday 11 April 1862, *Liverpool Journal*, 12 April 1862.

32   For the story of Susannah Watson see Smith, *A Cargo of Women*.

33   James Barnes: Central Criminal Court, First Session, 1850–51, 25 November 1850.

34   Shaw, *Convicts and the Colonies*, p. 154.

35   Francis Stapleton and Abraham West: *Derby Mercury*, 3 August 1831.

36   Angus McKay: information compiled by descendants, plus this author. Case papers at NAS AD14/50/256; Portsmouth Prison Register, 1847–52, TNAUK PCOM 2/105.

37   William Honeyman: *Edinburgh Evening Courant*, 28 December 1815. All Honeyman research carried out by Jill Roy and other descendants.

38   Case papers NAS JC 8/11; *Edinburgh Evening Courant*, 15, 23 September, 28 December 1815, 18 January 1816.

39   NAS AD14/16/48, JC13/42 1v, JC8/11 f154.

40   *Glasgow Herald*, 3, 10 May 1816; *Glasgow Chronicle*, 4 May 1816, NAS AD14/16/48; Precognition, JC26/379 Indictment, JC 13/42 Minute Book, Remission of Sentence JC8/11 r154r.

41   *Glasgow Herald*, 2 October 1815.

42   www.oldbaileyonline.org, Thomas Stacey, 8 September 1831, t18310908–1.

43 Gloucester Gaol Registers, 1815–79, at Gloucester Record Office for both men.

44 George Rawlinson: Hertford Lent Assizes 1862; *Hertford and Bedford Gazette*, 8 March 1862; Portland Prison Register 1862, PCOM 2/382.

45 As with many of the earlier ships, the *Bensley's* indent did not include the prisoners' crimes. Exactly who was guilty of highway robbery has been calculated from a mixture of criminal registers, calendars of prisoners for trial and newspaper reports.

46 www.genuki.org.uk/big/eng/GLS/StGeorge/Gaz1868.htm. Information on the parish of St George taken from the *National Gazetteer of Great Britain and Ireland* [1868] transcribed by a family researcher Colin Hinson for the GENUKI website in 2003.

47 Gloucester Gaol Register, GRO QGc 5/1; *Gloucester Journal*, April 1816; family background supplied by Pauline Connell and other members of the Barrett family.

48 Joseph Sowden: TNAUK ASSI 41/22, City of York and County of York Gaol Delivery, 12 July 1862.

49 Quigley: *Glasgow Chronicle*, 3 May 1816; *Glasgow Herald*, 3 May 1816.

50 www.eastlondonhistory.com/coiners.

51 Ibid.; Henry Mayhew, *London's Underworld*, pp. 13–19.

52 Mayhew, *London's Underworld*, pp. 319–20.

53 Ibid.

54 Ibid.

55 *Lancashire Gazette*, 23, 30 March 1816; Lancaster Lent Assizes 1816, Criminal Registers for Lancaster; *Sir William Bensley* and *Lord Melville* indents.

56 www.oldbaileyonline.org, 29 May 1816, t18160529–22.

57 www.oldbaileyonline.org, 3 April 1816, t18160403–87.

58 Central Criminal Court, Second Session, 1861–62, 16 December 1861, p. 145.

59 *Times*, 14, 21 January, 1 February, 22 March, 10, 11 April 1862; Central Criminal Court Sixth Session, 9 and 10 April 1861–62.

60 *Derby Mercury*, 14 February, 12, 26 March 1862. Also Marriage Certificate 230/1856, parish of Ashby de la Zouche, Leicestershire, plus information from the late Kath Francis, grand-daughter of Joseph Shaw.

61 www.oldbaileyonline.org.

62 Robson, *Convict Settlers*, p. 210.

63 Central Criminal Court, Sixth Session, 1846–47, trial of William Frederick Manvell.

64 *Times*, 19 January 1815.

65 Research in the parish registers for Bodenham's marriage to Eliza Keattch and the birth of their son, Harry, carried out by John Trevett, husband of a Bodenham descendant.

66 www.oldbaileyonline.org, Francis Bodenham, 11 January 1815, t18150111–91, consulted 17 December 2004.

67 www.oldbaileyonline.org, Henry Ellis, Edward Bowen, Sarah Franks, Sarah Pinnion, 3 December 1817, t18171203–18, consulted 17 December 2004.

68 TNAUK Assi 41/15, City of York Assizes, July 1831.

69 *Times*, 29 November 1861.

70 Central Criminal Court, First Session, 1861–62, 27 November 1861; *Times*, 18, 20 November 1861, 29 January 1862.

71 Eliza Dore trial reported in the *Times*, 30 March 1852, reproduced in Woods, *The Last Ladies*, pp. 81–83.

72 Johan Herrold: 16 August 1858, Central Criminal Court, Tenth Session, 1857–58. Thomas Barclay: *Times*, 11 July 1861; Central Criminal Court, Ninth Session, 1860–16.

73 *Staffordshire Advertiser*, 22 March 1862.

74 *Devizes and Wiltshire Gazette*, 24 July 1862.

75 SRNSW, *Ships' Indents, 1806–22*, compiled by James McClellan, printed by Pinewood Press, 1994. Based on Charles Bateson's figures for convicts delivered to New South Wales, my calculation is 8578 men for New South Wales, 1806–22 inclusive, which makes 307 soldiers for the same period 2.5 per cent of the whole.

76 HO 75/4, *Police Gazette; or, Hue & Cry*, October, November, December 1831; WO 25/2910, List of Deserters 17th Regiment of Foot, August–November 1831.

77 *Times*, 28 December 1831.

78 The *John's* printed indent had a space for 'prior offences', which included a record of the number of lashes they had received. Quigley's are shown as 150. ML ZF365.9544025/1 Reel FM4/10567, Printed Convict Indents 1830–34.

79 Philip Hilton, email to author, 26 May 2005.

80 Detailed information about the 1st/17th Foot (Leicestershire) Regiment which served in Australia between 1830 and 1836 can be found on a website of Australian colonial military history compiled by B. and M. Chapman and David Murphy, consulted by the author in 2005. See *Australia's Red Coat Settlers*, http://freepages.history.rootsweb.com.

81 SRNSW 4/2145 CSIL 32/4441, 32/4648.

82 Philip Hilton, 'Escape to Captivity', paper delivered at The Escape Conference, Strahan, Tasmania, June 2003. In the MS, footnote 42 on MS p. 14 gives 56 per cent as the number transported for desertion to Van Diemen's Land, based on Hilton's examination of AOTAS CON 31, CON 33 and CON 37.

83 The practice of branding deserters with the letter 'D', and 'BC' for bad character, was abolished in 1871. Vashti Farrer, 'Shot at Dawn . . . in the Public Interest', *Australian Financial Review*, 17 June 2005.

84 *Times*, 17 September 1847, p. 6.

85 *St Vincent* documents; *Lord Dalhousie* registers; prison registers at Portsmouth, Pentonville.

86 Charles Cozens, *Adventures of a Guardsman*, pp. 50, 63.

87 John Mitchel, *Jail Journal*, 1940 edition, cited in John Williams, *Ordered to the Island*: p. 55.

88 John Conway, TNAUK PCOM 2/110, Portsmouth Prison Register 1863.

89 Philip Hilton, email to the author, 26 May 2005, provides background on soldiers' marriages as well as the percentage who were married amongst the military convicts. He compares Robson's figure of 33 per cent for the whole of Britain with historian John Williams' figure of 24 per cent for Irish male convicts.

90 Richard Farrell: TNAUK PCOM 2/69 Pentonville Prison Register, 1860–62; names of wife and child in application for wives and families 1870, CO386/154, AJCP PRO Reel 987.

91 NAS AD 14/50/459, JC 26/938, JC 26/1850/586; *Glasgow Herald*, 28 February 1850; AOTAS *St Vincent* documents.

92 Jill Chambers, *Rebels of the Fields*. Chambers has published extensively and in detail on the Swing Riots.

93 Ibid.

94 Heights from *Sir William Bensley* indent op. cit.

95 A.J. Peacock, *Bread or Blood*, p. 63.

96 Ibid., p. 111.

97 A.J. Peacock is the expert on the Littleport bread riots and *Bread or Blood* is the landmark work on the subject. In addition, I have been fortunate to draw from the work of family historian Peter Curle, whose research has been published as *A Collection of Bits and Pieces on the Littleport and Ely Riots, 1816*. It includes personal details of the rioters which is not supplied elsewhere, plus the press coverage of the special commission established to try the Littleport rioters.

98 Curle, *Bits and Pieces*, p. 19; Peacock, *Bread or Blood*, p. 63.

99 Peacock, p. 12.

100 Gwyn A. Williams, *The Merthyr Rising*, p. 94.

101 Ibid., p. 88.

102 Ibid., Chapter 3.

103 Ibid., p. 90.

104 Ibid., p. 115.

105 Ibid., p. 117.

106 Ibid., pp. 120–21.

107 Ibid., p. 119.

108 Ibid., p. 116.

109 Ibid., p. 120.

110 Ibid., p. 176.

111 Figures for the number killed vary. These are taken from the *Times*, 20 July 1831.

112 Williams, *The Merthyr Rising*, p. 138.

113 Ibid.

114 Ibid., p. 124.

115 Ibid., p. 115.

116 Ibid., p. 159.

117 *Cambrian*, 2 July 1831, quoted in Williams, p. 159.

118 Williams, p. 165.

119 Ibid.

120 Ibid., pp. 165, 199.

121 Ibid., p. 193, quotes from Lewis Lewis as reported in the *Cambrian*, 20 August 1831.

122 Ibid., p. 114.

123 Ibid., p. 114, credits Eric J. Hobsbawm's *Bandits* (1969) with this telling phrase, which he says is 'classic' and 'familiar' in 'peasant' society. In the footnote, he compares Lewsyn to Zapata.

124 *John* indent.

125 Physical details from *St Vincent* documents.

126 Rudé, Chapter 2.

127 Robson, p. 56.

128 *Limerick Chronicle*, 18 July 1849, copy supplied by Nash descendant Dawn Nash Durbin.

129 Christopher O'Mahony (Director Limerick Regional Archives) and Valerie Thompson, (Sydney researcher), *Poverty to Promise: The Monteagle Emigrants, 1838–1858*, Crossing Press, Darlinghurst 1994, p. 6, for both direct quotes. Generally, the foregoing information is from the chapter entitled 'The Monteagle Background'.

130 *Limerick Chronicle*, 18 July 1849.

131 The *Limerick Chronicle* is the source of all details of the trial.

132 *Limerick Chronicle*, 18 July 1849.

133 Evidence of Laughlin Sharpe as reported in the *Limerick Chronicle*.

134 Monteagle to Lord Clarendon, 3 November 1848, quoted in O'Mahony and Thompson, *Poverty to Promise*, p. 5.

135 Cozens, *Adventures of a Guardsman*, p. 83.

136 Colin Arrott Browning was the surgeon concerned. He served on several voyages on convict transports and it was on the *Arab* in 1834 that he learned about the bribery of the hulk officers. Quoted in Charles Bateson, *The Convict Ships, 1787–1868*, p. 77.

137 Peter Cunningham, *Two Years in New South Wales*, p. 313.

138 Ibid., pp. 300–01.

139 L. Evans and P. Nicholls (eds), *Convicts and Colonial Society*, p. 168.

140 BPP, *Minutes of Evidence before the Select Committee on Transportation, 1837–38, Crime and Punishment*, Vol. III, p. 154.

141 Ibid., p. 156.

142 Ibid., p. 268.

143 Alexander Maconochie, *Report on the State of Prison Discipline in Van Diemen's Land*, quoted in C.M.H. Clark, *History of Australia*, Vol. III, p. 175, and in John West, *The History of Tasmania*, p. 464.

144 Cunningham, *Two Years in New South Wales*, p. 302.

CHAPTER 4 *A Convict Community*

1   Calculation based on Wray Vamplew, *Australian Historical Statistics*, pp. 104–05, and Carol Baxter (ed.), *General Muster of New South Wales 1814*, pp. xii–xiii.

2   William Bradley, *A Voyage to New South Wales, 1786–1792*, facsimile of the manuscript published by the Trustees of the Public Library of New South Wales in association with Ure Smith, Sydney 1969, p. 202; Watkin Tench, *A Complete Account of the Settlement at Port Jackson*, in *Watkin Tench 1788*, edited and introduced by Tim Flannery, Text, Melbourne 1996, p. 122.

3   Tench, *Watkin Tench 1788*, p.109; John Cobley, *Sydney Cove, 1795–1800*, Vol. 5, *The Second Governor*, Angus & Robertson, Sydney 1986, p. 34.

4   Cobley, *Sydney Cove*, p. 88.

5   These lines and more first appeared in *The History of New South Wales* by George Barrington, published in Britain in 1802. In 1852, the Reverend John West reproduced a much longer version in *The History of Tasmania*, pp. 369–70. In 1927, however, it was claimed that the author was 'a gentleman of Leicester' named Henry Carter (see note by A.G.L. Shaw in West's *History*, p. 647). The truth of the matter probably lies somewhere between the two, with Barrington or another convict speaking words to the effect quoted and Carter polishing the Prologue for publication.

6   Log of the *Sir William Bensley*, kept by Lieutenant Richard Bastard, ML FM4/2360.

7   Charles Bateson, *The Convict Ships, 1787–1868*. See in particular Chapter 9.

8   *Staffordshire Advertiser*, 6 January 1816; Stafford Calendar of Prisoners, Epiphany Sessions, 11 January 1816, William Salt Library, Stafford.

9   Detailed report of the case including transcripts of two letters written by Sorell in the *Times*, 7 July 1817.

10 Leonie Mickleborough, *William Sorell in Van Diemen's Land, 1817–24*. See Chapter 1 for details about Sorell and his relationships.

11 Bastard, *Sir William Bensley* log.

12 Bateson, *The Convict Ships*, pp. 207–08.

13 Information from Reeves descendant Lauris Crampton.

14 See Bateson for details of the *Friendship*; *Hobart Town Gazette*, 21 February 1818, for details of arrival of Mrs Brodribb and Mrs Wells; and Bateson, p. 382, for numbers on the *Friendship*. Comments about the free women on the *Friendship*, SRNSW 4/1740 Reel 6047 p. 65.

15 Mickleborough, *William Sorell*, pp. 11–16.

16 Macquarie to Bathurst, 4 April 1817, *HRA*, Series III, Vol. III, p. vii, cited in Mickleborough, *William Sorell*, p. 10.

17 Brodribb told Commissioner Bigge on 25 May 1820 that Macquarie promised him emancipation after he had been two years in the colony. *HRA*, Series III, Vol. III, p. 346.

18 *HRA*, Series III, Vol. III, p. 153, and Series III, Vol. IV, pp. 760–67.

19 William Thomas details collected in *Stapylton, With Major Mitchell's Australia Felix Expedition 1836*, ed. Alan E. J. Andrews, Blubber Head Press, Hobart 1986, pp. 238, 248.

20 1821 Petition of William Fisher, SRNSW 4/1862 Fiche 3207 p. 64; 1825 Muster records Frances and daughter Maria Fisher as coming free on the *Providence* in 1822. The 1828 Census also lists the family with the addition of another child. In the census, Maria is recorded as Born in the Colony.

21 Information supplied by descendants with NSWBDM registration numbers, including death of Thomas Plows, 3455/1860, St Peter's, Campbelltown.

22 Distribution of men from the *Sir William Bensley*, SRNSW 4/3496 Reel 6005 p. 79.

23 August 5, 12, 1822, SRNSW 4/1761 Reel 6055 pp. 94, 107.

24 August 9, 1822, SRNSW 4/3506 Reel 6009 p. 162.

25 September 30, 1822–September 30, 1823, Ashby on list of persons to whom convict mechanics have been assigned. SRNSW X53 Reel 3296 pp. 25, 39, 55, 70; *HRA*, Series III, Vol. III, pp. 233–34, Bell to Commissioner Bigge, 26 February 1820, and pp. 333–35. Read to Bigge 1820 cited in Mickleborough, p. 66.

26 Jill Roy with the assistance of fellow descendants Jan Irving, Janice Jackson, Shirley Stone and Michael Stone.

27 Diane Phillips, *An Eligible Situation*, particularly Chapters 2 and 3.

28 Mickleborough, p. 48.

29 Ibid., pp. 58–59.

30 Ibid., p. 157.

31 Extract from diary of the Reverend Robert Knopwood, 30 April 1817, supplied by a descendant.

32 Evidence of William Paterson to Commissioner Bigge, 30 March 1820, *HRA*, Series III, Vol. III, p. 841.

33 Irene Schaffer (ed.), *Land Musters, Stock Returns and Lists, Van Diemen's Land, 1803–1822*.

34 Ibid.

35 Death of Richard Butter [*sic*], 17 December 1827, age 51, Conditionally Free, Farmer, TASBDM 1624/1827 Rgd 34.

36 L.L. Robson, *A History of Tasmania*, pp. 217–18; Brodribb's participation in the 'Black Line' operation at p. 102 in Henry Melville, *The History of Van Diemen's Land*.

37 Lieutenant Archibald Bell, evidence to Commissioner Bigge, 27 November 1817, *The Evidence to the Bigge Reports*, Vol. 1, p. 88.

38 Gatehouse details in SR Archive Resources Index on CD-ROM published 2004.

39 *HRA*, Series III, Vol. III, p. 264.

40 Ibid., pp. 345–46.

41 *Hobart Town Gazette*, 9 January 1819.

42 *Hobart Town Gazette*, 23 January 1819.

43 *Hobart Town Gazette*, 9 December 1820.

44 *Hobart Town Gazette,* 11 January, 19 April, 8 February, 8, 15 March, 5 April, 1, 9, 12, 16, 19 April 1823.

45 *HRA*, Series III, Vol. III, pp. 257–59.

46 The dates of Brodribb's pardons are recorded in the entry for his son William Brodribb jnr in *ADB*, Vol. 3, MUP, Carlton 1969.

47 Richard Armstrong: AOTAS CON 31/1 p. 5, CON 13/1 p. 73; 1820 Convict Muster; Marriage TASBDM 677/1823 Rgd 36 and death of Sarah TASBDM 1016/1825 Rgd 34; Richard's death TASBDM 3571/1834 Rgd 34. Details on Sarah as a convict including the surgeon's comments from Philip Tardif, *Notorious Strumpets and Naughty Girls*, p. 277.

48 *Sir William Bensley* indent, SRNSW 4/4005 Reel 393; *Hobart Town Gazette*, 28 May 1818, 9 January 1819; AOTAS CON 31/45, CON 13/1 p. 245; and information supplied by descendant Carol Scott at website www.ballaratgenealogy.org.au/art/Yates.htm.

49 AOTAS CON 13/1 p. 73; conditional pardon dated 7 August 1821, SRNSW 4/4430 Reel 774, p. 156. No information has been discovered about what happened to Robert Groves after the early years. His conduct record notes that he received a 'Free pardon' No. 72, dated 4 June 1831, which presumably means an absolute pardon. This would allow him to return to England. He had been managing his widowed mother's farm in Berkeley at the time of his conviction. It is possible he returned home.

50 Long: AOTAS CON 31/27; further information supplied by Long descendant Linda Forbes, including that Mary Ann Fetters was the daughter of Jane Foreman.

51 Reeves ticket-of-leave, 17 July 1819. 1821 Muster records John Reeves renting a farm at Brown's River.

52 Roach: AOTAS CON 31/34; Court of Criminal Jurisdiction, SRNSW SZ781 and T1–15, *HRA*, Series III, Vol. IV, pp. 761–66; *Sir William Bensley* Punishment List 1817–21, ML AJCP HO 10/43 PRO Reel 77.

53 Penny: ticket-of-leave, 16 January 1818; 1820 Convict Muster; *Sir William Bensley* Punishment List, 1817–1821, ML AJCP HO 10/43 PRO Reel 77. Collins: SRNSW Petitions 1820 Fiche 3204.

54   John Burley's death recorded on his conduct record. AOTAS CON 31/1.

55   Sorell to Cimitiere, 25 March 1820, *HRA*, Series III, Vol. III, p. 95.

56   Sorell to Macquarie, 16 May, 1 July 1817, *HRA*, Series III, Vol. III, pp. 236, 264.

57   Joseph Easey research supplied by Peter Curle, *A Collection of Bits and Pieces on the Little-port and Ely Riots, 1816.*

58   Francis Bodenham: AOTAS CON 31/1, CON 13/1 p. 73; *Hobart Town Gazette*, 13 January, 18 July, 3 October 1818; *Sir William Bensley* Punishment List, 1817–21, AJCP PRO Reel 77, HO 10/43; *HRA*, Series III, Vol. IV, p. 57, regarding sailing on brig *Jupiter* for trial in Sydney; SRNSW Court of Criminal Jurisdiction X820 Reel 6023 p. 59; marriage to Sarah Franks 22 March 1819, TASBDM 319/1819. Sarah Franks: AOTAS CON 40/3 p. 1, CON 13/1 p. 14; Tardif, *Notorious Strumpets*, p. 306.

59   Major G. Druitt, Chief Engineer to Commissioner Bigge, 27 October 1819, in *The Evidence to the Bigge Reports*, Vol. 1, p. 7; *Sydney Gazette*, 18 November 1820.

60   *Evidence to the Bigge Reports*, Vol. 1, p. 39.

61   Jill Roy and her associates discovered correspondence about Honeyman in India at the British Library as follows: Z/P/186 Index to the Judicial Consultations; Correspondence Calcutta, P/134/53 and P/134/54, Marine Board Letter dated 15 June 1821, Calcutta, Letters dated 31 May, 1, 9, 15, 16, 21, 22 June 1821; Madras Public Proceedings Index A/P/2487, Marine Board letters dated 28 April, 1 May 1821 and Police letters dated 3 March, 13 March 1821.

62   Burns on the *Frederick*: *Hobart Town Gazette*, 14 February 1818; Jenkins and Baker: *Hobart Town Gazette*, 10 January 1818.

63   Thomas Harlow escape: *Hobart Town Gazette*, February 1818; seen hiding in the bush November 1819: *HRA*, Series III, Vol. III, pp. 731–32; *Sir William Bensley* Punishment List 1817–21, ML AJCP HO 10/43 PRO Reel 77; February 1820 picked up on the road, sentenced to two years in Newcastle, *HRA*, Series III, Vol. III, p. 82. Valentine Wood absconded: *Hobart Town Gazette*, 3 April 1818; Sorell's opinion, *HRA*, Series III, Vol. II, 8 August 1818, p. 479.

64   *Hobart Town Gazette*, 4, 11, 18 April 1818.

65   *Hobart Town Gazette*, 2, 9, 16, 23 May 1818.

66   SRNSW 4/3498 Reel 6006 p. 274.

67   The first significant examination of escapes was by Warwick Hirst, *Great Convict Escapes in Colonial Australia.*

68   SRNSW 4/1749 Reel 6051 p. 254.

69   William Honeyman's story was uncovered by Jill Roy, Dip. FHS (member), with the help of Jan Irving, Janice Jackson, Shirley Stone and Richard Stone. Much of it was published by Jill Roy in 'The Story of William Honeyman, 1792–1821'.

CHAPTER 5 *Outward Bound*

1   Wray Vamplew (ed.), *Australians: Historical Statistics*, p. 104.

2   John Molony, *The Native Born*, p. 24.

3   Hamish Maxwell-Stewart, 'The Search for the Convict Voice', p. 82.

4   J.D. Lang, *An Historical and Statistical Account of New South Wales*, 3rd edition, London 1852, Vol. I, p. 137.

5   Author anonymous, cited by F.G. Clarke, *The Land of Contrarieties*, pp. 155–56.

6   John Spurway, 'The Growth of Family History in Australia'.

7   For comments from convicts see Babette Smith, *A Cargo of Women*, p. 173.

8   John Lang, *Reminiscences of My Life and Times*, D.W.A. Baker (ed.), William Heinemann Australia, Melbourne 1972, p. 114.

9   John Hood, *Australia and the East* [1843], in Russel Ward, *The Australian Legend*, p. 61.

10   Ward, *The Australian Legend*, p. 129.

11   See Max Waugh, *Forgotten Hero*. Figures for convict population are on p. 52.

12   Surgeon's journal, TNAUK ADM 101/37, AJCP PRO Reel GETNO.

13   For a comprehensive examination of convict transports see Charles Bateson, *The Convict Ships, 1787–1868*.

14   The Northern Road ran 169 miles from Castle Hill to Windsor via Wiseman's Ferry, Wollombi and Patricks Plains. Building started in 1826 and was completed in 1831. At times gangs of 300 convicts were employed on the road. Frank Crowley, *A Documentary History of Australia*, Vol. 1, pp. 423–24.

15   Figures taken from Vamplew, *Australian Historical Statistics*, p. 4.

16   Joseph Williams: Hobart sentence, AOTAS CON 31/45; various records of transport to Newcastle, SRNSW 4/3504 pp. 7, 10, 35, 4/3504A, pp. 196, 257; assignment to Robert Howe, SRNSW 4/1811 pp. 180–2, 188, 4/1718 p. 193, 4/1875 p. 243, 4/3512 p. 681; 1825 Muster, 'government servant to Robert Howe'; 1837 Muster, 'with George Williams'; children, Elizabeth NSWBDM V1838356 22/1838, Emma NSWBDM V184014 24A/1840. George Williams printer of the *Australian*: R.B. Walker, *The Newspaper Press of New South Wales 1803–1920*, Sydney University Press, Sydney 1976, p. 6.

17   Robert Dye: AOTAS CON 31/9, CON 13/1 p. 74; James Jenkins: AOTAS CON 31/23 p. 3, CON 13/1 p. 73; marriage, occupation and death on NSWBDM 004049/1867.

18   Sentence for receiving in Court of Criminal Jurisdiction, SRNSW X820 Reel 6023 p. 59; gaoler at Port Macquarie referred to in SRNSW 4/1817 p. 54 and 4/1816 pp. 487–88 on Reel 6069.

19   SRNSW 4/1817 p. 54.

20   'Letters to Sheriff' re Bodenham as turnkey at Penrith, Letter 30/198 dated 6 October 1830, SRNSW 4/3896 Reel 1062 p. 456, and Letter 30/265 dated 17 December 1830 at p. 520.

21   Certificate of freedom, 29 July 1861, SRNSW 4/4299 Reel 985.

22   Smith, *Cargo of Women*, pp. 39–40.

23   Ibid. for the full story of Susannah Watson.

24   *Edinburgh Review*, 1819, in Crowley, *Documentary History*, Vol. 1, pp. 251–22; William Panton letter in the author's possession; J.D. Lang in Crowley, Vol. 1, pp. 422–23.

25   All 1832 assignments from the *John* in *NSWGG*, 1832, pp. 259–64, 309–14, referred to hereafter as *John* 1832 Assignment Lists; Thomas Bottoms, alias Swain, 1837 Muster 'with Samuel Terry, Bathurst'.

26   Isaac Fisher and William Taylor: *NSWGG*, 30 June 1832.

27   Molony, *The Native Born*, p. 48.

28   *The Uncensored Story of Martin Cash (Australian Bushranger) as told to James Lester Burke*. Transcription of the original manuscript in AOTAS.

29   Joseph Laycock: SRNSW ticket-of-leave 40/2352 Port Stephens, ticket-of-leave passport 42/0177, ticket-of-leave 45/2067 Port Stephens; Death NSWBDM V1848991 33B/1848.

30   CSIL Mineral Survey Department 1832–37, SRNSW 4/2193.2, 4/2341.1, 4/2264.2, 4/2301.1, 4/2382.2

31   *John* indent, SRNSW 4/4017 Reel 905.

32   *John* 1832 Assignment Lists.

33   Scone Bench Book, 3 April 1833, SRNSW 7/90 Reel 677.

34   Patricks Plains Bench Book, 5 November 1835, SRNS, 4/7685 Reel 679; 1837 Muster; *John* 1832 Assignment Lists; *John* indent.

35   1828 Census.

36   Return relating to iron gangs and road parties, 1836–41, SRNSW 4/6271 Reel 708.

37   Richard Nichols: *NSWGG*, June 1832; SRNSW ticket-of-leave 43/1657 dated 30 June 1843; details of marriage, children, son James' career, Richard's death in 1882 supplied by descendant Bronwyn Howell.

38   *John* indent; www.oldbaileyonline.org, Henry Alphan 8 September 1831, t18310908-3, consulted 16 November 2006; SRNSW ticket-of-leave 40/2139 and ticket-of-leave passport 42/303 dated 28 February 1842.

39   Cited by Ward, *Australian Legend,* p. 82. Leslie originally quoted by H.S. Russell, *The Genesis of Queensland*, Sydney 1888, p. 166.

40   Appendix to the Bigge Report reproduced in L. Evans and P. Nicholls (eds), *Convicts and Colonial Society, 1788–1868*, p. 31.

41   *The Uncensored Story of Martin Cash*, p. 8.

42   Ibid., p. 7.

43   Ibid., pp. 9–10.

44   Ibid., p. 11.

45   Ibid., p. 15.

46   Ibid., p. 29.

47   Ibid., p. 12.

48   Lewis Lewis (aka Lewsyn yr Heliwr): *NSWGG*, June 1832; SRNSW ticket-of-leave 40/2245 dated 8 October 1840 and ticket-of-leave passport 46/583 dated 10 June 1846. Note regarding death is recorded on the passport; conditional pardon No. 48/320 dated 31 December 1847, SRNSW 4/4455 Reel 785 pp. 243–44; application to bring out family, SRNSW 4/2550.1; two petitions dated 6 January 1841 and 1 September 1841, CSIL 41/4590, 41/6299 and AJCP CO201/311 pp. 226–241 Despatch 180, 19 September 1841. I am indebted to Perry McIntyre for the discovery of this and the other applications for families, which she had extracted for her own research.

49   Alan Atkinson, 'Four Patterns of Convict Protest', pp. 29–51.

50   Information from descendants Ken Vaughan and Kathy Wright.

51   1837 Muster; application to bring out family, SRNSW CSIL 39/13607, CSIL 39/13608 4/2550.1; AJCP, CO201/296 pp. 94–96 Despatch 18 dated 11 February 1840; SRNSW ticket-of-leave 41/0032, 40/1679; SRNSW 44242, ticket-of-leave passport 41/474; conditional pardon (second class) dated 7 February 1846 listed in *NSWGG*, 1846, p. 197; NSWBDM birth of Charlotte V1846 2096 32A/1846 and death of Harriet Hughes at Shellharbour, Albion Park, 457/1899.

52   Tom Vaughan: SRNSW ticket-of-leave 40/1736 dated 13 August 1835 and conditional pardon approved September 1847 but issued in 1849 No. 49/326; NSWBDM marriage of Thomas Vaughan and Mary Ann Croker No. 378, Vol. 27C; detailed information supplied by descendant Ken Vaughan, some of it drawn from the memoirs of pastoralist James Ritchie which were published by Jeanne Willis in the *Goulburn Evening Post*, 1976.

53   *Maitland Mercury*, 9, 13 September 1848.

54   Men in irons from Norfolk Island, SRNSW 4/6271 Reel 708.

55   Isaac Fisher: *NSWGG*, June 1832, assigned to Robert Cooper; *NSWGG*, 30 April 1845, p. 457; marriage, NSWBDM V185282 980/1852; death of Sarah, NSWBDM 18531519 39B/1853 at Goulburn; children with Elizabeth, NSWBDM 1854–60 Martha, Isaac, John, Nathaniel, Eliza at Goulburn; death NSWBDM 5809/1887 age 85 years at Argyle.

56   Ticket-of-leave passport 41/328 dated 5 August 1841, SRNSW 4/4242; ticket-of-leave number noted on the passport as 40/1767.

57   *NSWGG*, June and July 1832, for assignments on arrival; Francis ticket-of-leave, 40/1767 SRNSW 4/4142 Reel 937 and Abraham 43/4180 SRNSW 4/4180 Reel 950; 1837 for both men at Raymond Terrace; Francis death, NSWBDM 3177/1859, Abraham marriage V1853 2436 73C/1853 and death 3636/1871.

58   James Wilde, information supplied by descendants Bernard Chapman and Margaret Grant, including letter from Henry O'Brien to Colonial Secretary dated 12 September 1837, newspaper report of the Parramatta Quarter Sessions dated 14 August 1849, death certificate 05476 1866. Author's research. Case papers in trial of James Wild [*sic*] and Thomas Haw at Lincolnshire, Parts of Lindsey, Quarter Sessions 21 October 1831, Lincolnshire County Record Office LQS A/9/3, LQS A/1/537/1–5, 163, 176, 182, 212; TNAUK HO/17 51/1 Hq38; *John* indent; 1837 Muster; *NSWGG*, June 1832, 21 January 1835, 10 December 1839.

59   Theo Barker, *A History of Bathurst*, pp. 101–02.

60 *John* indent.

61 The Carters' Barracks file 1833–34 at SRNSW 4/2223 Reel 600 contains the authorities' calculations of boys arriving including: 40 on the *Heroine*, 70 on the *Lord Lyndoch*, three 11-year-olds and two 12-year-olds on the *Dunvegan Castle*.

62 The Female Orphan School still exists, standing beside the river on the campus of the University of Western Sydney.

63 Barker, *History of Bathurst*, pp. 61–62.

64 Ibid., pp. 95–96, citing ML Returns of the Colony 1833, 1834 and 1835; SRNSW Map 1374, *Sketch of the Allotments for small settlers and others into which it is proposed to divide part of the Government Reserve at Bathurst 20 June 1830*.

65 Superintendent of Carters' Barracks to Colonial Secretary, 11 June 1833, SRNSW CSIL from Carters' Barracks 4/2223 Reel 600.

66 Carter's Barracks Weekly Return of Punishments, October–December 1832, SRNSW 2/8313 Reel 2652.

67 Carters' Barracks, lists of boys 1833, SRNSW 4/2223 Reel 600.

68 *NSWGG*, 6 February 1844, 4 April 1845, 5 May 1846, 14 July 1846, 20 June 1848, 27 July 1849, 31 December 1849.

69 Patricks Plains Bench Books 1835 p. 27, SRNSW 4/7685 Reel 679.

70 Robert Howcroft per ship *Lord Lyndock*; George Allen, diaries 1830–51, ML MSS477 boxes 3 and 4—diary entries 1 February, 8 February, 24 March 1835. Entry for 14 February 1836 cited in Barrie Dyster, *Servant and Master*, p. 66.

71 'Extract from a letter from a settler' in Judith Johnson and Monica Anderson, *Australia Imagined*, p. 133.

72 A.G.L. Shaw, *Convicts and the Colonies*, p. 246.

73 Ibid., p. 247.

74 G.F. Davidson, *Trade and Travel in the Far East; or Recollections of Twenty-One Years passed in Java, Singapore, Australia and China*, 1846, in Crowley, Vol. 1, p. 532.

75 John Hirst, *Convict Society and its Enemies*, pp. 68–69.

76 David Kent and Norma Townsend, *The Convicts of the Eleanor*; Brian Walsh, 'Assigned Convicts at Tocal: "Ne'er-Do-Wells" or Exceptional Workers?', pp. 67–90.

77 Hirst, *Convict Society and its Enemies*.

CHAPTER 6 *The Bathurst Road*

1 SRNSW 9/6312, Clerk of the Peace; Supreme Court depositions 1838, Bathurst.

2 Ibid.

3 Philip Hilton has reached this conclusion. See 'Escape to Captivity', paper delivered at The Escape Conference, Strahan, Tasmania, June 2003. Hilton's finding is supported by the sample for this book.

4 Punishments etc. constructed from a mixture of *NSWGG*, 1832, 1833, 1834, 1836 and 1838; and Quigley's conduct record in Tasmania, AOTAS CON 33/68 p. 17020.

5 Peter Chinn, *The Thin Red and Blue Lines*, p. 23. Whether this stockade was called 18 Mile Hollow or 20 Mile Hollow has been a matter of some debate. In the records I consulted it was always 20 Mile Hollow.

6 Ibid., p. 29, in particular the detailed extract from the *Saturday Magazine*, November 1836. A Dr Reid from the 88th Regiment was a surgeon at No. 2 Stockade for some time in the 1830s. He testified in several Supreme Court cases during this period.

7 Ibid., p. 27, for the numbers at Mount Victoria and opening of No. 2 Stockade Cox's River.

8 Thomas Cook, *The Exile's Lamentations or Biographical Sketch of Thomas Cook*.

9 Peter MacFie, 'Dobbers and Cobbers'.

10 Sue Rosen, *Men at Work*, p. 200.

11 Ibid., pp. 201–3.

12 Cook, *The Exile's Lamentations*, p. 30.

13 The 17th Regiment of Foot arrived in New South Wales in 1830 and continued there until March 1836 when it left for India. David Murphy, letter reproduced in *The Push from the Bush*, pp. 85–86.

14 AOTAS CON 33/68 p. 17020.

15 Stacey's record compiled from *NSWGG*, 1833, pp. 167, 189, 247, 478; AOTAS CON 37/4 p. 1358.

16 *Sydney Gazette*, 22 February 1834; Stacey's Van Diemen's Land conduct record, AOTAS CON 37/4.

17 Details of the *Phoenix* wreck on Sow and Pigs Reef and subsequent purchase by Governor Brisbane in ML A1559–62 p. 124 and SRNSW 4/7025 pp. 24–25; details of its closure as a prison in 1838 in SRNSW CSIL 28/2513 and enclosures in 4/2428 Reel 2425.

18 Details of the escape plan in SRNSW 4/2231 CSIL Letter 34/6484 and accompanying report and Stacey depositions.

19 Superintendent of Carters' Barracks to Colonial Secretary, 11 June 1833, SRNSW CSIL 4/2223 Reel 600.

20 W.W. Burton, Notes on Criminal Cases, Supreme Court of New South Wales, February 1834, SRNSW 2/2412 pp. 181–98.

21 Macquarie University website, www.law.mq.edu.au/scnsw/, *Decisions of the Superior Courts of New South Wales, 1788–1899*, published by the Division of Law, Macquarie University.

22 Samuel's record reconstructed from the *NSWGG*; certificate of freedom 46/0009, SRNSW 4/4402 Reel 1021.

23 George Rowney death, NSWBDM 9935/1888.

24 This reconstruction of Crooks' record is a blend of entries in the *NSWGG*, 1832, p. 260, and 1835, pp. 89, 487, plus a list of his punishments noted by the Superintendent of Convicts on his petition dated 27 April 1846, SRNSW 4/2736.2 Reel 2266.

25 SRNSW COD 207, 'Report Relative to the Road to Bathurst', Sir Thomas Mitchell, Bathurst, 21 October 1833.

26 *Sydney Herald*, 4 February 1836.

27 *Sydney Gazette*, 4, 6 February 1836; *Australian*, 23 February 1836.

28 Wheeler's record reconstructed from *NSWGG*, 1833, 1834 and 1835; SRNSW 4/8390 Reel 2401, Clerk of the Peace Quarter Sessions depositions Campbelltown No. 10 p. 401; SRNSW 4/5673, 4/5626 Reel 672, Cawdor and Stonequarry Bench Book July 1834, 16, 22 June, 20 July 1835; SRNSW Supreme Court Papers and Informations 1835, T164.

29 Wheeler's petition dated 12 May 1846, SRNSW CSIL 46/3739 with 46/3799 in 4/2736.2 Reel 2266.

30 Ibid.

31 Wheeler marriage, NSWBDM V1847361 32C/1847; death, NSWBDM 3669 1870.

32 Invermein Bench Book, 30 October 1833, SRNSW 7/90 and 4/7533 Reel 677. *John's* indent records the 200 lashes.

33 Invermein Bench Book, 26 November 1833.

34 Ibid.

35 *Sydney Herald*, 20 February 1834.

36 *Australian*, 17 February 1834.

37 *Australian*, 28 February 1834.

38 *Sydney Gazette*, 15 February 1834.

39 *Monitor*, 14 February 1834.

40 *Monitor*, 28 February 1834.

41 Ibid.

42 *Monitor*, 11 March 1834.

43 *Australian*, 18 May 1838; *Sydney Herald*, 24 May 1838.

44 Quigley's conduct record, AOTAS CON 33/68 p. 17020.

45 Petition to Sir George Grey, Secretary of State for the Colonies.

46 TNAUK HO10/4 AJCP Reel 77, Convicts from Norfolk Island to Van Diemen's Land.

47 Quigley: indent of the *Governor Phillip*, 1 November 1845, AOTAS CON 16/3 p. 188.

48 Conduct record, AOTAS CON 33/68 p. 17020; *Sydney Morning Herald*, 6 August 1845 for verdict relating to armed robbery.

49 Stacey's conduct record on Norfolk Island can be found in AOTAS CON 37/4 p. 1358.

50 *Monitor*, 11 March 1834.

51 *The Uncensored Story of Martin Cash*, p. 8.

52 Letter from a convict in Perth to his brother in England, *Cornhill Magazine*, April 1866, in Frank Crowley, *A Documentary History of Australia*, Vol. 2, pp. 84–85.

53 Norma Townsend, 'A "Mere Lottery"', p. 73.

54 A.G.L. Shaw, *Convicts and the Colonies*, p. 216.

55 Stephen Nicholas and Peter R. Shergold, 'Convicts as Workers', in Stephen Nicholas (ed.), *Convict Workers*, pp. 11, 180–83, 195; John Hirst, *Convict Society and its Enemies*, pp. 57–69.

56 Raymond Evans and William Thorpe, 'Power, Punishment and Penal Labour: Convict Workers and Moreton Bay', pp. 96–99.

57 Hamish Maxwell-Stewart, 'Convict Workers, Penal Labour and Sarah Island', p. 143.

58 Ullathorne's ordination and despatch for New South Wales in Frank Clune, *Norfolk Island*, p. 144.

59 Frances O'Donoghue, 'The Vicar-General and Norfolk Island', pp. 60–61.

60 J.B. Polding, *The Letters of John Bede Polding OSB*, p. 105.

CHAPTER 7 *An Unclean Thing*

1 Alison Adburgham, *A Radical Aristocrat*, O'Connor's diary note at p. 1.

2 Ibid., p. 151.

3 Ibid., p. 28.

4 John Ritchie, 'Towards Ending an Unclean Thing', pp. 144–64.

5 John Hirst, *Convict Society and its Enemies*, p. 24.

6 C.M.H. Clark, *A History of Australia*, Vol. II, p. 321.

7 Ibid., p. 336.

8 Ibid., pp. 334–35.

9 *Times*, 26 September 1837, extract in Frank Crowley, *A Documentary History of Australia*, Vol. 1, p. 529.

10 Jonathan King, *The Other Side of the Coin*, p. 14.

11 Hirst, *Convict Society*, p. 189.

12 King, *Other Side of the Coin*, p. 23.

13 Ibid., p. 22.

14 John Ritchie, *The Wentworths: Father and Son*, p. 180.

15 Ibid., pp. 177–78.

16 Judith Johnson and Monica Anderson, *Australia Imagined*, p. 35.

17 Crowley, *Documentary History*, Vol. 1, pp. 251–52.

18 *Edinburgh Review*, 1819, in Crowley, Vol. 1, p. 334.

19 Hirst, p. 10.

20 Ibid, Chapter 1 generally.

21 Eris O'Brien, *The Foundation of Australia, 1786–1800*, p. 340.

22 Hirst, p. 27.

23 Ibid., p. 17.

24 Quoted in G.D. Page, 'An Analysis and Exploration of the Varying Opinions, Between 1788 and 1960, on the Character of the Convicts Transported to the Eastern Australian Colonies', p. 26.

25 Ralph Clark, quoted in Anne Summers, *Damned Whores and God's Police*, Penguin, Melbourne 1975, p. 267.

26 Crowley, Vol. 1, p. 193.

27 Richie, *The Wentworths*, p. 171.

28 *Report from Select Committee on Secondary Punishment 1831–32*, in Norma Townsend, 'A "Mere Lottery"', p. 66.

29 BPP, 1836, Vol. XI, Paper No. 512, 27 June 1836, in Crowley, Vol. 1, p. 528.

30 *Report From the Select Committee of the House of Commons on Transportation; Together With a Letter From the Archbishop of Dublin on the Same Subject and Notes by Sir William Molesworth, Bart., Chairman of the Committee* [1838], Libraries Board of South Australia facsimile edition, Adelaide 1967.

31 L. Evans and P. Nicholls (eds), *Convicts and Colonial Society, 1788–1868*, p. 64.

32 *Times*, 25 December 1839 (written by Bourke in 26 December 1838).

33 Summary Jurisdiction Act, in Townsend, 'A "Mere Lottery"', p. 66.

34 *Report from the Select Committee on Transportation Together with the Minutes of Evidence, Appendix and Index, Ordered by the House of Commons to be Printed*, 3 August 1838, p. 11.

35 Ibid., p. xxii.

36 Evans and Nicholls, *Convicts and Colonial Society*, p. 65.

37 Townsend, p. 68.

38 Ibid.

39 Reverend Richard Johnson to Henry Rickes, Esq., 15 November 1788, in George Mackaness (ed.), *Some Letters of Rev. Richard Johnson etc.*, Mackaness, Sydney 1954, Pt. 1, p. 24.

40 Reverend William Henry to London Missionary Society, 29 August 1799, *Historical Records of New South Wales*, Vol. II, p. 715.

41 Evidence of the Reverend Robert Knopwood to Commissioner Bigge, in Evans and Nicholls, p. 41.

42 Hirst, p. 25.

43 *Report from the Select Committee on Transportation*, 1838; Richard Whateley, 'Substance of a Speech on Transportation Delivered in the House of Commons on 19 May 1840', quoted in Page, 'An Analysis and Exploration of the Varying Opinions …', p. 28.

44 BPP, *Select Committee on Transportation, 1837–38*, Appendix to Evidence, the Reverend H.T. Stiles, 'Observations on the State of Norfolk Island'.

45 A.G.L. Shaw, *Governor Sir George Arthur, Bart, 1784–1854*, pp. 66–67.

46 Father William Ullathorne to Dr Brown of Downside, 10 January 1838, in Frances O'Donoghue, 'The Vicar-General and Norfolk Island', p. 61.

47 Ibid.

48 Ullathorne, *The Catholic Mission in Australia*, extract in Crowley, Vol. 1, p. 530.

49 F.G. Clarke, *The Land of Contrarieties*.

50 M.G. Fawcett, *Life of the Right Hon. Sir William Molesworth Bart., M.P., F.R.S.*, 1901, cited by John Richie, 'Towards Ending an Unclean Thing', pp. 144–64.

51 Ibid., p. 150.

52 Ibid., pp. 144–64.

53 *Sydney Herald*, 9 November 1837.

54 Gipps to Glenelg, 18 July 1838, *HRA*, Series I, Vol. XIX, p. 504.

55 *Australian*, July 1838.

56 Gipps to Glenelg, 18 July 1838.

57 *Times*, 9 April 1839.

58 *Sydney Herald*, 28 May 1838, reported in Clark, *History of Australia*, Vol. II, p. 346.

59 O'Donoghue, 'The Vicar-General and Norfolk Island', p. 64.

60 W.B. Ullathorne, *Autobiography*, 1891, republished as *From Cabin-Boy to Archbishop*, 1941, quoted in O'Donoghue, p. 62.

61 Clark, Vol. II, p. 345.

62 Peter Chinn, *The Thin Red and Blue Lines*, p. 30.

63 Quarter Sessions, Sydney, 4 July 1836, Case No. 1, SRNSW 4/8468.

64 Shaw, *Convicts and the Colonies*, p. 303.

65 Clark, Vol. II, p. 345.

66 Ritchie, 'Towards Ending an Unclean Thing', pp. 144–64.

CHAPTER 8 *A Pervading Stain*

1 Henry Button, *Flotsam and Jetsam*, 1909, in Patricia Fitzgerald Ratcliff, *The Usefulness of John West*, p. 196.
2 Details of West's British missions in Ratcliff, *The Usefulness of John West*, particularly Chapters 8, 9 and 10.
3 Ibid., p. 165.
4 Ibid., pp. 165–66.
5 Ibid., p. 166.
6 Ibid., p. 161 and n. 14 p. 479.
7 *Colonial Times*, 6 July 1852, in ibid, p. 400.
8 Ratcliff claims that West's belief transportation to Van Diemen's Land was about to end was created by reading the 'first' Molesworth report, which she identifies as the one addressed to his constituents in Leeds and containing a letter from Archbishop Whateley (as opposed to the official printing in the BPP). However, this version was not published until October 1838, when West was about to sail. A.G.L. Shaw, *Convicts and the Colonies*, pp. 272–73.
9 Ratcliff, p. 170.
10 John Sibree, 'The Claims of British Colonies on the Aid of British Christians', 1838, cited by Ratcliff, p. 165.
11 W.B. Ullathorne, *The Catholic Mission in Australia*, 1837, in Frank Crowley, *A Documentary History of Australia*, Vol. I, p. 530.
12 Lloyd Robson, *A History of Tasmania*, Vol. I, p. 454.
13 Crowley, *A Documentary History of Australia*, Vol. 2, p. 43.
14 Stephen Judd and Kenneth Cable, *Sydney Anglicans*, pp. 26–27.
15 Ibid., p. 42.
16 Patricia Curthoys, 'State Support for Churches 1836–1860', p. 33.
17 Ibid., p. 31.
18 Ratcliff, p. 3.
19 Michael Roe, *The Quest for Authority in Eastern Australia, 1835–1851*, p. 15.
20 Alan Atkinson, *The Europeans in Australia: A History*, Vol. 2, p. 336.
21 Figures taken from the *Ross Almanack 1838*, cited by Ratcliff, p. 191.
22 Crowley, Vol. 2, p. 82.
23 Ibid., pp. 82–83.
24 John West, *The History of Tasmania*, pp. xii–xiii.
25 Ibid., p. 613.
26 Ratcliff, p. 400.
27 Ibid., p. 181.
28 Conclusion expressed by reviewer of Dr Lang's book in the *Times*, 26 September 1837, in Crowley, Vol. 1, pp. 528–29.
29 The phrase belongs to the Reverend W.T. Stiles, who accompanied Ullathorne to Norfolk Island, BPP, *Select Committee on Transportation, 1837–38*, Appendix 40, Vol. 3, p. 267.
30 *Launceston Examiner*, 8 May 1847.
31 Ian Brand, *The Convict Probation System*, Chapter 6.
32 *Cornwall Chronicle*, 21 November 1846.
33 Ibid.
34 The League was formalised in March 1849.
35 *Launceston Examiner*, 28 July 1847.
36 Lloyd Robson quoted in Anne McLaughlin, 'Against the League', p. 80.
37 *Launceston Examiner*, 21 April 1847.
38 *Reply to Thirty-Nine Reasons for the Continuance of Transportation as set forth by Mr Williamson* in *Launceston Examiner*, 1 May 1847, cited by C.M.H. Clark, *A History of Australia*, Vol. III, p. 424.
39 Ratcliff, p. 380.
40 Ibid., p. 337.

41   *Launceston Examiner*, 23 August 1848; Letter from Theodore Bartley, JP, Richard Dry, JP, and W.R. Pugh, JP, to Governor Denison 21 August 1848. Both sources cited in Catie Gilchrist, 'Space, Sexuality and Convict Resistance in Van Diemen's Land'.

42   Robson, *History of Tasmania*, p. 497 and p. 611 n. 34.

43   West's hopes to go to London in ibid., p. 497; Anne McLaughlin, 'Against the League', p. 88; Ratcliff, p. 380.

44   West, p. 233.

45   *Times*, 22 May 1851.

46   Correspondence between Denison and Grey, 13, 21, 23, 27 December 1850, in Shaw, *Convicts and the Colonies*, p. 322.

47   Dan Huon, 'The Origins of the Launceston Anti-Transportation Leagues 1847–1849', p. 115.

48   The *Hashemy* disembarked exiles in Sydney in June 1849. Victoria received four boatloads of exiles between 1847 and 1849, and Moreton Bay received one in 1849 and one in 1850. Details in Charles Bateson, *The Convict Ships, 1787–1868*, pp. 393–95.

49   Gregory Picker, 'A State of Infancy', pp. 226–41.

50   Michael Sturma, *Vice in a Vicious Society*, p. 53.

51   West, p. 230.

52   Ratcliff, pp. 547–48.

53   Robson, p. 498.

54   Ratcliff, pp. 547–48.

55   Crowley, Vol. 2, p. 228.

56   Shaw, Introduction to West, p. xvii.

57   Ibid., p. xvii.

58   West took certain memoranda about his early days in Launceston with him when he left the church years later, leaving a note to say he had them. The Reverend Charles Price had been the sole Congregational preacher before West arrived in Launceston and started a rival chapel. Price's Church Day Book, which might have revealed much about the acrimony that developed between West's group and Price's followers, also mysteriously vanished. It was returned anonymously to the Queen Victoria Museum in Launceston in the 1980s with the relevant pages torn out. Ratcliff, pp. 173, 215.

59   Denison to Deas Thomson, 24 March 1851, ML A1531–2, in Lloyd Robson, 'Review of A.G.L. Shaw', p. 111.

60   Robson, 'Review of A.G.L. Shaw', p. 111.

61   Shaw, Introduction to West, p. xi.

62   West, pp. 512–521.

63   Ibid., p. 226.

64   Shaw, Introduction to West, pp. xiv, xx.

65   Speech at Congregational Union Meeting, reported in the *Launceston Examiner*, 23 December 1843, quoted in Shaw, Introduction to West, p. xvi.

66   Richard Flanagan, *A Terrible Beauty*, quoted in McLaughlin, p. 77.

67   Huon, 'Origins', p. 107.

68   *Sydney Morning Herald*, 13 December 1873, quoted in Shaw, Introduction to West, p. xxi.

69   Reverend Philip Palmer to Secretary of State, 29 April 1846, AOTAS CO 280/203/549, in Ian Brand, *The Convict Probation System*, p. 37.

70   Wilmot to Stanley, 2 November, 2 December 1843, CO 289/2163, in Shaw, *Convicts and the Colonies*, p. 298.

71   BPP, Papers relating to Convict Discipline and Transportation, 1847, in L. Evans and P. Nicholls (eds), *Convicts and Colonial Society, 1788–1868*, p. 93.

72   Ibid.

73   Brand, *Convict Probation System*, p. 1.

74   Ibid., p. 147.

75   Ibid., pp. 147–48.

76 Ibid., p. 148.

77 Ibid., p. 149.

78 Ibid., p. 149.

79 Ibid., p. 154.

80 Ibid., p. 155.

81 Ibid., p. 152.

82 Ibid., p. 152.

83 Ibid., p. 156.

84 Ibid., p. 159.

85 Ibid., p. 160.

86 Ibid., p. 160.

87 James Hardy Vaux, *Memoirs*, 1819, in Evans and Nicholls, *Convicts and Colonial Society*, p. 164.

88 Thomas Cook, 'Lamentations of an Exile', unpublished manuscript, ML A1711.

89 *Sydney Morning Herald*, 15 September 1845; *Maitland Mercury*, 13 September 1845.

90 SRNSW CSIL 46/3980, CSIL 46/5843, 4/2736.2 Reel 2266.

91 For example, cases of 'unnatural crime' reported in Britain: Thomas Wood sentenced to two years at the Assizes, *Gloucester Journal*, 4 August 1831; Joseph Wheeler sentenced to twelve years for 'buggery with another man' at Winchester Assizes, 14 July 1862; Opening of Midland Circuit at Lincoln Calendar of cases for trial includes three for 'unnatural offences', *Times*, 6 December 1861; Inquiry into Unnatural Crime on the *Captivity* hulk at Portsmouth June 1811, AJCP ML M821.

92 Brand, pp. 114, 129.

93 Mr Park to Dr Robertson, Oatlands, 4 March 1846, Inclosure 21 in No. 9, Despatch 54, cited in Gilchrist, 'Space, Sexuality and Convict Resistance in Van Diemen's Land'.

94 Robert Pringle Stewart at Norfolk Island, 1846, 'on the doors being opened, men were scrambling into their own beds from others, in a hurried manner', in ibid.

95 Mr E.S. Hall to Dr Robertson, 23 February 1846, Inclosure 12 in No. 9, Despatch 54, Sir John Eardley-Wilmot to Lord Stanley, 17 March 1846, BPP, *Crime and Punishment Transportation, 1843–47, Vol. 7,* in ibid.

96 Henry Phibbs Fry, *A System of Penal Discipline*, in ibid.

97 Crowley, Vol. 2, p. 22.

98 *Launceston Examiner*, 5 May 1847, written by 'Christianos' and addressed 'To the Freemen of Tasmania'.

99 J. Syme, *Nine Years in Van Diemen's Land, Comprising an Account of its Discovery, Possession, Settlement, Progress, Population, Value of Land, Herds, Flocks etc.; An Essay on Prison Discipline; and the Results of the Working of the Probation system; with Anecdotes of Bushrangers*, 1848, reproduced in Crowley Vol. 2, pp. 122–23.

100 William Penny: 1819 List 9:2, Irene Schaffer (ed.), *Land Musters, Stock Returns and Lists, Van Diemen's Land, 1803–1822*; conduct record, AOTAS CON 31/34 p. 5, CON 13/1 p. 73; 1820 and 1821 Musters; Sir William Bensley Punishment List, HO 10/46 PRO Reel 77; TASBDM Marriage Rgd 36 427/1820, Death Rgd 35 442/1860.

101 AJCP TNAUK HO 10/43 Reels 77–78, Tasmanian Musters 1817–21 and *Sir William Bensley Punishment List*. Information about the move of Thomas Reeves to South Australia provided by descendant Lauris Crampton.

102 Long's death 17 December 1853. Information supplied by descendant Linda Forbes.

103 AOTAS CON 35/1 p. 97, CON 31/6 p. 131 and CON 13/1 p. 74, all as James Clephane; *Sir William Bensley* Punishment List 1817–21, listed as Henry, ML AJCP HO 10/43 Reel 77; 1824 Muster Van Diemen's Land listed as James Clephane 'Missing' ML AJCP HO 10/46 PRO Reel 78.

104 Andrew Clephane to New South Wales Colonial Secretary, September–October 1832, enclosing certificate from John Payne, master of the brig *Nereus*, that Charles Clephane had asked him to support the application and offering to transport Andrew Clephane to Van Diemen's Land. SRNSW 4/3506 Reel 6009 p. 325.

105 AOTAS CON 35/1.

106 AOTAS SC 41/1, Supreme Court Record Book of Persons Tried in Criminal Cases, 1824–31. Note on conduct record says, 'Pardoned by Colonial Secretary', letter 20 February 1829, 4488/29.

107 Marriage: 1940/1832 Rgd 36; Birth of William 1835, Andrew b. 1833 in Tasmanian Pioneers Index; Death of Charles Clephane, 17 March 1852, at Launceston, age 57, 543/1852 Rgd 35.

108 Conditional pardon No. 85, 24 February 1832, noted on conduct record, AOTAS CON 31/1 p. 149.

109 AOTAS CON 31/1 p. 149.

110 Correspondence and documents in the possession of the Barrett family. This and other research into the life of Joseph Barrett was carried out by descendants Pauline Connell née Barrett, Gayle Proctor and Grant Barrett.

111 Mary Dodd per *Sir Charles Forbes*, AOTAS CON 40/3, MM 33/1; TASBDM marriage of Joseph Barrett and Mary Dodd, 24 March 1831, 1654/1831 Rgd 36.

112 AOTAS CON 40/3, MM 33/1.

113 Shropshire Archives, Quarter Sessions Records, QR 355/153, QR 355/3. Research by Barrett descendants.

114 *Shrewsbury Chronicle*, 6 January 1837.

115 Conduct record for Mary Barrett per *Platina*, AOTAS CON 40/2, CON 18/25.

116 Ibid. The discovery of Mary's return to England and her subsequent re-transportation is entirely the work of Barrett descendants.

117 Obituary of Abraham Barrett, *Launceston Examiner*, 27 October 1899.

118 Extract from Stefan Petrow, 'Going to the Mechanics', 1998, p. 145, supplied by Pauline Connell.

119 Family information supplied by Barrett descendant Pauline Connell; Joseph Barrett, Gentleman, died 28 March 1865 at Launceston, TASBDM 835/1865 Rgd 35.

120 M.M.H. Thompson, *The First Election*.

121 Sturma, p. 53, for details of *Peoples' Advocate* change of mind.

122 Clark, Vol. III, p. 452; West, p. 239, for Wentworth's change of mind.

123 Evans and Nicholls, p. 122.

124 John Manning Ward, *James Macarthur, Colonial Conservative, 1798–1867*, p. 157.

125 Grey to Fitzroy, 3 September 1848, in *Sydney Morning Herald*, 22, 26, 27, p. 157.

126 G.C. Mundy, *Our Antipodes*, 1852, in Crowley, Vol. 2, p. 154.

127 Ward, 159–60.

128 *Sydney Morning Herald*, 12 June 1849, in Frank Crowley, Vol. 2, pp. 154–55. Lowe's speech has been converted to first person to increase its impact.

129 McLaughlin, 'Against the League', p. 111; *Hobarton Guardian*, undated, cited by Anne McLaughlin, p. 84, as located at GO 33/77 p. 955.

130 BPP, 1850, in Crowley, Vol. 2, pp. 173–75.

CHAPTER 9 *Best Forgotten*

1 Pamela Statham, 'Swan River Colony, 1829–1850', in C.T. Stannage, *A New History of Western Australia*, p. 181.

2 L. Evans and P. Nicholls, *Convicts and Colonial Society, 1788–1868*, pp. 216–25.

3 For comprehensive details of the Parkhurst juvenile convicts see Andrew Gill, *Forced Labour for the West* and *Convict Assignment in Western Australia, 1842–1851*.

4 Charles Bateson, *The Convict Ships, 1787–1868*, pp. 374–76.

5 Petition from Delegates of the Eastern Colonies on the Subject of Transportation 1863, enclosure in Sir John Young Governor of New South Wales to Duke of Newcastle, 21 April 1863, in Evans and Nicholls, *Convicts and Colonial Society*, pp. 265–66.

6 BPP, *Select Committee on Transportation*, Minutes of Evidence, 1861.

7 Ibid.

8   John West, *The History of Tasmania*, p. 518.

9   C.M.H. Clark, *A History of Australia*, Vol. III, p. 421.

10 Toni Johnson Woods, 'Virtual Reality', in Ian Duffield and James Bradley (eds), *Representing Convicts*, p. 47; Lauchlan McKinnon details at www.adb.online.anu.edu.au, consulted January 2007.

11 For the decision, *Times*, 10 June 1861. For the evidence, BPP, *Select Committee on Transportation*, Minutes of Evidence, 1861.

12 A. McArthur, 'Three Letters to the Editor of the Daily News', 1864, in Evans and Nicholls, pp. 266–67.

13 H. Willoughby, *Transportation: The British Convict in Western Australia*, 1865, in Frank Crowley, *A Documentary History of Australia*, Vol. 2, pp. 494–95.

14 H. Grellet, *The Case of England and Western Australia in Relation to Transportation*, 1864, in Evans and Nicholls, pp. 267–68.

15 Ibid., p. 267.

16 Anthony Trollope, *Australia*, Vol. 2, pp. 195–96.

17 See for examples Evans and Nicholls, pp. 259–63.

18 Duke of Newcastle to Governor Fitzgerald, in Evans and Nicholls, p. 242. See also 'A Statement of Settlers' Grievances, 1855', pp. 243–44.

19 Rica Erickson, *The Bride Ships*, pp. 12–13.

20 Bateson, *The Convict Ships*, pp. 374–75, 396, 297.

21 WA Criminal Registers; Rica Erickson and Gillian O'Mara, *Dictionary of Western Australians*.

22 For further details see F.H. Broomhall, *The Veterans*.

23 Trollope, *Australia*, Vol. 2, pp. 179–180.

24 Thomas Tomlinson, AJCP ML, Central Criminal Court, 13 May 1862, Seventh Session, 1861–62, p. 14; SROWA Acc. 128 Criminal Registers for the *Lord Dalhousie* Prisoner 7565; Erickson and O'Mara, *Dictionary of Western Australians*; Convict Ticket-of-leave Register Toodyay, SROWA, ACC.721/3, digitisation WAGS, 2004; WABDM marriage 4093/1876; four children at York, 1876–81; death of Sarah Ann Tomlinson, 10975/1881 and death of Thomas Tomlinson, age 50, 436/1891.

25 Josiah Brown convictions in Bedford Gaol Register, Bedfordshire, and Luton Archives and Records Service, online database at http://apps.bedofrdshire.gov.uk, consulted 23 June 2006.

26 J.F. Mortlock, *Experiences of a Convict*, p. 76; William Gates, one of the American 'patriots' who was transported to Van Diemen's Land, also noted that flogging was preferred to solitary confinement: 'this sort of punishment [solitary confinement] is considered the hardest that can be inflicted, and they had far rather take the quota of lashes from the cat, than the week in solitary'. Quoted in Cassandra Pybus and Hamish Maxwell-Stewart, *American Citizens, British Slaves: Yankee Political Prisoners in an Australian Penal Colony, 1839–1850*, p. 115.

27 Charles Campbell, *The Intolerable Hulks*, pp. 105–09.

28 Alexandra Hasluck, *Royal Engineer*, p. 54.

29 Ibid., p. 60.

30 Thomas Gorman: Central Criminal Court, London, 16 September 1857, Eleventh Session 1856–57, AJCP ML; *Dalhousie* registers SROWA Acc. 128/Reg. 32, 43 and SROWA Acc. 1156/Reg. 29.

31 Ticket-of-leave information from Erickson and O'Mara.

32 Hampton to Newcastle, 19 February 1863, BPP, 1863, vol. XXXIX [3224], pp. 24–25.

33 Mortlock, *Experiences of a Convict*, p. 223.

34 Broomhall, pp. 89–104 *passim*.

35 Convict ticket-of-leave Register, Toodyay, ACC.721/31 SROWA. Index and Register digitised by WAGS.

36 AJCP ML CO386/154 1870 Reel 987 p. 184.

37 Entry for Richard Farrell per *Lord Dalhousie* in Erikson and O'Mara, p. 183.

38   Portsmouth Prison Register, TNAUK PCOM 2/110, Prisoner No. 8250; Toodyay Register.

39   Portsmouth Prison Register; Toodyay Register.

40   Millbank Prison Register, 1861–62, Prisoner 4040, TNAUK PCOM 2/45; Portland Prison Register, 1862, Prisoner 1692, TNAUK PCOM 2/389; Accession 128 SROWA; marriage WABDM 3399/1872; death of Henry Milford WABDM 256/1892.

41   Accession 128 SROWA; Erickson and O'Mara; WABDM marriage Caleb Stapley and Jane Maria Murray 3197/1870 and death of Caleb Slapley [sic] No. 7006/1874. With thanks for their help to Stapley descendants direct and indirect, Neville Thomas, Terry Stapley, Marie Young and Brian Saunders.

42   List of Prisoners' Property for the *Lord Dalhousie*, SROWA ACC 1156 V14, Part 2.

43   WA Prison Registers, Prisoner 7551; Erickson and O'Mara; family information supplied by Jennifer Cook, descendant of David Sowden Ledger.

44   Letter from Jennifer Cook to the author, 15 May 2005.

45   *Hertford and Bedford Gazette*, 8 March 1862.

46   Portland Prison Register, 1862, TNAUK PCOM 2/389, Prisoner No. 1917; WA Prison Registers, Prisoner 7525; Erickson and O'Mara; family information supplied by descendant Lorraine Clarke.

47   Correspondence with Lorraine Clarke, 2005–07.

48   WA Prison Registers, Prisoner 7518; Erickson and O'Mara; family information including details of Agnes Atkinson's background supplied by Reeves descendant Kerry Allbeury.

49   Ibid.

50   WA Prison Registers, Prisoner 7538; Erickson and O'Mara; WABDM for marriage, births and deaths of Annie Elizabeth Sherry, Henry Sherry and their children; *West Australian*, 28 October 1885.

51   Ibid.

52   WABDM marriage of John Waldock and Ann Elizabeth Sherry at Quindanning, 181/1888; death of John Waldock, age 57, 2343/1900; death of Annie E. Waldock, 31/1909.

53   Trollope, Vol. 2, p. 207.

54   Letter from a convict in Perth to his brother in England, published in *Cornhill Magazine*, April 1866, in Crowley, *A Documentary History of Australia*, Vol. 2, pp. 84–85.

55   Kennedy to Newcastle, 16 March 1860, in Evans and Nicholls, p. 271.

56   Comptroller General's Report for 1861 in Kennedy to Newcastle, 4 February 1862, reproduced in ibid., p. 273.

57   Annual Report, enclosure in Hampton to Newcastle, 19 February 1863, BPP, 1863, in Evans and Nicholls, p. 261.

58   Trollope, Vol. 2, p. 207.

59   Publishing history of *Oliver Twist* online at www.pbs.org/wgbh/masterpiece/olivertwist, consulted 20 March 2007.

60   Trollope, Vol. 2, pp. 182, 207.

61   Ibid., p. 207.

62   www.aboutdarwin.com, consulted 20 March 2007.

63   Elof Carlson, 'Scientific Origins of Eugenics', State University of New York at Stony Book, www.eugenicsarchive.org, consulted 20 March 2007.

64   TNAUK CO201/392 fols 3 *et seq.*, in Michael Roe, *The Quest for Authority in Eastern Australia, 1835–1851*, p. 161.

65   www.museocriminologico.it, consulted 20 March 2007.

66   Warwick Hirst, archivist Mitchell Library, quoting from Collection of Stevenson letters in the *Australian*, 26 February 1994.

67   C.L. Bacchi, 'The Nature–Nurture Debate in Australia 1900–1914', pp. 199–200.

68   Ibid., p. 211.

69   W.H. Knight, *Western Australia, its History, Progress, Condition and Prospects; and its Advantages as a Field of Emigration*, 1870, in Erickson, *The Bride Ships*, p. 84.

70　Erickson, p. 82.

71　Ibid., p. 84.

72　Erickson, 'The Brand on His Coat' and other sources at http://en.wikipedia.org/wiki/
Ex-convict_school_teachers_in_Western_Australia.

73　Jenny Gregory, 'The Gallops of Dalkeith', p. 50.

74　Erickson, p. 179.

75　Mortlock, p. 220.

76　WA Prison Registers; Erikson and O'Mara.

77　Erickson, p. 179.

78　Family details supplied by Mrs Kath Francis, grand-daughter of Joseph and Maria Shaw.

79　Telephone conversation between Mrs Kath Francis and the author, 19 August 2004.

80　A.G.L. Shaw, *Convicts and the Colonies*, p. 358.

81　Mortlock, p. 227.

82　Ibid., pp. 229–30.

83　See Chapter 2.

CHAPTER 10 *Distinctions of Moral Breed*

1　On 14 December 1852, the Secretary of State Sir John Pakington signed the despatch that ended transportation. Duke of Newcastle to Denison, 7, 22 February 1853, cited by L.L. Robson, *A History of Tasmania*, Vol. 1, pp. 505–06.

2　Pakington to Denison 14 December 1852 in Robson, *A History of Tasmania*; and see Robson's analysis of correspondence of T.F. Elliott, Assistant Under-Secretary for the Colonies to Lord Grey in 1852, Robson, pp. 507–08.

3　Celebration details in Robson, p. 506.

4　Surgeon's journal *St Vincent*, 1853, ML AJCP ADM 101/66 Reel 3209.

5　The men's tickets-of-leave are recorded the English prison registers. See, for instance, TNAUK PCOM 2/105 Portsmouth Prison Register 1847–1850.

6　TNAUK HO 8/99 Register of Convict Hulks, 1849.

7　Portsmouth Prison Register 1847–50 and surgeon's journal, *St Vincent*.

8　TNAUK PCOM 2/136 York Hulk Register, ML AJCP Reel 5988; Portsmouth Prisoner Register 1847–1850.

9　TNAUK HO 23/4 Leicester Gaol Register.

10　Charles Bateson, *The Convict Ships, 1787–1868*, p. 370; Ellen O'Neil: AOTAS CON 15/6, CON 41/29, CON 19/9.

11　Surgeon's Journal, *St Vincent*.

12　*St Vincent* indent, AOTAS CON 14/47.

13　Figures from an analysis of conduct records for the *St Vincent* in AOTAS CON 33/115.

14　John Mitchell: AOTAS CON 33/115.

15　Denison to Pakington, 26 November 1852, cited in Robson, p. 502.

16　Michael Nash: AOTAS CON 33/115, CON 18/59, CON 14/47. Family information supplied by descendant Dawn Nash Durbin.

17　Christopher O'Mahony and Valerie Thompson, *Poverty to Promise: The Story of the Monteagle Emigrants, 1838–1858*, Crossing Press, Darlinghurst, Sydney 1994.

18　Kidd's conduct record, AOTAS CON 33/115; James Kelly entry in *ADB* Online, www.adb.online.anu.edu.au, consulted 18 February 2007.

19　William Kidd: AOTAS CON 33/115.

20　Patrick Brian: AOTAS CON 33/115; POL 324/3; marriage of Patrick O'Brien and Catherine Morrissey TASBDM 1332 (456) 1857; research plus family information and photograph supplied by descendants Carl O'Brien and Anne Grant.

21　Henry Taperell: AOTAS CON 33/115, plus information from descendant, Sue Tooth.

22　*Grey River Argus*, 7 July 1866.

23　Information supplied from her research by Taperell descendant Sue Tooth.

24　Eliza Morrison: AOTAS CON 41/26, CON 15/6, CON 19/8.

25   John Hobbs: AOTAS CON 33/115.

26   Application to marry, AOTAS CON 52/7 p. 179; Eliza Morrison's death noted on her conduct record, AOTAS CON 4126.

27   Biographical entry for Eliza Dore in Christine Woods, *The Last Ladies*, pp. 80–83. Eliza's conduct records, AOTAS CON 41/37, CON 15/8.

28   Ellen O'Neil: AOTAS CON 41/29, CON 15/6, CON 19/9.

29   John O'Neil: AOTAS CON 33/115, CON 18/59, CON 14/47.

30   *Hobart Mercury*, 8 August 1856.

31   *Hobart Mercury*, 5 September 1856.

32   *Tasmanian Daily News*, 4 September 1856.

33   AOTAS CON 41/29; Hospital record, Vol. 35/6 No. 4927/1865.

34   Patricia Ratcliff, *The Usefulness of John West*, pp. 437–39; C.M.H. Clark, *A History of Australia*, Vol. III, p. 423; see Chapter 8 for West's obituary.

35   W.A. Brodribb, *Recollections of an Australian Squatter, 1835–1883*, pp. 70–72, plus further information from Brodribb descendant Mrs Jo Watson.

36   A.G.L. Shaw, 'John West's Tasmania', p. 90.

37   Frank Crowley, *A Documentary History of Australia*, Vol. 2, pp. 552–53.

38   Anthony Trollope, *Australia*, Vol. 1, p. 225.

39   Crowley, *Documentary History*, Vol. 2, p. 534.

40   *Statistics of Tasmania 1857* and *House of Assembly Journals 1857*, cited in Henry Reynolds, 'That Hated Stain', p. 19.

41   Alan Atkinson, *The Europeans in Australia*, Vol. 2, p. 337; for decline in churchgoing Atkinson cites Hans Mole, *The Faith of Australians*, Sydney 1985, pp. 53–55.

42   Michael Roe, *The Quest for Authority in Eastern Australia, 1835–1851*. See particularly 'Part Three: A New Faith: Moral Enlightenment'; p. 150 for Harpur quote; p. 190, 'a drive for purity'; p. 193, necessity for the working man to respond; p. 190, a nation of such people must be wise and good and splendid; pp. 204–06 for elements of moral enlightenment including possible influence on bathing. See also Patricia Curthoys, 'A Provision for Themselves and Their Families?'; Marilyn Lake, 'The Politics of Respectability', p. 276.

43   Roe, *The Quest for Authority*, p. 205: 'the Australian working man took moral enlightenment for his own'.

44   Ibid., p. 204.

45   Reynolds, 'That Hated Stain', p. 31.

46   Trollope, *Australia*, Vol. 1, p. 230.

47   Roe, p. 195

48   Henry Reynolds, *Why Weren't We Told?*, p. 18.

49   Roe, p. 1.

50   See population figures in Roe, Appendix 1, p. 207. Also Trollope, Vol. 1, gives figures for 1870, p. 257.

51   Angus McKay: AOTAS CON 33/115, CON 14/47, CON 18/59.

52   McKay ticket-of-leave, *Hobart Town Gazette*, 17 July 1855; stealing sheep, *Launceston Examiner*, 16 June 1881; further research and family information from descendant Dr Christopher Riley.

53   Dr Christopher Riley.

54   Denison to J.S. Pakington, 30 October 1852, cited by Crowley, Vol. 2, p.53.

55   AOTAS POL 709, *Police Gazette* 1861–72.

56   Thomas Fleming: AOTAS CON 33/115, CON 37/9 p. 4056.

57   William Whittaker: AOTAS CON 33/115, CON 37/9 p. 4037.

58   Hamish Maxwell-Stewart, 'The Search for the Convict Voice', p. 87, n. 16. According to Maxwell-Stewart the Port Arthur Authority has concluded that, based on their figures, about 23 per cent or one in five spent time on the Tasman peninsula. (It could be argued that 23 per cent is nearer one in four.) In *Convicts and the Colonies* (p. 216), A.G.L. Shaw

concluded between one-fifth and one-quarter experienced secondary punishment. My calculations from this sample put it around 20 per cent. Research into recidivism, which distorts the figures, is required before an authoritative figure can be reached.

59   List of men supplied to the author by Sue Hood from the Port Arthur Historic Site.

60   Ducie Denholm, 'Port Arthur', p. 411.

61   Patrick Quigley: AOTAS CON 33/68, CON 21/1; Indent of the *Governor Phillip*, 1 November 1845, CON 16/3 p. 188.

62   Mary Fay per *Kinnear (2)*, AOTAS CON 41/19, CON 15/5, CON 19/7.

63   Patrick Quigley: marriage to Mary Fay at Westbury, TASBDM 1459/1853; death of Mary Quigley at Westbury, 605/1863; marriage to Christina Green at Westbury, 695/1863; death of Patrick Quigley, 582/1872.

64   Stefan Petrow, 'Claims of the Colony', p. 222.

65   *Hobart Mercury*, 21 July 1876, in David Young, *Making Crime Pay*, p. 31.

66   Young, p. 32 citing the *Hobart Mercury*, 18 April 1877 and 20 July 1877.

67   Young, p. 32.

68   Young, p. 32.

69   J.W. Beattie, undated, *Port Arthur, Van Diemen's Land; Hobart*, advertising for Tasman's Villa boarding house, in Young op. cit. p. 71.

70   Reynolds, 'That Hated Stain', p. 23.

71   Young, pp. 94–95 for details of the controversy over the film.

72   For Defeat of Establishment candidates for the municipal election see M.M.H. Thompson, *The First Election*, p. 15.

73   Calculations from population figures in Roe, p. 207. In 1841, on a conservative estimate that allocated only half those born in the colony to the convict/emancipist group, the figures were: convicts, emancipists and descendants, 61,098; free settlers and descendants, 69,757. By 1851, people born in the colony were simply lumped with those who arrived free in a single total making it much harder (no doubt deliberately) to calculate the likely size of those with convict connections. Again calculating conservatively and allocating only one-third of the increase in this category since 1841 to the convict camp, the population break-up in New South Wales is: convicts, emancipists and their descendants, 86,098; born in the colony and arrived free, 119,757. If the increase in population since 1841 was divided equally between arrived free and convict connections, the difference is less than 10,000. See Roe, p. 207.

74   Trollope, Vol. 1, p. 230.

75   *Sydney Morning Herald*, 11 February 1879.

76   Elena Grainger, *Martin of Martin Place*, p. 124. Details of William Bede Dalley in John Molony, *The Native Born*, p. 207.

77   Thomas Arnold to Sir John Franklin, 20 July 1836, in Arthur Penrhyn Stanley, *The Life and Correspondence of Thomas Arnold, D.D., Late Head-Master of Rugby School, and Regius Professor of Modern History in the University of Oxford*, 4th edition, 2 vols, B. Fellowes, London, 1845.

78   Babette Smith, *A Cargo of Women*, pp. 151–65.

79   See footnote 58 for details.

80   *Sydney Morning Herald*, 21 August 1848; *NSWGG*, 1847, pp. 313, 362; SRNSW 4/3216 No. 53/10633; NSWBDM V1853 742 106/1853, V1853 700 139/1853

81   Records of the New South Wales Benevolent Society at ML, Index to Admissions D563, CY 1801, Inmates Journal A7229, CY 1478A.

82   Thomas Stacey conduct record, AOTAS CON 37/4 p. 1358.

83   Conduct record, AOTAS CON 37/4; Thomas Stacey, Protestant, age 60, Free by Servitude, Admitted 23 June 1863, ship *John(3)*, died 1 May 1864 of Renal Vesical, Birthplace Middlesex, Trade Cook, 41 years in the colony. Listed in Joyce Purtscher (ed.), *Deaths at the General Hospital Hobart January 1864–June 1884*.

84   Trollope, Vol. 1, p. 235.

CHAPTER 11 *The Lost World*

1   J.B. Hirst, *Convict Society and its Enemies*, p. 213.

2   *Martin Cash: The Bushranger of Van Diemen's Land in 1843–4; The Uncensored Story of Martin Cash (Australian Bushranger) as Told to James Lester Burke*.

3   Muswellbrook Bench Book, 25 May 1836, SRNSW 4/5600 Reel 670.

4   Genesis of *For The Term of His Natural Life* in Introduction by Stephen Murray-Smith to 1970 edition, Penguin, p. 10, cited in David Young, *Making Crime Pay*, p. 160, n. 47.

5   Young, *Making Crime Pay*, p. 19.

6   M. Clarke, *Stories of Australia in the Early Days*, 1897, in Frank Crowley, *A Documentary History of Australia*, Vol. 3, pp. 31–32.

7   M. Clarke, *For The Term of His Natural Life*, Book Agencies of Tasmania, Hobart 1994.

8   Price Warung, *Tales of the Convict System*, pp. ix–xxxvi.

9   *Bulletin*, 21 January 1888.

10 Ibid.

11 Lloyd Robson, 'The Convict Cargo Re-Inspected', p. 31.

12 John West, *The History of Tasmania*, p. 517.

13 John Moloney, *The Native Born*, pp. 74–76; John Ritchie, *The Wentworths*, pp. 210–11; *Sydney Gazette*, 29 January 1842.

14 'The Day We Were Lagged', *Bulletin*, 21 January 1888.

15 Peter Spearritt, 'Australia Day, Australia Wide: A Sydney Spectacle', *Australian Society*, December 1988/January 1989, p. 18. See also Graeme Turner, *Making it National*, p. 68.

16 *New South Wales Legislative Assembly, Votes and Proceedings*, 1901, Vol. 6, p. 946, in Warung, *Tales of the Convict System*, p. xix.

17 Henry Reynolds, 'That Hated Stain', pp. 19–31.

18 West, *History of Tasmania*, cited in ibid., p. 23.

19 Reynolds, p. 31.

20 Anna Haebich, 'The Battlefields of Aboriginal History', p. 8.

21 Robert Hughes, *The Fatal Shore*, p. 593.

22 Robert Reynolds, *From Camp to Queer*, p. 30.

23 J.F. Mortlock, *Experiences of a Convict*, p. 141.

24 Hamish Maxwell-Stewart to the author, 1999.

25 Anne Summers, *Damned Whores and God's Police*, Penguin, Melbourne 1975; Miriam Dixson, *The Real Matilda*, Penguin, Melbourne 1976; Beverley Kingston, *My Wife, My Daughter and Poor Mary Ann*, Thomas Nelson, Melbourne 1975; Portia Robinson, *The Women of Botany Bay*, Macquarie University, Sydney 1988; Babette Smith, *A Cargo of Women*; Deborah Oxley, *Convict Maids*, CUP, Cambridge 1996; Kay Daniels, *Convict Women*, Angus & Robertson, Sydney 1998.

26 See Lauchlan McKinnon's evidence to the Select Committee on Transportation in Chapter 9.

27 New South Wales Parliament, Minutes of Evidence taken before the Select Committee on the Chinese Immigration Bill, August 1858.

28 Useful articles include D.L. Carrington, 'Riots at Lambing Flat, 1860–1861', R.B. Walker, 'Another Look at the Lambing Flat Riots, 1860–1861', P.A. Selth, 'The Burrangong (Lambing Flat) Riots, 1860–1861'.

29 *The Age*, 21 May 1857.

30 J.B. Hirst, *The Strange Birth of Colonial Democracy*, pp. 159, 161–62.

31 Andrew Markus, *Fear and Hatred*, p. 241.

32 Dan Huon, 'The Origins of the Launceston Anti-Transportation Leagues, 1847–1849', p. 94.

33 C.M.H. Clark, *A History of Australia*, Vol. II, p. 345.

34 John M. Ward, *Earl Grey and the Australian Colonies, 1846–1857*, Chapter VIII.

35 Ian Brand, *The Convict Probation System*, Enclosure No. 5, at pp. 147–60.

36 Those historians who have dealt with the anti-transportation in some detail include Michael Sturma, *Vice in a Vicious Society*; Lloyd Robson, *A History of Tasmania*, Vol. 1; and Hirst, *Convict Society*. Robson's work in particular suggests that, except for his untimely death, he would have pursued the subject vigorously.

37 Jan Kociumbas, '"Mary Ann", Joseph Fleming and "Gentleman Dick"'.

38 Ibid. See also Chapter 5.

39 Reynolds, *Why Weren't We Told?*, p. xiii.

40 Kociumbas, *Oxford History of Australia*, Vol. 2, p. 298.

41 John M. Ward, 'Charles Cowper', www.adb.online.anu.edu.au, consulted 3 June 2007.

42 A.W. Martin, *Henry Parkes*, p. 54.

43 Mark McKenna, *The Captive Republic: A History of Republicanism in Australia, 1788–1996*, CUP, Melbourne 1996, p. 71; for the biblical injunction see particularly 1 Corinthians 6.9.

44 C.M.H. Clark, *The Beginning of an Australian Intelligentsia*.

45 See C.N. Connolly, 'The Middling Class Victory in New South Wales, 1853–62'.

46 Ward, *Earl Grey and the Australian Colonies*.

47 Connolly, 'Middling Class Victory', p. 371.

48 Sturma, *Vice in a Vicious Society*, Chapter 3; C.M.H. Clark, *A History of Australia*, Vol. III, pp. 415–16.

49 Manning Clark describes John West as first taking up the convict question in 1847, missing entirely the press furore of 1846 as well as activity prior to that date. Clark, *History*, Vol. III, p. 423; Sturma, p. 52, describes the movement as a reaction to the arrival of Lord Grey's exiles.

50 Adam Jamrozik, *The Chains of Colonial Inheritance*, p. 39.

51 Russel Ward, 'An Australian Legend'.

52 Henry Reynolds, 'Racial Thought in Early Colonial Australia', p. 53.

53 Russel Ward, 'The Australian Legend Re-Visited', p. 179.

54 *Decisions of the Superior Courts of New South Wales, 1788–1899*, www.law.mq.edu.au/scnsw/Cases1838–39, published by the Division of Law, Macquarie University.

55 Jamrozik, *Chains of Colonial Inheritance*, p. 32.

56 Turner, *Making it National*, p. 69.

57 James Jupp, 'Identity', in R. Nile (ed.), *Australian Civilisation*, 1994, quoted in Jamrozik, *Chains of Colonial Inheritance*, p. 37.

58 Ibid., p. 32.

59 Charles Buller to Lord Stanley, November 1841, TNAUK, CO206/42 pp. 245f., cited by M.M.H. Thompson, *The First Election*, p. 12.

60 Russel Ward, *The Australian Legend*, p. 153.

61 Hirst, *Convict Society*, p. 169.

62 Emancipists' Petition enclosed with correspondence, Macquarie to Bathurst, 22 October 1821, *HRA*, Series I, Vol. X, p. 550.

63 Russel Ward, *The Australian Legend*, p. 16.

64 L.L. Robson, *The First A.I.F.*, pp. 2–3.

65 G.A. Wood, 'Convicts', pp. 196–97.

66 ML Am76, 1912. Handwritten manuscript annotated '24/5/12 for the B[ulletin] Xmas 18/-'. Photographic copy in possession of McCay's great-niece, Penelope Nelson.

67 See Tamsin O'Connor, 'Buckley's Chance: Freedom and Hope at the Penal Settlements of Newcastle and Moreton Bay', in *Exiles of Empire*, Special Convict Issue, *Tasmanian Historical Studies*, Vol. 6, No. 2, 1999, p. 124.

bibliography

NEWSPAPERS

Great Britain

Chester Chronicle
Derby Mercury
Devizes and Wiltshire Gazette
Edinburgh Advertiser
Edinburgh Evening Courant
Glasgow Chronicle
Glasgow Herald
Gloucester Journal
Hertford and Bedford Gazette
Lancashire Gazette
Liverpool Journal
Maidstone and Kentish Journal
Manchester Guardian
Police Gazette; or, Hue and Cry
Preston Chronicle
Reading and Oxford Gazette
Salisbury and Winchester Journal
Salopian Journal
Shrewsbury Chronicle
Staffordshire Advertiser
Stamford Mercury
Surrey Gazette
Sussex Advertiser
Times, London
Worcester Journal
York Herald

Australia

Australian
Bulletin
Cornwall Chronicle

Hobart Courier
Hobart Mercury
Hobart Town Gazette
Launceston Examiner
Maitland Mercury
Monitor
Sydney Gazette
Sydney Morning Herald (*Sydney Herald* before 1841)
Tasmanian Daily News
West Australian

MANUSCRIPTS

United Kingdom
The National Archives, Kew
Assize Records ASSI 5–6, ASSI 11/25–26, ASSI 21/60–64, ASSI 23/10, ASSI 26/1, ASSI 27, ASSI 33–34, ASSI 41, ASSI 45, ASSI 31–34, ASSI 26–28, ASSI 21–23, ASSI 57, ASSI 61
Millbank Prison Register 2/29–30, 2/45
Pentonville Prison Register 2/62, 2/69, 2/70
Portsmouth Prison Register 1847–52 PCOM 2/105, 2/110
Portland Prison Register PCOM 2/382, PCOM 2/389
Gibraltar Hulk PCOM 2/11, PCOM 2/132, HO 8/101
York Hulk Register PCOM 2/136
Leicester Gaol Register HO23/4
Register of Convict Hulks 1849–52 HO/99–111
Lancaster Prison Governor's Journal 1816 PCOM 2/442, 1862 PCOM 2/445
Calendars of Quarter Sessions and Assizes, Liverpool PCOM 2/319, PCOM 2/335
Calendars of Quarter Sessions and Assizes for West Riding, Yorkshire PCOM 2/414, Hampshire 2/418, Lancashire PCOM 2/328
Calendar for Quarter Sessions and Assizes for Newcastle PCOM 2/344
Palatanate Depositions of Lancashire 1826–35 PL 27/10, PL 27/14, PL 27/16
HO 75/4 *Police Gazette: or, Hue and Cry*
HO 6/1 Recommendations from Judges and Recorders
WO 25/2910 List of Deserters
The Trial at large of (the Poachers by name) for the Wilful Murder of Wm. Ingram . . . likewise the Trial of W.A. Brodribb, Gentleman for administering an Unlawful Oath, Gloucester Lent Assizes 1816 before the Hon. Mr Justice Holroyd, to which is prefixed An Introductory Narrative . . . and a Plan of the Ground, printed and sold by D. Walker and Sons, Journal Office, Westgate Street, Gloucester 1816. Available at The National Archives

County Record Offices
Gloucester Gaol Registers 1815–79, GRO Q/Gc 5/1–7, Q/Gc 6/1–7
Gloucester Gaol Chaplains' Journals 1806–72 Q/Gc 15/1–6
Gloucester Gaol Governors' Journals 1793–1873 Q/Gc 3/1–3
Gloucestershire Calendars 1790–1878 Q/SG 2
Lincolnshire County Record Office Calendars and Quarter Session Records LQS A/9/3; LQS A/1/537/1–5, 163, 176, 182, 212; TNAUK HO/17 51/1 Hq38
Staffordshire, William Salt Library, Stafford, Calendars of Prisoners 1816–49
Somersetshire Record Office, Taunton, List of Prisoners in Ilchester Gaol QAG1/15/3–4; Calendars of Prisoners 1815–54 DD/MT/19/1/1–2
Bristol Record Office: Quarter Session records JQS/P/692–94, JQS/P/618, JQS/D/47
Manchester Archives at the Manchester Library, Quarter Sessions M116/2/4/43, M116/2/4/51, M116/2/4/53, M/116/2/4/134–37

Lancashire Record Office, Preston, Prosecutors Bills QSP/3153/60, QSP/2769/91, QSP/3165/151, QSP/2701/16–18; Calendars QJC 5–7, QJC 9–10; Petitions QSP 3132/44, QSP 3123/107, QSP 3153/60, QSP 3153/64, QSP 3158/107–08; Depositions PL 27/9–16

Derbyshire Record Office, Calendars of Prisoners Q/SP/8/17–28, Q/SP/10/5–8, Q/SP/12–15

Worcestershire Record Office: Calendars of Prisoners 1847–62

National Archives of Scotland, Edinburgh

Declarations and Precognitions AD14/15/49, 53; AD14/16/2, 16, 35, 48; AD 14/30/349; AD 14/31/16, 175, 182; AD 14/47/355, 512; AD14/48/42, 80, 236; AD14/50/98, 252, 256, 276, 459, 466–67, 475, 472, 477, 601; AD 14/52/251; AD 14/61/149, 329; AD 14/62/23, 31, 174, 244, 249

Minute Books Circuit Court of Justiciary, Glasgow JC13/40–42, 64, 69, 90, 92, 99–100

Minute Books Circuit Court of Justiciary, Ayr JC12/29, 49

Minute Books High Court of Justiciary, Edinburgh JC 8/11–16, 25–26, 53, 57, 58, 60, 67

Minute Books Circuit Court of Justiciary, Perth JC 11/88, 93–95, 101

Indictment JC 26/1850/586

Australia

Mitchell Library

AJCP Criminal Registers HO 26/21 22 Reels 2735–36; HO 27/11–12 Reels 2757–59; HO 2739–42 Reels 2779–84; HO 27/78–99 Reels 2818–34; HO 27/125–33 Reels 2847–51

AJCP HO 10/1–2 Reels 59–66; HO 10/43–51 Reels 77–80 Musters 1817–41

AJCP HO 10/46, Reel 78

AJCP HO 10/43 PRO Reel 77 *Sir William Bensley* Punishment List 1817–21

AJCP CO 54/1 No. CO 386/154 Register of Applications for Wives 1834–42

AJCP ADM 101 Surgeons' Journals

AJCP Berkshire Record Office M713, M866

AJCP Hertford Record Office M1176 Reel 6570

AJCP Bedfordshire Record Office M821, Inquiry into Unnatural Crime on the *Captivity* hulk at Portsmouth June 1811; Quarter Sessions Records, Prison Returns; M591 Log of the *Sir William Bensley* 1816–17

AJCP Cheshire Record Office Quarter Session Orders for Transportation M845–46

AJCP Printed Convict Indents 1830–34, ZF365.9544025/1 Reel FM4/10567

NSWGG 1832–63

NSW Governor's Despatches to Secretary of State for Colonies, Vol. 2, March 1817–18 A1191, CY 815

NSW Benevolent Society Admissions Indexes D562–4, Inmates Journal A7229–31

New South Wales Parliament, Minutes of Evidence taken before the Select Committee on the Chinese Immigration Bill, August 1858

BPP, *Crime and Punishment, Transportation*, Minutes of Evidence Before the Select Committee on Transportation, 1837–38, 1861, 1863

BPP, *Report from the Select Committee of the House of Commons on Transportation*; together with a letter from the Archbishop of Dublin on the same subject and Notes by Sir William Molesworth, Bart., Chairman of the Committee, 1838, Libraries Board of South Australia facsimile edition, Adelaide 1967

HRA, Series III, Vols I–V; Series I, Vol. XIX

State Records NSW (a selection)

ARK (Archives Resources Kit), Index to Colonial Secretary's Papers 1788–1825, searchable by name and subject, published by SRNSW 2004

Index to Colonial Secretary's Correspondence, Convicts and Others 1826–77, compiled by Joan Reese

Index to letters sent re convicts 1826–55, compiled by Joan Reese

Index to letters from Sheriff

Musters and other papers relating to convict ships 1790–1849

Fiche 3204 Petitions 1820

Fiche 3207 4/1862 Petitions 1821

4/1740 Reel 6047 Enquiry re the *Friendship*

4/1749–61 Reels 6051–55 Correspondence from Superintendent of Convicts

4/1802 Reels 748, 6066 re Melville Island

4/2145 1832 Chronological (*John* Mutiny investigation)

4/2261 from Sheriff 1834

4/2282.2 Reel 2201 Miscellaneous Persons 'B' 1835

4/2284.1 Miscellaneous Persons 'M' 1835

4/2771.1 Miscellaneous Persons 'M' 1847

4/2399.2 Engineer 1838

4/7104 Norfolk Island

4/2761 and 4/2762.1 Reel 2266 Convicts 1847

4/2371.4 Police Newcastle 1837

4/2775, 4/2776, 4/2777, 4/2779.1 Police 1847

4/2817 Police 1848

4/2867.4 Police 1849

4/2736.2, Reel 2266 Petitions 1846

4/2193.2, 4/2341.1, 4/2264.2, 4/2301.1, 4/2382.2 CSIL Mineral Survey Department 1832–37

4/3794 Reel 749 Letters to Moreton Bay 1824–31

4/3896–902 Reels 1062–65 Letters to Sheriff 1828–50, 4/1817 Reel 6069, 4/6571 Letters to Sheriff 1847–49

4/6271 Reel 708 Men in irons from Norfolk Island

4/6271 Reel 708 Return relating to Iron Gangs and Road Parties 1836–41

COD 207 '*Report relative to the road to Bathurst*', Sir Thomas Mitchell, Bathurst

4/2223 Reel 600, 4/2223, Reel 600, 2/8313, Reel 2652 Carters Barracks

4/3025 List of Prisoners at Blackheath Stockade 1847

Principal Superintendent of Convicts bound indents 1788–1835 and printed indents 1830–42

Tickets-of-leave online index at www.sag.org.au

State Records of New South Wales online databases for Tickets-of-Leave Passports, Ticket-of-Leave Exemption, Conditional Pardons, Certificates of Freedom, Convict Bank Accounts, Quarter Sessions Cases 1834–37 indexes all online at www.records.nsw.gov.au

Convict Death Register 1828–79

Sydney Gaol Entrance Book 1831–47 for prisoners sentenced to death and for prisoners transported 1837–47

Cockatoo Island: Returns 1843–56 Reels 606, 608–11, Registers Reels 1258, 2081–85, General Index Reel 605

Shipping and Distribution lists of convicts 4/3496–98, 4/3502–6 Reels 6005–09, 4/3896–900 Reels 1062–64 (Port Macquarie, Moreton Bay, Norfolk Island), Reels 4/4005–06, Reels 393–94, 4/4014 Reel 398, 4/4017 Reel 905 (1829–32 *Princess Royal* and *John (3)*) Reels 662, 769–70 Norfolk Island Lists

Bathurst Bench Books 1825–36 2/8223–25

Invermein (Scone) Bench Book 1833–37 7/90, 4/7553 Reel 677, 4/56–66 Reel 678–79

Patricks Plains (Singleton) Bench Book 1835, 4/7685 Reel 679, 1839–44 4/5662, 5/7686 Reels 680–01

Muswellbrook Bench Book 1832–36 9/2690, 4/5599–600, 4/5600 Reel 670, 4/5601; 1838–43 Reel 671

Newcastle Bench Book 1833–38 SZ80, 4/5607–08 Reels 2721–22

Port Macquarie Bench Book 4/5637–39 Reels 2723–24

Port Stephens Bench Book 4/7571 Reel 2737

Vale of Clywdd Bench Book 1836–39 4/5673 Reel 669

Cawdor and Stonequarry Bench Book July 1834–35 4/5673, 4/5626 Reel 672

Windsor (North Richmond) Bench Book 1836–40 4/5697 Reel 682

Persons Tried Hyde Park Barracks X707 Reel 662

Clerk of the Peace Quarter Sessions depositions 1832–39

Clerk of the Peace, Index to Quarter Sessions 1839–49

Clerk of the Peace, Supreme Court depositions 1838 Bathurst 9/6312

Judge Advocates Bench 1815–21 SZ775 COS 236

Court of Criminal Jurisdiction SZ777–803, X820 Reel 6023

Supreme Court Papers and Informations 1835 T164

W.W. Burton, Notes on criminal cases, Supreme Court of New South Wales, February 1834, 2/2412

Bathurst Gaol Index 1846–68 4/8501, Bathurst Gaol Entrance Book 1837–44 4/8490 Reel 2320

Monthly return of summary trials before Benches of Magistrates X708–09 Reel 662

Decisions of the Superior Courts of New South Wales, 1788–1899, published by the Division of Law, School of History and Classics, Macquarie University, www.law.mq.edu.au/scnsw, consulted 2004–07

Archives Office of Tasmania

St Vincent (3), CON 33/115, CON 18/59, CON 14/47

Governor Phillip indent 1845 CON 16/3

Assignment Lists and papers CON 13/1

Conduct Records Local convictions CON 37/8–10

Description Records 1817–53 CON 18/59

Supreme Court Record of Persons Tried in Criminal Cases 1824–31 SC 41/1

Macquarie Harbour Commandant's Letterbook 1830–32 CON 85, CSO 43/1

Colonial Secretary to Commandant Port Arthur 1834 CON 86/1

Return of Convicts embarked for Port Arthur 1834 CON 126

Register of Prisoners received at Port Arthur March–April 1852 CON 90

Register of Prisoners Discharged (from a Penal Station) CON 88/1

Colonial Secretary Correspondence 1831 including returns from Port Arthur CSO 1/511–11180, CSO 512/11190–204, CSO 513/11206–21

TAS Papers 92 (PT 2) 93 Reel CY8508

Colonial Secretary Correspondence Indexes 1824–36 CSO 3/1

Conduct Registers of Male Convicts arriving on non-convict ships or locally convicted CON 37/9

Convict Deaths CON 63–64

Decisions of the Superior Courts of the Nineteenth Century Tasmanian Superior Courts, published by the Division of Law, Macquarie University School of History and Classics, University of Tasmania www.law.mq.edu.au/sctas, consulted 2004–07

Western Australia

List of Prisoners' Property for the Lord Dalhousie SROWA ACC 1156, V14, Part 2

Convict Registers for the *Lord Dalhousie* SROWA Acc 128

Convict Ticket of Leave Register Toodyay, SROWA ACC.721/31, WA Index and Register digitised by WAGS

Printed Manuscripts

Ships' Indents 1806–22, SRNSW, compiled by James McClellan, printed by Pinewood Press, 1994

Regulations of the Penal Settlement at Port Arthur, 1st edition, Item 4672 Ferguson's *Bibliography of Australia*, published by H.A. Evans and Son, Melbourne 1966

Victoria, Prisoners: Committals–Trials, 1 July 1851 – 30 June 1853, The Heraldry and Genealogy Society of Canberra Inc., Facsimile Series No. 2

New South Wales, Criminals Condemned to Death Since 1840, Legislative Assembly, 20 April 1860, includes Name Index, The Heraldry and Genealogy Society of Canberra, Facsimile Series No. 3

ELECTRONIC PRIMARY SOURCES AND INDEXES

Bedford Gaol Register 1801–1879, Bedfordshire and Luton Archives and Records Service, online database at http://apps.bedfordshire.gov.uk, consulted 23 June 2006

National Library of Wales, online database of nineteenth-century prisoners convicted, www.llgc.org.uk/index.php?id=670

Lincolnshire Convicts transported to Australia, Gibraltar and Bermuda, searchable database from records in the Lincolnshire Archives, www.lincolnshire.gov.uk/section.asp?catId=6722

Proceedings of the Old Bailey, London 1674–1834, www.oldbaileyonline.org/

Prisoners sentenced to death and transportation, Yorkshire 1830–1839, biographical compilation by Jill Chambers, 2005 on CD-ROM

Criminal Petitions Index 1819–1839 Pt 1–4, from TNA HO17/40–79, CD-ROM compiled by Jill Chambers, 2004

Census of New South Wales 1828, CD-ROM ed. Keith Johnson and Malcolm Sainty, published by the Library of Australian History, 2001

Liverpool Asylum Index Pt 1 1859–1883 and Pt 2 1882–1894, CD-ROMs compiled by Liverpool Genealogy Society, 2004

Convict Employer Registers 1843–1845, Bench Books for Argyle District–Berrima/Throsby Park 1826–27 and Argyle District–Goulburn Plains 1827–35, Liverpool 1824–26, CD-ROM compiled and edited by Margot Crestani and Pamela Valentine for Liverpool Genealogy Society, 2003

Colonial Convict Movements 1827–53 Index, CD-ROM published by Descendants of Convicts, Melbourne, November 2003

Convicts Permissions to Marry 1810–51, CD-ROM indexed by Lesley Uebel, Registered No. CPM22

Index to records from collections of 39 family history societies and institutions of Australia and New Zealand, CD-ROM, published by AGCI, 2004, managed by SAG, Sydney

NSWGG, 1832–63, Index, CD-ROM published AGCI 2005, managed by SAG, Sydney

NSWBDM online index, www.bdm.nsw.gov.au

Convict Ticket-of-Leave Register Toodyay ACC 721/30 CD-ROM published by WAGS in conjunction with State Records of Western Australia, 2004

Convict Ticket-of-Leave Register Toodyay ACC 720/31 digitised original CD-ROM published by WAGS in conjunction with SROWA, 2006

Tasmanian Convicts, the complete list from the original records, CD-ROM produced by AOTAS in conjunction with the Genealogical Society of Victoria, 2004

Tasmanian Pioneer Index Births, Deaths and Marriages 1803–1899, CD-ROM published by Macbeth Genealogical Services Pty Ltd with permission of TASBDM

Tasmanian Federation Index Births, Deaths and Marriages 1900–30, CD-ROM published by Macbeth Genealogical Services with permission of TASBDM, 2006

Tasmanian Papers, Index to Tasmanian Collection of Records 1830s to 1930s in the Mitchell Library, including 1794 Norfolk Island and 1823–1848 New South Wales, CD-ROM compiled by Kiama Family History Volunteers Group, 2002, published by Macbeth Genealogical Services

Victoria Registry of Births, Deaths and Marriages online index, http://online.justice.vic.gov.au

WABDM online index, www.justice.WA.gov.au/F/familyhistory

Western Australia Fremantle Prison searchable convict database, www.fremantleprison.com.au/history/history6.cfm

York Assizes 1785–1851 online database compiled from the Assize Calendars by The City of York and District Family History Society, http://yorkfamilyhistory.org.uk/casehistories.htm

Australian Dictionary of Biography, www.adb.online.anu.edu.au, consulted 2006–07

PUBLISHED

Adburgham, Alison, *A Radical Aristocrat: Sir William Molesworth of Pencarrow*, Tabb House, Padstow, Cornwall 1990

Alexander, Alison, 'The Legacy of the Convict System', *THS*, Vol. 6, No. 1, 1998

Alexander, Alison, 'A Turbulent Career, Jane Hadden', in *Pros and Cons of Transportation: A Collection of Convict Stories*, Tasmanian Family History Society, Hobart Branch, Hobart 2004

Atkinson, Alan, 'Four Patterns of Convict Protest', *Labour History*, No. 37, 1977

Atkinson, Alan, *The Europeans in Australia: A History*, Vol. 1, *The Beginning*, OUP, Melbourne 1997

Atkinson, Alan, *The Europeans in Australia: A History*, Vol. 2, *Democracy*, OUP, Melbourne 2004

Atkinson, Alan, and Marian Aveling (eds), *Australians 1838*, Fairfax, Syme & Weldon Associates, Sydney 1987

Bacchi, C.L., 'The Nature–Nurture Debate in Australia, 1900–1914', *Historical Studies*, Vol. 19, No. 75, October 1980

Barker, Theo, *A History of Bathurst*, Vol. 1, *The Early Settlement to 1862*, Crawford House Press, Bathurst 1992

Bateson, Charles, *The Convict Ships, 1787–1868* [1959], Library of Australian History, Sydney 1985

Baxter, Carol J (ed.), *1814 General Muster of New South Wales*, ABGR in association with SAG, Sydney 1987

Baxter, Carol J (ed.), *1823, 1824, 1825 General Muster List of New South Wales*, ABGR in association with SAG, Sydney 1999

Brand, Ian, *The Convict Probation System: Van Diemen's Land, 1839–1854*, ed. M.N. Sprod, Blubber Head Press, Hobart 1990

Brodribb, W.A., *Recollections of an Australian Squatter, 1835–1883* [1883], John Ferguson, Sydney 1978

Brooke, Alan, and David Brandon, *Bound for Botany Bay: British Convict Voyages to Australia*, The National Archives of Great Britain, Richmond, Surrey 2005

Broomhall, F.H., *The Veterans: A History of the Enrolled Pensioner Force in Western Australia, 1850–1880*, Hesperian Press, Carlisle, WA 1989

Butler, A.G., *The Digger: A Study in Democracy*, Angus & Robertson, Sydney 1945

Butlin, N.G., C.W. Cromwell and K. L. Suthern (eds), *1837 General Return of Convicts in New South Wales*, ABGR in association with SAG, Sydney 1987

Campbell, Charles, *The Intolerable Hulks: Shipboard Confinement, 1776–1857*, Fenestra Books, Tucson 2001

Carrington, D.L., 'Riots at Lambing Flat, 1860–1861', *JRAHS*, Vol. 46, Pt 4, October 1960

Cash, Martin, *Martin Cash: The Bushranger of Van Diemen's Land in 1843–4: A Personal Narrative of his Exploits in the Bush and his Experiences at Port Arthur and Norfolk Island*, J. Walch & Sons, Hobart 1972

Cash, Martin, *The Uncensored Story of Martin Cash (Australian Bushranger) as Told to James Lester Burke*, compiled and edited by Joan Dehle Emberg and Buck Thor Emberg, Regal Publications, Launceston *c.* 2000

Chambers, Jill, *Rebels of the Fields: Robert Mason and the Convicts of the Eleanor*, self-published, Herts 1995

Chinn, Peter, *The Thin Red and Blue Lines: A History of the Military and Police Presence in the Blue Mountains Between the Nepean and Cox's Rivers, 1814–2005*, Springwood Historical Society, Springwood 2006

Clark, C.M.H., with the assistance of Leslie Pryor, *Select Documents in Australian History, 1788–1850*, Angus & Robertson, Sydney 1950

Clark, C.M.H., *Select Documents in Australian History, 1851–1900*, Angus & Robertson, Sydney 1955

Clark, C.M.H., 'The Origin of the Convicts Transported to Eastern Australia, 1787–1852',

Historical Studies of Australia and New Zealand, Vol. 7, Parts 1 and 2, November 1955–May 1957

Clark, C.M.H., *A History of Australia*, Vol. II, *New South Wales and Van Diemen's Land, 1822–1838*, MUP, Carlton 1968; Vol. III, *The Beginning of an Australian Civilization; 1824–1851*, MUP, Carlton 1973

Clark, C.M.H., *The Beginning of an Australian Intelligentsia*, The Second Herbert Blaiklock Memorial Lecture delivered at the University of Sydney on 19 July 1972, The Wentworth Press, Sydney 1973

Clark, Keith M., *Convicts of the Port Phillip District*, K.M. & G. Clarke, Waramanga ACT 1999

Clarke, F.G., *The Land of Contrarieties: British Attitudes to the Australian Colonies, 1828–1855*, MUP, Carlton 1977

Clune, Frank, *Norfolk Island*, Angus & Robertson, Sydney 1967

Cochrane, Peter, *Colonial Ambition: Foundations of Australian Democracy*, MUP, Carlton 2006

Conlon, Anne, '"Mine is a Sad Yet True Story": Convict Narratives, 1818–1850', *JRAHS*, Vol. 55, Pt 1, 1969

Connolly, C.N., 'The Middling Class Victory in New South Wales, 1853–62', *Historical Studies*, Vol. 19, No. 76, April 1981

Cook, Thomas, *The Exile's Lamentations or Biographical Sketch of Thomas Cook*, Sydney 1841, ML A1711 CY Reel 919

Cozens, Charles, *Adventures of a Guardsman*, Richard Bentley, London 1848

Crowley, Frank, *A Documentary History of Australia*, Vol. 1, *1788–1840*, Vol. 2, *1841–1874*, Vol. 3, *1875–1900*, Thomas Nelson, Melbourne 1980

Cunningham, Peter, *Two Years in New South Wales* [1827], David S. Macmillan (ed.), Angus & Robertson in association with RAHS, Sydney 1966

Curle, Peter, *A Collection of Bits and Pieces on the Littleport and Ely Riots 1816*, self-published, Gloucestershire n.d.

Curthoys, Patricia, 'A Provision for Themselves and Their Families? Women Depositors of the Savings Bank of New South Wales, 1846–1871', *JRAHS*, Vol. 84, Pt 2, December 1998

Curthoys, Patricia, 'State Support for Churches, 1836–1860', in Bruce Kaye (ed.), *Anglicanism in Australia: A History*, MUP, Carlton 2002

Denholm, Ducie, 'Port Arthur: The Men and the Myth', *Historical Studies*, Vol. 14, No. 56, 1971

Dixson, Miriam, *The Imaginary Australia: Anglo-Celts and Identity, 1788 to the Present*, UNSW Press, Sydney 1999

Duffield, Ian, and James Bradley, eds., *Representing Convicts: New Perspective on Convict Forced Labour Migration*, LUP, Leicester 1997

Dyster, Barrie, *Servant and Master: Building and Running the Grand Houses of Sydney, 1788–1850*, UNSW Press, Sydney 1989

Eastley, Robyn, 'Using the Records of the Tasmanian Convict Department', *Tasmanian Historical Studies*, Vol. 9, 2004

Erickson, Rica, *The Bride Ships: Experience of Immigrants Arriving in Western Australia, 1849–1889*, Hesperian Press, Carlisle, WA 1992

Erickson, Rica, and Gillian O'Mara, *Dictionary of Western Australians*, Vol. IX, *Convicts in Western Australia, 1850–1887*, UWA Press, Nedlands 1994

Evans, L., and P. Nicholls (eds), *Convicts and Colonial Society, 1788–1868*, 2nd edition, Macmillan, Melbourne 1984

Evans, Raymond, and William Thorpe, 'Power, Punishment and Penal Labour: Convict Workers and Moreton Bay', *Historical Studies*, Vol. 25, No. 98, April 1992

Flanagan, Richard, *A Terrible Beauty: History of the Gordon River Country*, Greenhouse, Melbourne 1985

Fletcher, Brian, *History in New South Wales, 1888–1938*, UNSW Press, Sydney 1993

Gibson, J.S.W., *Quarter Sessions Records [Britain] for Family Historians: A Select List*, 2nd edition, Federation of Family History Societies, Plymouth 1989

Gilchrist, Catie, 'Space, Sexuality and Convict Resistance in Van Diemen's Land: The Limits of Repression?', in *ERAS*, the online journal of postgraduate students, School of Historical Studies, Monash University, Melbourne, Edition 6, at www.arts.monash.edu.au/eras/edition_6, consulted 17 September 2006

Gill, Andrew, *Forced Labour for the West: Parkhurst Convicts Apprenticed in Western Australia, 1842–1851*, Blatellae Books, Marylands, WA 1997

Gill, Andrew, *Convict Assignment in Western Australia, 1842–1851*, Blatellae Books, Marylands, WA 2004

Gillen, Mollie, *The Founders of Australia: A Biographical Dictionary of the First Fleet*, Library of Australian History, Sydney 1989

Grainger, Elena, *Martin of Martin Place: A Biography of Sir James Martin*, Alpha Books, Sydney 1970

Gregory, Jenny, 'The Gallops of Dalkeith: A Re-Examination of a Pioneer Family', *The Push From the Bush*, No. 22, April 1986

Griffiths, Tom, 'Past Silences: Aborigines and Convicts in our History-Making', *Australian Cultural History*, No. 6, 1987

Haebich, Anna, 'The Battlefields of Aboriginal History', in Martyn Lyons and Penny Russell (eds), *Australia's History: Themes and Debates*, UNSW Press, Sydney 2005

Hammond, J.L. and B. Hammond, *The Village Labourer, 1760–1832*, Longmans Green, London 1913

Hancock, W.K., *Australia* [1930], Jacaranda Press, Brisbane 1966

Hasluck, Alexandra, *Royal Engineer: A Life of Sir Edmund DuCane*, Angus & Robertson, Sydney 1973

Hasluck, Alexandra, *Unwilling Emigrants: Letters of a Convict's Wife*, Fremantle Arts Centre Press, Fremantle 2002

Hawkins, David T., *Criminal Ancestors: A Guide to Historical Criminal Records in England and Wales*, Sutton Publishing, Stroud, Gloucestershire 1996

Hazzard, Margaret, *Punishment Short of Death: A History of the Penal Settlement at Norfolk Island*, Hyland House Publishing, Melbourne 1984

Hiener, J.E., 'Martin Cash: The Legend and the Man', THRA, *Papers and Proceedings*, Vol. 14, No. 2, January 1967

Hilton, Philip, 'Escape to Captivity', paper delivered at The Escape Conference, Strahan, Tasmania June 2003

Hirst, J.B., *Convict Society and its Enemies: A History of Early New South Wales*, George Allen & Unwin, Sydney 1983

Hirst, J.B., *The Strange Birth of Colonial Democracy*, Allen & Unwin, Sydney 1988

Hirst, Warwick, *Great Convict Escapes in Colonial Australia*, Kangaroo Press, Sydney 1999

Hopkins, Harry, *The Long Affray: The Poaching Wars in Britain*, Macmillan, London 1986

Horner, J.C., 'The Themes of Four Tasmanian Convict Novels', THRA, *Papers and Proceedings*, Vol. 15, No. 1, June 1967

Hughes, Robert, *The Fatal Shore*, Collins Harvill, London 1987

Huon, Dan, 'The Origins of the Launceston Anti-Transportation Leagues, 1847–1849', THRA, *Papers and Proceedings*, Vol. 44, No. 2, 1997

Jamrozik, Adam, *The Chains of Colonial Inheritance: Searching for Identity in a Subservient Nation*, UNSW Press, Sydney 2004

Johnson Woods, Toni, 'Virtual Reality', in Ian Duffield and James Bradley (eds), *Representing Convicts: New Perspective on Convict Forced Labour Migration*, LUP, Leicester 1997

Johnston, Judith, and Monica Anderson, *Australia Imagined*, UWAPress, Nedlands 2005

Judd, Stephen, and Kenneth Cable, *Sydney Anglicans: A History of the Diocese*, Anglican Information Office, Sydney 1987

Karskens, Grace, *The Rocks: Early Life in Sydney*, MUP, Carlton 1997

Kaye, Bruce, general editor, *Anglicanism in Australia: A History*, MUP, Carlton 2002

Kent, David, and Norma Townsend, *The Convicts of the Eleanor: Protest in Rural England, New Lives in Australia*, The Merlin Press–Pluto Press Australia, Annandale, NSW 2002

King, Jonathan, *The Other Side of the Coin: A Cartoon History of Australia*, Cassell Australia, Sydney 1976

Kingston, Beverley, *The Oxford History of Australia*, Vol. 3, *1860–1900*, OUP, Melbourne 1988

Kociumbas, Jan, *The Oxford History of Australia*, Vol. 2, *1770–1860*, OUP, Melbourne 1992

Kociumbas, Jan, '"Mary Ann", Joseph Fleming and "Gentleman Dick": Aboriginal–Convict Relationships in Colonial History', *JACH*, Vol. 3, No. 1, April 2001

Lake, Marilyn, 'The Politics of Respectability: Identifying the Masculinist Context', in Penny Russell and Richard White (eds), *Pastiche 1, Reflections on Nineteenth Century Australia*, Allen & Unwin, Sydney 1994

Lambert, Ronald D., 'Reclaiming the Ancestral Past: Narrative Rhetoric and the "Convict Stain"', *Journal of Sociology*, Vol. 38, No. 2, 2002

MacFie, Peter, 'Dobbers and Cobbers: Informers and Mateship Among Convicts, Officials and Settlers on the Grass Tree Hill Road, Tasmania, 1830–1850', THRA, *Papers and Proceedings*, Vol. 35, No. 3, September 1988

McLaughlin, Anne, 'Against the League: Fighting the "Hated Stain"', *THS*, Vol. 5, No. 1, 1995–96

Markus, Andrew, *Fear and Hatred: Purifying Australia and California, 1850–1901*, Hale & Iremonger, Sydney 1979

Martin, A.W., *Henry Parkes: A Biography*, MUP, Carlton 1980

Maxwell-Stewart, Hamish, 'Beyond Hell's Gates: Religion at Macquarie Harbour Penal Station', *THS*, Vol. 5, 1997

Maxwell-Stewart, Hamish, 'Convict Workers, Penal Labour and Sarah Island: Life at Macquarie Harbour, 1822–1834', in Ian Duffield and James Bradley (eds), *Representing Convicts*, LUP, Leicester 1997

Maxwell-Stewart, Hamish, 'The Search for the Convict Voice', *THS*, Vol. 6, No. 1, 1998

Maxwell-Stewart, Hamish, 'The Life And Death of James Thomas', *THS*, Vol. 10, 2005

Mayhew, Henry, *London's Underworld* [1862], Peter Quennell (ed.), Bracken Books, London 1983

Melville, Henry, *The History of Van Diemen's Land, From the Year 1824–1835 Inclusive During the Administration of Lieutenant-Governor George Arthur*, George Mackaness (ed.), Horwitz-Grahame, Sydney 1965

Messner, Andrew, 'Contesting Chartism From Afar: Edward Hawksley and the People's Advocate', *JACH*, Vol. 1, No. 1, April 1999

Mickleborough, Leonie, *William Sorell in Van Diemen's Land, 1817–24: A Golden Age?*, Blubber Head Press, Hobart 2004

Milliss, Roger, *Waterloo Creek: The Australia Day Massacre of 1838, George Gipps and the British Conquest of New South Wales*, UNSW Press, Sydney 1994

Molesworth, Sir William, *Report from the Select Committee of the House of Commons on Transportation, Together With a Letter From the Archbishop of Dublin on the Same Subject and Notes* [1838], State Library of South Australia, Adelaide 1967

Molony, John, *The Native Born: The First White Australians*, MUP, Carlton 2000

Mortlock, J.F., *Experiences of a Convict* [1864–65], G.A. Wilkes and A.G. Mitchell (eds), Sydney University Press, Sydney 1965

Nicholas, Stephen (ed.), *Convict Workers: Reinterpreting Australia's Past*, CUP, Cambridge 1989

O'Brien, Eris, *The Foundation of Australia, 1786–1800*, Sheed & Ward, London 1937

O'Connor, Tamsin, 'A Zone of Silence: Queensland's Convicts and the Historiography of Moreton Bay', in Ian Duffield and James Bradley (eds), *Representing Convicts: New Perspective on Convict Forced Labour Migration*, LUP, Leicester 1997

O'Donoghue, Frances, 'The Vicar-General and Norfolk Island', *The Push from the Bush*, No. 17, April 1984

O'Farrell, Patrick, *The Irish in Australia*, rev. edition, UNSW Press, Sydney 1993

Page, G.D., 'An Analysis and Exploration of the Varying Opinions, Between 1788 and 1960, on the Character of the Convicts Transported to the Eastern Australian Colonies', BA thesis, University of New England, Armidale 1961

Peacock, A.J., *Bread or Blood: Agrarian Riots of East Anglia, 1816*, Victor Gollancz, London 1965

Petrow, Stefan, 'Claims of the Colony: Tasmania's Dispute with Britain over the Port Arthur Penal Establishment, 1856–1877', THRA, *Papers and Proceedings*, Vol. 44, No. 4, December 1997

Phillips, Diane, *An Eligible Situation: The Early History of George Town and Low Head*, Karuda Press, Jamison Centre, ACT 2004

Picker, Gregory, 'A State of Infancy: The Anti-Transportation Movement in New Zealand, 1848–1852', *New Zealand Journal of History*, Vol. 34, No. 2, October 2000

Pickering, Paul A., 'The Oak of English Liberty: Popular Constitutionalism in New South Wales, 1848–1856', *JACH*, Vol. 3, No. 1, April 2001

Polding, J.B., *The Letters of John Bede Polding OSB*, Vol. 1, The Sisters of the Good Samaritan, Glebe, NSW 1994

Purtscher, Joyce (ed.), *Deaths at the General Hospital Hobart January 1864–June 1884*, self-published, Mount Stuart, Tasmania 1999

Pybus, Cassandra, and Hamish Maxwell-Stewart, *American Citizens, British Slaves: Yankee Political Prisoners in an Australian Penal Colony, 1839–1850*, MUP, Carlton 2002

Ratcliff, Patricia Fitzgerald, *The Usefulness of John West: Dissent and Difference in the Australian Colonies*, The Albernian Press, Launceston 2003

Reynolds, Henry, 'That Hated Stain: The Aftermath of Transportation in Tasmania', *Historical Studies*, Vol. 14, No. 53, October 1969

Reynolds, Henry, 'Racial Thought in Early Colonial Australia', *Australian Journal of History and Politics*, Vol. 20, No. 1, 1974

Reynolds, Henry, *Why Weren't We Told? A Personal Search for the Truth About our History*, Penguin Books, Melbourne 2000

Reynolds, Robert, *From Camp to Queer: Remaking the Australian Homosexual*, MUP, Carlton 2002

Richmond, Barbara, 'John West and the Anti-Transportation Movement', THRA, *Papers and Proceedings*, Vol. 2, No. 1, 1952

Ritchie, John (ed.), *The Evidence to the Bigge Reports, New South Wales Under Governor Macquarie*, Vol. 1, *The Oral Evidence*, and Vol. 2, *The Written Evidence*, Heinemann, Melbourne, 1971

Ritchie, John, 'Towards Ending an Unclean Thing', *Historical Studies*, Vol. 17, No. 67, October 1976

Ritchie, John, *The Wentworths: Father and Son*, MUP, Carlton 1997

Robson, L.L., *Australia and the Great War, 1914–1918*, Macmillan, Melbourne 1969

Robson, L.L., 'Review of A.G.L. Shaw (ed.), *The History of Tasmania* by John West', THRA, *Papers and Proceedings*, Vol. 20, No. 2, June 1973

Robson, L.L., *The Convict Settlers of Australia: An Enquiry Into the Origin and Character of the Convicts Transported to New South Wales and Van Diemen's Land, 1787–1852* [1965], MUP, Carlton 1976

Robson, L.L., *A History of Tasmania*, Vol. 1, *Van Diemen's Land from the Earliest Times to 1855*, OUP, Melbourne 1983

Robson, L.L., *The First A.I.F.: A Study of its Recruitment, 1914–1918*, MUP, Carlton 1982

Robson, Lloyd, 'The Convict Cargo Re-Inspected', *Bulletin of the Centre for Tasmanian Historical Studies*, Vol. 2, No. 1, 1988

Roe, Michael, *The Quest for Authority in Eastern Australia, 1835–1851*, MUP, Carlton 1965

Roe, Michael, 'The Establishment of Local Self-Government in Hobart and Launceston, 1845–1858', THRA, *Papers and Proceedings*, Vol. 14, No. 1, December 1966

Rosen, Sue, *Men at Work: Penal Ideology and Nation Building on the Great Western Road*, Heritage Assessment and History, Epping, NSW 2007

Roy, Jill, 'The Story of William Honeyman, 1792–1821', *Descent* (Journal of the Society of Australian Genealogists), Vol. 26, No. 4, December 1996

Rudé, George, *Protest and Punishment: The Story of the Social and Political Protesters Transported to Australia, 1788–1868*, The Clarendon Press, Oxford 1978

Sainty, Malcolm and Johnson, Keith (eds), *1828 Census of New South Wales*, Library of Australian History, Sydney 1980

Schaffer, Irene (ed.), *Land Musters, Stock Returns and Lists, Van Diemen's Land, 1803–1822*, St David's Park Publishing, Hobart 1991

Selth, P.A., 'The Burrangong (Lambing Flat) Riots, 1860–1861: A Closer Look', *JRAHS*, Vol. 60, Pt 1, March 1974

Shaw, A.G.L., 'Convicts and Their Crimes', *Sydney Morning Herald*, 27 June 1953

Shaw, A.G.L., *Convicts and the Colonies: A Study of Penal Transportation From Great Britain and Ireland to Australia and Other Parts of the British Empire* [1965], MUP, Carlton 1976

Shaw, A.G.L., *Governor Sir George Arthur, Bart, 1784–1854*, MUP, Carlton 1980

Shaw, A.G.L. ,'John West's Tasmania', *Bulletin of the Centre for Tasmanian Studies*, Vol. 3, No. 1, 1990–91

Smith, Babette, *A Cargo of Women: Susannah Watson and the Convicts of the Princess Royal*, UNSW Press, Sydney 1988 (Rosenberg Publishing edition, Kenthurst 2005)

Snowden, Diane, 'A White Rag Burning: Irish Women Who Committed Arson in Order to Be Transported to Van Diemen's Land', doctoral thesis, University of Tasmania, May 2005

Spearritt, Peter, 'Celebration of a Nation: The Triumph of Spectacle', *Historical Studies*, Vol. 23, No. 91, October 1988

Spurway, John, 'The Growth of Family History in Australia', *The Push From the Bush*, No. 27, 1989

Stannage, C.T. (ed.), *A New History of Western Australia*, UWA Press, Nedlands 1981

Sturma, Michael, *Vice in a Vicious Society: Crime and Convicts in Mid-Nineteenth Century New South Wales*, UQP, St Lucia 1983

Tardif, Phillip, *Notorious Strumpets and Naughty Girls*, Angus & Robertson, Sydney 1990

Taylor, Sandra, 'Who Were the Convicts? A Statistical Analysis of the Convicts Arriving in Western Australia in 1850/51, 1861/62 and 1866/68', MA thesis, UWA 1978

Therry, R., *Reminiscences of Thirty Years' Residence in New South Wales and Victoria* [1863], Sydney University Press, Sydney 1974

Thompson, M.M.H., *The First Election: The New South Wales Legislative Council Election of 1843*, self-published, Goulburn, NSW 1996

Townsend, Norma, 'The Molesworth Enquiry: Does the Report fit the Evidence?', *Journal of Australian Studies*, No. 1, June 1977

Townsend, Norma, 'A "Mere Lottery": The Convict System in New South Wales Through the Eyes of the Molesworth Committee', *The Push from the Bush*, No. 2, October 1985

Trollope, Anthony, *Australia* [1873], 2 vols, Hippocrene Books, New York 1987

Turner, Graeme, *Making it National: Nationalism and Australian Popular Culture*, Allen & Unwin, Sydney 1994

Vamplew, Wray (ed.), *Australians: Historical Statistics*, Fairfax, Syme & Weldon Associates, Sydney 1987

Walker, R.B., 'Another Look at the Lambing Flat Riots, 1860–1861', *JRAHS*, Vol. 56, Pt 3, September 1970

Walsh, Brian, 'Assigned Convicts at Tocal: "Ne'er-Do-Wells" or Exceptional Workers?', *JACH*, Vol. 8, 2006

Ward, John M., *Earl Grey and the Australian Colonies, 1846–1857*, MUP, Carlton 1958

Ward, John M., *James Macarthur, Colonial Conservative, 1798–1867*, Sydney University Press, Sydney 1981

Ward, Russel, *The Australian Legend* [1958], OUP, Melbourne 1970

Ward, Russel, 'An Australian Legend', *JRAHS*, Vol. 47, Pt 6, December 1961

Ward, Russel, 'The Australian Legend Re-Visited', *Historical Studies*, Vol. 18, No. 71, 1987

Warung, Price, *Tales of the Convict System: Selected Stories of Price Warung*, ed. B.G. Andrews, UQP, St Lucia 1975

Waugh, Max, *Forgotten Hero: Richard Bourke, Irish-Born Governor New South Wales, 1831–1837*, Australian Scholarly Publishing, Melbourne 2005

West, John, *The History of Tasmania* [1852], A.G.L. Shaw (ed.), Angus & Robertson, Sydney 1981

Williams, Gwyn A., *The Merthyr Rising*, University of Wales Press, Cardiff 1988

Williams, John, *Ordered to the Island: Irish Convicts in Van Diemen's Land*, Crossing Press, Darlinghurst 1994

Wood, G.A., 'Convicts', *JRAHS*, Vol. VIII, Pt IV, 1922

Woods, Christine, *The Last Ladies: Female Convicts on the Duchess of Northumberland, 1853*, self-published, Claremont, Tasmania 2004

Young, David, *Making Crime Pay, The Evolution of Convict Tourism in Tasmania*, THRA, Hobart 1996

index